D1607796

Women of God and Arms

Women of God and Arms

Female Spirituality and Political Conflict,
1380–1600

Nancy Bradley Warren

PENN

UNIVERSITY OF PENNSYLVANIA PRESS

Philadelphia

Copyright © 2005 University of Pennsylvania Press
All rights reserved
Printed in the United States of America on acid-free paper

10 9 8 7 6 5 4 3 2 1

Published by
University of Pennsylvania Press
Philadelphia, Pennsylvania 19104-4112

Library of Congress Cataloging-in-Publication Data

Warren, Nancy Bradley.
  Women of God and arms : female spirituality and political conflict,
1380–1600 / Nancy Bradley Warren.
      p.   cm.
  Includes bibliographical references and index.
  ISBN-10: 0-8122-3892-3 (cloth : alk. paper)
  ISBN-13: 978-0-8122-3892-1
    1. Christian women—Religious life—Europe—History—To 1500. 2. Christian
women—Europe—History—To 1500. 3. Women in politics—Europe—History—To 1500.
4. Christian women—Religious life—Europe—History—16th century. 5. Christian
women—Europe—History—16th century. 6. Women in politics—Europe—History—
16th century.
BV4527.W36   2005
274′.05′082—dc22   2005042317

For William Andrew Warren

Contents

Introduction

WHEN I WAS FINISHING the archival research for this project, I came across an eighteenth-century French manuscript in the British Library (London British Library MS Add. 25,351) containing copies of accounts of "funeral ceremonies, performed chiefly in the Netherlands, in honour of sovereigns and princes."[1] Among the obsequies described in this collection are those of Isabel of Castile "faites en la ville de Bruxelles . . . par ordre de L'Archiduc Philippe son gendre" [performed in the city of Bruxelles . . . by order of her son-in-law the Archduke Philippe].[2] Because chapters of this book concern both Isabel of Castile and the Burgundian Low Countries, I decided to have a look. To my delight, I found present in miniature in this account of Isabel's funeral ceremonies precisely the set of intersections that is at the heart of this book—women's multifaceted roles in the overlapping religious and the political spheres, and the interconnections at once dynastic and cultural linking England and the Continent, both of which inform the processes of representation and identity formation that animate political action in the medieval and early modern periods.

Isabel of Castile was, famously, both a pious and a warlike queen, very much a woman of God and arms. The account of her obsequies reflects both of these aspects of her reign. It begins by announcing the date and place of the death of the "tres haulte tres Excellente et tres Catholicque Dame Doyne Ysabeau Reyne D'Espagne" [very high, very excellent, and very Catholic Lady Isabel queen of Spain]. It then goes on immediately to describe her and her husband Ferdinand jointly as the conquerors "par armes" [by arms] of "les Mores" [the Moors] of the "Royaulme de Grenade et ses appertenances" [kingdom of Granada and its territories] (fol. 16v). This "holy war" to retake territories on the Iberian peninsula from Islamic rulers—the so-called "reconquest"—foregrounds the degree to which religion and political action, especially warfare, go hand in hand in the medieval and early modern periods. This connection is quite evident in the overlap of both the Hundred Years' War and Franco-Burgundian civil strife with the papal schism, political conflicts under consideration in the first three chapters of this book. The violent animosity between Catholics and Protestants characteristic of English domestic and foreign affairs under Henry VIII, Mary I, and Elizabeth I that I examine in the book's final chapters further bears witness to the inseparability of the religious and political spheres. Overall, this book constitutes an exploration of the central roles played by "women of God"—female saints, devout lay women, and monastic women—as "women of arms"—rulers, fighters, diplomats, and participants in propaganda—in all of these events as well as in the larger religio-political systems in which they unfolded.

The appellation "tres Catholicque" for Isabel invokes her identity as Isabel "la Católica," the construction of which I explore in chapter 4. Calling Isabel "tres Catholicque" draws attention to the reserves of symbolic capital located in medieval female spirituality. Such symbolic capital enabled and underwrote not only Isabel's independent political action—including in some cases armed action—but also that of women as diverse as Joan of Arc, Colette of Corbie, Margaret of York, and Elizabeth I. The politically valuable symbolic capital of medieval female spirituality was not, however, only available to holy women themselves. The fact that the obsequies described in the text were ordered by Isabel's son-in-law Philippe, whose somewhat controversial inheritance of Isabel's realms through his marriage to her daughter Juana is outlined in the text, reveals that this resource could be accessed as a legitimating force by others. As the following chapters will demonstrate, mobilizing female spirituality for purposes of political legitimation is a phenomenon repeatedly witnessed in Burgundian, French, and English as well as Spanish affairs throughout the fourteenth, fifteenth, and sixteenth centuries.

The anonymous reporter of Isabel's obsequies discourses at length on the decoration of the church and the order of the funeral procession. The descriptions highlight the importance of ceremony in mobilizing religion for purposes of political legitimation. Philippe's obsequies for his mother-in-law harken back to the elaborate processions, entries, and other public displays of religious devotion that were central to the self-representational strategies of his Burgundian forebears; it is with such strategies that I concern myself in the first two chapters. Isabel's funeral also recalls the pageantry, often religious in nature, that is a hallmark of English political culture under the Tudors and that I interrogate in chapters 5 and 6.

Toward the end of the account, we learn that the "Roy Darmes thoison dor dit a hault voix par trois fois assavoir le premier vers l'Autel le visage, et les deux aultres vers le Roy, 'vive Don Philippe et Doyne Iehanne par la grace de Dieu Roy et Royne de Castille, de Leon, et de Grenade, Prince et Princesse Darragon et Cecille'" [the King of Arms of the Order of the Golden Fleece said in a loud voice three times—that is to say, the first time facing the altar and the other two towards the king—"Long live Lord Philippe and Lady Jeanne by the grace of God king and queen of Castile, Leon, and Granada, prince and princess of Aragon and Sicily"] (fol. 23v). Much as the herald's pronouncement, made first towards the altar, publicly gives Philippe's kingship a sacramental, divine stamp, the church provided both a physical site and a symbolic means for the creation of political authority for rulers ranging from John the Fearless to Henry VIII to Elizabeth I. Furthermore, just as Isabel's holiness was part of her legacy to Philippe and Juana upon which Philippe capitalized in the public ceremonies of mourning, so too female spirituality consistently played a prominent part in identity formation and representation for English and Burgundian rulers.

Because the obsequies were designed not only to mourn Isabel's death but also to celebrate Philippe's accession, the text spends a considerable amount of time sketching out Isabel's family tree and emphasizing his dynastic claim. In the process, it foregrounds the ways in which the internal and external politics of England and several Continental realms were interwoven. Blood and marriage linked the English dynasties of Lancaster and York with those of France, Burgundy, Flanders, and Castile, creating tangled networks of alliances and animosities. Also created as a byproduct of this network of marriage and kinship were cultural anxieties about national identity, lineage, and gender.

Various threads of these tangles are visible in the account of Isabel's funeral ceremonies. The writer identifies Isabel, "fille au Roy de Castille, et femme de Fernande Roy d'Aragon" [daughter of the king of Castile and wife of Ferdinand, king of Aragon], as the mother of three daughters alive at the time of her death. The eldest of these is Juana ("Jehanne"), married to "Philippe Archiduc de Bourgogne," who is in turn identified as "fils de Maximilien d'Austrice Roy des Romains et de Dame Marie Ducesse de Bourgogne" [son of Maxilian of Austria, king of the Romans, and Lady Marie, duchess of Burgundy] (fol. 16v). The marriage of Philippe and Juana united the Habsburg empire with the holdings of Castile and Aragon; it also reawakened anxieties about female rule and the place of women in lineages, questions that smoldered in England as well as in Spain in the fourteenth, fifteenth, and sixteenth centuries. The herald's pronouncement of Philippe and Juana's accession discussed above subtly responds to such anxieties by emphasizing that, although Juana is Isabel's "heretiere" [heir] (fol. 16v), Philippe takes precedence in rule.

The reference to the marriage of Maximilian to Marie of Burgundy recalls the earlier consolidation of the Habsburg empire. It also evokes the political landscape examined in the book's opening chapters—the heroic, albeit ultimately unsuccessful, political efforts of Marie's father Charles the Bold to create a Burgundian state independent of France and allied with England. To this end, he married Margaret of York, sister of Edward IV of England, whose political spirituality I discuss in Chapter 2. To complicate matters further, though, Charles also claimed the right to the throne of England through his mother, Isabel of Portugal, a descendent of John of Gaunt, duke of Lancaster.

The account goes on to mention the marriages of Isabel's other daughters. With much less detail than is lavished on Juana and Philippe, it states that the second daughter "avoit Espose le Roy Don Manuel de Portugal" [married King Manuel of Portugal]. Then, tersely, it states "la tierche at espose Arthur Prince de Galles Laquelle a ce Iour estoit vefue" [the third married Arthur Prince of Wales; she is now a widow] (fol. 17r). The brevity of this reference belies the enormity of the consequences of this third daughter's marital career. This third daughter is of course Katherine of Aragon, who, after being widowed by Arthur, prince of Wales, would go on to marry his brother, so becoming the first wife of Henry VIII. Henry's efforts to divorce her would not only set in motion the English Reformation but would also redraw the map of political alliances throughout Europe, events I examine toward the end of the book.

Katherine of Aragon's arrival in England provides the occasion to consider another sort of linkage that connected England and Continental realms. England, France, Burgundy, Spain, and the Low Countries were joined through frequent textual and cultural exchanges as well as by ties of kinship and political alliance. The Spanish humanist writer Juan Luis Vives accompanied Katherine to England, and he wrote for her daughter—the future Mary I—a treatise entitled *The Instruction of a Christian Woman*. This text, originally in Latin, was quickly translated into Spanish; it was also soon translated into English by Richard Hyrd. As I discuss in the third chapter, it became one of the most popular texts in Tudor England, circulating alongside the also popular translations of the French works of Christine de Pizan. Significantly, in all of these texts, we find negotiations of national identity, gender, and authority. Furthermore, as my analysis of these texts demonstrates, female spirituality travels across

national boundaries and through centuries as an important tool for coming to terms with fraught political issues.

This book thus examines far-reaching questions concerning the participation of female spirituality in diverse political systems. As its interdis-
ciplinary subject matter requires, it treats a wide generic range of sources:
hagiography, chronicles, monastic records, devotional treatises, military
manuals, political propaganda, and texts traditionally designated as literary.
My overarching aim is to interrogate the vital cultural work performed by
manifestations of female spirituality at the intersections of civic, international, and ecclesiastical politics.

The first chapter focuses on St. Colette of Corbie (1381–1447), reformer
of the Franciscan friars and the Poor Clares. St. Colette was a profoundly
political saint, both during her lifetime and afterward. Her participation
in the internal politics of the Church and the Franciscan Order were inextricably interwoven with her involvement in the complex political networks
joining England, France, Burgundy, and the Low Countries. To examine
Colette's political engagement and its larger cultural significance, I interrogate her efforts to reform the friars of Dole and her repeated attempts
to found a nunnery in her natal town. The resistance of the friars and the
persistent opposition of the Benedictine monks of Corbie highlight anxieties about female authority, both religious and secular. These encounters
also underline the importance of spiritual, symbolic profit in the religio-
political sphere.

Just as social authority and symbolic capital were key issues for
the Benedictine monks at Corbie and for Colette's opponents within the
Franciscan order, so too were they of prime importance to the dukes and
duchesses of Burgundy. The Burgundians were, with their proclivity for
pageantry and ceremony, past masters of self representation. At junctures
when their authority faced serious challenges, members of the house of
Burgundy often lent their social prestige and financial resources to Colette's
foundations, especially those in Poligny, Auxonne, Dijon, and Ghent. My
analysis of Burgundian involvement with these monastic communities
demonstrates that the spiritual returns the dukes and duchesses received
served to advance their efforts to obtain representational credit, so also
advancing, through the cycle of interconvertibility, Burgundian power.

The second chapter continues to examine the Burgundian dynasty,
but expands the focus to address Burgundy's relationships with England
as well as with France by examining the career of Margaret of York, duchess of Burgundy. Margaret of York, sister of Edward IV and wife of Charles

the Bold, was a famously pious woman. Her interest in religious books, patronage, and reform has led some scholars to argue that her piety was in fact the primary component of her role as duchess of Burgundy, replacing the "political" activities that were the province of the dukes. Margaret's spiritual interests were not, however, necessarily contrary to the political, dynastic concerns that occupied her husband Charles and his successor Maximilian. Rather, Margaret's spirituality offered another avenue for pursuing precisely such concerns. Just as St. Colette found opportunities for political advantage and political agency in her religious practices (even as her brand of female spirituality was mobilized by others for their own political aims), so Margaret too found in the very forms of female spirituality deemed appropriate to a woman of her station ways of achieving her political goals. Indeed, her devotional practices as well as her religious patronage bear witness to her very politicized identity as an authoritative duchess of Burgundy during a tumultuous period in Burgundian affairs.

To illustrate this claim, I examine Margaret's gifts to religious institutions, her devotion to such saints as St. Anne, St. Agnes, and St. George, and her use of monastic reform as a diplomatic aid in negotiating Anglo-Burgundian alliances. Of particular interest in understanding Margaret's political spirituality is a text called *Le dyalogue de la ducesse de bourgogne a Ihesu Crist* (London, British Library MS Add. 7970) written for Margaret by Nicholas Finet. This devotional treatise explicitly connects Margaret's monastic patronage and reforms with the "bien conmun" [common good] and, accordingly, with the political success of the house of Burgundy. In this chapter I also turn my attention to Anne d'Orléans, the cousin of Louis XI and sister of Louis XII of France, who became abbess at Fontevraud. Anne and Margaret came from similar circumstances but clearly led very different sorts of lives. Strikingly, however, for Anne, as for Margaret, monastic reform became a strategic political tool. When Anne became abbess in 1477, she continued the reform efforts begun by her predecessor Marie de Bretagne, capitalizing on the Fontevrauldine legacy of Anglo-French unity at the very time when her royal relations were competing with Margaret and the Burgundians to forge alliances with England. Anne too worked to create a spiritual union to cement a political one, striving to spread Fontevrauldine reforms to England to recoup property and influence lost during the Hundred Years' War.

The third chapter considers a different form of political action undertaken by a holy woman. It interrogates the legacy of Joan of Arc and its influence on English political and literary culture in the fifteenth and sixteenth centuries, focusing in particular on the nexus of Joan of Arc, Christine de Pizan, and Margaret of Anjou. Christine de Pizan, though Italian by birth and supported by Burgundian as well as Valois patrons, identified strongly with France and the French royal cause. Indeed, she exhibited particularly strong animosity toward the English. Given Christine's sympathies, her work enjoyed surprising popularity in England in the fifteenth and sixteenth centuries, a time when France and the status of the English claim to France were extremely difficult issues. Furthermore, her most popular texts, *L'Epistre d'Othea*, *Le Livre de faits d'armes et de chevalerie*, and *Le Livre de la cité des dames*, emphasize many of the most troubling problems that faced the English monarchy: military training, the conduct of war, proper governance, and—crucially for the ever-fraught issue of royal succession, the catalyst for so much of the domestic and international conflict in this period—women's place in lineages.

In this environment, the cultural pressures provided by Christine and her texts, troubling through they may have been, were in fact quite productive. Strategic manipulations of the figure of Christine, combined with targeted transformations of her works, provided opportunities for retroactive revisions of the gender boundaries and national boundaries Christine and her countrywomen Joan and Margaret destabilized. At the center of this process of making politically congenial truth out of political trauma is the creation of an identity for Christine as a cloistered woman religious. Female monasticism—the same form of religious life that provided entrées into political life for St. Colette and Margaret of York—becomes, in the hands of English redactors of Christine's work, a way to limit women's political power and save martial masculinity.

The climate in which Isabel of Castile had to shape a creditable model of female rule, and in which she had to justify her involvement in military and empire-building pursuits, was as hostile to female participation in such endeavors as those encountered by Margaret of Anjou and Margaret of York, and it is to Isabel that I turn my attention in Chapter 4. To combat such antagonism, Isabel masterfully manipulated the "symbolics of power."[3] Her perspicacious mobilizations of medieval female spirituality and sanctity did much to advance her symbolic politics and thus to consolidate her royal authority.

Isabel cultivated a persona of pious queenship grounded in traditional ideologies of female conduct and models of women's devotion. In this way, she aligned herself with convention, downplaying potentially controversial aspects of her reign. Female spirituality and sanctity served to clothe

Isabel's power in a nonthreatening guise, so making it culturally accept-able. Paradoxically, in order to increase her ability to rule independently, Isabel and her supporters adopted strategies in some respects very like those employed by the English writers who "cloistered" Christine de Pizan, aligning Isabel with ideologies that often minimize women's autonomy. I explore this contradictory dynamic in my reading of the Augustinian friar Martín de Córdoba's *Jardín de nobles donzellas*, written for Isabel just be-fore she became queen and printed for wider consumption late in her reign at a moment of dynastic crisis.

At the same time, Isabel's representational program transformed accepted models of female spirituality and sanctity to validate her own less-than-traditional political participation and military leadership. New, strongly politicized exemplars were built on the framework of medieval sainthood to authorize in Isabel behavior not typically condoned for women. Once again, as we see in the cases of Colette of Corbie, Margaret of York, and Christine de Pizan, female spirituality's political value proves to be multivalent and malleable. The anonymous text *La Poncella de Fran-cia*, written for and dedicated to Isabel, textually "canonizes" Joan of Arc centuries before her official recognition as a saint. Through careful shap-ing of Joan's history in ways favorable to Isabel's cause, this text engages aspects of medieval female hagiography to frame Isabel's pursuits as a "woman of arms," especially her involvement in the reconquest, as holy missions endorsed by God.

Chapters 5 and 6 address the period spanning the reigns of Henry VIII and Elizabeth I as one characterized by the liminality present in the spaces between historical periods and between cultural groups.[4] The per-sistence of medieval religion, and particularly of medieval female spiritu-ality, was a crucial factor in the constant transformations that characterized what it meant to be English and the ways in which it was possible to per-form English identity on the larger stage of European politics. The fifth chapter considers the case of the visionary nun Elizabeth Barton. Barton is, of course, known for her opposition to the Henrician Act of Supremacy and the royal divorce, but her visions' disruptive political power did not end with the King's Great Matter. Just as the controversy surrounding the divorce spilled over into, and indeed largely shaped, Henry VIII's foreign policy, so too her revelations took on international importance as Henry endeavored to secure England's position in the European political sphere.

Elizabeth Barton was, furthermore, fundamentally involved in the what Peter Lake and Michael Questier call the "struggle for the control of

. . . central ideological, rhetorical, and material weapons."[5] In fact, she was inescapably involved in this competition, because medieval female spirituality was such a rich source of precisely the symbols and tropes for which the struggle was waged. The battle was a particularly fierce one, because the very definition of English identity was at stake. To elucidate the nature of this ideological struggle, and to highlight the extraordinary importance of Elizabeth Barton's participation in it, I analyze in detail one of her revelations from 1532. This revelation recounts the removal of the consecrated host from Henry VIII at a mass held during his negotiations at Calais with Francis I. Quickly and widely disseminated, it struck at the heart of Henry VIII's foreign policy and, perhaps even more significantly, at the heart of his representation of the English monarchy.

Like Joan of Arc, Elizabeth Barton supported a vision of divinely ordained political authority in England in opposition to the vision of a reigning English monarch. Elizabeth, though, did so from within rather than from without. She thus participated in the sort of intellectual exile that Edward Said attributes to the "nay-sayers," to those "individuals at odds with their society."[6] During Elizabeth I's reign, intellectual exile increasingly became, for many English monastics, physical exile as well. The sixth chapter addresses the long-term implications of the dissolution of the monasteries for Elizabethan politics as I interrogate emerging models of national identity. Cultural manifestations of female spirituality, and especially the locus of the cloister, became radically contested territory. I focus in particular on the Brigittine nuns of Syon, who fled first to the Low Countries, then to France, and finally to Lisbon. Using postcolonial theories of diaspora, I explore the formation of a Catholic understanding of "Englishness" that competed with the English identity shaped by Protestant nationalist narratives. Histories produced by Syon in exile bear witness to a dissident version of the immediate, medieval past and its religion, one that undercuts the triumphalism of Elizabethan propaganda.

Moving from ideological conflict to more direct political action, I consider the *Life of Sister Marie Champney* (London, British Library MS Add. 18,650) and documents concerning Marie's fellow nun-in-exile Elizabeth Sanders. Marie and Elizabeth's stories reveal that nuns of Syon returned illegally to England to work for the Catholic cause, allied themselves with Spain and the Catholic League against Elizabeth I, and quite possibly even engaged in armed plots against the queen. The cases of these women religious emblematize the ways in which Syon, and by extension female spirituality firmly rooted in medieval traditions, took part in the conflict concerning the nature of English identity and the structure of the English monarchy.

The chapters are arranged more or less chronologically, but I move quite deliberately back and forth across the medieval / early modern "divide" within chapters. One of my central aims, in fact, is to demonstrate that the divide does not really exist. I seek to breach the temporal boundary that so often separates work on these periods and to complicate the Catholic / Protestant dichotomy frequently invoked in drawing a line between the Middle Ages and the early modern era. The book begins in France and arrives in the conclusion in the New World, traveling by way of Burgundy, the Low Countries, Spain and England. Again, however, I move freely across national boundaries within chapters, since I desire to transcend the political borders (both those on maps and those within universities) that tend to isolate work on England, the Iberian Peninsula, and the Continent.

In the course of these temporal and geographical trajectories, female religious practices emerge as distinct forms of female political agency, the possibilities of which and the cultural meanings of which themselves incorporate both continuity and transformation. My argument, fundamentally, is that female spirituality is an arena in which women can themselves engage, and can be engaged by others, in political actions. This book is occupied with the crucial task of grasping what remains the same, as well as what changes, in defining the terms, the stakes, and the identities of the participants in the cataclysmic national and international conflicts played out in this arena in a period spanning just over two hundred years.

I

Monastic Politics: St. Colette of Corbie, Franciscan Reform, and the House of Burgundy

Colette of Corbie as a Political Saint

In 1946, in the aftermath of World War II in France, a curious pamphlet was published to mark the upcoming five-hundredth anniversary of the death of St. Colette of Corbie. The document, entitled *Sainte Colette de Corbie et l'action catholique féminine française*, first presents a brief biography of the saint. Then, however, it turns to its more immediate purpose of advancing a concerted postwar effort to return French women to the domestic sphere by holding up St. Colette as an example of ideal femininity. The politically active fifteenth-century virgin and traveling monastic reformer is stunningly transformed into a patroness of home, hearth, and maternity. The clerical writer of the pamphlet, a Capucin named Pierre Damien, declares:

Il est opportun d'attirer vers Sainte Colette le regard et le coeur des femmes de France, en ce moment où selon la parole de Sa Sainteté Pie XII, sonne dans le monde l'heure de la femme. Ecoutons encore la voix du Saint Père: "La femme vraiment femme ne peut voir ni comprendre à fond tous les problèmes de la vie humaine autrement que sous l'aspect de la famille. C'est pourquoi le sens affiné qu'elle a de sa dignité la jette dans l'inquiétude chaque fois que l'ordre social ou politique menace de porter préjudice à sa mission maternelle, au bien de la famille."[1]

[It is opportune to draw the notice and the hearts of the women of France to St. Colette at this moment when, according to the word of His Holiness Pius XII, the hour of the woman sounds in the world. Let us listen again to the Holy Father's voice: "In the end the true woman can neither see nor comprehend all the problems of human life otherwise than from the perspective of the family. That is why the refined sense she has of her dignity throws her into turmoil each time the social or political order threatens to bring prejudice to her maternal mission, to the good of the family."]

As odd as this particular twentieth-century invocation of St. Colette may seem, it is in fact part of a tradition that would not have seemed particularly strange to Colette herself or to her later-medieval contemporaries. Pierre Damien is, after all, using this female saint to legitimate a political agenda (albeit one that does not harmonize especially well with Colette's life and work) and to shore up political authority during troubled times. Indeed, just over 500 years earlier, during an equally tumultuous period of French history, St. Colette was mobilized in similarly propagandist fashion by John the Fearless, duke of Burgundy. In 1414, after an unsuccessful Burgundian attempt to retake Paris, outright civil war resumed between the Burgundians and Armagnac forces. The Armagnacs enjoyed a string of military successes through the spring and summer of 1414; John's duchess Margaret and their children were reportedly even menaced at Dijon and Rouvres by enemy soldiers. It was in June of this turbulent summer, perhaps partially in recompense for Colette's intercessory prayers that reportedly helped to save Margaret and the Burgundian heirs from the Armagnacs, and perhaps also to gain public support in an important town at a time when his power was in jeopardy, that John granted to Colette, who already enjoyed considerable local popularity for her reputed sanctity, a disused arsenal at Poligny to found a convent of her order there.

John's support for Colette's foundation at Poligny in fact had more political benefits for his cause than he himself would ever know. Colette put the community "sous la protection de Jésus crucifié" [under the protection of the crucified Jesus],[2] not a terribly surprising choice given the traditional Franciscan emphasis on Christ's passion displayed in Colette's spirituality and writings. She also had erected in the garden there a large stone cross so that the passion would be perpetually remembered. Furthermore, she expressly wished that the convent church be "dédiée sous le vocable de Notre-Dame-de-Pitié" [dedicated to Our Lady of Compassion].[3] After John's murder at Montereau in 1419, the foundation's connections with Christ's passion and Marian compassion were turned to his benefit. Shortly after his death, in an extraordinarily audacious legitimating move that transformed politically motivated murder—some would even say well-deserved revenge—into holy martyrdom, a tableau was displayed at the convent representing the descent from the cross. According to a description of the painting from 1783 (which indicates that the tableau in the nunnery then—presumably the one present now—is most likely the copy of an older one), "sous la figure du Christ c'est le duc lui meme tué a Montereau et percé de coups quil est" [the duke himself, who was killed at Montereau and pierced with blows, is depicted in the guise of Christ]. In the features of the Virgin Mary holding the body of the crucified Christ, "la duchesse de Bourgogne est representée" [the duchess of Burgundy is represented], although whether the duchess in question is John's mother Margaret of Flanders or his wife Margaret of Bavaria is a subject of some debate. Henry de la Baume is "representé . . . sous l'habit de St. françois" [represented . . . in the habit of St. Francis], and Pierre de Vaux, Colette's confessor and after her death the author of her *vita*, also appears, wearing "l'habit et les simbols de St Antoine de Padoüe" [the habit and symbols of St. Anthony of Padua]. Weeping, St. Colette "baise la main du Christ" [kisses Christ's hand], taking the position traditionally occupied in depictions of the descent from the cross by Mary Magdalene, another female saint who, as I shall discuss below, is used to serve the Burgundian political agenda. In the background behind Colette, Marie de Corbie "est representée . . . sous l'habit de Ste Claire" [is represented . . . in the habit of St. Clare].⁴ John's death is thus mapped onto the crucifixion as the notorious duke, surrounded by the entire Colettine "family," receives saintly, even divine, status.

The twentieth-century use of St. Colette by Pierre Damien and the fifteenth-century efforts of the Burgundians in Poligny highlight ongoing intersections of secular politics and female spirituality, intersections that permeate the history of St. Colette, her monastic reforms, and her foundations. St. Colette, founder of a reformed branch of the Poor Clares, was born in 1381 in the shadow of the great Benedictine abbey of St. Pierre in Corbie and died in Ghent in 1447, already widely revered as a saint. Colette, who lived in one of the most disturbed regions at one of the most fraught periods of European history, was a profoundly political saint, both during her lifetime and afterward; indeed, in her work on St. Colette, Elisabeth Lopez has astutely observed "the reciprocal influence of religious and political domains."⁵ As a monastic reformer who needed papal authorization for her efforts, Colette was enmeshed in the struggles instantiated by the rivalries of two, and for a time three, popes. These rivalries intersected with international political conflicts as well as with political strife in France. Furthermore, in her campaign of monastic reforms, she frequently found herself in the thick of clashes within the Franciscan Order, both those involving competing branches of the Franciscan reform movement and those between Observant and Conventual Franciscans. These contests too resonated with contemporary French and European political developments. In fact, Colette's participation in the internal politics of the Church and the Franciscan Order was inextricably interwoven with her involvement in the complex networks of political alliances and animosities among England, France, Burgundy, and the Low Countries.

As both Pierre Damien's pamphlet and the Burgundian involvement with the Colettine house at Poligny reveal, female spirituality is quite valuable as a source of symbolic capital available to advance political aims. Indeed, John the Fearless considered the symbolic benefits accruing from his support of Colette's foundation in Poligny worth accepting rather substantial material losses to obtain, since "la maison, les mazières et meiz" [house, outbuildings, and quarters] that he donated were worth more than 24,000 francs.[6] The Chambre de Comptes at Dijon objected strenuously to the gift, but John overrode them, issuing letters patent in which he commanded that they "faire lever et oster le empeschem*ent* et faire laisser jouir icelle abbesse et ses di*c*tes sueurs de no3 don" [remove the impediment and allow this abbess and her said sisters to enjoy our gift]. He further ordered that, "pour ce nous . . . de n*os*tre cuer desirons laugmenta-ci*on* du diuin se*r*uice" [because we . . . in our heart desire the increase of divine service], the monastery "soit fonder et ediffie en la place de no3 di*c*tes maisons maisieres et mex" [be founded and built in the place of our said houses, outbuildings, and quarters].[7]

Colette's life, works, and "afterlife" demonstrate, however, how very complicated such useful sources of symbolic capital can be; while valuable, female spirituality and sanctity are also highly malleable and not always easily controllable. What is useful in one context may be quite threatening, even dangerously counterproductive, in another. Gendered elements of Colette's spirituality and reforms caused trouble for her within the Church and the Franciscan Order. Particularly problematic were her strict application of Franciscan ideals to women and men alike, the authority given to women in her reform movement, and the emphasis she placed on women's abilities both spiritual and temporal. This combination of factors provoked anxieties concerning the proper roles of women in public and spiritual life not unlike those lurking behind Pierre Damien's and Pope Pius XII's pronouncements on the appropriate, domestic roles of women in 1946. The relationships between Colette and powerful secular political figures demonstrate, however, that the same gendered elements also did much to make Colette and her foundations especially attractive to dukes, duchesses, and even kings.

Symbolic Capital and Monastic Identity

Colette's early history is dominated by conflict, both with the local clergy of her hometown of Corbie and with the Benedictine abbey of St. Pierre, which loomed large in Corbie's religious landscape. Her reputation for holiness spread while she was quite young, and when she was about seventeen years old, many women started visiting her to receive spiritual advice, to the great displeasure of local clerics. Jean de Boissy, bishop of Amiens, was called in, and he compelled her to cease and desist these "conférences spirituelles" [spiritual conferences], since "divers membres du clergé" [various members of the clergy] felt it was not "convenable" [suitable] for a woman without education to teach about religious matters.[8] At about the same time that she drew clerical objections for her role as a spiritual advisor, she was orphaned. Dom Raoul de Roye, abbot of Corbie, was made her guardian. He wanted to marry her off, but she eventually prevailed upon him that she should be allowed to enter religion.[9] Colette tried the Benedictines and Urbanist Claresses, finding neither to her satisfaction, and eventually she was enclosed as an anchoress. After approximately four years, she was released from her vows as an anchoress and emerged from her anchorhold. Accompanied by the Franciscan Henry de la Baume, she gained an audience with Pope Benedict XIII at Nice, was professed on the spot as a Franciscan nun, and was authorized to begin founding reformed houses of Claresses.

Colette's first attempt to found a nunnery after her audience with the pope was in her natal town, and a few years before her death, she tried once more to found at Corbie. Both attempts failed, continuing her history of troubled relations with the town and the Benedictine monastery there. I turn now to the circumstances of these failed foundations at Corbie, because they highlight themes that run throughout her career. Colette's efforts to found at Corbie, and the objections made to them, foreground the inseparability of the political, the material, and the symbolic realms; indeed, they demonstrate, to adopt Fredric Jameson's well-known formulation, that in Colette's monastic reforms and foundations there is nothing that is not social, historical, and political.[10]

Colette's first attempt to start a nunnery was accompanied by a great deal of disapproval both from the townspeople of Corbie and from the monks of St. Pierre. Some of these difficulties stemmed from the Franciscan reform movement's connection with the Avignon papacy. Colette and Henry de la Baume, associated with "un pape accusé d'entretenir le schisme" [a pope accused of sustaining schism] were widely deemed undesirable by the citizens of Corbie (*Petite vie*, 36). In 1445, however, during the stormy period of the Council of Basle and the reign of the antipope Felix V (the former Amédée de Savoie), Colette returned to her birthplace to attempt her foundation once again, and this time she had the support of some of the most influential figures of the age. Her allies included Philippe de Saveuse, governor of Amiens and servant of the Duke of Burgundy, who obtained a papal bull giving license for the foundation from the Roman pope Eugene IV, whom the Burgundians supported (although they did have permission to continue relations with the house of Savoy).

In spite of Colette's powerful supporters and her alliance with the "right" side of the ecclesiastical schism this time, the monks of St. Pierre objected once again, much in the same vein as the first time around. In both cases, they complained because they feared that their revenues would dwindle if a new convent were founded in Corbie.[11] Colette tried to assuage their fears by assuring them that her convent would not accumulate property. Since the nuns would live in strict accordance with St. Clare's vision of absolute poverty, the monks would suffer no loss of revenue. Indeed, she claims in a letter to the monks at Corbie that they and the town would benefit from the foundation: "je crois devant Dieu que ladite construction sera à l'honneur de Dieu et de vous, et à la recommandation de votre monastère et au profit d'icelui ainsi qu'au réconfort de vous et de tous les habitants de la ville" [I believe before God that the said construction will be to your honor and God's, and to the renown of your monastery and its profit, as well as to your comfort and that of all the inhabitants of the city].[12] The benefits in question are spiritual and symbolic, accruing from the nuns' embracing a life of austere poverty and their devotion to the ideals of St. Francis and St. Clare. Colette's personal commitment to such ideals, as well as the kinds of benefits such commitment can convey, are evident in another letter that she wrote to Jeanne Labeur, a nun in her foundation in Ghent. In this missive, Colette extols the essential virtue of poverty, saying, "Ô sainte Pauvreté, parement de notre rédemption; précieux joÿau; signe certain qui donne le Roÿaume du Ciel!" [O holy Poverty, ornament of our redemption; precious jewel; sure sign that grants the Kingdom of Heaven!].[13] She exhorts her nuns, "Or, mes Tres aimées soeurs,

aimés, aimés cette noble vertue a L'exemple de jésus-christ, de notre Glorieux Pere St. françois, et de notre mere Madame Sainte Claire" [There-
fore, my very dear sisters, love, love this noble virtue in the example of
Jesus Christ, our glorious father St. Francis, and our mother St. Clare].[14]
A document known as "l'entention de Seur Colette," written for the nuns
at Ghent, demonstrates the extraordinary stress Colette places on an Evangelical mode of life. Colette writes, "nous ÿ sommes tenûes et obligies
comme aux commandemens aux autres consaulx de la sainte eûangele qui
litteralement ne sont pas mis en nre fourme de vie selonc que requiert lestat
de nre profession. Nous ÿ sommes plus tenues que les autres cpiens." [We
are held and obliged to the other counsels of the Holy Gospel that are not
literally included in our form of life according to the requirements of our
profession as we are held to the commandments. We are held to them to
a greater extent than other Christians are.][15]

The monks of Corbie did not agree with Colette's assessment of the
situation and appealed to the Parliament of Paris, which took their side.
Colette's powerful friends then stepped into the fray. She enlisted the aid of
Charles VII, king of France, calling on his "douce et piteuse miséricorde"
[sweet and compassionate mercy] and appealing to his loyalty toward his
"très nobles prédécesseurs rois très chrétiens" [very noble predecessors the
very Christian kings].[16] Charles responded on Colette's behalf with a writ
dated July 29, 1446; even the queen of France and the dauphin weighed
in, sending letters of their own in support of Colette's foundation (*Belle
vie*, 250). Colette, able in this case, as in many others, to command support from rival parties, also requested help from her frequent benefactors
the Duke and Duchess of Burgundy, who, as I shall discuss shortly, found
much profit for themselves in supporting Colette's reforms and foundations. Duke and duchess alike wrote to the monks, pleading Colette's cause
(*Belle vie*, 247, 250).

Colette's ability to muster support from high-ranking political figures
emphasizes the importance of the relationships among the material, symbolic, and spiritual spheres. That the monks of Corbie ignored not only
all of the pleas and decrees sent to them but also a new papal bull order-
ing them to allow Colette's foundation to proceed, and the arrival of three
papal commissioners further demonstrates the significance of such conver-
gence (*Belle vie*, 252). The rhetoric of Colette's letters to the monks and to
Jeanne Labeur similarly highlight such interconnections, while suggesting
as well the malleability of female spirituality. Colette's descriptions of the
nuns' poverty, couched in precisely the terms of material value (profit,

ornament, precious jewel) that such praise of poverty seems to reject, suggest the ready exchangeability of value among the material, symbolic, and
spiritual realms. Her language puts into sharp relief the "perfect interconvertibility" of economic and symbolic capital to which Pierre Bourdieu
makes reference.[17] Poverty, as a distinctive, indeed, a defining feature of
Colette's conception of Franciscan monastic identity, becomes, somewhat
paradoxically, subject to the kinds of "economic calculation" that, as
Bourdieu observes, "extend[s] . . . to all the goods, material and symbolic,
without distinction, that present themselves as *rare* and worthy of being
sought after in a particular social formation."[18]

    Colette's secular supporters in her conflict with the monks were well
positioned to take advantage of the ready convertibility of material and
symbolic resources. They engaged, consciously or unconsciously, in precisely the sort of economic calculation that Bourdieu describes as they
pleaded Colette's cause. In effect, they exchanged their social clout for spiritual "credit." As the case of the house of Burgundy examined below reveals,
such credit could have temporal payoffs, including the advancement of
self-representational efforts, the legitimation of political authority, and,
perhaps, concomitant increases in material wealth.

    The same interconvertibility of resources from which Colette's sup-
porters stood to benefit also lies at the root of the monks' persistence in
their objections to Colette's foundation in Corbie. There is no denying
that the Benedictines had their own financial interests at heart. It is telling
that they reacted to Colette's reassurances concerning the poverty of her
nuns by turning that apparent plus into a minus. Clothing their self-interest
in concern for the local populace, they countered her argument by saying
that a house subsisting purely on alms could not exist in Corbie without
doing real harm to the indigent who relied on those alms (*Hagiographie*,
532). The spiritual and symbolic profits resulting from the commitment of
Colette and her nuns to poverty were, however, actually a more serious
danger for the Benedictine monks than any immediate financial damages
that Colette's foundation might cause. In this cultural environment, symbolic capital, which is granted to those who can provide "the best material
and symbolic *guarantees*,"[19] is "perhaps *the most valuable form of accumula-
tion*."[20] Whether or not Colette's foundation were to cut into the monks'
revenues directly, the strict female house would likely diminish the monks'
social authority and political power (power witnessed, for instance, by
their successful appeal to the Parliament of Paris) through a devaluation
of the symbolic capital in which that authority and power were grounded.

The Colettine foundation would inflict such damage by pointing up what Lopez has called the "essential contrast" between the luxurious Benedictine mode of life—and the abbey of St. Pierre at Corbie was very well to do indeed—and the austere Franciscan one.[21] The very financial assets that the monks initially desired to protect were thus, in fact, a liability, and the very elements of female spirituality that provided benefits to Colette's supporters (and to Colette herself as well as her nuns) were detrimental to the Benedictines of St. Pierre. Because the distinctive, evangelical qualities of Colette's reformed order were perceived as providing the "best guarantee" of spiritual and symbolic returns in an age in which ecclesiastical wealth and corruption were under fire, Colette's foundation had the potential to upset more than the monks' balance sheet;[22] the symbolic diminutions that the Colettines' poverty could effect might well thus have radically upset the balance of power both socially and spiritually.

In the fraught environment of the first half of the fifteenth century, Colette's opponents had at their disposal the ideal tool to wield against a holy woman whom they perceived as a threat, that is, accusations of heresy and sorcery. The Benedictine brethren wasted no time. "Plusieurs déclarènt qu'elle se trompait dans ses dévotions. Certains l'accusèrent de sorcellerie, assurant qu'un démon familier lui fournissait des caractères magiques." [Several declared that she was deceived in her devotions. Some accused her of sorcery, asserting that a demonic familiar furnished her with magic characters.][23] The monks of St. Pierre were, significantly, not alone among Colette's adversaries in resorting to such accusations. On at least two other occasions, those unhappy with her efforts at foundation and reform accused her of heresy. Once, two learned clerks made a public announcement calling her "hérétique, sentant mal de la foi" [heretic, with a stinking faith] and, most damning, "favorable des opinions des Pragois"—that is, they claimed she was a partisan of Jerome of Prague, a particularly dangerous accusation in the context of the condemnation and execution of Jerome and his associate Jan Hus at the Council of Constance. On another occasion, when she was returning from doing "aucunes choses nécessaires pour la religion" [certain things necessary for religion] she was denounced as being affiliated with the "bigards" [beghards] or "frères du libre esprit" [brethren of the Free Spirit] (*Hagiographie*, 442–43).

The monks of Corbie and Colette's other opponents, in accusing her of heresy and sorcery, resemble Joan of Arc's captors and judges, a resemblance not at all surprising when one considers that Joan was a contemporary of Colette. Indeed, there are reports, albeit unconfirmed, that the

two holy women met in 1429.[24] Interestingly, Colette's opponents also mirror Joan's in that they move easily between registers in their accusations,
further illuminating the political importance of intersections among the
material, spiritual, and symbolic. Just as Joan's interrogators in her trial
slide seamlessly between accusations of heresy and improper use of material goods (for instance, her acquisition of money and horses, her supposedly sumptuous male attire[25]), so too do Colette's enemies move from
making charges of transgressions in the spiritual realm to charges of misconduct in the material realm. In order to neutralize the value of Colettine
poverty, which, as we have seen, was so problematic for the monks of St.
Pierre, Colette's enemies denounced her, devoted though she was to strict
Franciscan ideals, for being "une riche femme, pleine d'or, et d'argent,
pretant à usure et maintenant (le) charge (à) trois ou quatre, comme à
Paris, à Bruges et à Gand" [a rich woman, well appointed with gold and
silver, a usurer lending at a charge of three or four times, like in Paris,
Bruges, and Ghent] (*Hagiographie*, 495).

   The parallels between Joan and Colette are instructive; both Colette's
opponents and Joan's captors and judges resorted to the same strategy because they needed to accomplish the same thing. They needed to discredit
a holy woman to recoup their own authority and the symbolic capital
upon which that authority is founded. That they both turned to accusations
of heresy and sorcery illuminates the very political nature of the threat
posed by the holy women. As R. I. Moore does, I would call attention to
Max Weber's analysis of religion, politics, and economics in classical China,
in which he observes that the prosecution of heresy emerged when con-
flicting claims, ideas, and religious practices "appeared to become a political threat to the prevailing order."[26] Although Colette enjoyed papal
approval (albeit approval complicated by the Schism) for her reformist
undertakings, to many male religious she was an embodiment of female
power that jeopardized proper order, both spiritual and social, in the ecclesiastical political system. At the same time, however, secular political figures
found in her and her houses useful resources for reinforcing their own
partisan visions of proper order, so demonstrating the complexities of the
valuable symbolic capital of female spirituality.

Monastic Reforms and the Politics of Gender

Although papal bulls contradict the account advanced during her canonization proceedings that Benedict XIII authorized her at their initial meeting

to reform the First as well as the Second Order of St. Francis, her reforms undeniably did spread to the friars.[27] In her interactions with the male branch of the order, issues of female power and questions of proper order once again come to the fore, as do the politics of poverty. One of the first male communities to fall under Colette's scrutiny was that at Dole, which was founded in 1372 as an Observant house. As Douillet points out, however, the designation of Observant "indicated the aspirations of some rather than the general state of the community."[28] The pope, upon learning of abuses at Dole, put the house in the hands of Colette and her helper in the reform process, Henry de la Baume. Not all in the community took kindly to being reformed; in particular, a faction led by Jean Foucault, who had been three times "gardien du monastère" [guardian of the monastery], objected strenuously and brought a civil case against Colette.[29]

While money and property are certainly important concerns in this conflict, as they are for the monks of Corbie, issues of symbolic capital, social authority, and political power once again "hide" under cover of material economics. Although the case should have, by rights, fallen under canon law, the well-connected and locally influential Foucault and his partisans managed to bring the affair before the Parliament of Dole, where they, like their Benedictine brethren who had resorted to the Parliament of Paris, initially framed their case in financial terms (*Petite vie* 56). The friars represented themselves as a persecuted party being banished from a house that legitimately belonged to them.[30] In the friars' opposition to Colette, material motives were certainly a factor, as they were with the Benedictines of St. Pierre, albeit, in both cases, not the only—or necessarily the most important—factor. Jean and his followers, although by name Observants, lived like Conventuals; indeed, according to contemporary accounts, Jean was quite well off. They were thus probably reluctant to give away their property and goods in accordance with the requirements of Colette's reforms. Accompanying naked financial interest, though, were deeper concerns involving Colette's status as an abbess, her authority vis-à-vis the friars, and the power of women within the Franciscan Order.

To understand these concerns, it is necessary to understand some of the rather unusual dimensions of Colette's reform movement. Colette's brand of monastic reform had much in common with the Observant movement. Colette's foundations, however, were endowed by papal bulls with special privileges.[31] At the Council of Constance, the Observants, wishing to escape the control of the Conventuals, had received permission to owe their obedience to Observant "vicars provincial." Unlike the other Observants, Colette's houses maintained technical obedience to the Minister

General of the Order. In spite of this technical obedience to the Minister General, Colette was basically free to create her own reform.[32] In fact, the Minister General Guillaume de Casal's introduction to Colette's *Constitutions* places her above even her own law in enacting her reforms. He writes, "Te autem in xpo dilectissimam filiam ut ea possis implere propter que videris a domino yhu xpo vocata, hiis statutis nullatenus obligatam esse declaro: eos enim qui altiori dei spiritu aguntur non esse sub lege apostolus predicavit." [You, however, most beloved daughter in Christ, in order that you might accomplish that to which you seem to be called by the Lord Jesus Christ, are not bound by these statutes, for the Apostle instructed that those who are led by the higher spirit of God are not subject to the law.][33]

In her desire to preserve the strictest standards of St. Francis and St. Clare, Colette set up for her nuns a program of negotiated obedience to the ministers of the order in which obedience depends on the ministers' sympathy with the goals of her reforms and her narrowly defined version of Franciscan identity. In "l'entention de Suer Colette" she tells the nuns to obey "aux successeurs de saint francoÿs" [the successors of St. Francis], that is to say, "le ministre general" [the minister general].[34] She then qualifies this exhortation, saying that if "par temptation dyabolique" [through diabolic temptation] the "dit successeur" [said successor] is not in sympathy with the strict Franciscan ideals of the reform and "nous vaulsist empechier, où permittre où faire empechier, où qui ne nous vaulsist pas preserver ne deffendre de ceux qui nous vauldroient empeschement faire" [would impede us, would permit or cause impediment, or would not defend us from those who would impede us], then the nuns should pray to God, the Virgin Mary, St. Francis and St. Clare. The nuns should not stop with prayer but should also seek a temporal solution, turning first to "monsigneur le cardinal qui sera nostre protecteur" [monsignor the cardinal who will be our protector] and, afterward, if necessary, to "nre Saint pere le pape" [our Holy Father the pope] for a "remede convenable" [suitable remedy].[35] A letter written to Colette by the same Minister General Guillaume de Casal who gave her such scope in her reforms suggests the degree to which the Colettine nuns' obedience to the minister was indeed a provisional, negotiated one. It also perhaps displays Casal's ambivalence about his endorsement of Colette's independent authority. He disapprovingly remarks, "il me semble que vos filles n'osent pas obéir ni acquiescer à mes mandements et persuasion sans votre spéciale permission. Je crois qu'elles le font comme n'étant pas accoutumées et n'ayant pas l'expérience." [It seems to me that your daughters dare not obey or acquiese to my commandments and persuasions without your special permission. I believe that they do it as though unaccustomed to it and inexperienced in it.][36]

Colette's status in her quasi-independent reform was, as her frequent designation as "mère"[mother] suggests, that of "abbess general" over friars as well as nuns.[37] Indeed, her maternal, abbatissal jurisdiction over male religious is amply demonstrated in a letter that she wrote to the friar Jehan Lanier revoking his status as confessor for her community of nuns at Puy. Making reference to his "feublesse et ensiennete" [weakness and old age], Colette notifies Jehan of his dismissal. She cites as grounds for her action the reports she has received indicating that he can no longer "bonement . . . faire lofice" [perform his office well]. She forestalls any argument about the installation of his replacement, stating bluntly, "cest mon plaisir et ma valont[e] . . . que enfint soit il fait" [it is my pleasure and my will . . . that in the end it shall be so].[38]

Such maternal power over male clerics in the Colettine tradition was, furthermore, not limited to Colette herself as "abbess general." Other abbesses in Colettine communities could wield such authority as well, as emerges in the letter Mahaut de Savoie wrote to St. Colette concerning the foundation of a chantry at the Colettine nunnery at Poligny. Blanche de Savoie was buried there, and Mahaut funded two chaplains to say masses for Blanche's soul. Mahaut writes that if it should transpire that "aucuns dyceulx chapellains ou tous deux" [either of these chaplains or both of them] were "defectueux de faire leur deuoir" [delinquent in performing their duty] then "labbesse du conseil de leur visiteur ou confesseur et de sez seurs discretes les puisse destituer et deposer et aultrez elire et presenter" [the abbess, with council of their visitor or confessor and of her sage sisters, may deprive and depose them and elect and present others].[39]

Colette herself was additionally empowered to approve conventual elections; in this regard, her power over friars as well as nuns was not simply abbatissal but mirrors that of a diocesan bishop.[40] Not surprisingly, such independent authority caused trouble with at least one bishop. In addition to facing protests from "administrateurs intéressés" [interested administrators] concerned about loss of rents, and from local clergy as well as religious foundations worried about loss of income, Colette ran into episcopal objections when she attempted to establish her community at Amiens. The bishop of Amiens naturally took the side of the local clergy and religious, but he also was greatly concerned to ensure "son autorité" [his authority] over "ces religieuses nouvelles" [these new women religious] (*Belle vie*, 242).

The nature of Colette's personal power and of female power more broadly construed within the order, with all the spiritual and symbolic ramifications such power carried, were perhaps the greatest issues for Jean Foucault and his adherents at Dole in their resistance to her reforms, as their choice of tactics after the Parliament of Dole ruled against them reveals. Jean decided that if reform were inevitable, a reform led by men was preferable to one led by a woman. So, he allied himself with the Observants, even though their requirement for absolute poverty was virtually identical to that mandated by Colette. The Observants, always seeking to increase their influence within the order, included Dole in a list of houses to be approved by the Council of Constance to owe obedience to vicars provincial, a move designed to take control out of Colette's hands. This strategy too proved unsuccessful for Foucault and his supporters at Dole, since the community became irrevocably Colettine. The conflict did, however, get the attention of many friars in Burgundy, who opposed the autonomy Colette had managed to secure thanks, at least to some degree, to the help of the house of Burgundy. Her reforms finally even provoked the Minister General to whom Colette and her houses technically owed obedience. He too wanted to check Colette's growing power, so he forbade all foundations in Burgundy without his direct authorization (*Petite vie*, 56). This move on the Minister General's part led Colette skillfully to play the secular political system against the ecclesiastical one as she began a program of foundations in Bourbon territories.

The nature of Colette's power as abbess, the role of women within the order, and the contested construction of the Franciscan "chain of command," were likewise key factors in her famous encounter with a "rival" reformer, John of Capistrano. In the 1440s, the Franciscans needed to elect a new minister general. The interim was an Observant Franciscan, and the Observants were working hard to unify the Italian and Burgundian branches to ensure the election of an Observant rather than a Conventual to fill the post permanently. Thus, in France and Italy, the reformed friars were striving to unify themselves as well as to bring houses of nuns under their wing (*Petite vie*, 76). In addition to the similarity between the Colettines and the Observants in their strict adherence to Franciscan ideals of absolute poverty, an affinity that likely made the Colettines seem an easy target for assimilation under the Observant umbrella, Colette's houses drew particular attention because of their autonomy from other reform movements. John of Capistrano, sent as a papal legate to the duke of Burgundy, paid a visit to Colette to demand the absorption of her communities into the larger Observant reform movement. This development would have entailed the friars' taking over the direction of the monasteries and the appointment of confessors. The friars would also have had the power to dismiss abbesses elected by the communities—all powers held by Colette herself under her *Constitutions* (*Petite vie*, 76).

That John of Capistrano had a special concern with, and a very different vision of, the proper construction of female authority in religion can be seen by comparing his *Declaratio Primae Regulae s. Clarae*, followed by Observant communities of nuns in Italy, to Colette's *Constitutions*. Colette emphasizes the authority of the abbess over the sisters and the absolute necessity for obedience to the abbess. Although the abbess "is not the creator of the law, she possesses juridical power to apply it."[41] Capistrano, on the other hand, focuses at length on the abbess's capacity to love the sisters, her humility, and her patience. As Lopez notes, for Capistrano, "The essential aspect of the abbess's charge is not so much to govern, organize, and manage, as to love and help the sisters."[42] While Colette's construction of the abbess's authority resembles that of a Benedictine abbot, who holds the place of Christ in a monastery, Capistrano's idea of the abbess's role is closer to that set out by a fifteenth-century English translator of the Benedictine Rule for women. This English writer, also seeking to limit the possibilities for female authority in religion, describes the abbess as meek, mild, "bowsum," and child-like rather than maternal.[43]

Colette eventually prevailed over John of Capistrano, just as she did at Dole. He capitulated, allowing her reforms to continue as an autonomous movement. In spite of Colette's victories in the short term while she lived, however, the anxieties caused by the power accorded to women—particularly authority over men—in the Colettine reforms persisted. Indeed, Colette's quasi-episcopal, abbatissal status became still more potentially threatening in its representation in the *Vie de Sainte Colette*, composed by Pierre de Vaux soon after the saint's death. He attributes to Colette apostolic status, which she merited thanks to her punctilious observance of the apostolic mode of life. For instance, he recounts that when she was talking with a group of nuns about the virtues of humility and poverty, "les douze apôtres s'apparurent et vinrent en sa présence, et s'asseyaient sur la terre auprès d'elle" [the twelve apostles appeared and came into her presence, and seated themselves on the ground next to her] (*Hagiographie*, 485). Then, to demonstrate "la société et conformité qu'elle avait à eux et leur sainte vie, ils se tinrent en sa présence jusqu'en la fin de l'exhortation" [the fellowship and conformity she had with them and their holy life, they remained in her presence until the end of her exhortation] (*Hagiographie*, 486). In her *vita*, Colette becomes, in effect, one of the apostles, an "apostoless" like Mary Magdalene, and so is represented as having a kind of authority (that is, authority to speak on spiritual matters) jealously guarded from women in the fifteenth century. Significantly, in this regard, her apostolic status has a linguistic component. Pierre de Vaux recounts an incident that occurred when Colette was traveling with a group of nuns in "une étrangère région" [a foreign region]. Some armed men fell upon the party, speaking "rudement et épouvantablement" [rudely and horribly]. Colette, "qui, par la grâce du Saint-Esprit, comme les glorieux apôtres, entendait toutes langues" [who by the grace of the Holy Spirit understood all languages like the glorious apostles], responded to them "doucement et bénignement" [sweetly and benignly], and their evil designs were transformed into "amour et charité" [love and charity] (*Hagiographie*, 418–19). It is especially striking that her divine enabled command of languages is said to extend even to Latin, the clerical language of authority: "Les apôtres toutes langues parlaient et entendaient. Pareillement, tous langages du monde, *et latin*, et allemand, et autres, par la grâce de Dieu, elle entendait" [The apostles spoke and understood all languages. Likewise, by the grace of God she understood all the world's languages—both *Latin* and German was well as others] (*Hagiographie*, 488, my emphasis).

In the end, the Observant friars finally got their "revenge," so to speak, on Colette, whose power and influence had clearly not died with her. At the end of the fifteenth century, direction of the order passed to the Observants. In renewing their reforms, they made a great deal of use of Colette's writings to further their own religio-political aims, finding her text to be "un bon instrument de reprise en main des couvents décadents" [a good instrument to take decadent convents in hand]. They took care, however, that "le nom de l'auteur, soeur Colette" was erased from these texts [the name of the author, sister Colette] (*Petite vie*, 78). The action of the Observants not only highlights their desire to minimize Colette's authoritative legacy and the power of women in the Franciscan Order, but it also points to Colette's mastery of textual as well as spiritual and symbolic exchanges. Just as Colette's *vita* attributes to her a command of spoken languages, including Latin, we see in her prolific career as the author of letters and monastic texts a powerful command of the written language as a vehicle to enforce her will (as the letter dismissing Jehan Lanier illustrates) and to establish her particular version of Franciscan reform (as the letter to Jeanne Labeur and "l'entention de Seur Colette" demonstrate). By erasing Colette's

authorship of her texts while using the texts themselves for their own purposes, the later fifteenth-century Observants achieve the kind of "takeover"
of Colette's symbolic capital and political power that Jean Foucault and
John of Capistrano had been unable to accomplish during her lifetime.

Female Spirituality and Burgundian Legitimacy

In the face of difficulties with ecclesiastical authorities like those she encountered at Corbie and Dole, Colette clearly made the most of her connections with politically influential figures. Colette was quite skillful in
parlaying the symbolic capital available from her spirituality and her distinctive brand of monastic identity into the material and political support
she needed to found convents and enact reforms. Important political figures also made the most of their connections with her and her reform
movement; the house of Burgundy in particular took a keen interest in
Colette and her nuns. A fascinating symbiosis existed between Colette and
the Burgundians. From their very beginnings, Colette's reforms and foundations owed much of their success to Burgundian support, and the Burgundians also owed a great deal of their success in self-representation at
critical junctures to St. Colette and her foundations.

The Burgundian-Colettine alliance began with Henry de la Baume,
who accompanied Colette to her audience with Pope Benedict XIII that
began her career of monastic reforms. Henry came from a family with a
history of service to the house of Burgundy. One of his brothers, Jean de
la Baume, was "écuyer-échanson" to John the Fearless, and another brother,
Jacques, was "écuyer-bannaret."[44] Henry also was, as his name indicates,
from Baume, which belonged to Blanche de Genève, countess of Savoy.
Blanche, in turn, was a vassal of Burgundy for Chalon; she had other strong
ties to the house of Burgundy as well. Her niece Louise married Guillaume
de Vienne, "le premier chambellain de John-sans-Peur" [the first chamberlain of John the Fearless] (*Petite vie*, 46), and another niece, Mahaut,
also became the niece of Margaret, duchess of Burgundy, when she married Louis de Bavière (*Belle vie*, 100). It was, furthermore, Blanche who
acted as the initial liason between Colette and Margaret, duchess of Burgundy, who, together with her husband John the Fearless, became such
avid patrons of Colette's reforms and foundations.[45]

Just as social authority and symbolic capital were key issues for the
Benedictine monks at Corbie and for Colette's opponents within the

Franciscan order, so too were they of prime importance to the dukes and duchesses of Burgundy. Roger Chartier has observed that the "authority of a constituted power or the power of a group . . . depends on the credit given to (or withheld from) the representations they propos[e] of themselves."[46] The dukes and duchesses of Burgundy, with their proclivity for pageants, civic ceremonies, and conspicuous consumption, were extraordinarily skilled practitioners of self-representation. As did its adversary the dauphin in the late 1420s, though, the house of Burgundy at times needed, in spite of its great power, to shore up and legitimate its authority, which faced frequent and sometimes serious challenges. Much as the dauphin strategically supported Colette's contemporary Joan of Arc, at critical junctures, the Burgundians often lent their social prestige and financial resources to Colette's foundations. The spiritual returns they received served, in turn, to advance their efforts to obtain representational credit, so enhancing Burgundian power and authority. The malleability of this source of symbolic capital is once again evident. While Colette was able to mobilize such resources to advance her own aims in the Church and the Franciscan Order (and indeed faced significant opposition for doing so), she and her reformist agenda were also subject to another sort of "takeover," somewhat like that effected by the later fifteenth-century Observants, as they were mobilized by secular political figures in the service of very different aims beyond her control.

Female sanctity and holiness were not unusual sources of representational credit for the Burgundians to embrace in the fifteenth century. In the fourteenth century, as André Vauchez has observed, during the height of the Great Schism "imperiled hierarchies" turned to holy women to legitimate and shore up their crumbling authority.[47] English kings—the sometimes-allies of the Burgundian dukes—turned, Lancastrian and Yorkist alike, to St. Birgitta and the Brigittine Order as they worked to pose creditable self-representations.[48] The Burgundians themselves have a history of reliance on female sanctity in self-legitimating discourses, as a chronicle describing the origins of the house reveals. Entitled "Extrait daulcuns Registres anciens et aultres ensseignemens troues en la tresorie de poligni et ailleurs touchant pluisieurs rois princes et aultres personnes saintes issus de la tresnoble et tresancienne maison La maison de Bourgongne" [Extract of certain ancient registers and other documents found in the treasury of Poligny and elsewhere concerning several kings, princes, and other holy persons of the very noble and very ancient house of Burgundy],[49] this text locates the beginnings of the house of Burgundy in salvation history. In this account, the king and queen converted to Christianity by Mary Magdalene upon her arrival in Marseille fourteen years after Christ's resurrection are none other than the king and queen of Burgundy, and it is their heir who is born through her intercession: "La tresglorieuse Magdeleine par sa predication conuertit a marselle le roy et la roine de bourgongne Et depuis furent baptises par St Maximin a aix en prouuence Et eurent vng filz par la pryere de ladicte Magdeleine." [The very glorious Magdalene converted the king and queen of Burgundy at Marseille through her preaching. And then they were baptised by St. Maximin at Aix-en-Provence. And they had a son through the prayer of the said Magdalene.][50] Thus, the Burgundian rulers have a direct connection with Christ through the "apostoless" Mary Magdalene (as the *Vie de Sainte Colette* suggests, a figure not unlike the "apostolic" St. Colette in some regards), and so become part of an ancient tradition of legitimate Christian rule. [51]

In addition to their clear usefulness as sources of the valuable symbolic capital of female sanctity and holiness, Colette and her reformed nunneries presented certain practical advantages to the Burgundians in their representational efforts. Colette, preferring as she did to found in urban settings, gave the dukes of Burgundy ideal opportunities to take advantage for propagandist purposes of her growing reputation for sanctity as well as the contemporary taste for strictly regulated, austere forms of monasticism. By associating themselves with her foundations, they rode the rising tide of her cult, tapping into her popularity to cultivate good will for themselves among the townspeople—a goal in which the house of Burgundy was perennially interested, as is revealed, for instance, by John the Fearless's effort to gain a reputation as a reform-minded populist in Paris even as he crushed an uprising seeking reforms in Liège.

Even more importantly, the Burgundians' endeavors to facilitate Colette's monastic foundations, their endowments of them, and their ongoing connections with them provided opportunities for urban displays of popular acclaim which added to their representational credit and bolstered their political legitimacy at critical times and places. Such combinations of public display and public worship were particularly valued by the dukes of Burgundy, who skillfully manipulated intersections between secular politics and religious devotion. For example, extracts from Philip the Good's accounts found in Paris, Bibliothèque Arsenal MS 3902 include an entry from 1423 recording the duke's gift of "mille liures de lire" [a thousand pounds] to be distributed among the "gens deglise" [people of the church] of Dijon "et autres villes de duche" [and other cities of the duchy] to reward them for the "loyaute et bon aucueil" [loyalty and good welcome] that they showed to the duke "par plusieurs processions messes et autres suffrages de devotion" [by several processions, masses, and other acts of devotion].[52]

John the Fearless's first direct involvement with Colette and her reform movement provides a case in point, highlighting his own political astuteness (astuteness clearly evident in his later support of the Colettine house at Poligny discussed above) as well as the symbolic value of what she had to offer. The fact that John would support Colette's efforts at all emphasizes the extraordinary usefulness of Colette to the Burgundian cause at a time when the political situation looked quite dismal for the duke. John was known early on as a supporter of Franciscan reform movements. Shortly before Colette began her first foundation at Besançon in January 1408, however, he had a falling-out with the Observant Franciscans with whom Colette was, at least at the beginning of her career, closely identified. In 1407, John's conflict with Louis d'Orléans over control of the royal government spilled into the ecclesiastical arena. Louis supported the pope in Avignon, Benedict XIII, the same pope who first authorized Colette's reforms and foundations. Since John opposed Louis, he correspondingly turned against Benedict XIII as well as against those allied with the Avignon papacy—including the Observant friars of Paris, who were doubly damned in John's eyes since amongst them was a group associated with Guillaume Josseaume, a known partisan of Louis. After the murder of Louis on November 23, 1407, John "écarte les observants franciscains, soupçonnés, en bloc, d'être des suppôts de l'ennemi armagnac" [separated himself from the Observant Franciscans, who were suspected as a whole to be supporters of the Armagnac enemy] (*Petite vie*, 38–39).

The Burgundian-Armagnac quarrel that was renewed in 1410 following the brief truce brokered by the 1409 Peace of Chartres burgeoned into full-scale civil war in 1411. The Burgundians initially enjoyed some military success, but the Armagnacs made an alliance with the duke of Clarence, who in 1412 brought armies to their aid. John, seeing the writing on the wall, accepted the mediation of the count of Savoy and on July 14, 1412, concluded the Congress of Auxerre. This agreement restored the conditions of the Peace of Chartres, but John was no more devoted to it than he had been to the earlier treaty.

It is at this difficult juncture in the summer of 1412 that John made St. Colette and her foundations a part of his personal efforts to solidify his authority. While John had been at odds with Franciscan reformers, Colette and John's duchess Margaret had been busy establishing a connection that would prove quite fruitful through the years. Blanche de Genève accompanied Colette from Rumilly, where she had fled following her initial failure at Corbie, to Besançon; there she seems to have introduced Colette to the duchess. In Besançon in 1408, Margaret, who was understandably anxious about the repercussions of the assassination of Louis d'Orléans the previous year (in spite of Jean Petit's justification) and, perhaps, about the state of her spouse's soul, became involved in Colette's project of establishing a nunnery in this important Burgundian city where "le Parlement venait d'y être transféré" [the Parliament had recently been transferred] (*Belle vie*, 102). John was certainly aware of the striking success of the foundation in Besançon, where Colette had been received with a triumphal entry.[53] After establishing her house there, Colette had gone to Dijon, where she petitioned Margaret to intercede with John to give her a site for a nunnery at Auxonne. The desired location was the "Vielle Monnaie" [Old Mint] or "Maison des sous" where both Philip the Bold and John the Fearless had illegally minted their own currency.[54]

Even given his recent quarrel with the Franciscans, John saw in Colette's request, in light of his troubles and her triumph at Besançon, the opportunity to turn this facility where illegitimate coin had been made into a locus where symbolic capital to advance his own political cause could be produced. On August 3, 1412, less than a month after agreeing to the hated Congress of Auxerre, John issued letters patent conferring the "Vieille Monnaie" to Colette to found "un monastère de Cordelières de Sainte-Clère" [a monastery of reformed Franciscan nuns]. In the letters, John expresses the conventional pious desire that he, his "très chère et très aimée compagne la duchesse" [very dear and beloved companion the duchess] as well as his heirs and successors "soyons participans ès messes, oraisons, prières et autres oeuvres de charité et bienfaiz, qui se feront au dict monastère" [be participants in the masses, prayers, and other works of charity and good that will be performed by the said monastery].[55]

Whatever the spiritual payoff may have been, John's gift, which was quite generous since the expenses for the foundation were heavy, was amply rewarded in this world.[56] Colette's coming to Auxonne was every bit the success her arrival at Besançon had been. She entered the city, accompanied, significantly, by Guillaume de Vienne, John's first chamberlain, and "the citizens of Auxonne came out to meet her and greeted her with joyous acclamations."[57] In fact, her entry on October 28, 1412, calls to mind one of the famous Burgundian "joyeuses entrées." The people of Auxonne

greeted Colette, her Burgundian escort, and the accompanying procession
with cries of "Noël! Noël! à la bonne Soeur Colette" [Noel! Noel! to
good Sister Colette].[58] This celebration echoed the greetings which were
traditional practice at royal and ducal entries, as when Philip the Good
later entered Paris in 1420 and, according to the chronicler Georges Chastellain, "Lors pouvoit-on oyr gorges et voix démener bruit diversement,
et les enfans crier 'Noël!'" [One could hear throats and voices raise a var-
ied clamor, and the children cry "Noel!"].[59] The procession at Auxonne
served, as has been said of the "joyeuses entrées," to "strength[en] the
bond" between duke and city, thus boosting the duke's authority. [60]

The usefulness of Colette in strengthening relationships between the
dukes of Burgundy and politically vital cities is especially evident in Ghent,
a city where the Burgundians faced ongoing challenges to their authority
from prosperous burgesses. In the 1430s and 1440s Philip the Good faced
particularly troubled times in the cities of Flanders. After the 1435 Treaty
of Arras, "the duke's authority was undermined as a result of the break
with the English."[61] Insurrection against the duke broke out in Bruges in
1436 and was not effectively put down until 1438. Although Ghent did
not support Bruges in its uprising, conflict flared there as well (and would
erupt into open rebellion in 1447) as clashes continued between burgesses,
who wanted local independence for the wool staple, and Philip, who desired unification under his control.

Colette and her nuns once again provided the house of Burgundy
with a chance to gain representational credit and popular support in a time
and at a place when both were sorely needed. For many years Colette had
enjoyed a fervent following in Ghent, and there was longstanding desire
among the bourgeois of Ghent for Colette to establish a nunnery there.
Papal authorization had been granted on June 26, 1427, to Hélène Sclap-
per to undertake the foundation, and fundraising had begun almost immediately, followed in short order by construction. The continuing war
involving England, France, and Burgundy, as well as frequent outbreaks
of unrest in Flanders, delayed the arrival of the nuns, however.[62] Fortu-
nately for the Burgundians, Colette and the long-awaited sisters arrived in
Ghent in August 1442, and Odette, "une fille naturelle du duc de Bourgogne" [an illegitimate daughter of the duke of Burgundy] was installed
as abbess at the convent, which was named Bethlehem. Colette remained
in residence at Bethlehem for some time, and she and Odette received
"des centaines de visites de personnes de la ville et de la région" [hundreds
of visits from people of the town and the region], so forming "nouvelles

amitiés" [new friendships] that were undoubtedly beneficial to the Burgundians (*Belle vie*, 240).[63]

Colette's Vision of St. Anne, or the Multiple Values of Female Sanctity

I turn in closing to a final example that demonstrates the ready trans-
formability and the multi-faceted usefulness of female holiness. In addition to being extraordinarily committed to absolute poverty, Colette was
passionately attached to virginity. In fact, her *vita* reports that because of
"l'excellent amour qu'elle avait à pureté de coeur et de corps" [the excellent love she had for purity of heart and body], she had special reverence
for "des saints et saintes . . . qui avaient gardé virginité" [male and female
saints . . . who had kept their virginity] (*Hagiographie*, 412–13). Accordingly,
she disdained to show special devotion to the thrice married St. Anne,
from whom Colette "ne demandait point aide et secours" [did not demand
aid]. One day, however, while Colette was praying, St. Anne appeared to
her in a vision, "menant avec elle toute sa noble progéniture, c'est à savoir
ses trois filles et leurs glorieux enfants" [bringing with her all her noble
progeny, that is to say her three daughters and their glorious children]
(*Hagiographie*, 413).

This vision had several consequences for Colette herself, for her reform movement, and for particular foundations. In these consequences
we see, once again, the spiritual, the symbolic, and the material circulating freely, highlighting the interconvertibility of resources in disparate,
though firmly interconnected, spheres. Following the vision, Colette "con-
çut une singulière dévotion" [conceived a singular devotion] to St. Anne,
whom she adopted as "son intercesseresse et avocate envers sa très-noble
et sainte lignée" [her intercessor and advocate with her very noble and
holy lineage] that she might receive heavenly aid in executing her reforms
(*Hagiographie*, 413). St. Anne thus became, in effect, for Colette on a celestial plane what Colette was for the Burgundians on earth—that is, a way
of tapping into divine authority to legitimate one's own authority and
advance one's own political agenda.

The vision also led Colette to decide to admit widows as well as virgins to her order. St. Anne's status provided impeccable justification for
the validity of this decision, and Colette's personal authority for crafting
her distinctive versions of monastic reform and Franciscan identity was

further bolstered. Furthermore, this divinely inspired change of heart had the practical consequence of enabling a whole group of politically and socially powerful women to participate directly in Colette's reform movement, with all the advantages such participants brought with them.

Finally, Colette's new devotion to St. Anne prompted her to dedicate convent churches and chapels to St. Anne at several of her foundations (*Hagiographie*, 414 n.1). Because the cult of St. Anne was extremely popular in the later Middle Ages, the connections of Colette's houses with St. Anne had the advantageous potential to increase interest in and material support for these foundations. Indeed, the chapel of St. Anne at the Colettine house at Besançon appears to have been a prestigious, desirable location for burial (*Hagiographie*, 414).[64]

The symbolic capital available in Colette's vision of St. Anne and the holy kindred was not, though, available only to Colette herself and her foundations. Indeed, this vision took on a very different meaning, and was turned to very different purposes, by the Burgundians in the sphere of secular politics. When Charles the Bold became duke in June 1467, he sought to marry Margaret of York, since in order to crush his nemesis Louis XI of France he desired a renewal of the ties between Burgundy and England through an alliance with Margaret's brother Edward IV. This marriage, which took place on July 3, 1468, had been achieved only with difficult and protracted negotiations. The Burgundians were consequently anxious to publicize it in grand fashion, as the famously lavish celebrations described by chroniclers make evident. In spite of the attendant political advantages, however, the nuptials were a source of some ambivalence, not only in England but also, apparently, at home as well, since the Burgundian chronicler Georges Chastellain goes to great lengths to justify Charles's marriage with one so at odds with his "vraie nature originale françoise" [true, original French nature].[65] In this environment, St. Colette's vision was conveniently available to suggest the divine approval of the nuptial union joining England and Burgundy. The apparition of the thrice-married St. Anne and her offspring was easily connected to the marriage of Charles and Margaret, since the marriage was his third. An illumination in a manuscript of the *Vie de Sainte Colette* depicts Charles and Margaret with St. Colette as witnesses to the revelation.

In a final transaction in which material resources are exchanged for spiritual credit, which in turn bolsters political legitimacy, Margaret presented this richly decorated, valuable manuscript, in which she describes herself, in an inscription written in her own hand, as "Votre loyalle fylle

Margarete d'Angleterre" [your loyal daughter Margaret of England],[66] to the Colettine convent of Bethlehem in Ghent. Significantly, this convent had been founded by members of the merchant class, among whom there was a long-standing devotion to St. Colette and whose good will was so crucial to the maintenance of Burgundian authority in this wealthy and politically important town. Margaret's gift thus illustrates the value of keeping alive, even after Colette's death, the connection between the house of Burgundy and this saintly source of politically useful symbolic capital.

Indeed, Margaret, like Charles before her, actively pursued the cause of Colette's canonization, a cause which, unfortunately for the Burgundians and, perhaps, unfortunately for Colette and her foundations as well, was not accomplished until 1807. I do not wish to suggest that Charles's or Margaret's interest was entirely motivated by politics—nor do I wish to attach such purely calculating motives to earlier Burgundian interest in Colette and her foundations. The increase in Colette's renown and prestige which would have resulted from her canonization would, though, clearly have been to the Burgundians' symbolic benefit as Charles, and later Margaret on her stepson-in-law Maximilian's behalf, battled Louis XI and pursued expansionist aims, just as the spread of her fame, enhanced by her Burgundian-supported foundations, had been beneficial for their predecessors. Furthermore, had Charles or Margaret been able to see her canonization through, such successful efforts might also, in a continuation of the Colettine-Burgundian symbiosis, have helped to prevent her "erasure" by the Observants when they gained control of the Franciscan Order in the late fifteenth century.

2

Strategic Saints and Diplomatic Devotion: Margaret of York, Anne d'Orléans, and Female Political Action

Piety and Politics

A chronicle relating the history of the house of Burgundy found in Paris, Bibliothèque Arsenal MS 3602 opens by foregrounding the Burgundian ancestry of the Frankish queen St. Clotilde: "Saincte Clotilde fut fille du roy de Bourgyne laquelle ayant epouse Clovis Roy de France fut cause que led*ict* clovis receut le sainct sacrement de baptesme et fut le premier roy de france Chrestien." [St. Clothilde was the daughter of the king of Burgundy; having married King Clovis of France, she caused the said Clovis to receive the sacrament of baptism, and he was the first Christian king of France.][1] This chronicle provides another example of the Burgundians' strategy of using female holiness to legitimate political authority adopted by the dukes and duchesses in their involvement with St. Colette and her nuns.[2] According to this chronicle's version of Burgundian history, thanks to Clotilde, the title of "most Christian king" so beloved by the kings of France could only be claimed via a Burgundian connection. The narrative would even, perhaps, suggest that the house of Burgundy had a better claim to that appellation than did the French monarchs with whom they were so often at odds!

Charles significantly turned to this same scene from the Burgundian past at the celebration of his marriage to Margaret of York. As Jehan de Haynin reports in his account of the festivities, "The hall . . . of the chamberlains was hung with a superb tapestry showing the coronation of King Clovis, called Lois, the first Christian king of France." He also indicates that the tapestries, which gave Clotilde a slightly different Burgundian pedigree than the aforementioned chronicle, portrayed "the renewal of the alliance between him and King Gundobad of Burgundy; the wedding of King Clovis to Gundobad's niece; his baptism with the Holy Ampulla."[3] Like the thrice-married St. Anne in Colette's vision embraced, as I discuss in the previous chapter, by Margaret and Charles, St. Clotilde delivered an air of holy legitimacy to the union.

In addition to reminding the great and powerful of Europe that this marriage was a divinely blessed one (not to mention reminding them that the claim to the throne of France was always on the minds of the English and Burgundians alike), this tapestry had other significant resonances with the circumstances of the marriage whose celebration it graced. Charles and Margaret's marriage, like that of Clovis and Clotilde, cemented an extremely important international alliance. The marriage between the sister of Edward IV of England and the powerful duke was meant to secure a strong relationship between England and Burgundy, a relationship important for both England and Burgundy in opposing Louis XI. It was also accompanied by the first stable trade agreement between the two powers for more than thirty years.[4]

In spite of her role as the "link" cementing the connection between Edward and Charles, Margaret was no mere pawn in politico-economic affairs controlled by men. As we shall see, Margaret's activities following her marriage make it extraordinarily fitting that a tapestry depicting Clotilde — a royal wife who turned her spirituality to political ends — was present at the celebration of her marriage to Charles. Indeed, Margaret of York's own political career, like that of Clotilde, began in earnest with her marriage. Some scholars downplay Margaret's political role during and after Charles's lifetime, a view which, I would argue, stems from a rather limited vision of what constitutes "political" participation in the later medieval and early modern periods.[5] Margaret was intimately involved with diplomacy, financial management, and administration, including military administration. She seems to have handled all these tasks with considerable skill. During one of Charles's long absences, she "led the resistance against a French invasion of Artois and negotiated with the Flemish cities for the mobilization of troops."[6] She also engaged, on more than one occasion, in negotiating terms between England and Burgundy.[7] After Charles's death, Margaret "took upon herself a heavy load of responsibility for the maintenance and administration of all her dower property," occupying herself with "upholding law and order, collecting aides and taxes and maintaining all the property of the demesne."[8] Such evidence demonstrates that both during her marriage and throughout her widowhood Margaret took great interest in politics, concerning herself both with the fortunes of the Burgundian duchy and those of the Yorkist dynasty in England.

Like Clotilde, Margaret of York was a very pious woman. She was quite interested in religious patronage and reform, demonstrating special attraction to the Augustinians, the Brigittines, the Observant Franciscans, and, as we have seen, the Colettines. She presented several works of art to churches in Binche, Mons, Ghent, Bruges, and Malines, and her accounts show numerous donations to hospitals and monasteries.[9] Furthermore, many of the books that she owned treated religious subjects.[10]

Margaret's interest in religion has led some scholars to argue that her piety was the prime component of her role as duchess of Burgundy, replacing the "political" activities that were the province of the dukes. In his discussion of the portraits of Margaret found in her books, Thomas Kren observes, "Whereas the depictions of Philip and Charles in their books often show a mighty ruler ceremoniously presiding at his court, those of Margaret emphasize the spiritual life."[11] Similarly, Jeffrey Chipps Smith argues that while Charles the Bold's portraits "depict him as a patron of culture, leader of his loyal knights, and wise administrator," those of Margaret depict her "as a devout and pious duchess: setting an example . . . [and] showing her personal relationship with Christ."[12]

Somewhat ironically, the *dukes* of Burgundy are often cited as masters of using religion to serve political ends. Walter Prevenier and Wim Blockmans observe that the "dukes manipulated the church most where their own provinces were involved, namely by appointing countless bishops who were politically favourably disposed to the Burgundian state."[13] They also indicate that "Charles the Bold's unsuccessful attempt to bring the borders of the Burgundian state into line with those of a newly formed church province" is "[p]roof of the fact that the dukes wanted to carry intervention in church policy a step further." While they attribute ducal "support of the bishops, abbeys and churches" to a mixed desire to "displa[y] their piety" and to "us[e] the church as one of the means towards the aim of controlling society" they, and other scholars, attribute Margaret's religious activities to uncomplicated piety or, at the most, to a rather slightly politicized desire to set an example.[14]

Margaret's religious interests clearly occupied much of her time and were, as Kren notes, appropriate to "the expectations of a woman of her rank." Such interests were not, however, necessarily contrary to the "political and dynastic concerns" that he, like many scholars, claims occupied Charles alone.[15] Rather, Margaret's religious interests were another avenue for pursuing precisely such political and dynastic concerns. The spiritual life was in Margaret's case an extremely effective way of accessing and enacting political power. Christine Weightman claims that Margaret, like her mother Cecily of York, found no conflict between piety and determined promotion of her family fortunes.[16] I would go one step further to contend that Margaret in fact found piety quite useful in promoting her political aims.[17] Her devotional practices as well as her religious patronage bear witness to her very politicized identity as an authoritative, active duchess of Burgundy. Indeed, Margaret adopted and even enlarged upon the sorts of political strategies John the Fearless and Philip the Good put into practice in their involvements with St. Colette and her foundations. Margaret of York demonstrates the extraordinary degree to which forms of piety long associated with and upheld as desirable for women—monastic patronage, Marian devotion, devotion to the saints—can prove to be not only spiritually satisfying practices but at the same time also powerful, unexpected opportunities for political agency.

Donation, Devotion, and Burgundian Dominion

That Margaret's spirituality may be seen not as a replacement for, but instead as an integral part of, her political agency emerges in a depiction of her found in her manuscript copy of *Benoit seront les miséricordieux*. In this illumination, Margaret kneels in prayer accompanied by St. Margaret and surrounded by the Church Fathers Jerome, Gregory, Ambrose and Augustine. These men point to the church represented in the center of the miniature, recognizable as Saint Gudule in Brussels. "Behind Saint Gudule, views of Notre Dame du Sablon, a gate, and the town hall have been magically relocated northward. . . . Margaret's position seems bound by the flanking walls to a spot south of Saint Gudule—a spot that in the 1470s belonged within or immediately adjoined the precinct of the great Coudenberg, a ducal palace."[18] Smith calls attention to the significance of the setting, saying that it is "hardly accidental." He continues, "Margaret is depicted as the Duchess of Burgundy and perhaps also as the vicaress of Christ, guardian of the church and her people."[19] This portrayal of Margaret in the guise of a vicaress of Christ simultaneously foregrounds her role as a vicar of ducal authority, especially since Charles was known to align himself with Christ in his role as duke.[20]

Such a depiction of the duchess hints at Margaret's skill in using her own spirituality to serve Burgundian authority. Such skill was readily evident in her presentation of a richly illuminated manuscript of the *Vie de Sainte Colette* to the Colettine nuns in Ghent, a gift which, as we have seen, had great symbolic benefits for the Burgundian cause.[21] This was not to be her only politically useful devotional gift. When Charles began the siege of Neuss, Margaret accompanied him from Brussles to Maastricht. She subsequently traveled alone to Aachen, where she donated a crown to the statue of the Virgin Mary in the cathedral.[22] Margaret was entitled to wear a crown not as duchess of Burgundy but by virtue of her status as the sister of King Edward IV of England, an entitlement that Jean Squilbeck notes "might cause her husband, who aspired to royal consecration, to take umbrage."[23] If her wearing a crown did in fact displease Charles by reminding him that he had not yet attained the rank he desired, she chose a remarkably astute manner of divesting herself of one, especially in light of Charles's recent history with the city of Aachen.

Following the sack and looting of Liège in 1468–1469, towns throughout Europe feared Charles's wrath. Aachen, which had sent cannon to Liège to replace those that the duke had destroyed, had good reason for concern, since Charles "considered seriously the possibility of an attack on Aachen immediately after the sack of Liège."[24] The civic authorities attempted to appease Charles by offering him apologies and the keys to their city while he was in Maastricht in November 1468, and they later also sent him a gift of wine. Ultimately, Charles settled with Aachen; the city gave him 80,000 Rhenish florins in exchange for his pardon. Aachen was also required to allow the duke and his men to enter the city freely. In June 1469, the duke signed a treaty with the city which placed it "under Charles's special protection and safeguard."[25]

Richard Vaughan reports that Charles only visited Aachen personally a single time, in August 1473. He notes, "The citizens' attitude to him on that occasion is illustrated by the fact that as soon as he had departed the town authorities, in the presence of an imperial herald, solemnly removed his 'Privy Chamber' and a tent with his arms on it, which he had left standing in the market place."[26] Margaret's donation of her crown in Aachen, a mere year later, thus likely had multiple meanings for the citizens of the city, who had such a troubled past with Charles. On the one hand, the duchess's crown on the Virgin's head in the cathedral might have been seen as a reconciliatory gesture, a sign of the special, protective bond between the duchy and the city. On the other hand, it might metonymically have represented Burgundian authority, signifying the divine legitimacy of ducal rule. As Blockmans has observed, "On a political level, Aachen was the place where the German kings had been crowned; although negotiations . . . to bestow royal dignity on Duke Charles had failed, he remained ambitious. Margaret's crown in Aachen can be understood as yet another expression of her husband's claim."[27] Indeed, while Harry Schnitker argues that the primary meaning of Margaret's donation is as a gesture of her humility, he notes that "the distinction between intense faith and public ceremonial and between religious devotion and political gesture was not yet made."[28] Margaret's donation was thus an especially adept mobilization of "the ceremonial . . . symbols which were seen . . . to accompany temporal lordship"; indeed, it furthered what Robert B. Rigoulot has called the "assiduous" Burgundian collection and deployment of "the 'marks of sovereignty.'"[29]

The saints to whom Margaret showed special devotion further reveal the political valences of her spirituality. She was naturally attached to her patron saint, St. Margaret, but she also exhibited great fondness for St. Barbara, St. Anne, and St. Agnes, all saints who had particular importance in Ghent.[30] Charles's relationship with Ghent had been famously difficult since the beginning of his reign as duke. Indeed, the difficulties stretched back to the time of his father, Philip the Good. Philip had boasted of his defeat of the rebellious townspeople of Liège, Bruges, and Ghent, but, as Vaughan points out, "the radical elements, in Liège and Ghent especially, had by no means been suppressed by Philip the Good."[31] Upon becoming duke, Charles made his solemn entry into Ghent in 1467 on the rather unwisely chosen feast-day of St. Lieven. His entry disrupted the civic festivities traditionally held on the feast-day; as a result, riots ensued that "represented a direct threat to his authority."[32] Charles was only able to escape by promising concessions to the rioters' demands.

Charles was not to wait long to exact his revenge for his humiliating experience on the occasion of his solemn entry. In January 1468, he punished the city by publicly destroying the Great Privilege of Ghent, so depriving the citizens of "all semblance of civic autonomy." He also reimposed the much-detested *quellote* and had *echevins* favorable to his cause appointed with no electoral participation by the citizens.[33] Having reasserted his political authority in Ghent through harsh measures, Charles turned to representational matters. As Roger Chartier has argued, political authority stands or falls on the acceptance or rejection of the self-representations it poses;[34] as we have seen, the disruption of Charles's representation of his authority at his initial entry led to palpable threats to that authority and to a reduction (albeit a temporary one) of that authority. Following the elaborately choreographed, symbolically freighted ceremony of the destruction of the Great Privilege, Charles was faced with the delicate task of holding on to his newly rescued power while papering over the rift between the Burgundian duchy and the resentful citizens of Ghent. In other words, Charles not only had to make sure his authority was secure, but he also had to make sure it was publicly celebrated and, at least in appearance, welcomed by the very citizens upon which it had been imposed so mercilessly.

Charles, like his Valois predecessors, thus needed to establish his sovereignty "not through law-making and the exercise of political power alone, but by cultivating the beliefs, traditions and ritual which, in the medieval polity, tied the monarch to his people and give his authority its quasi-sacerdotal character."[35] The duchy needed to employ effective, congenial representational strategies to prevail in the city, and in carrying out such endeavors Margaret played a major political role. On May 20, 1469, just on the heels of the restoration of the *quellote*, Margaret entered the city, followed eleven days later by Charles himself. As Peter Arnade observes, "The ritual interaction between Gentenars and the ducal family expressed in these two entries ameliorated but did not eradicate the discord produced by the entry that had gone awry. The 1469 entries . . . certainly restored the much desired image of consensus, but only at the expense of Ghent's public life."[36]

Margaret's religious activities were perhaps even more important in Burgundian political maneuverings in Ghent than was her entry in 1469. Margaret's special devotion to St. Barbara, St. Agnes, and St. Anne did a great deal to enhance the image of consensus set up by the entries; even more crucially, her devotional practices helped to shape a new version of urban, public life beneficial to the ducal cause. As early as 1472, both Margaret and her step-daughter Mary were members of the important guild of St. Barbara in Ghent.[37] St. Barbara was the patron saint of two politically important trades, the builders and the gunners. She was also extraordinarily popular in the Low Countries. Margaret's preference for this saint thus served to make common cause with citizens who repeatedly rebelled against Burgundian rule in the fifteenth century.

The cult of St. Anne, like that of St. Barbara, was also extremely popular in Ghent in the second half of the fifteenth century. In the aftermath of the war between Philip the Good and Ghent, local civic and religious authorities advocated "[s]econd and third marriages and renewed childbearing . . . through the cult of St. Anne" to replenish the city's de-pleted population.[38] Margaret was the third wife of Charles the Bold, so the cult would have held an obvious attraction for her. Given the circum-stances of the cult's promotion in Ghent, though, Margaret's veneration of this saint, and her membership, from 1473, in the local guild of St. Anne, had distinct advantages for the Burgundian cause. Margaret's mem-bership in the guild of a saint whose cult was promoted to renew the city following the defeat at Burgundian hands emphasized the harmonious reconciliation of the city with the duchy. Margaret may well have vicari-ously represented her husband's authority in Ghent; as Weightman says, Charles needed "to maintain a high presence in the city" and so "Margaret and Mary were obliged to remain there for long periods."[39] Margaret's publicly celebrated devotion to St. Anne also suggested, though, that she was, like the saint, a beneficent intercessory figure. She was in the position to be identified, as Queen Anne of England had been during Richard II's dispute with the city of London, as a mediatrix who would intercede for the citizens with her wrathful husband.[40] So, while Charles established that he was a ruler whose authority should not be challenged, Margaret's asso-ciation with St. Anne helped to indicate that the Burgundians also had the best interests of the city at heart. St. Anne was particularly useful in this regard, since, as Kathleen Ashley and Pamela Sheingorn point out, this saint "tended to be appropriated by the wealthy bourgeoisie who formed the patrician oligarchies of many late medieval towns, for Anne and her hus-band Joachim, were understood to be members of that class."[41] This was, of course, precisely the class whose support the Burgundians most needed and whose privileges had been most restricted by Charles's punishments.

Margaret's affinity for St. Agnes also did much to enhance a new, pro-Burgundian form of civic life in Ghent. In 1469, the year of the rec-onciliation between Charles and the city, a group of rhetoricians received permission to worship in the Borluut family's chapel of St. Agnes in the church of Sint-Jan. Parish officials "recognized the right of 'a confraternity and society in the form of a guild of the most excellent and pure Virgin, Saint Agnes'" to hold services there.[42] Rhetoricians' confraternities held an extremely important place in public life in fifteenth-century Ghent. They have been "[i]nterpreted variously . . . as play groups, literary societies, inheritors of the sacred dramatic traditions of the medieval clergy, and pioneers of the secular literary esprit."[43] Their activities were central to Burgundian representational strategies, since they performed dramas with political current resonances and participated in Burgundian entries. As

Arnade has noted, the creation of the St. Agnes confraternity in 1469 parallels the creation of the De Fonteine rhetoricians' confraternity in the
equally troubled period preceding the war between Ghent and Philip the
Good. He observes, "More than just coincidental, these two dates suggest
how the new ritual groups were closely associated with the erosion of political autonomy once enjoyed by Ghent's citizens and the expansion of power
. . . of a political bloc . . . more favorable to Burgundian supremacy."[44]

The St. Agnes confraternity was composed of wealthy and influential
townspeople, as is demonstrated by its right to hold services "in the chapel
of the Borluuts, Ghent's most important patrician family, in the city's
most powerful parish church."[45] Given the importance of the rhetoricians'
confraternities in Burgundian self-representation, and given the social
prominence of the members of the St. Agnes confraternity in particular,
Margaret's financing of a convent devoted to none other than St. Agnes
in Ghent was an astute choice. Blockmans argues that Margaret's patronage of the convent of St. Agnes reveals a "special preference for a figure
revered as the patron of young women and children."[46] This is perhaps
true, but Margaret's patronage also reveals a special preference for a figure
revered, like St. Anne, by powerful citizens of Ghent whose support was
vital to the Burgundian cause.

Even long after Charles's death Margaret was raising religious monuments to Burgundian authority in Ghent. In 1498, she donated 100 *lb.* to
found a chapel of St. George there. Blockmans again views her act as one
motivated by interest in "children, childbearing, and family," noting that
the foundation "refers to her loyalty to Duke Charles, who especially ven-
erated this saint, patron of the Order of the Garter."[47] More than simple
loyalty to Charles and his memory was at stake, though. St. George was a
figure of great military and civic significance in Ghent, and the 1490s were
a time in which it would have been extremely valuable to the Burgundian
cause for Margaret to emphasize the connection between this saint and the
duchy. Relations with the town were again rocky, since during the preceding years Ghent had once again been at war with the duchy, the Habsburg
rulers being no more popular with Ghent's citizens than their predecessors.[48]

The patron saint for the military confraternity of the crossbowmen of
Ghent was none other than St. George. Philip the Bold had entered the
confraternity in 1369, and all his Burgundian and Habsburg successors were
members as well.[49] Unlike shooting confraternities elsewhere in the Low
Countries, though, the St. George crossbowmen were not bound by a charter specifying that they owed particular military duties to the Burgundian

dukes. As Arnade points out, Ghent's crossbowmen did not call themselves "our lord's archers" as their counterparts in Bruges did. He continues, "Assistance to both Ghent and the count of Flanders might be expected, but it was never explicitly incorporated" in the confraternity's legal records.[50] Margaret's foundation of a chapel dedicated to the crossbowmen's patron saint would therefore have been a useful step in helping to secure their loyalty at a militarily uncertain time, especially since Charles's successor Maximilian was, like Charles, known for his devotion to St. George.[51]

St. George also had international political importance. He was not only the patron of the crossbowmen of Ghent, but he was also, perhaps even more famously, the patron saint of England. Margaret's making a public gesture of her attachment to this saint so strongly associated with England in 1498, might be interpreted as a statement directed as much to the English as to the citizens of Ghent. Margaret of York had been intimately involved in the Perkin Warbeck affair, which in 1498 was in the final stages of collapse.[52] By founding a chapel of St. George in the Low Countries, the place from which Warbeck hailed, in the very city where Charles the Bold had received his insignia of the Order of the Garter from Edward IV in January 1469, Margaret may have been thumbing her nose at Henry VII and insisting on the ongoing validity of the Yorkists' claim — the party, Margaret presumably wished to suggest, favored by St. George.[53]

Divine Diplomacy

After the accession of Henry VII, relations between England and Burgundy were often tense, at times even openly hostile, and Margaret worked to aid efforts by both Lambert Simnel and Perkin Warbeck to overthrow Henry. Before the advent of the Tudor dynasty, however, she had spent much of her career trying to foster Anglo-Burgundian alliances. As in the Low Countries, where she advanced the Burgundian cause through her monastic patronage and her participation in guilds devoted to strategically important saints, so too in her role as a diplomat negotiating between England and Burgundy she found productive opportunities in the realm of female spirituality.

Margaret's husband Charles the Bold's relations with England were complex. He was tied by blood to the Lancastrian line through his mother Isabella of Portugal, a granddaughter of John of Gaunt. At key moments, he made the most of this connection, even going so far as to identify himself as English. In a letter written to Sir John Wenlock and the magistrates at Calais, Charles styled himself as more authentically English than the English themselves, swearing, "par St. George, lequel me cognoit estre meilleur Anglois, et plus desirer le bien de iceluy royaume que vous et tous les autres Anglois ne sont" [by St. George, who knows me to be a better Englishman, and more desiring of the good of that realm, than you and all the other Englishmen].[54]

Charles also emphasized his English heritage and affinity to political advantage by flaunting his membership in the Order of the Garter. Edward's presentation of the Garter to Charles, and Charles's acceptance of it, provided a strong symbolic confirmation of the bond between England and Burgundy. The fulsome, albeit rather formulaic, language of Edward's commission for the presentation of the Order to Charles as well as that of Charles's certification of his receipt, underlines the value of this international union. Edward, calling himself, significantly, "par la grace de dieu Roy dangleterre et de france" [by the grace of God king of England and France], addresses the duke as "treshauls & puisant prynce nostre tresame frere Charles duc de bourgougne" [very high and powerful prince our well-beloved brother Charles, duke of Burgundy]. In describing Charles's election as a member of the "confreres cheualiers & compaignons dudict ordre" [confraternity of knights and companions of the said order], the commission refers to the "glorieuses merites" [glorious merits] of Charles's "vertuous haultesse & noblesse dont la Renommee ses partout espandu" [virtuous high nobility which is renowned everywhere]. Charles in turn hails Edward as "nostre treshonnore Seigneur & frere le Roy dangleterre" [our very honored lord and brother the king of England] and certifies that he has sworn "le serment" [the oath] required by the Order's statutes according to the agreed conditions.[55]

In both 1471 and 1472, and indeed likely every year after Charles's election to the Order in 1469, the Burgundian court celebrated the Feast of the Garter on St. George's Day. At Trier in the autumn of 1473, Charles wore his Garter on a ceremonial occasion. Then, in 1475 during the siege of Neuss, he again wore the Garter on the eve of St. George's Day, subsequently attending a mass "wearing the sky blue robes of the Order, powdered with Garters."[56] He had good reason to publicize his ties to England at this moment, since, through Margaret's diplomatic efforts, Edward IV "had mustered the largest English army ever assembled for the invasion of France."[57] Charles's attachment to St. George, and the Anglophilia it implied, evidently got the attention of Louis XI. In the printed version of Louis XI's declaration of war against Charles the Bold, one of the reasons given for taking up arms is that Burgundian troops raiding on the Norman coast "had joined forces with the English . . . and even raised 'the ensign of the red cross . . . the ancient ensign of England and the English' on French soil."[58]

Although linked to the Lancastrians by blood, Charles had aligned himself with the Yorkist dynasty when he married Edward IV's sister. He was, however, eminently willing to play both sides of the Lancastrian / Yorkist conflict in the interest of keeping open the possibility of pressing his own claim to the English throne. In 1470, when Edward was forced into exile and Henry VI returned to the throne, Charles finessed his allegiance, "proclaiming his intention to maintain the alliance intact, reminding them of his Lancastrian descent, declaring his readiness to recognize whatever dynasty the nation might itself establish."[59] In spite of his professions of Lancastrian loyalty, Charles did secretly assist Edward IV to regain the throne of England. But, he did not abandon his Lancastrian heritage, with all the opportunities it might potentially provide for him. When Henry VI died, Charles obtained a renunciation from Isabella of her title to succeed to the throne of England in favor of his own. He also made a secret declaration that, although he would refrain from asserting his right for the time being, "he did not consider himself banned from putting it forth when occasion might arise."[60]

Charles was not alone in having flexible loyalties in the course of Anglo-Burgundian affairs. Edward IV, in spite of his affinity for Burgundian court culture, was no steadfast supporter of his Burgundian brother-in-law.[61] As we have seen, early in 1475, thanks to Margaret's skilled diplomatic negotiations, Edward IV had sent troops to the continent to invade France while Charles turned his attention to fighting in the Rhineland. Later that year, however, unhappy with the meager support Charles was providing to the English in the struggle against France, Edward signed the treaty of Picquigny with Louis XI. This treaty cut his ties to Charles the Bold "in spite of Margaret of York's protestations."[62]

Edward's defection to Louis in 1475 set the stage for Margaret's return to England in 1480 to negotiate with her brother on behalf of Maximilian to renew the Anglo-Burgundian alliance. Maximilian clearly had great confidence in Margaret; as Luc Hommel reports, Maximilian gave his mother-in-law full power and authority to conclude negotiations for the treaty.[63] Such confidence was not misplaced, as Margaret proved to be an adept ambassador under fairly trying circumstances.[64] Edward's strong attraction to the Burgundian court and its customs, as well as the legacy of Charles's self-styling as an Englishman devoted to St. George, provided the backdrop for a subtle, yet effective, part of Margaret's diplomatic strategy. Margaret not only seems to have encouraged Edward's interest in the trappings of sophisticated Burgundian court culture, perhaps hoping to increase his attachment to the duchy, but she also sparked his interest in Burgundian religious culture.

As part of the foundation for a political and economic alliance between England and Burgundy, already united by marriage and blood as well as by courtly taste, Margaret strove to forge a spiritual alliance as well. At the heart of this strategy was Margaret's encouragement of Edward's interest in the strict monastic orders to which she and her Burgundian relatives were so devoted.[65] From the beginning of his reign Edward had showed favor to the Brigittines, an order that also received significant support from Margaret. For instance, in the first year of his reign, Edward IV repealed Henry VI's grant that had given possessions belonging to the Brigittine house of Syon to King's College, Cambridge. Indeed, Edward's generosity to Syon was so great that he became known as the house's "second founder."[66] Margaret nudged Edward to expand the horizons of his monastic patronage to other austere religious orders, especially the Observant Franciscans.

As A. G. Little has noted, in spite of the Observant Friars' popularity on the Continent, the order was introduced into England quite late. Furthermore, the reason for their eventual introduction in 1481 differed from those that drove the Observants' rapid spread elsewhere. Little argues that "the introduction of the Observants into England was due neither to a demand for reform among the friars of the province nor to protests of the laity against their moral conduct, but to the king acting under suggestion from abroad."[67] This suggestion almost certainly came from his sister Margaret during the course of her diplomatic visit, since Edward obtained a papal bull for an Observant foundation at Greenwich—significantly, the site of his "favorite residence"[68]—on the heels of that visit in January 1481. Furthermore, Margaret may have hoped to strengthen the spiritual connection between England and Burgundy by founding additional houses in England of this order, which had such a strong presence in Burgundian territories and of which she was such a stalwart supporter.[69] Together with a group of English nobles, she obtained a papal bull dated September 24, 1481, giving approval for the foundation of three additional Observant houses in England.

Although these additional houses were never founded, the community at Greenwich flourished.[70] Pious reasons may well have motivated Margaret's encouragement and Edward IV's decision to establish the community; in addition to the spiritual benefits the foundation provided, the house of Observant Friars at Greenwich also became a living reminder of, and a consecrated monument to, the link between England and Burgundy. Much as Margaret made politically advantageous gifts of the manuscript of the *Vie de Sainte Colette* and her crown, so too she astutely gave a beautifully illuminated gradual to the Greenwich friars.[71] Her generous gift underlines the community's value to her cause, while its use within the community would have served as a reminder to the friars of that cause.

Ties linking the Franciscan community at Greenwich to the Low Countries, as well as to other areas under Burgundian influence, were quite strong. The duty for providing for the foundation fell on John Philippi, who was the former provincial vicar of Burgundy and who had been re-elected as vicar-general of the Observants in June 1481. He appointed friar Bernard of Lochen (or Blochen) as his commissary and sent other friars from Ostend in the Low Countries to England. As Little notes, the original Greenwich friars probably were all foreign, and even more than ten years after the foundation "the recruits came mostly from abroad."[72] Evidence from ordination lists indicates that many of these foreigners came from the Low Countries and other areas dominated by the Burgundians. Friars who came from Malines (one of Margaret's dower towns) and Aachen appear with particular frequency.[73]

The population and administration of the house of Observants of Greenwich by friars from Burgundian-dominated areas, although not necessarily done at Margaret's direction, recalls the long-standing Burgundian practice of giving religious appointments to those having strong pro-Burgundian political sympathies.[74] Prevenier and Blockmans see the desire to increase ducal influence as motivating the Burgundian selection process in making religious appointments; candidates were chosen with an eye toward extending Burgundian influence "not only to the church as an institution, but also to the congregations who could sometimes hear political messages from the pulpit."[75] In this case, the foundation at Greenwich, filled with pro-Burgundian friars, had the very useful potential to extend Burgundian influence to those at the center of English royal power.

Margaret's diplomatic negotiations with Edward IV, in which the Observant Franciscans seem to have played an important role, were extremely successful, if only in the short term. That Margaret found it useful

in achieving diplomatic success to encourage Edward IV to support the
Observant Friars is not surprising when one considers the political benefits
the Burgundians had reaped over the years from supporting houses of
the Colettines, another Franciscan reform movement.[76] In fostering her
brother's interest in this religious order to advance her political cause, it is
also possible that Margaret was heeding advice given to her in a devotional treatise entitled *Le dyalogue de la ducesse de bourgogne a Ihesu Crist*.

The *Dyalogue*, by Nicolas Finet, was presented to Margaret around
1470, and it survives in London, British Library MS Add. 7970. It consists
of a conversation between Margaret, called "la ducesse" [the duchess], and
"Ihesucrist" [Jesus Christ] in which Margaret seeks information on how
to live in this world to ensure her salvation in the next. The text presents
instruction on prayer and contemplation as well as conventional sorts of
conduct instructions concerning such matters as dress. The conversation
between Margaret and Christ also reveals considerable concern with the
roadblocks to spiritual advancement faced by the wealthy and powerful.
The *Dyalogue* correspondingly spends much time outlining how "ceux qui
sont en prelacions et seignouriez" [those in positions of prelacy and lord-
ship] ought to turn their power to beneficial ends while avoiding the snares
of worldliness.[77]

As it turns out, according to the *Dyalogue*, a political life and a spiritual life are not necessarily incompatible. Indeed, when combined properly, they can form a mutually reinforcing system in which political power
can serve spiritual development while devotional acts can have political
benefits. Significantly, Christ explains that support for monastic reform
movements and reformed orders is particularly useful in this mutually reinforcing system. Early in the text, Jesus acknowledges Margaret's difficult
spiritual position, saying, "Ma fille tu as longtamps este et es encorez en
cestuy monde gra*n*t dame seur Edouuart roy dengleterre fe*m*me & espeuse
de Charles duc de bourgongne" [My daughter, you have long been, and
still are, a great lady in the world, sister of King Edward of England and
wife of Charles, duke of Burgundy] (*Dyalogue* fol. 9v-10r). However, Christ
points out that she has by and large avoided the dangers of her elevated
status, continuing, "a present tu fais tresagement car tu te applicques du
tout a deuocion et aux choses espirituelles en delaisant autant quil est licite
touttes ponpes terriennes et a ornemens" [presently you do very wisely
because you apply yourself entirely to devotion and to spiritual things,
leaving aside all earthly pomp and ornaments to the extent that it is permitted to you] (*Dyalogue*, fol. 10r). He tells Margaret that it is particularly

fortunate that she spends more time with and converses more readily with "les personnes deuotes et religieuses obseruans leurs rigles" [devout people and nuns who observe their rules] than "auec les princes et barons" [princes and barons] (*Dyalogue*, fol. 10r). This praise for Margaret's activities might seem to imply a separation of the political and religious realms, and it might seem to be an encouragement for her to eschew the "masculine" realm of politics for the more traditionally and acceptably "feminine" one of piety. In fact, however, Margaret's support for the devout and her involvement with observant religious turn out to be politically beneficial acts, even political duties.

When Margaret asks Jesus for advice on how the powerful should conduct their affairs, He advises her that such people must exercise their offices in a careful and God-fearing manner. They must exhibit prudence and diligence, avoiding pride and vanity as well as calling frequently upon Him.[78] They must not seek "leur propres prouffis delices et honneurs" [their own profits, delights, and honors] but rather seek "tous iours le prouffit du bien commun" [always the advancement of the common good] (*Dyalogue*, fol. 30r-30v). The common good is the most divine, Christ tells Margaret, and supporting monastic reform movements—especially those of the friars—is one of the best ways to advance such a cause. Jesus advises Margaret:

Tu feras ce que poras qui en toy sera pour le bien conmun en tous ces affayres principalement en lestat de lesglise et espirituel affin que les cloistres soyent reformes et la reguliere obseruance soit en vigeur meismement es quatre ordes des mendians qui ont a preschier aux aultres Car par leur reguliere et examplire vie et conuersacion poroient croistre plusieurs grans biens. (*Dyalogue*, fol. 98v–99r)

[You shall do what you can that will advance the common good in all these affairs, principally in the spiritual state of the church, so that cloisters may be reformed and regular observance may exist with the same rigor in the four mendicant orders who must preach to others. Because their regular and exemplary life and conversation may foster great benefits]

Monastic reform is indeed so important both spiritually and politically that Christ will brook no excuses from Margaret for not undertaking it. Even bodily weakness and age must not stand in the way.[79] He tells her that if she personally cannot accomplish reforms, then she should exhort her "mary prince trespuissant saige et vaillant" [husband, a very powerful, wise, and valiant prince] to "acconplir ce que dit est" [accomplish that which is said] (*Dyalogue*, fol. 99v-100r). Furthermore, if she protests that her husband "na point de pooir ne iuridicion sur les gens deglise" [does not have power or jurisdiction over the people of the church] to compel them, he must obtain such authority "de par nostre saint pere le pape sure lesdittes personnes pour les reformer" [from our Holy Father the pope over these said people to reform them] (*Dyalogue*, fol. 100r–100v). Margaret appears to be persuaded, saying, "[I]e ne doubte pas certainement que ce ne fut chose moult prouffitable au bien ciuil de reformer leur couuens deformes" [Certainly I do not doubt that there is anything so profitable to the civic good as to reform their dissolute convents] (*Dyalogue*, fol. 100v–101r).

In the *Dyalogue*, the "bien civil" or "bien conmun" and the good of the house of Burgundy dovetail nicely. Not only does Margaret engender political as well as spiritual benefits through supporting monastic reform, but such activities also give added legitimacy to the Burgundian cause, since the Burgundians, as rulers, are behaving in accord with a divinely sanctioned model of rule. This stance harmonizes well with the merging of religious and political authority found in the illumination (discussed above) of Margaret as the vicaress of Christ found in *Benoit seroient les misericordieux*, also written for Margaret by Nicholas Finet.

Margaret died on November 23, 1503. Her support for religious foundations and her involvement with monastic reforms were important parts of her legacy, suggesting the degree to which she followed the advice of the *Dyalogue*. As the Burgundian chronicler Molinet reports, Margaret "fut fort regrettée plainte et plourée des religioux réformées et de plusieurs personnes dévotes, euxquelles elle donna de ses biens largement" [was greatly lamented with complaints and tears among reformed religious and numerous devout people to whom she had been so generous with her goods].[80] Numerous epigraphs helped keep alive the mutually informing political and spiritual benefits the duchess's devotional activities had fostered. These epigraphs were often found on the walls of monastic foundations who had been recipients of her largesse.[81] A characteristic example was located in the church of the Chartreux of Louvain. Speaking as though in Margaret's voice, in language that closely resembles the ideal model of rule set out in the *Dyalogue*, the text states:

Interea qua cura, rogas? Fuit unica cura
Viros fovere sacros, sacrasque feminas.
Quid docti? Doctis templorum confero curas
Quibuslibet, legem modo norint sacram.
Quid sibi magnates? Sibi quid Simonis alumni?
Male audiunt, petentes quod dari est nefas.[82]

[You ask what my task was during this time? It was solely the care of men and women consecrated to God. And what of the learned? To them I gave benefices, on the condition that they observe sacred law. And what of the nobles? And what of the disciples of Simon? They were badly received, because they were seeking something that is forbidden to give.]

The Latin epitaph on her tomb similarly describes her as "Juris, Religionis, Reformationis, pietatis, mire fautrix mechlinie oppido suo" ["A marvellous and devoted Patroness of Justice, of Religion and of Reform in her dower town of Malines"] [83]

Margaret chose to be buried in a Franciscan habit, having been received, at the end of her life, into the Third Order of St. Francis. Her burial site, in the Church of the Observant Franciscans of Malines, as well as her tomb itself, underline the ongoing connections between the Burgundian dynasty and this strict monastic order, so perpetuating the political and spiritual benefits produced by the connection. According to a sixteenth-century observer of her tomb, on one side of the choir was a statue of Margaret, kneeling, being presented by St. Margaret. On the other side, "Icelle dame couche morte sur une natte enveloppée dung suaire, une couronne sur son chief avec trois cordelliers l'administrans. Le tout faict d'allebastre, et y a ung ange . . . " [This lady lies dead on a bier draped with a shroud, a crown on her head, with three Franciscan friars ministering to her. The whole is made of alabaster, and there is an angel . . .].[84] This angel, which wears a crown and holds a lozenge bearing the arms of England and Burgundy surmounted by a crown ("tenans ses armes en Lozenge"), is a fitting final claim for the divinely approved authority of the house of Burgundy and its divine blessed union with England.[85]

Rival Reforms

One might imagine that Margaret of York's crafting of political agency through pious practices, especially her pursuit of diplomatic success by means of monastic foundation and reform, was idiosyncratic, a unique strategy of one equally devoted to her God, her families (both natal and conjugal), and their dynastic aims. Alternatively, given the history of the house of Burgundy with St. Colette and her reforms, one might suspect that Margaret's strategies were peculiarly Burgundian. However, the case of Anne d'Orléans demonstrates that the involvement of women of God in affairs typically thought to be the province of men of arms was a more widespread cultural phenomenon than the examples I have treated thus far in the first two chapters might suggest. Indeed, as I hope to show in subsequent chapters, this was a phenomenon that informed, and indeed in important respects shaped, political life throughout Europe in the later medieval and early modern periods.

Margaret of York's contemporary Anne d'Orléans came from a strikingly similar background. Like Margaret, Anne was sister to a king, in this case Louis XII of France. She was also connected by blood to an important ducal dynasty, that of Brittany.[86] Like Margaret, Anne, too, was a woman of great piety. Her piety, however, found expression through a very different form of religious life; Anne entered the abbey of Fontevraud at age 14, where she became abbess following her cousin Marie de Bretagne's death in 1477.[87] Though coming from similar familial circumstances, Margaret and Anne thus lived very different sorts of lives.

Strikingly, though, for Anne, as for Margaret, piety was intimately connected with, and in fact was a vital component of, political action. As it did for Margaret, monastic reform became for Anne a kind of diplomatic tool, one that she used on the side of the Burgundians' great adversaries the French who were engaged in competing efforts to forge alliances with England in the late 1470s and early 1480s. The order of Fontevraud, with its history of Anglo-French connections and its long-term engagement in royal politics on both sides of the Channel, provided an ideal platform from which to pursue amicable relations between England and France.

The abbey of Fontevraud and its English daughter houses were from their earliest years enmeshed in power struggles and coalition building in England as well as between England and France. Fontevraud's second abbess was Matilda of Anjou, the widow of William, eldest son of Henry I of England. She was also the aunt of Henry Plantagenet, duke of Anjou, who became Henry II of England in 1154. Tradition holds that Matilda planned the expansion of the order into England, an effort that may well have been undertaken for political ends. Berenice Kerr observes, "It is not improbable that Henry Plantagenet had himself approached Matilda about a Fontevraud foundation in England. He had been in England in 1148–9 to assess the political situation. Perhaps he saw advantages in colonizing England with foundations from Fontevraud."[88]

If Henry was hoping to use monastic foundation to consolidate support for his kingship in England, his chosen strategy proved to be a good one. Kerr persuasively argues that "founding a monastery was . . . an act of royal service. Subjects wishing to demonstrate their loyalty . . . would thus be likely to choose an order which either had the king's approval or was identified with him in some way."[89] The patrons for the first English Fontevrauldine foundation were the count and countess of Leicester. The countess, Amice, had a "lively interest in the order." and probably encouraged her husband Robert to establish the house."[90] The date of the foundation, however, "also implies political considerations." Robert gave lands and revenues to Fontevraud for the foundation of an English priory sometime after 1147, likely in 1153. This gift "marks the definitive reconciliation of the count of Leicester, who in 1136 had taken the side of King Stephen, with Henry Plantagenet. The foundation of an English daughter-house of the great abbey in Poitiers is one of many indicators of the Angevin party's triumph in England."[91]

Connections between the English monarchy and the abbey of Fontevraud remained strong well beyond the early years of the order. As Alfred Jubien points out, "The sovereigns of England and of the house of Anjou-Plantagenet were extremely generous to Fontevraud Abbey";[92] even after the onset of the Hundred Years' War, support continued, although rents were not always paid regularly. For instance, the twenty-second abbess, Blanche de Harcouty, had to seek the help of her cousin Charles VI of France, who wrote to Richard II saying, "Vous prions et requerons tres instamment, et de cuer . . . que pour amour et contemplacion de nous et des choses dessus touchées, vous vueillez vostre et nostre dicte cousine faire paier et contanter des dictz arrerages et aussi la dicte rente, doresnavant" [We pray, and require most urgently, from our heart . . . for love and contemplation of us and for those matters discussed above, henceforth you will have your and our cousin paid and made good the said arrears and also the said rent].[93] Furthermore, English Fontevrauldine houses suffered less than some of the other alien priories during the Hundred Years' War.[94] When Edward III declared war on France in 1337, the only property considered to be "of alien ownership" was that held directly by the mother house of Fontevraud; additionally, the "rupture of relations" between the priory of Amesbury and Fontevraud was "even in time of war . . . curiously incomplete."[95]

As late as 1486, Alice Fisher, prioress of Amesbury, sent the abbess Anne d'Orléans a ring with an amethyst stone and "a silk purse of English work" as a "sign of submission."[96] In response to her gifts, Alice received a "friendly letter . . . outlining the nature of the Order, confirming her in her office, and enjoining her to observe the statutes and to keep the obits of Robert d'Arbrissel, Henry II, Richard I, and Eleanor of Aquitaine."[97] An early sixteenth-century manuscript from Amesbury, Oxford MS Bodleian Library Add. A. 42, mentions the statutes of Fontevraud, a reference that "gives reason to suspect that the connection with Fontevraud was not only continued beyond 1486 but that the statutes of the order were still of importance in regulating life within the convent during the early sixteenth century."[98]

French influence in English Fontevrauldine priories did inevitably decline through the course of the Hundred Years' War, however, especially since the abbess was unable to exercise her duties as visitor in the English houses during the war. When Anne d'Orléans became abbess and began to work to spread the reforms begun by her predecessor, her efforts to export the reforms to England were accompanied by efforts to regain property and strengthen influence lost during the war years. In early 1479, preparations got underway for "a mission to the English houses." Anne planned for one of the priors of the order "to go to England with a courteous letter of introduction to Edward IV, explaining the nature and history of the Order, and seeking the renewal of customary payments out of the Exchequer, license to visit the convents in his kingdom, and other benefits."[99] Anne also investigated the early years of Fontevraud's presence in England in order to renew claims to her English holdings. She had a terrier showing the English property "so far as Angevin documents could show it" drawn up, and "several ancient charters were hunted up and viewed."[100]

Anne's projected "mission to England" coincided with a very tense time in relations among England, France, and Burgundy, transpiring at exactly the moment Maximilian sent Margaret of York to England to try to detach Edward IV from Louis XI. At this juncture, Louis likely needed all the help he could get to try to hold on to his ally. Indeed, that at this political juncture Anne sought to remind Edward IV of the "nature and history of the Order," and that she explicitly focused attention on the Angevin-Plantagenet era (a technique she also employed in her letter to the prioress of Amesbury with her mentions of Henry II and Eleanor of Aquitaine), strongly suggest that the efforts to spread the Fontevrauldine reforms to England may have been prompted by political affairs beyond those of the order's internal politics. Although Anne's kinsman Francis II, duke of Brittany, engaged, like Charles the Bold of Burgundy, in struggles for power independent of the French king, Anne was also linked by blood to the French monarch. Furthermore, Anne was likely to be favorably disposed to the king's cause, since like her predecessor Marie, she had received much royal aid in the difficult process of launching reforms.[101] This history of royal support, which enabled Anne to obtain new privileges for the order, get old ones renewed, and expand the scope of reforms, gave her good reason to cooperate with the French monarch in his political aims, especially when they coincided so well with her own.

Anne's letter to Edward IV served a purpose similar to that served by the tapestries depicting the wedding of Clovis and Clothilde at the marriage of Charles and Margaret: it represented a return to a sacred moment in the past to advance a political end in the present. Anne's strategy also resembled that of Henry II when he sought to have Fontevrauldine priories established in England. In these early days of the order, as Chibnall observes, "the spiritual filiations always underline, and sometimes precede, territorial conquests."[102] Anne evidently hoped much the same thing would be true in the later fifteenth century, although her desire was that spiritual affiliation might advance not only the recapture of Fontevrauldine territory in England but also a diplomatic conquest leading to an alliance between England and France.

Unfortunately, we do not know what transpired in the course of Anne's "mission to England"; indeed, we do not even know whether her agent ever made the trip.[103] Furthermore, Edward IV ultimately did rejoin Burgundy, albeit rather half-heartedly and without much long-term effect on the course of events on the Continent. What may be most significant about Anne's plans to spread her reforms to England at this particular moment, and about the way she chose to present those plans to the English king, is that her letter to Edward IV, like his sister's support for the Observant Friars in England, gives evidence for a powerful, but heretofore largely unacknowledged, mode of feminine political action.

The Sword and the Cloister:
Joan of Arc, Margaret of Anjou, and Christine de Pizan in England, 1445–1540

Gender, National Identity, and Anglo-French Politics

For St. Colette of Corbie, female spirituality provided symbolic capital with which she could advance her political aims within the Church and the Franciscan Order. Her holiness and that of her reformed nuns were also symbolic resources available to the Burgundian dukes and duchesses as they pursued the expansion of their territory and the consolidation of their authority. Margaret of York and her French contemporary Anne d'Orléans further demonstrate the ways in which religious patronage, devotional practices, and monastic reform could become an important mode of political action for women. In this chapter, we turn our attention to another, quite different form of political action by one of the most famous holy women of later medieval Europe. Joan of Arc's divinely inspired act of taking up the sword on behalf of France during the Hundred Years War, and her consequent death at the stake after her condemnation by Anglo-Burgundian ecclesiastical authorities, created a legacy that endured through centuries. That this woman of God moved directly into the sphere of men of arms inspired both derision from her political enemies and praise from such politically engaged writers as her contemporary Christine de Pizan and the later anonymous Spanish author of *La Poncella de Francia*.[1] Furthermore, Joan's spectral presence haunted Anglo-French relations long after she herself was not present to lead French armies against the English.

During her lifetime and afterwards, Joan of Arc challenged the English at a faultline between gender identity and national identity. In the second half of the fifteenth century and the first half of the sixteenth century, two other French women fractured that faultline still further: Christine de Pizan and Margaret of Anjou. The careers of these women intersect in significant ways. Among the most obvious, although not, as I shall argue, the only, connections are the facts that Margaret owned a copy of Christine's *Faits d'armes* and Joan, as I mentioned, became the subject of Christine's celebratory *Ditié de Jehanne d'Arc*.

The years between 1445 and 1540 witnessed not only Margaret of Anjou's arrival in England as Henry VI's queen and Joan of Arc's official rehabilitation by the Church, but also the height of Christine de Pizan's popularity in England. This popularity might initially seem rather surprising, since Christine, though Italian by birth and supported by Burgundian as well as Valois patrons, identified strongly with France and the French royal cause. Indeed, she exhibited particularly strong animosity toward the English, who, as she claims in the *Lamentacion sur les maux de la France*, were the "natural enemies" of the French.[2] Given Christine's sympathies, and given that in this era of English history France and the status of the English claim to France were extremely difficult issues, Christine's work would seem unlikely to be attractive to English audiences.[3] Furthermore, her most popular texts, *L'Epistre d'Othea*, *Le Livre de faits d'armes et de chevalerie*, and the *Le Livre de la cité des dames*, emphasize many of the most troubling problems facing the English monarchy during the later medieval and early modern periods: military training, the conduct of war, proper governance, and—crucially for the ever-fraught issue of royal succession, the catalyst for so much of the domestic and international conflict in this period—women's place in lineages.[4]

English interest in Christine and her work in this particular textual environment is neither an accident of history nor evidence of perverse literary tastes. Although Christine's works foreground politically difficult matters, the English found value in these texts in their efforts to advance their political causes. The *Livre de faits d'armes et de chevalerie* has, for instance, an ironic history of being used to justify English efforts to take French territories, as I shall discuss. In addition to such direct benefits, Christine's texts provided a paradoxically welcome kind of cultural provocation. Ian Moulton has observed, "In the patriarchal ideology of the period, the English nation was in many ways identical with English manhood. . . . [N]otions of manhood and effeminacy were frequently bound up with the opposition between the native and the foreign."[5] In confronting the challenges that politically active French women presented to English nationhood and English manhood, English redactors of Christine's works seized the chance to make a virtue of necessity, engaging in elaborate containment strategies that turn threats into defensive assets.

The cultural pressures provided by Christine and her texts, troubling though they may have been, were in fact quite productive. Strategic manipulations of the figure of Christine, combined with targeted transformations of her works, provided opportunities for retroactive revisions of the very things Christine and her countrywomen destabilized.[6] Christine and her texts thus represented both distressing symptoms of anxieties concerning gendered and national identity—in psychoanalytic terms they might be viewed as iterations of an unfinished trauma—and a potential remedy for those symptoms.[7] L. O. Aranye Fradenburg has asserted, "History makes its truths in accordance with desire and its defenses."[8] English redactors of Christine's texts found ways of processing political trauma to produce politically desirable "truth." The English versions of the *Faits d'armes*, *Othea*, and *Cité des dames* achieve this metamorphosis through a dynamic of simultaneous celebration of and minimization of women's political roles, joined with valorizations of male heroism and masculine authority. This contradictory combination ultimately works to maximize the political benefits available from Christine's works by textually modeling solutions to the sorts of troubles exacerbated by Christine, her writings, and the activities of her compatriots Joan of Arc and Margaret of Anjou. These solutions rely in large part upon invocations of religiously inflected ideologies and ideals of feminine conduct. In the end, English versions of Christine's texts solidify the mutually informing gender boundaries and national boundaries that the originals so often disturb.[9]

Arms and the Woman

Issues of gender figure prominently, both in practical and representational terms, in the entwined histories of Anglo-French relations and English royal succession in the later Middle Ages. During the Lancastrian era, English kings engaged in a delicate balancing act between contradictorily gendered models of monarchical inheritance. Representations of the Lancastrian claim to the throne of England often mobilized paradigms of apostolic succession and sacerdotal kingship, excluding women from the line of succession. This was an exclusion upon which the Lancastrians insisted even more forcefully once the Yorkists appeared on the scene, since the Yorkist claim to the throne through Lionel, duke of Clarence (an elder son of Edward III than the Lancastrian progenitor John of Gaunt, duke of Lancaster) depended at two points on succession through women: Lionel's daughter

Philippa and great-granddaughter Anne Mortimer. Such insistence would, ironically, come to haunt the Lancastrian-descended Tudors in the reign of Henry VIII.

Simultaneously, though, Lancastrian representations of the English claim to the throne of France often brought to bear the example of the Incarnation as a case in which a virtuous woman legitimately transmits a divine inheritance to her son.[10] Such an argument was necessary since the Lancastrian kings depended for their claim to the French throne on a connection through the female line.[11] They therefore needed to validate the role of women to pass on the right of succession but not, crucially, to inherit that right. This argument concerning women's critical yet attenuated roles in lineages was of course also important in Yorkist claims to the English monarchy, for the genealogical reasons outlined above.

When the young Henry VI came to the throne, the problematic place of women in transmitting the right to rule, and the vexed task of trying to represent as wholly masculine an authority that depends in some regard on women, no longer seemed such pressing issues. His father Henry V had not only successfully consolidated his claim to the English throne but had also, through the Treaty of Troyes, been named the legal successor to the French throne. Indeed, genealogical propaganda representing the dual monarchy that circulated at the time of Henry VI's accession focused on his descent through the *male* English and French lines, lines founded by saintly kings.[12]

During Henry VI's reign, however, women once again muddied the waters of Anglo-French relations and English royal politics, causing even more serious problems than those stemming from contradictory Lancastrian representational strategies. In particular, Joan of Arc, visionary, cross-dressing virgin, and at least temporarily successful military leader, prompted what might be called a crisis of English monarchical masculinity during the reign of the child-king. As Steven Weiskopf has observed, Joan provoked a "fear that the powerful body of the English monarchy, once represented by Henry V" was "being unmanned 'bi litel and lytel."[13] Because her dispatch at the stake provided only fleeting—if ever effective—resolution, Joan represented for the English not simply a temporary but rather an ongoing problem, one exacerbated by her rehabilitation. She continued, even long after her death, to disturb the already-conflicted, related formations of gendered and royal identities.

To make matters worse, the consequences of English losses in France in the 1430s and 1440s led to another difficult French woman's arrival on the scene. In 1445, in an effort to make peace and shore up the English claim, Henry VI wedded Margaret of Anjou, niece of Charles VII. The political necessity of women emerged once again, and with it resurfaced the dangerous possibility that women would choose to wield for themselves the power they more properly should hand over to men.

When Henry VI and Margaret of Anjou married, John Talbot, earl of Shrewsbury, presented Margaret with a magnificent manuscript (now London, British Library MS Royal 15 E VI) as a nuptial gift. This large, lavishly illuminated manuscript contains several chivalric romances and chansons de geste—the *Roman d'Alexandre*, the *Chanson d'Aspremont*, *Gui de Warrewick*, and *Le Chevalier au cygne* among others—as well as military and political treatises, including Christine de Pizan's *Faits d'armes*.[14] Additionally, at the beginning of this manuscript is an elaborate full page genealogical chart (Figure 1) depicting Henry VI's claims to the thrones of England and France which focuses, as did the earlier genealogical propaganda mentioned above, on the male line in both cases.

This chart's rather obfuscatory emphasis on the male line tacitly admits to a key aspect of the masculinist crisis, since, as we have seen, the hereditary claim to the French throne rested on descent through the female line.[15] Likewise suppressed is Margaret's importance, given the realities of English losses, for English hopes of consolidating any sort of actual power in France. Although women's necessity was once again, unwelcomely, in the political picture, Margaret of Anjou herself is literally *not* in the genealogical picture representing the English dual monarchy, as Michel-André Bossy has observed. Rather than being named or portrayed in the family tree, she is "translated into emblems," particularly into a bouquet of marguerites positioned in the center of the bottom margin.[16] Significantly, Bossy notes that in the genealogical chart, "a pointed appendage beneath the portrait of Henry VI suggestively penetrates the parted flowers. . . . [The] iconographical message is unmistakable: the queen's function in this table of lineage is procreative—she is to produce a son and heir for Henry VI."[17]

This image announces what is in fact an important subtext of the gift manuscript as a whole. It emphasizes that, as the Virgin Mary does in Lancastrian invocations of the Incarnation, women are to play passive, transmissive functions, functions that are subordinate to the dominant roles of men in the political sphere. This emphasis is further reinforced by the collection of chansons de geste and romances, texts that embody the simultaneous celebration of women in carefully circumscribed roles, the occlusion of female agency, and the glorification of male heroism. These

Figure 1. Royal genealogy. MS Royal 15 E VI fol. 3r. By permission of the British Library.

selections feature female passivity and procreativity while celebrating the valiant actions of "Des preux qui par grant labeur / Vouldrent acquerir honneur / En France en Angleterre / Et en aultre mainte terre."[18]

The suppression of women's independent political power that takes place iconographically in the opening genealogical chart and textually in the chansons de geste is mirrored by the treatment of Christine de Pizan in illuminations for the *Faits d'armes* in this manuscript. As Bossy has also observed, the version of the *Faits* in MS Royal 15 E VI is *not* one of those which erases Christine's authorship.[19] The illumination that introduces the treatise, however, is not what other manuscripts of the *Faits* would lead one to expect. The scene that is typically found at the beginning of the text, a portrayal of Christine conferring with Minerva (Figure 2), so indicating her authority to write on military and political matters, is missing. The conference between Christine and Minerva is replaced by a depiction of Talbot receiving the sword of marshal of France.[20] The male marshal displaces martial women; this scene, like the genealogical chart, masks female agency. Men are represented as the rightful possessors both of political authority and the military means (in the phallic sword) to protect, enforce, and legitimate that authority.

Bossy discusses the importance of these iconographic revisions for Talbot's own political ambitions.[21] I would argue, though, that there are even larger political implications to the similar treatments of Margaret and Christine in the Royal manuscript. Both of these French women provided something necessary or expedient to the English cause. Margaret played an important role in English hopes of shoring up their claims in France. Similarly, Christine's *Faits d'armes*, although written to educate a French prince to fight against the English, provided, as I mentioned earlier, advantageous justification for the English to use in pressing their claim to French territories. In her explication of just causes of war, for instance, Christine says that among the lawful grounds for military action are the need to recover "lands, lordships, and other things stolen or usurped for an unjust cause."[22] In the *Boke of Noblesse*, written about 1450 and then revised in 1475, William Worcester cites precisely this passage to justify a new English invasion of France, as I discuss below.[23] Furthermore, Henry VII later found the *Faits* to be a similarly useful tool for supporting his own renewed interest in the English claim to France, as William Caxton's epilogue to his printed translation of the *Faits* reveals.[24]

Therefore, in spite of, or, more accurately, because of, their usefulness, both Margaret of Anjou and Christine de Pizan were in the dangerous position of being able to claim a kind of political agency for themselves. To make matters worse, they might readily have been perceived as actually having staked such a claim. Rather than working to shore up the English position in France, for instance, Margaret of Anjou pursued a contrary political role from the beginning of her marriage, pressing Henry VI into capitulating to French interests by securing the English surrender of Maine and Anjou.[25] Christine represents, in a sense, the textual equivalent of Margaret's independent undertakings. In the prologue to the *Faits d'Armes*, she goes to great lengths to make a case for the legitimacy of her writing about traditionally masculine military and political matters, since to do so is "chose non accoustumee et hors vsage a femme" [unexpected and not customary for a woman]. To support her case, Christine invokes the example of "dame minerue" [Lady Minerva] who "trouua . . . lart et la

Figure 2. Christine de Pizan and Minerva. *Faits d'Armes*. London, MS Harley 4605 fol. 3. By permission of the British Library.

maniere de faire le harnois de fer et dacier" [discovered the art and method
of making armor of iron and steel]. Christine then identifies herself with
the "hault deesse" [high goddess], saying, " je suis comme toy femme ytal-
ienne" [I am, like you, an Italian woman]. [26]

Thus, one might regard Christine and Margaret, as French women
who intervene in "properly" masculine affairs, as similar embodiments of
the fused threats of feminine political agency and foreign puissance. The
parallel iconographic treatments of Margaret and Christine in the Royal
manuscript address these threats by conveying a message that women
should participate in the politico-military sphere only indirectly. Talbot's
wedding gift emphasizes that, as Fradenburg states, women should "dra-
matiz[e] the masculinity of the warrior by being what he is not and by
watching his efforts from another place."[27] Even more pointedly, the manuscript suggests that *English* men—Henry VI and Talbot himself—are the
legitimate recipients of power that passes through the hands of *French*
women, who should graciously transmit, rather than wield as their own,
that which they possess.

The connection that I am suggesting between Margaret of Anjou and
Christine de Pizan as joint representations of gendered and ethnic threats
is not as tenuous as it might initially seem. A sort of "missing link" connecting Margaret and Christine is Joan of Arc. Joan, that source of ongoing anxieties about gender and English national identity, hovers on the
scene like a returning manifestation of that which has been culturally repressed. Her afterlife thus colors fifteenth- and sixteenth-century perceptions of women's participation in the realms of war and government.

Margaret of Anjou is, in fifteenth-century historical sources, explicitly
linked to Joan of Arc.[28] In fact, according to a commentary of Pope Pius
II, Margaret even compared herself to Joan in a speech to her troops. She
reportedly declared, "I have often broken their [the English] battle line. I
have mowed down ranks far more stubborn than theirs are now. You who
once followed a peasant girl, follow now a queen."[29]

Christine too has quite a direct link with Joan. Her last known work
is the *Ditié de Jehanne d'Arc*, a text filled with anti-English rhetoric. The
Ditié is also replete with accounts of Joan that foreground the resonances
between matters of gender and Anglo-French politics. Not content merely
to celebrate English losses on the battlefield, Christine highlights Joan's
symbolic emasculation of the English as well. She describes Joan as one
who simultaneously overcomes English dominance in France and masculine dominance in the military sphere. She gleefully declares:

Hee! quel honneur au femenin
Sexe! Que Dieu l'ayme il appert,
Quant tout ce grant peuple chenin,
Par qui tout le regne ert desert,
Par femme est sours et recouvert,
Ce que C^m hommes [fait] n'eussent,
Et les traictres mis á desert!
A peine devant ne le creussent.[30]

["Oh! what honour for the female sex! It is perfectly obvious that God has special regard for it when all these wretched people who destroyed the whole kingdom—now recovered and made safe by a woman, something that 5000 *men* could not have done—and the traitors have been exterminated. Before the event they would scarcely have believed this possible" (*Ditié*, 46, emphasis in original)]

Explicitly emphasizing the anxiety-provoking spectacle of a woman in armor, Christine calls Joan a "fillete" ["little girl"] of just sixteen years "A qui armes ne sont pesans" (*Ditié* 273–75) ["who does not even notice the weight of the arms she bears" (*Ditié*, 46)]. Christine also draws attention to Joan's power over men as their military commander when she says, "Et de noz gens preux et abiles / Elle est principal chevetaine" (*Ditié*, 285–86) ["And she is the supreme captain of our brave and able men" (*Ditié*, 46)]. If Joan surpasses even noble, capable, and brave French men, just think of the implications for the defeated English! Furthermore, Joan outdoes even that paragon of chivalry embraced as progenitor by the English (as well as by the French) monarch, Hector; Christine exults of Joan, "tel force n'ot Hector n'Achilles!" (*Ditié*, 287) ["Neither Hector nor Achilles had such strength!" (*Ditié*, 46)].

Deborah Fraioli asserts that "It is unlikely that she [Christine] intended her poem to be read by the English," and she observes that there is not "any evidence that the poem ever reached England in medieval times."[31] Surviving manuscripts of the *Ditié* suggest, however, the possibility that an English audience may have been aware of the poem and its authorship—after all, it begins "Je, Christine" [I, Christine]—in the fifteenth century. The *Ditié* was written in "Anglo-Burgundian or 'enemy' territory";[32] furthermore, one of the manuscripts containing the *Ditié*, MS Berne 205, can be connected with the town of Sens. Until its surrender to Charles VII on January 7, 1430, Sens was an Anglo-Burgundian stronghold. This manuscript additionally bears indications "that the *Ditié* was pressed into service as royalist propaganda . . . within six months of its composition."[33] Propaganda of this type seems likely to have registered with the Anglo-Burgundian forces, especially given the Anglo-Burgundian faction's own highly developed program of propaganda production.

Even if Christine did not intend the poem for an English audience, and even if the poem did not actually reach England, there were plenty of politically and literarily savvy Englishmen on the Continent where the *Ditié* did circulate. Members of this potential English audience who may have encountered the poem abroad include such figures as John Talbot, and, as I shall discuss below, John Fastolf; both of these men knew other texts of Christine's, and they both imported some of her works into England. Furthermore, although we cannot definitively prove English knowledge of Christine's *Ditié*, Christine, as a French woman claiming both expertise in military matters and the right to voice strong political opinions against the English, still has a suggestive connection with Joan.

John Talbot, who gave the manuscript containing Christine's *Faits* to Margaret of Anjou, would have had an especially personal knowledge of—and likely a particular animosity toward—Joan of Arc. He was one of the chief commanders at the battle of Patay, where he was captured when the French army, inspired by Joan, crushed the English forces. Given these connections, I contend that, consciously or unconsciously, the legacy of Joan of Arc shapes the way in which Christine's text, at once so problematic and so useful, is "packaged" for Margaret of Anjou. The agenda underlying this packaging may be detected in the fact that the portrayal of Minerva and Christine so pointedly omitted from the *Faits* in the gift manuscript depicts Minerva wearing the armor she invented and carrying an upraised sword. For Talbot, and for the politically besieged English male aristocracy he represents, a female figure in armor would, understandably, suggest a model of feminine politico-military action and concomitant masculine impotence that he, as well as others of his status, would likely rather forget and rather that Joan's strong-willed countrywoman Margaret not consider in reading the *Faits*. The omission of Christine accompanied by the armed Minerva from Margaret's manuscript is, however, fraught with irony, since Margaret did become more or less literally the "woman in armor" Talbot's gift takes such pains to suppress.[34] The unsuccessfully repressed figure of Joan in a sense returned to full life in the person of Margaret.

Christine in the Cloister

The Joan-Margaret-Christine connection does not end with MS Royal 15 E VI. In an environment in which negative associations of Margaret with Joan were rapidly solidifying, there is also a further connection between Joan and Christine that likely played a role in shaping English treatments of Christine's work.[35] Many manuscripts of Christine's texts came to England via John Fastolf, who may well have become acquainted with her work during his service in France to the Lancastrian regime.[36] In addition to making Christine's work on chivalry, good governance, and military theory known to later generations of translators and disseminators, including Anthony Woodville, Lord Rivers; Stephen Scrope; and William Worcester (who used the *Faits d'armes* in his *Boke of Noblesse*),[37] Fastolf, like John Talbot, would have had plenty of experience with Joan of Arc to pass on to these men as well. Fastolf was one of the commanders at Patay, where Talbot was taken prisoner. In fact, in the autumn of 1441 or the spring of 1442, Fastolf had to "rebut a charge, laid before the king and his peers by the aggrieved Lord Talbot, of conduct unbecoming a knight of the Garter at the battle of Patay."[38]

Such experiences, shared with the next generation, would have resonated with the long-lived legacy of Joan, who remained a significant figure in the political landscape through the reign of Henry VI and into that of Edward IV.[39] These unpleasant remembrances of Joan would have coincided with increasing awareness of Margaret of Anjou's independent-minded political agency, so fostering ever more intense anxiety about maintaining embattled constructions of English masculine and political authority. The combined corrosive effects of Joan of Arc's afterlife and Margaret of Anjou's actions may well have prompted an imaginative, common textual solution to the uneasiness they stirred up. English versions of the works of that other difficult French woman, Christine de Pizan, proved in the mid-fifteenth century to be a remarkable vehicle for the recuperation of English manhood and monarchy.

Because both Scrope and Worcester are closely linked with Fastolf, P. G. C. Campbell's assertion, made long ago, that Fastolf may be behind the transformation of Christine de Pizan into a life-long nun—a claim present in Scrope's *Othea* and Worcester's *Boke of Noblesse*—has special political relevance.[40] In a move with a venerable tradition of use to neutralize politically problematic women (witness the monk of Canterbury's desire to shut Margery Kempe in "an hows of ston"[41]), Christine is put into the secure enclosure of a religious foundation, so conveniently removing her from the role of active, knowledgeable participant in the politico-military sphere.[42] Scrope and Worcester thus achieve textually the fulfillment of the desire to contain female political agency and military skill, a feat much more difficult to accomplish with the dead but not forgotten Joan or the living Margaret of Anjou.

Scrope seems to have written his translation of the *Othea* around 1450; as Curt F. Bühler observes, he was not the only later medieval or early modern Englishman to find Christine's *Othea* worth rendering in English. Since this text was, somewhat unusually, translated three times in the later fifteenth and early sixteenth centuries, it is worth pausing to consider what might have been so attractive about the *Othea*.[43] One possibility has to do with the *Othea*'s politically useful celebrations of women's position in lineages and female virtue. These celebrations seemingly take place within the boundaries of a perceived masculine hierarchy and so superficially replicate the focus on a passive, transmissive female role found in the opening genealogical chart of MS Royal 15 E VI.[44]

Christine's *Othea* presents the goddess of prudence, Othea, instructing the fifteen-year-old Hector of Troy in "those things which are necessary / To great valor and contrary / To the opposite of Prowess."[45] She is an ideal manifestation of virtuous female behavior, because she enacts just the sort of transmissive function envisioned as appropriate for women. The opening lines of the text position Othea as one who "addresses hearts great in valor" as she declares to Hector, "I desire / Your great profit. . . ." She adds, "By my letter I wish to counsel / You. . . . " (*Othea*, 35). She thus passes on her knowledge to the "prototype of the . . . chivalric hero"[46] who will be the one to put the theories she expounds actively into practice. In this, she does just what Talbot evidently hoped Margaret of Anjou would do with the *Faits d'armes* for the royal heir she was to produce. One of Scrope's three dedications for his translation of the *Othea*, found in MS M. 775 in the Pierpont Morgan Library, is to a "hye princesse," a dedication that suggests perhaps Scrope too may have envisioned such a role for an English noblewoman.[47]

Furthermore, in many of its glosses and allegories, the *Othea* transforms the feminine, even the potentially threatening figure of the politically and militarily active woman, into something securely under the control of the masculine, thus making it "safe" to praise. For instance, in the gloss on the text concerning Minerva, a text which focuses on her invention of armor, that invention is transferred firmly into Hector's hands. He is called son of Minerva because he, in Scrope's Middle English, "couthe sette armure wel a-werke"; according to Scrope, "it was *his ryghte crafte*" (*Epistle* 23, emphasis added). The craft of arms, though it originates with Minerva, belongs properly, rightly, to the male hero who actually performs deeds of arms, setting "armure wel a-werke."

The text's treatments of women's place in lineages, their virtue, and their transmissive roles prove, however, to be problematically double-edged, working in some ways against the political agenda the text is mobilized to serve. The *Othea* proves to be as difficult to contain within a masculinist political and ideological framework as Joan of Arc and Margaret of Anjou were. For instance, the treatment of female lineage in the *Othea* is not straightforwardly useful for the English monarchical cause as it might initially seem. On one level, the text helpfully portrays Hector, called son of Minerva, as the legitimate masculine heir to the divine qualities she, and her fellow goddess Othea, his instructor, pass on. On another level, though, the text celebrates not simply women's transmissive functions but also assertively independent female figures. For instance, as Jane Chance has observed, in the *Othea* Christine "rewrite[s] the genealogy of the gods from a female perspective."[48] This rewriting famously includes a series of allegories that "feminizes" the masculine Christian trinity using the goddesses Diana ("we shall take for Diana God of Paradise"), Ceres ("we shall take for Ceres, whom the good knight should resemble, the blessed Son of God"), and Isis ("There where it says that the good spirit ought to resemble Isis, who is a planter, we may understand the holy conception of Jesus Christ by the Holy Spirit in the holy Virgin Mary") (*Othea*, 59–60). Here is a version of women's place in a divine genealogy far distant from the one advanced by the "suggestively parted marguerites" in the illumination that precedes Margaret's copy of the *Faits*.

That the *Othea* begins and ends with accounts of the value, even the necessity, of specifically female knowledge and wisdom heightens the work's disquieting suggestions that women may capably take on roles other than passive, transmissive ones. The first text is Othea's initial address to Hector, and the gloss on this text begins, "Othea in Greek can be taken from the wisdom of woman" (*Othea*, 36). The accompanying allegory opens, "As prudence and wisdom are mother and conductress of all virtues, without which the others could not be well-governed, it is necessary to the chivalrous spirit that it be adorned with prudence" (*Othea*, 38). The final text concerns the instruction of Caesar Augustus by the Cumaean Sibyl, and here the gloss explains that Caesar "learned to know God and belief from a woman" (*Othea*, 120). The last word of the allegory for this text is, as Chance notes, *sapiencia*.[49] As she points out elsewhere, this is "wisdom written by a woman."[50]

The possibilities for female political and military action presented by the *Othea* are especially problematic. Helen Solterer has written that the representation of female knights and female martial ambition in the

Tournoiement as dames "seems to lock women into a passive position," but at the same time the text "conjures up the possibility that they could be represented otherwise."[51] Similarly, while the *Othea* would seem to show women who possess military skill, political ability, and vital cultural knowledge in safely passive, transmissive roles, it also calls to mind the possibility that women might break out of these roles into the realm of action.[52]

Strikingly, the "most powerful figures" in the text are "mothers, female warriors, and female scholars."[53] Immediately after being described as Minerva's son, Hector is told to embrace the goddess Pallas and so "reap with your prowess." Othea further advises, "All will go well for you if you have her; / Minerva sits well with Pallas" (*Othea*, 51). The gloss elaborates, "So she is named Minerva in that which appertains to chivalry, and Pallas in all things which appertain to wisdom" (*Othea*, 51), demonstrating in a single sentence the superlative skills of women in the martial and intellectual spheres. Such descriptions foreground the very things that Scrope's translation would evidently rather strategically minimize: women's powerful maternal presence in lineages, women's military abilities, and women's intellectual capacity.

The possibilities for feminine political and military action raised by the *Othea* had, I would argue, especially troubling resonances in the mid-fifteenth century in light of Margaret of Anjou's increasing power in the English court. In the 1450s, Margaret was beginning to adopt the very sorts of political authority that the *Othea* suggests women can successfully wield, and such figures as Pallas and Minerva emphasize precisely the "Joan-like" roles that Margaret was starting to embrace. When Scrope's translation was first circulating, Henry VI experienced his initial period of incapacitating disability. At this juncture, Margaret "attempted to conceal his condition and then tried to prevent a council or regent from taking power by securing it for herself." Reports also came to light in January of 1454 "that she had 'made a bille of five articles, desiryng those articles to be graunted [by parliament].'" This bill "would have given her 'the whole ruele of this land'" and would have enabled her to name various high officers of state, including the treasurer, normally chosen by the king himself.[54]

The difficulties raised by women's participation in matters of war and politics in the *Othea* make Scrope's representation of Christine as a patron of scholarly male clerics who are said to be the text's real authors particularly significant. Scrope, after dedicating the translation to Fastolf, writes: "And this seyde boke, at the instaunce & praer off a fulle wyse gentyl-woman of Frawnce called Dame Christine, was compiled & grounded by the famous doctours of the most excellent clerge the nobyl Vniuersyte off Paris" (*Epistle*, Appendix A, 122–23).[55] Jennifer Summit points out that the "fiction of Dame Christine" as "a cloistered religious woman" and as a pious woman who requests work from authors rather than an author herself, gains popularity "because it upholds a gendered model of authorship that makes masculine communities into centers of authorized textual production and displaces literate women into the margins."[56] A similar argument can be made for this representation of Christine in relation to a gendered model of military and political power, particularly since the exclusion of women from these spheres was perceived as a critical need in later medieval and early modern England. To return to Fradenburg's formulation, Christine in the cloister is definitively in "another place" than that of the male warrior. As a pious patron of male scholars, Christine performs the only role that women should take on in the "properly" masculine arenas of war and politics—that of enabling male action and supporting male authority.

Scrope further emphasizes the necessity of denying women an independent role in the practices of war and statecraft by listing at some length in his preface the male classical and patristic sources for the text's material: "Vyrgyl, Ouyde, Omer . . . Hermes, Plato, Salomon, Aristitles, Socrates, Ptholome . . . Austyn, Jerom, Gregorie, Ambrose . . . the Holy Ewaunngelistes and Epistollys and othyr holy doctours." To much the same end, he tellingly changes the title from the *Epistle of Othea to Hector* to the *Book off Knyghthode* or the *Boke off Cheuallry* (*Epistle*, Appendix A, 122–24). The removal of Othea and her authorship of the epistle from the title mirrors the displacements of Christine to the nunnery and the role of textual patron; it similarly recalls the omission of the image of Minerva in armor in Margaret's copy of the *Faits*. At the same time, Scrope's introduction of references to knighthood and chivalry further occlude female knowledge in matters of arms and policy in favor of masculine military and political skill. This move resembles the replacement of the image depicting Christine's instruction by the goddess with one portraying Talbot receiving the marshal's sword.

Scrope's preface contains another detail that reveals his need to contain the possibilities for female power suggested by the text of the *Othea*. After describing "Dame Christine" as the patron of the text, he goes on, somewhat oddly, to celebrate at length the career of the Frenchman John, duke of Berry, for whom he says Christine intended the work. Scrope praises his "victories, dedis of cheualrie and of armys," his skill in "grete police vsyng," and his "spilrytuell and gostly dedys." The duke's success is, furthermore, hyperbolically increased when he is said to have lived "C yeers" in which time he "flowrid and rengnyd in grete wor-chip and ren-ovnne of cheualrie" (*Epistle*, Appendix A, 122–23). For Scrope, it seems, it is better to praise the successes of a French man in arms and diplomacy than to admit a French woman's skill in such matters. The juxtaposition of Christine, turned into a pious patron of clerics, with the politically and militarily successful French duke serves to reinforce gender roles deemed culturally appropriate.

William Worcester's *Boke of Noblesse* was initially composed at about the same time as Scrope translated the *Othea*, and like the *Othea*, the *Boke* makes a case for the validity of including women in lineages in a safely con-tained, transmissive role. Such a cause was understandably important for Edward IV, to whom a revised version of the *Boke* was presented in 1475, not only for the renewal of the English claim to France but also for the legitimation of the Yorkist claim to the English throne.[57] At the opening of the *Boke of Noblesse*, Worcester addresses the royal reader—initially Henry VI, later Edward IV—lamenting the loss, in 1450, of "youre verray right and true title in the inheritaunce of the saide Reaume of Fraunce and the Duche of Normandie" (*Boke of Noblesse*, 3). He then goes on to elaborate, at some length, the genealogical bases for the English right to claim such territories, an account in which women feature prominently. For instance, Worcester, like Anne d'Orléans, finds politically useful material in the Anjou-Plantagenet era. In regard to "King Harry the seconde of Englande" he argues, "So in conclusion he was, be right of his moder dame Maude, the empresse, king of Englonde and duke of Normandie, and, be right of his father Geffrey Plantagenest, erle of Anjou and of Mayne and Torayne; be right of his wiffe dame Alienor, duke of Guien" (*Boke of Noblesse*, 24).

In addition to the genealogical justifications for the English king's retaking what the French had purportedly usurped by "umbre of the said fenied colour of trewes, ayanest alle honoure and trouthe of knighthode" (*Boke of Noblesse*, 25), Christine de Pizan's *Faits d'armes* is, as I mentioned earlier, explicitly quoted in justifying the renewal of the war in France. When Worcester first invokes her text, mistitled the *Tree of Batailles* (after one of Christine's chief sources), he seems to regard her as the author of the text. He uses such phrases as "dame Cristyn makithe mencion," "dame Cristen seiethe and moevithe," and "dame Cristin saiethe" (*Boke of Noblesse*, 6), suggesting her authorship even though by referring to her as "dame" Christine he may allude to her cloistered status.

Thus, at the beginning of the *Boke*, it seems that women can safely be included and even celebrated in making a case for the English cause. They are, after all firmly situated in lineages in relation to male heirs; similarly, "dame Christine"'s theories of war are balanced by accounts of the heroic actions of English men in France. For example, the royal addressee is reminded of the "actis and dedis in armes of so many famous and victorious Kingis, Princes, Dukis, Erles, Barounes, and noble knights" (*Boke of Noblesse*, 3). Worcester likewise exhorts the king to have "in remembraunce the victorious conquestis of youre noble predecessours," the first mentioned of which is none other than "the vaillaunt knight Hector of Troy" whose "steppis in conceitis of noble courage of the mighty dedis in armes" are held up as a model (*Boke of Noblesse*, 20). The parade of noble predecessors leading up to the account of Henry VI's French coronation treats in some detail the exploits of John, duke of Bedford, in France. Strikingly, any mention of Joan of Arc, who featured so prominently in Bedford's activities in France, is scrupulously omitted (or, perhaps, once more unconsciously repressed) as the narrative skips from Bedford's victory at the battle of Vernelle in 1424 to the coronation itself, so preserving a pleasant fantasy of English, masculine, heroic success (*Boke of Noblesse*, 18–20).

The reality of the English situation in France after 1450, and the intensifying crisis of English masculinity that this situation, as well as Margaret of Anjou's growing power and Henry VI's growing disability, provoke, prevent such a rosy view from holding. Indeed, Worcester's yoked concerns with English masculinity and martial ability are subtly evident even in the opening paragraph of the text, which declares that the "litille epistle is wrote and entitled to courage and comfort noble men in armes to be in perpetuite of remembraunce for here noble dedis" (*Boke of Noblesse*, 1). In a discussion of the Order of the Garter and past English victories in France, Worcester breaks in with a long commentary on the sad current state of affairs. After praising the skill of Bedford, John Chandos, and John Radcliffe, he complains that such heroes were not to be found in 1449–1450, which he describes as "the brief seson of the sodeyne and wrecchid intrusion late had by the *unmanly* disseising and putting oute of Fraunce, Normandie, Angew, and Mayne, withe the duchies of Gasquien and Guyen" (*Boke of Noblesse*, 48, emphasis added). Furthermore, Worcester indicates his anxiety about the current decline of English male prowess when he laments that these lost territories could have been held if only there had been sufficient men of arms "of the lyonns kynde as to have bene of soo egir courage and so *manly* and stedfast as they were before this time" (*Boke of Noblesse*, 48, emphasis added).

Later, Worcester also bemoans the contemporary lack of military training for young English men, who now "wastyn gretlie theire tyme in suche nedelese besiness" as learning "the practique of law or custom of lande, or of civile matier" (*Boke of Noblesse*, 77).[58] Once again, the issue seems to be not merely the need for the "grettir defens of youre roiaumes" (*Boke of Noblesse*, 76) but also the need to defend English masculinity itself. Worcester writes: "So wolde Jhesus they so wolle welle lerned theym to be as good men of armes, chieveteins, or capetains in the feelde that befallithe for hem where worship and *manhode* shulde be shewid, moche bettir rathir then as they have lerned and can be a captaine or a ruler at a sessions or a shire day" (*Boke of Noblesse*, 78, emphasis added). Worcester holds a view of masculinity similar to that espoused by the sixteenth-century poet William Goddard in *A Mastiff Whelp*. In satire 62, Goddard mocks "maiden-chaunged Mick" who is enjoined, "Come use thy pyke; tha'st use'd too long thy —."[59] As Moulton observes of this poem, "masculinity is *not* seen primarily in biological terms"; Mick "is a man not because he has a prick but because he knows how to use a pike."[60] Mick has been transformed into a woman as a consequence of neglecting the use of his pike; Worcester fears much the same fate for aristocratic young Englishmen who turn away from arms to the study of law and custom.

It is in this context that we must consider a Latin note about Christine de Pizan written in the margin of the *Boke*. When her *Faits d'Armes* is invoked once again, we are told that the "dame Cristyn," previously quoted as the apparent author of the so-called *Tree of Batailles*, is in fact "domina praeclara natu et moribus, et manebat in domo religiosarum apud Pasaye prope Parys" [lady distinguished in birth and manners, and she lived in the nunnery at Poissy near Paris], and that she sponsored the compilation of "plures libros virtuosos, utpote *Liber Arboris Bellorum*" [several virtuous books, of course the *Tree of Battles*] by "plures clericos studentes in universitate Parisiensi" [several clerics studying at the University of Paris].[61] Not only are Christine's authorship and her authority to speak on military matters reassigned to men, but, having purportedly spent her life in the nunnery of Poissy, she is firmly excluded from the spheres of political and military affairs. In order to make sure that English men are not made effeminate, to the detriment of the English nation, Worcester insists on the pure masculinity of these crucial realms of action constitutive of English manhood and monarchy. In an instance of the "rewriting of history" that "retroactively giv[es] . . . elements their symbolic weight by including them in new textures,"[62] Christine is assigned a properly feminine "supporting role" as she is, like St. Colette in the hands of the fifteenth-century Observant Franciscans, stripped of her authorship and her agency. Christine's role here is also much like the one unsuccessfully constructed in the Royal manuscript for Margaret of Anjou, whose military and political activities contributed greatly to the tumult of the textual environment in which the *Boke* was produced and circulated. The revision of Christine in the *Boke* thus advances the larger revisionary project of reclaiming not only lost English territory in France but also English martial masculinity lost along with it.

Plus ça change . . .

Although a dividing line is often drawn between the medieval and early modern periods in the reign of Henry VIII, this Tudor descendant of the Lancastrian monarchs faced many of the same problems that his ancestors did concerning genealogy, monarchical legitimacy, masculine authority, and English identity. In addition to facing challenges similar to those encountered by fifteenth-century rulers, Henry and his partisans found similar ways of coping with them. In particular, Christine de Pizan once again provided a paradoxical remedy to mutually reinforcing gendered and nationalistic anxieties.

In 1521, Henry Pepwell published *The Boke of the Cyte of Ladyes*, Brian Anslay's translation of Christine's *Cité des dames*. Christine de Pizan's *Livre de la cité des dames* is perhaps simultaneously the most and least overtly "political" of her three works with which I am concerned. It is overtly political in that it seeks to redress misogynist traditions about women's virtues and abilities, and it is overtly political in its allegorical framework of the construction, population, and government of a city. The *Cité* also spends a great deal of time, especially in Part I, on women who take active roles in military and governmental affairs, women including the Babylonian queen Semiramis; the Amazons Thamiris, Menalippe, Hippolyta, and Penthesilea (who, significantly, seeks to avenge the death of none other than Hector of Troy); and the French queen Fredegund.[63] Furthermore, highly valuable kinds of knowledge, including the knowledge that makes military and political action, and indeed even civilization itself, possible, are said to have originated with women: law with Carmentis and armor with Minerva, for instance.[64] In spite of its extensive revisionings of history and cultural norms, however, the *Cité* actually seeks to create an alternative, parallel system rather than to intervene too directly in the existing political system (which in many regards, particularly in respect to traditional gender hierarchy, Christine actually supports). The text might therefore have been perceived, especially by later medieval and early modern male readers, as a far less political work than the *Faits d'Armes* or the *Othea*.

The *Cité* did take on pointedly contemporary political significance in England during the reign of Henry VIII, however. In Pepwell's edition of Anslay's translation, women once again function to aid the dynastic aims of men as a text by a woman about women is made to serve a transmissive, masculinist function. As Summit has shown, Pepwell's prologue, with great relevance to current events at court, "describes his work as a printer by using the tropes of patrilineage and aristocratic succession"; by offering to print the book in the name of Richard Grey, earl of Kent, Pepwell gives Kent "a way to perpetuate his name and influence through the mechanical reproduction of the press, despite his failure to do so through biosocial means."[65] Such textual possibilities for the continuation of a male line "might have been imagined to appeal" to a court extraordinarily preoccupied with lineage and reproduction, given that Henry VIII still lacked a legitimate heir by 1521.[66]

This dynastic crisis in the Henrician court had a counterpart in ongoing uneasiness about English masculinity and the proper role of women in civic affairs. In fact, such anxieties manifest themselves in Pepwell's prologue when he refers to his hesitance to publish a text praising the "excellence" of "gentylwomen" since "people lewde" make it a practice "theyr prowesse to dyspyse."[67] An extremely popular text contemporary with Pepwell's edition of Anslay's translation was the *Instruction of a Christian Woman*, written by the Spanish humanist Juan Luis Vives in 1523 and translated soon afterward into English by Richard Hyrd.[68] Both the original and the translation were dedicated to Katherine of Aragon, queen of England, daughter of Isabel of Castile, and mother of the Princess Mary (the future Mary I), for whose instruction the text was intended. This treatise makes clear that "Women are temperamentally unsuited to public life because in such a situation they are disposed to become proud, headstrong, and combative."[69] For instance, Vives poses a rhetorical question to "you women that wyll medle with comen matters of realmes and cites / and wene to gouerne peoples and nacions," asking, "Wene you it was for nothying / that wyse men for bad you rule and gouernance of countreis and that saynt Paule byddeth you shall nat speke to congregacyon and gatherynge of people."[70]

Tudor-era chronicles demonstrate, furthermore, that concerns about feminine power and foreign puissance were still culturally connected in perceptions of women's participation in affairs of state. Action by women implied the emasculation of men; in these chronicles one sees that "individual masculine weakness" was indeed perceived "as a national concern."[71] An early translation of Polydore Vergil's *English History*, written not long after the Latin text's composition in 1512–1513, describes at some length the capture and execution of "Joane Puselle, more fitt, as the brute went, to practise magike than martial affaires."[72] Even as Vergil denies Joan's martial fitness, his narrative calls attention to her ongoing pernicious (at least from an English perspective) influence. In this account, she continues to cause trouble for the English after her execution:

But the Frenche men to this day will not heare but that she was sent of God from heaven to expell thenemy out of their countrey; for they affirme that she dyed a virgin. After her fall the Frenche failed not in courage . . . and . . . so annoyed their enemies, that, dispeyring to winne the same, they [the English] departed of their owne accorde. The affaires of England grewe by this meane, from day to day, through Fraunce, woorse and woorse. (*English History*, 39)

Joan is here perceived as a source of increased French courage and as the catalyst for English defeats in France even after she was no longer leading armies against them. Indeed, one might argue that the length at which and the vehemence with which she is discussed in a text written nearly 100 years after her death suggest that she was *still* causing trouble for the English. In Vergil's *English History*, one sees in action the expected consequences of the "English effeminization" that Moulton finds to be a prevailing concern in early modern antitheatrical tracts—that is, one sees that a "weakness of English manhood" does "leave the nation defenseless against foreign foes."[73]

Edward Hall, whose chronicle is heavily indebted to the work of Polydore Vergil, attempts to manage the damaging consequences of Joan's afterlife in England by transforming the connected upheavals in gender and politics she caused for the English into gendered, political trouble for the French. He says that French glorification of "This wytch or manly woman" is in fact a "blotte" on "the Frenche nacion" since her successes highlight the shameful failures of the French king and armies. He writes:

What more rebuke can be imputed to a renoumed region, then to affirme,write &
confesse, that all notable victories, and honorable conquestes, which neither the
kyng with his power, nor the nobilite with their valiauntnesse, nor the counsaill
with their wit, nor the commonaltie with their strenght, could compasse or obtain,
were gotten and achived by a shepherdes daughter, a chamberlein in an hostrie,
and a beggars brat.[74]

Margaret of Anjou too remained a key focus for fears about the involvement of women in the politico-military sphere, in spite of the fact
that sympathy for the Lancastrians had become the order of the day with
the rise of the Tudor dynasty. As Patricia-Ann Lee notes, beginning with
Robert Fabyan's *New Chronicles of England and France* (originally completed in 1504, with a continuation in 1509, and published for the first
time in 1516), Margaret of Anjou becomes "both the precipitating factor
and to some extent the cause" of the fall of the house of Lancaster.[75] The
impetus for the Lancastrian decline is seen in Tudor chronicles as resting
squarely in Margaret's interventions in the properly masculine realms of
war and government. Indeed, the same translation of Vergil's *English History* that describes Joan as more fit for magic than martial affairs describes
Margaret as "very desirous of renowne" as well as "full of policie" and
"councell." Furthermore, Margaret is said to possess "all manly qualities"
disastrously combined with a feminine bent for "mutabilitie and chaunge"
(*English History*, 71). Even more damningly, "this Margarete, wife unto
the king" purportedly "warred much more happily by her owne conduct
and authoritie then by the kinges" (*English History*, 109). The anti-Margaret
sentiments are rounded out with the terse assessment that "by meane of a
woman, sprange up a newe mischiefe that sett all out of order" (*English
History*, 70). This Margaret thus closely resembles the feminine usurpers of
masculine political prerogatives who, according to the *Instruction of a
Christian Woman*, "knowe neyther measure nor order" and who "wyll be
ruled in nothynge after them that be experte" (*Instruction of a Christian
Woman*, h2v).

Joan of Arc and Margaret of Anjou are not the only politically active
women who show up as focal points for gendered and nationalistic anxieties in Tudor texts. Margaret of York, duchess of Burgundy, although
English by birth, was also perceived throughout the Tudor era as a troubling, "foreign" female who arrogated to herself a properly masculine
role, in the process causing all manner of problems for the English monarchy. As I discuss in the previous chapter, Margaret took a hands-on role
in Burgundian as well as Yorkist affairs. From the perspectives of Henry

VII and Henry VIII, her political activities made her in effect the latest incarnation of Joan of Arc. As early as 1493, following a four-year period of uneasy alliance with the Burgundians, Henry VII himself wrote to Sir Gilbert Talbot concerning Margaret's participation in plots supporting pretenders to the English throne. This letter stresses not only the duchess's "great malice" but also her foreign connections, making reference to "her promise to certain aliens, captains of strange nations, to have duchies, counties, baronies, and other lands, within this our royaume to induce them thereby to land here."[76] Similarly, just before launching into an extended recitation of Margaret's involvement in plots against the king, Hall emphasizes her extraordinary devotion to her stepdaughter Mary's children and Burgundian heirs after Mary's death as well as her involvement in administering Burgundian affairs. For these reasons, he says, Margaret "was highly reputed and estemed & bare great aucthoritie & swynge through all Flaunders and the lowe countries therto adiacent" (*Hall's Chronicle*, 430).

Margaret of York's malice and monstrosity are similarly persistent themes in Tudor chronicles, where her evildoing is frequently framed in strongly gendered language. In his account of the plot of the pretender Lambert Simnel to overthrow Henry VII, Vergil writes, for example, that Margaret "pursued Henry with insatiable hatred and with fiery wrath never desisted from employing every scheme which might harm him [Henry VII] as a representative of the hostile faction."[77] He also discourses at length on Margaret's involvement with another pretender, Peter (aka Perkyn) Warbeck, who claimed to be Richard, duke of York. In this section, he reports the speech of Dr. William Warham, sent to Flanders as Henry VII's envoy to the Archduke Philip, noting that Warham accuses Margaret of "monstrous designs" ("monstra pararet" [*Anglica Historia*, 70–71]). As Christine Weightman points out, Margaret's improperly masculine martiality once again emerges in familiar form in the *Twelve Triumphs of Henry VII*, in which Bernard André, the tutor of Prince Arthur, pejoratively compares Margaret to Menalippe, queen of the Amazons.[78]

Hall, whose chronicle was published during the reign of Henry VIII, is perhaps the most hostile of all toward Margaret of York. He famously describes her as the "diabolicall duches" (*Hall's Chronicle*, 462) and says that she is "lyke one forgettyng bothe God & charite, inflamed with malice diabolicall instinction." He also claims that she "inuented & practised all mischiefes, displeasures and damages that she could deuyse against the kyng of England" (*Hall's Chronicle*, 430).[79] The perceived horrors of Margaret's political endeavors become even more clear when Hall blusters,

"And farther in her fury and frantyke moode (accordying to the saying of the wise man, there is no malice equiualent nor aboue the malice of a woman) she wrought all the wayes possible how to sucke his bloud and compasse his destroccion" (*Hall's Chronicle*, 430). For Hall, Margaret of York was not simply on the wrong side of the political fence. His outrage is framed in pointedly gendered terms. Her political interventions are at once proof of her typically feminine malice and evidence of a fundamentally transgressive nature that leads her into the properly masculine political realm, and so, given her fundamental incapacity for these masculine pursuits, into madness and inhuman monstrosity.

So, in such a textual environment, why translate and publish a text like Christine de Pizan's *Cité des dames*, which does so much to argue *for* the fitness of women to participate in all aspects of public and political life? Much as do earlier English treatments of Christine's works, Pepwell's edition of Anslay's translation manipulates the text in ways which are, in many respects, at odds with the original content but which do much to serve contemporary masculinist political agendas. For instance, although Anslay's translation makes no effort to hide Christine's authorship, Pepwell's prologue describes the book as being "by Bryan Anslay, / Yoman of the seller / with the eyght kynge Henry."[80] This description minimizes the female authorial role—and with it female political authority—much as Scrope's revised titles for the *Othea* do. Pepwell's prologue similarly makes the work of praising women the work of men rather than the work of women themselves; it "elevate[s] Grey to the role of champion of women, which the text itself gives to de Pizan."[81] Implicit in these moves is the fundamental idea that the defense of women and their "city," like the defense and government of the realm, should be done by men rather than by women, who should remain passive.

Finally, and most significantly, Pepwell's edition continues the tradition of "cloistering" Christine. In the woodcut depicting Christine in her study, she is dressed in traditional widow's garb (Figure 3). This attire, with its barb and veil, presents a portrait that "closely resembles the iconography of religious women from woodcuts that Pepwell had previously printed of Saints Bridget and Catherine of Siena" (Figure 4).[82] This depiction of Christine illustrates the ways in which Pepwell's text, like MS Royal 15 E VI, uses iconography to suggest a model of proper feminine conduct. The woodcut of the "cloistered" Christine points to what women like Joan of Arc, Margaret of Anjou, and Margaret of York, all still causing trouble in the pages of Tudor chronicles as well as in the political culture of the

Figure 3. Christine de Pizan in her study. From the British Library copy of *The Boke of the Cyte of Ladyes*, published by Henry Pepwell, 1521. By permission of the British Library.

Figure 4. St. Birgitta. From the British Library copy of *The Dyetary of Ghostly Helthe*, published by Henry Pepwell, 1521. By permission of the British Library.

Tudor court, *should* have been doing rather than meddling in public affairs. Pepwell uses the figure of Christine to imply that, as *Instruction of a Christian Woman* asserts directly, while a woman's husband is alive, she should devote herself to "honesty of body / and great loue towarde her husbonde" (*Instruction of a Christian Woman*, i2v). Then, after her husband has died, she must in effect become the bride of Christ (also the proper model of behavior to emulate for a woman like Joan who does not marry), engaging in works of charity and contemplation while obediently conforming all aspects of her life to the will of the one "that is successour unto her husbande / that is immortall god vnto mortall man" (*Instruction of a Christian Woman*, r2r).

The woodcut, like the earlier textual constructions of Christine as a religious woman and textual patron, functions to remove an active, knowledgeable woman from the politico-military sphere.[83] In the culture of the Tudor court, such symbolic efforts to solve the political problem of women demonstrate the process described by Slavoj Žižek in which people "try to do away with" the consequences of something "through which breaks historical necessity" but which is perceived as "arbitrary."[84] Here, that necessary, arbitrary "something" with unwelcome consequences is the ongoing, vital role played by women in the constructions of political power and the desired identities of the English monarchs at home and abroad. As Žižek further notes, when, inevitably, repetition occurs of that event or thing of which the consequences have been denied, "it is finally perceived as an expression of the underlying historical necessity."[85] One might argue that such a realization definitively overtook Tudor England with the accession and triumphal reign of Elizabeth I.

In closing, I would like to point out that the long English tradition of "cloistering" Christine and making her into a bride of Christ is in some regards as fraught with irony as is the presentation of the *Faits d'Armes* to Margaret of Anjou or the culmination of the Tudor dynasty, with its anxieties about female political participation, with the reign of Elizabeth I. Saints Birgitta of Sweden and Catherine of Siena, whom Christine resembles in Pepwell's woodcut, were in fact extraordinarily politically active and influential women. Furthermore, the version of this fiction that consigns Christine specifically to the nunnery of Poissy is particularly ironic. English redactors of Christine's texts who forced this monastic "profession" upon her with the intention of removing her from the realms of military and political action were evidently not aware of the profoundly political nature of the house of Poissy. This monastic community was a royal foundation where the French king's aunt was the abbess and his sister was a nun, and where Christine, who did reside there late in life (although not as a nun), had ready access to the propagandist texts she used in composing the *Ditié de Jehanne d'Arc*. As Henry VIII would come to learn with the visionary Benedictine nun Elizabeth Barton, and as Elizabeth I (a queen who herself crafted modes of political action with the raw material of virginal female spirituality) would come to learn with the Brigittine nuns of Syon, female political agency is inescapably present even—perhaps especially—in the cloister.[86]

4

Religion and Female Rule: Isabel of Castile and the Construction of Queenship

The Symbolics of Power

Juan Luis Vives vehemently believed that women were unfit for political participation, as we have already begun to see from our examination of Richard Hyrd's English translation of the *Instrucción de la mujer cristiana*. Perhaps even more troubling to Vives, both socially and spiritually, than female political agency was female participation in military affairs. When Vives turns his attention to "arms and the woman," he wonders, "qué tienen que hazer las armas con las doncellas" [what ought arms to have to do with young women], and goes on to say, quite severely:

Hágote saber que no es muy católico el pensamiento de la muger que se ceva en pensar en las armas y fuerças de braços del varon. ¿Oy qué lugar seguro puede tener entre las armas la flaca y desarmada castidad? La muger que en estas cosas piensa beve poco a poco la ponçoña, sin que la sienta; y la que ha passado o passa por ello me lo diga: mortal es esta infición.[1]

[I make known to you that the thoughts of a woman who concerns herself with arms and with men's feats of arms are not truly Catholic. What secure place can weak, defenseless chastity find in the midst of arms? The woman who thinks of such things drinks poison little by little, without feeling it, and that which has happened or does happen because of it tells me that the infection is fatal.]

If it is perceived as something irreligious and dangerous to the all-important virtue of chastity for a woman even to *think* about matters of arms and other male pursuits, how much more troubling for a woman actually to engage in such activities herself! Vives in effect believes that to be a woman of God *and* a woman of arms is impossible.

Clearly the climate in which Isabel of Castile had to shape a creditable

model of female rule, and in which she had to gain acceptance for her involvement in the military and empire-building pursuits so important in
her reign, was as profoundly hostile both to female political authority and
female military participation as those encountered by Christine de Pizan,
Margaret of Anjou, and Margaret of York. Indeed, directed as it was to
Isabel's daughter Katherine for her daughter Mary, who, Vives likely realized, might be destined to rule one day (as she in fact did, as Mary I of
England), the *Instrucción* easily reads as an expression of such hostility and
a pointedly negative reaction to the very politically active model of queenship that, as we shall see in this chapter, Isabel crafted.[2] Similar hostility
characterized Isabel of Castile's first meeting with her confessor, Hernando
de Talavera. As José de Sigüenza reports, Isabel declared that she and her
confessor should both kneel, in accordance with the tradition for monarchs. Talavera responded, however, that he would remain seated but Isabel
must kneel "porque este es el tribunal de Dios, y hago aquí sus vezes"
[because this is God's tribunal, and I act here in His stead].[3] Such a re-
figuring of hierarchy, to which (perhaps surprisingly) Isabel consented,
demonstrates that from a clerical perspective even a queen is a "daughter
of Eve," marked by the innate intellectual, moral, and spiritual inferiority
inherited by all women.

Talavera's insistence on Isabel's kneeling directs us to realize that the
"symbolics of power" and the actual nature of power are very closely
related.[4] Indeed, Pierre Bourdieu observes that the "symbolics of power"
are in fact fundamental to the exercise of power. He writes that political
power "is the product of subjective acts of recognition and, in so far as it
is credit and credibility, exists only in and through representation."[5] Isabel,
in spite of her acquiescence to Talavera, was a master at manipulating the
symbolics of power to maximize her real power in an environment that
sought in many respects to deny it to her. In fact, Barbara Weissberger has
demonstrated that even Isabel's submission to Talavera, both at their initial encounter and afterward, should not necessarily surprise us after all,
since it had its advantages for Isabel. She argues that in Isabel's correspondence with her confessor, the queen exhibited an "epistolary humility"
that was "a kind of consciously complicit manipulation of the paradigm
of dominance and submission structurally embedded in the confessor-
penitent relationship."[6] She further demonstrates that such manipulation
served in the end to empower Isabel.[7]

Isabel's astute manipulations did not end with the confessor/peni-
tent relationship. As Peggy Liss argues, "Isabel was clearly wise in the

ways of image-making, highly respectful of the power of public opinion at all levels, and adept in courting and molding it."[8] In her image-making, Isabel mobilized female spirituality and sanctity in many perspicacious ways that enabled her to enhance the legitimacy of her role as a ruling queen. She cultivated a persona of pious queenship (rather like the epistolary persona she crafts in her letters to Talavera) centered on traditional ideologies of female conduct and established models of women's devotion.[9] In this way, she aligned herself with convention, downplaying the potentially controversial aspects of her reign. Female spirituality and sanctity served to clothe Isabel's political power in a non-threatening guise and so make it culturally acceptable. Paradoxically, by aligning Isabel with ideologies that often seek to minimize women's authority, such representational efforts actually increased her power. This contradictory process is at work in the Augustinian friar Martín de Córdoba's *Jardín de nobles donzellas*, a text that associates Isabel with very conventional feminine virtues and devotional practices.[10]

At the same time, Isabel's representational program also transformed accepted models of female spirituality and sanctity to validate her own less-than-traditional political participation and military leadership. Holy models of virtuous but unorthodox conduct were crafted to authorize behavior in Isabel that was not typically condoned for women. Furthermore, in marshalling the symbolics of power to Isabel's advantage, new, politicized exemplars of sanctity were built on the traditional framework of medieval sainthood. In particular, Joan of Arc was textually "canonized" centuries before her official recognition as a saint in the anonymous text *La Poncella de Francia*.[11] Through careful shaping of Joan's history in ways favorable to Isabel's cause, this text engages aspects of medieval female hagiography to frame Isabel's military, dynastic, and empire-building pursuits as holy missions endorsed by God. This strategy aims to increase acceptance of such unorthodox female activities and so, concomitantly, to increase Isabel's real ability to carry out these missions. In this instance, female spirituality and sanctity do not function to put a non-threatening face on female power. Rather, their function is more like that of Joan of Arc's banner inscribed with the names of Jesus and Mary, proclaiming boldly her power's divinely sanctioned legitimacy. Both representational strategies create an identity for Isabel as a woman of God—a practitioner of traditional feminine piety in the first case, a quasi-saint in the second. In doing so, they enhance her ability to take political action as a "woman of arms"—a ruler, a military strategist, and the architect of conquest and reconquest.

Paradoxical Tactics

The Augustinian friar Martín de Córdoba's *Jardín de nobles donzellas* has affinities with several generic traditions: the mirror for princes, the female conduct book, the catalogue of famous lives. Unlikely though it might seem given this combination, it is also an astute work of political propaganda. Its presentations of advice for a female monarch, its models of feminine virtue, and its dicta on proper feminine comportment entwine to serve a pro-Isabelline agenda, especially at two key moments: that of the text's initial composition and circulation in 1468–1474 and that of its first printing in 1500, late in Isabel's reign, by Juan de Burgos of Valladolid.[12] Both the period between 1468 and 1474 and the closing years of the fifteenth century were tumultuous times when Isabel had great need for effective representational strategies. The *Jardín* exhibits a "patriarchal ideology" abundantly evident in its uncritical presentations of misogynist stereotypes.[13] It also uses a rather "cautionary tone" in promoting female rule.[14] But this text played a key role in helping Isabel to achieve crucial representational tasks during these fraught periods.

That Martín de Córdoba is firmly in Isabel's camp politically is evident from the very first sentence of the prologue, which dedicates the text "A la muy clara & seeníssima señora doña Ysabel de real simiente procreada, infanta legítima heredera delos reynos de Castilla & León" [To the very glorious and most serene lady Isabel descended of royal line, legitimate heir of the kingdoms of Castile and Leon] (*Jardín*, 135). As part of the dedicatory opening, Martín goes on to put himself in the humble posture of "besando aquellas manos dignas de regir las riendas deste reyno" [kissing these hands worthy to govern the reigns of the realm] (*Jardín* 135). Thus, from the very first words, the *Jardín* stakes a claim for Isabel's hereditary right to be queen as well as for her worthiness to rule.[15]

Harriet Goldberg, who prepared the critical edition of the *Jardín*, concedes that there is "no doubt that Fray Martín supported Isabel's claim to the throne and opposed Enrique IV."[16] She downplays the political significance of the text on two counts, however, saying that its argument for female rule is rather beside the point since there was no male heir.[17] She also argues that "by 1468 . . . Fray Martín would have been allying himself with an already successful cause and therefore flogging a dead horse."[18] I believe that the lack of a male heir by no means would resolve cultural anxieties about female rule. On the contrary, such a situation seems particularly likely to *increase* fears about living under a woman's authority.

The unusual nature of Isabel and Ferdinand's relationship also surely had the potential to raise the level of anxiety even higher during the early years of Isabel's reign. As Ronald Surtz points out, following Isabel and Ferdinand's marriage in 1469, an agreement was drawn up in January 1475, shortly after Isabel's succession, that granted Isabel alone "the proprietorship of the crown of Castile." As a result, "Ferdinand, against centuries of patriarchal tradition, was theoretically subordinated to Isabella."[19] Isabel's succession and the resolution of questions concerning the legitimacy—in dynastic and gendered terms—of her reign were not as settled in the period leading up to her succession as Goldberg implies. The ways in which the *Jardín* proceeds in representing women generally and Isabel specifically are precisely targeted to address questions about both kinds of legitimacy during the years between 1468 and 1474, questions that arose again, albeit in somewhat modified form, at the end of the fifteenth century when the *Jardín* was first disseminated as a printed text.

On the one hand, Martín spends a fair amount of time discussing anti-feminist material in spite of his allegiance to Isabel; the *Jardín* might therefore seem to be a rather unsuccessful attempt to aid the queen's cause.[20] On the other hand, I would argue that the ways in which the text paradoxically rehearses notions of female inferiority while arguing for Isabel's fitness to rule creates a tension that in the end serves Isabel well, whether Martín de Córdoba fully or consciously planned it that way or not. Although he supports Isabel's cause, Martín, as a professed religious and one dependent on Isabel's patronage, quite probably had anxieties of his own about female rule and its concomitant reversals of masculine and clerical dominance over women. Such anxieties do indeed complicate the text's pro-Isabelline agenda at times, leaving the reader to wonder whether Martín shares more than he might want to admit with those less well-informed subjects ("Algunos . . . menos entendidos") who object to female monarchs ("auían a mal quando algund reyno o otra pulicía viene a regimiento de mugeres" [*Jardín*, 136]) against whom he claims to defend Isabel.

Isabel's representational strategy was, however, often characterized by her alignment with ideological paradigms that would seem to deny her power as a way to craft political power within them, as her relationship with her confessor Talavera suggests. Some of Isabel's representational efforts were thus "tactical" in Michel de Certeau's sense of the term.[21] Although as a member of the royal family Isabel was hardly socially disadvantaged, as a woman she did occupy "tactical" positions in relation to the masculinist framework that structured political power in the fifteenth and sixteenth centuries. Her representational strategy thus included insinuations "into the other's place, fragmentarily, without taking it over in its entirety."[22] Accordingly, the *Jardín* reinforces but at the same time tactically destabilizes, if only provisionally, dominant ideologies, turning those ideologies to purposes to which they might otherwise seem contrary. The text thus enables Isabel, at least episodically, to possess forms of political agency not regularly available to women and to escape the negative consequences of taking on such roles experienced in various situations, as we have seen, by Joan of Arc, Margaret of Anjou, and Christine de Pizan.

Martín's account of the positive qualities "natural" to women is every bit as conventional as the misogynist commonplaces that he reiterates. He begins Part 2 by explaining that women have three good conditions: "ca son las mugeres vergonçosas, son piadosas, son osequiosas" [these are modest, pious, attentive women] (*Jardín*, 193). That women should be modest, should show pity, and, as he elaborates, should show devotion to God, compassion "de próximo" [to one's neighbor], and care for house and family is precisely the sort of advice found in a great deal of medieval conduct literature for women (*Jardín*, 203). Martín stresses that while these qualities are desirable in all women, they are particularly necessary for highborn women in general and for Isabel in particular.[23] His model of queenship is in this fashion reassuringly crafted as simply an extension of accepted standards of female virtue, models of female conduct, and practices of female piety.

This strategy of reassurance through invocation of familiar norms appears in Martín's description of the importance of devotion to God for princesses and queens. He writes, "Assí todas las mugeres deuen ser enesta guisa por deuoción a Dios obsequiosas, quánto más deuen ser las reynas & princesas, las quales deuen ser enxenplo a todos de honrrar & seruir a Dios" [Just as all women ought to be in this fashion attentive in devotion to God, so much the more queens and princesses, who must be an example to all in honoring and serving God] (*Jardín*, 204). He continues by outlining precisely what royal women's devotional practices should include to make them shining examples to their people, a list that recalls types of spiritual activities typically recommended to women by medieval clerics: hearing Mass daily, reciting prayers, hearing sermons, having "lecturas honestas and santas" [honest, holy texts] read to them, conversing with learned and wise men ("letrados & sabios") who will instruct them in "cosas diuinales" [divine matters], thinking of the next life and the account they will have to render before God, and speaking of Paradise (*Jardín*, 204–5).

In Martín's paradigm, princesses and queens are ordinary women writ large; their roles are simply traditionally feminine ones enacted on a more prominent stage. This representation of what a queen should be and do implies both that her power will be under the control of "proper" authorities (especially clerics) and that she will be subject, through sermons, readings, and directed conversations, to ongoing reinforcements of ideologies that will further keep queenly power in check.

Furthermore, Martín resorts to comfortingly nonthreatening feminine roles in outlining how queens should make use of the carefully delimited power permitted to them. In his disquisition on pity, he turns to a version of queenship with a long history, writing that "la reyna" [the queen] must be "a sus vasallos piadosa" [merciful to her subjects], acting as their "madre" [mother] and "abogada" [advocate] (*Jardín*, 199). Martín continues, "Pues como enel reyno celestial el Rey, Jhesu Cristo, es juez & la Virgen Reyna es abogada, así ha de ser enel reyno terrenal, que el rey sea juez & la reyna abogada. . . . Assí Hester conel rey Assuero, que abogó por el pueblo de Ysrael & lo libró de muerte" [Then, just as in the kingdom of Heaven Jesus Christ is the judge and the Virgin Queen is the advocate, so too it should be in the earthly kingdom—the king shall be the judge and the queen the advocate. . . . It was thus with Esther with King Ahasuerus; she interceded for the people of Israel and saved them from death] (*Jardín*, 201). Like Esther, queens are supposed to use feminine influence with the king on behalf of petitioners; like the Virgin Mary, they are supposed to intercede with the king, who occupies a position like that of Christ sitting in judgment, to mitigate wrath and encourage mercy. Shaping the queenly role as that of a maternal intercessor and advocate, with Queen Esther and the Virgin Mary as models, is, as Paul Strohm has shown, an effective way of managing female political power.[24]

While Martín's accounts of women's good conditions and ideal roles for queens are profoundly conventional, nothing in the *Jardín* is more conventional than his emphasis on virginity, purity, and chastity. The centrality of chastity to Martín de Córdoba's definition of female virtue and his plan for proper feminine—and especially queenly—conduct emerges quite early in the text.[25] The third section of the *Jardín* hammers home the vital importance of female chastity with particular vigor. Martín lingers over a parade of pagan and Christian women who died to preserve their chastity, and follows this with a list of chaste widows (*Jardín*, 256–64). Following the views of Jerome in *Against Jovinianus*, he goes so far as to claim that chastity is the female virtue that matters above all others:

Todas las virtudes enla muger, avn que estouiesse vn montón dellas fasta el cielo, sin castidad no son sino como escorias & ceniza contra el viento, ca la muger que no es casta, avn que sea hermosa, se haze fea, antes fallarés que quanto es más fermosa, tanto más la suziedad la afea & deturpa. . . . Avn que sea deuota & roya los altares & dé quanto tiene a pobres, si casta no es, todo es enella perdido. (*Jardín*, 255)[26]

[Even if a woman's virtues might have mounted to the heavens, without chastity they are nothing but dross and ashes in the wind; because the woman who is not chaste, even if she is lovely, makes herself foul, and the more beautiful she is, the greater the filth and corruption. . . . Although she be devout and kneel before altars and give all she has to the poor, if she be not chaste, all of this is lost for her]

In his insistence that chastity is the most important feminine virtue, Martín could not adopt a more traditional ideological stance. The emphasis that Martín gives not just to chastity but especially to virginity and its value throughout the text might seem to work against Isabel, who married in 1469 and gave birth to her first child in 1470.[27] Furthermore, because the rhetoric of chastity was often a vehicle for asserting masculine control of women's bodies and their productive as well as reproductive capacities, a text that stresses the necessity of female chastity to such an extent would not appear to offer a queen much material to help her make a case for her personal power and legitimate authority as a ruler.

In spite of these evident difficulties, virginity and chastity were particularly important resources for Isabel on several fronts. These virtues were perhaps the ultimate source of symbolic capital for women in the later medieval period. As Sherry Ortner has observed, virginity and chastity are "particularly apt" for symbolizing a woman's mystical or spiritual value,[28] a sort of value extremely important for Isabel's self-representation as a divinely approved monarch. Martín in fact helps Isabel make the most of the ideology of virginity, a tool somewhat tricky for her to wield as a married woman and mother. He explicitly indicates that virginity's value does not reside purely in physical intactness. He observes, "la virginidad más está enel ánima que enel cuerpo" [virginity resides more in the soul than in the body] and declares that the virginity of St. John is no more worthy than the matrimony of Abraham (*Jardín*, 184–85). Furthermore, the value of physical intactness can, in his view, be eroded by improper behavior: "Vn moça avn que sea virgen, si es desvergonçada, no la quieren por muger" [Even if a girl be a virgin, if she is immodest, men will not want her for a wife] (*Jardín*, 197). Martín's framing of virginity as a spiritual disposition and his warning about its potential devaluation by nonphysical means resemble positions espoused in many medieval treatises on virginity. While Martín's argument breaks no new ground in this regard, it is quite valuable for Isabel precisely because it is so orthodox. The *Jardín* presents a competing orthodox view of virginity to counteract the commonly-held idea that marriage and maternity are the negative opposites of virginity. The text in this way gives Isabel a firm foundation for a "virginal" identity and increases the symbolic capital available to her.[29]

Associations with virginal purity had concrete political advantages for Isabel in shaping arguments in favor of the legitimacy both of female rule and of her succession to the throne. Such arguments were sorely needed in the years leading up to Isabel's coronation. Enrique IV and his half-sister Isabel, long at odds, reconciled on September 19, 1468, at Toros de Guisando, when Enrique disinherited Juana and named Isabel as his heir. Their concord was not, however, fated to be long-lived. Trouble began shortly after their reconciliation when Enrique accepted Alfonso V of Portugal as a husband for Isabel without her permission. Isabel decided independently to marry Ferdinand rather than Alfonso, and, on October 12, 1468, she "wrote to Enrique: 'By my letters and messengers I now notify Your Highness of my determined will concerning my marriage.'"[30] She had waited until mere days before the wedding to write to him because, she claimed, "she had been informed that he, 'following the counsel of some,' had sought to impede Fernando."[31] When Enrique IV's efforts to arrange the marriage he desired for Isabel failed, he changed his mind about who should succeed him. According to Enriquez de Castillo, the king "determinó de tornar sobre la hija, e ayudarla para subcediese ella y no la hermana" [decided to turn toward his daughter, and help her to succeed rather than his sister].[32] Indeed, in the late fall of 1470, shortly after the birth of Isabel's first child, Enrique sent out a manifesto that disinherited Isabel and renamed Juana as his heir.[33] His manifesto was made official in a ceremony held on November 26, 1470, to reverse the agreement of Toros de Guisando. At this time, Enrique "declared Isabel a dissolute woman who, acting without the king's counsel and disdaining Castile's laws, had lost her shame and coupled with Fernando, Prince of Aragón, who was so closely related that they could not wed without papal dispensation, which she had scorned. She had married an enemy for the perdition of Castile; she was no wife, but a concubine."[34]

The significance of the *Jardín*'s stress on virginity, purity, and chastity is heightened by Enrique's representation of Isabel as a dissolute harlot as well as by the conflicted political environment of the years between 1468 and 1474. By idealizing Isabel's virginal sexuality, the *Jardín* helps further her political success by representing her—though not technically intact—as the antidote to Enrique IV, whom pro-Isabelline sources in turn portray as sexually corrupt, tainted by hints of effeminacy and homosexuality. Isabel's supporters dubbed Enrique "el Impotente" [the Impotent One],[35] and, according to one chronicle, "Llega el Monarca en su afeminación a ir de madrugada a casa de su nuevo favorito Pancheco a distraerle en su enfermedad cantando acompañado de la cítara" [He was called the Monarchess for his effeminate custom of going at dawn to the house of his new favorite Pancheco to distract him from his infirmity by singing accompanied with the guitar].[36]

Significantly, Martín equates Isabel with the Virgin Mary in her purity *and* in her legitimate royal descent. He addresses Isabel as the "señora Princesa" [Lady Princess], saying that she "es de linaje real, como la Virgen que fue fija de reys" [is of royal lineage, like the Virgin who was the daughter of kings] and that she is "doncella, como hera la Virgen quando concibió al fijo de Dios" [a young woman, like the Virgin when she conceived the son of God] (*Jardín*, 164). Isabel enjoys a divine right to the throne as a member of a "linaje real" and as a "fija de reys," a right not simply legitimated but even sanctified by her association with the Virgin Mary. Isabel's virginal purity grants her a concomitant spiritual fitness that underwrites her rule; both heredity and morality justify her claim to the throne.

Isabel's virginal identity also allows her to distinguish herself from her rival for the throne Juana, frequently identified (at least by Isabel's supporters) as a bastard contaminated by her mother's lasciviousness.[37] Indeed, Martín calls attention to the way in which a woman's unchastity has a detrimental effect on her descendants, saying, "Si la muger no es casta, avn que sea generosa, deturpa así & a su linaje & toda su hidalguía se torna en prouerbio & escarnio" [If a woman be not chaste, even if she be noble, she and all her lineage are defiled, and all her line becomes the subject of gossip and shameful scandal] (*Jardín*, 255). In advising women, and especially queens, to be faithful to their husbands, Martín again raises the issue of heirs and succession in a way that seems particularly pointed. He writes, "Estos & tales enxemplos ayan las nuestras reynas para amar a sus maridos & será gran prouecho, no sola mente a ellos, mas a todo el reyno, que avrán hijos de bendición que suscedan a sus padres & mantengan el reyno en paz & justicia" [Our queens have these such examples to love their husbands, and it will be a great advantage, not only to them, but to the entire kingdom to have legitimate children to succeed their parents and to maintain the kingdom in peace and justice] (*Jardín*, 268). This assessment strikingly resonates with the strong desire among Isabel's supporters to portray Juana as illegitimate and as the heir, not to the throne, but to a legacy of corruption, sexual misbehavior, and social disorder in the realm.

Martín has still more barbs in store. In his discussion of St. Cecilia's chastity he uses language that seems designed to make even sharper the contrast between the chaste, legitimate Isabel and the sullied, illegitimate Juana. He says, "Más clara fue Santa Cecilia por que fue virgen porque fue *hija re rey*. Ser *hija de reyna* es claridad ajena, que viene de sus parientes; ser virgen & casta as claridad propria, que le viene de su propria virtud" [St. Cecilia was more glorious for being a virgin than for being a king's daughter. To be a *queen*'s daughter is not a virtue of one's own but one that comes from one's parents; to be a virgin and chaste is one's own glory that comes from one's own virtue] (*Jardín*, 269–70, my emphasis). Goldberg wonders in passing whether "the change from 'hija de rey' to hija de reyna" might be "significant," going on the observe that "this designation was reserved at the time for Juana la Beltraneja, daughter of Enrique IV" (*Jardín*, 270 n. 4). I believe the shift in phraseology is indeed highly significant, even if it was made unconsciously, given Martín's clear political allegiances. Just because one is the offspring of royalty, Martín indicates, one does not necessarily possess any innate virtue. Indeed, in Juana's case, that which "viene de sus parientes" would likely be something fairly undesirable. The chaste, pure Isabel, though, enjoys the best sort of "claridad," stemming from her "propria virtud"—virtue that underwrites the legitimacy of her reign. While in his earlier comparison of Isabel and the Virgin Mary, Martín represented Isabel as being, like Mary, a king's daughter and a member of the royal line, he here takes a different approach to the question of the legitimacy of Isabel's succession. He covers all his bases, suggesting not only that Juana may be merely the *queen*'s daughter (not the king's) but also that direct descent from the monarch (which Juana could make a case for having while Isabel, as Enrique's half-sister, could not) is in the end less important than being chaste and virtuous.

Martín thus makes queenly political roles fit within roles normally accepted for women; he in effect outlines a model of queenship for Isabel that implies she will do nothing as queen outside of the bounds of orthodox, feminine virtue and propriety. Martín's soothing portrait of Isabel's role would have served well to address anxieties, like those so prominent in the *Instrucción*, about the monstrosity of female rule current not only

in the years leading up to her accession to the throne but also at the end
of her reign. By 1500, when the *Jardín* was first printed, Isabel had been
queen for 26 years and there would have been little need to revisit questions about the legitimacy of her succession. However, the reassurances
that the *Jardín* presents concerning female rule did have immediate relevance. As a result of a series of dynastic misfortunes, issues of female succession and female rule were once again much on people's minds at the
close of the fifteenth century. Isabel and Ferdinand's only son Juan had
died on October 4, 1497, and in 1498 his widow Margaret, who was pregnant at the time of his death, miscarried. Isabel's eldest daughter, also
named Isabel, and her husband Manoel arrived from Portugal to take up
the succession. Isabel (the daughter) was pregnant at the time, and on
August 24, 1498, she delivered a son, Miguel. Although she died in childbirth, the arrival of a son would seem to have solved the problems facing
Isabel's line; Miguel, however, died on July 20, 1500. The next in line for
the throne was Isabel's daughter Juana, who, as I discuss in the introduction, was married to Philip of Burgundy. In light of rumors that circulated
about Juana, her quick temper, and her troubled relationship with her
husband, reassurances regarding female rule would have been especially
apposite for those wishing to keep a firm hold on the throne of Castile for
Isabel's progeny.

The very limitations of Martín's carefully scripted version of queenship may well have encouraged opponents of female rule to accept it, and
to accept Isabel herself and her daughter as her successor. Such limitations
in fact paradoxically enabled Isabel to craft a role as queen that far exceeds
the circumscribed one set forth in the *Jardín*. As I shall demonstrate, the
maternal roles of intercessor and advocate became for Isabel a foundation
on which to build a politically engaged and powerful form of queenship.[38]
Furthermore, while the *Jardín*'s promotion of received feminine virtue,
devotion, and conduct had clear political benefits for Isabel, the text does
not rely purely upon convention in outlining what constitutes a good
queen and how she should behave. Martín slips some unusual additions or
modifications to accepted models of female virtue into sections otherwise
filled with apparently simple commonplaces. Significantly, such passages
tend to work to suggest the legitimacy of Isabel's military involvement and
her at times authoritarian enforcement of her power. Such justifications
were particularly beneficial for Isabel in relation to her participation in the
campaign to retake Granada, in which she was intensively involved.[39]

As the campaign to retake Granada unfolded, Isabel did play the uncontroversial role of lady in whose service knights fought,[40] but her role exceeded that of a figurehead. She was directly involved in war-related economic policy, as in 1482, when she "assessed all cities, villages, and religious orders a stipulated number of knights and foot" to fund the siege of Loja.[41] She also took an active role in war-related diplomatic missions.[42] Isabel's involvement was not, however, confined to such "behind the scenes" roles, important though they were to the war effort. In 1484, the extraordinary extent of her personal engagement became clear. According to Pulgar's *Crónica*, Isabel was so determined to pursue the war that she did not defer to Ferdinand, who wanted to suspend the campaign against Granada in order to recover the counties of Rosellón and Cerdaña from France. Instead, she went to Córdoba independently to organize the year's campaign.[43] Isabel's participation in the war extended to hands-on direction of military strategy. Palencia reports that in 1484 an armada was fitted out "following the Queen's opinion" to prevent Muslim troops sent from Morocco from coming to the aid of Granada.[44] During the long years of war against Granada, Isabel spent a great deal of time in military encampments, as in the summer of 1487, when she was present at the siege of Málaga from May through Málaga's surrender in August.[45] Similarly, she spent months with the troops outside the walls of Granada itself. As did Margaret of Anjou, Isabel appeared before and addressed her troops, and she "even rode with them at the start of individual campaigns."[46]

Martín obviously could not have foreseen precisely what forms Isabel's involvement in the reconquest would take, nor how the war would play out through the closing quarter of the fifteenth century, when he wrote the *Jardín* in 1468–1474. Isabel, however, had a long-standing, well-known interest in the reconquest. Her involvement with the war preceded her accession to the throne by many years, as is indicated by the papal bull of indulgence she received in 1458, for having contributed 200 *maravedís* to the year's campaign against Granada.[47] It is plausible, therefore, that Martín's knowledge of Isabel's interest, combined with his own interest as a professed religious in encouraging the extirpation of heresy and a "return to orthodoxy,"[48] prompted him to suggest particular stances and actions to Isabel.

Toward the end of the *Jardín*'s prologue Martín strongly encourages Isabel to participate in war against the Muslims, mentioning Granada directly. He says to Isabel, with a dig at Enrique IV:

no sola mente rigese la república en tienpo de paz con justicia, mas avn en tienpo de guerra, por armas le defensase & avn dilatase más tierras conquistando como fizieron vuestros antecesores que conquistaron las Españas & oxearon los moscas suzias de Macometo & los persiguieron con espada fasta el reyno de Granada, donde agora están por la negligencia delos modernos príncipes. (*Jardín*, 139–40)

[Not only must the realm be governed justly in times of peace, but even in times of war; it must be defended with arms and its conquests even expanded, as did your ancestors who conquered the Spanish realms and scared off the filthy Moorish flies and pursued them with the sword as far as the kingdom of Granada, where they remain now through the negligence of modern princes]

Martín seems to have realized that for a woman ruler to succeed in advancing the reconquest he so desired, some finessing of his carefully delimited version of queenly power and proper conduct would be necessary.

Martín's subtle efforts to open the door for a stronger form of queenship that would allow the queen to enforce absolute authority, even to use force if necessary, appear in his discussion of why monarchs must fear God's power, honor His wisdom, and love His mercy. He advises Isabel that she should observe religious feasts with Masses, sermons, vespers, and canonical hours, and that she should say the creed morning and evening "creyendo ala mañana & ala noche firmemente lo que la sancta Yglesia nuestra madre cree, refiriendo su fe alos sabios maestros & doctores dela sancta Yglesia" [firmly believing morning and night that which our Holy Mother Church believes, referring your faith to the learned masters and doctors of the Church] (*Jardín*, 218–19). In the midst of this advice, which encourages Isabel's submission to clerical authority, he tells Isabel that she must love and honor God particularly zealously because monarchs "son lugar tenientes de Dios." This statement puts her at least on par with, and potentially above, those "sabios maestros & doctores dela Sancta Yglesia" (like, for instance, Talavera, who invoked his status as God's representative to subordinate Isabel at their first meeting) to whom she is advised to defer (*Jardín*, 218–19). Such a construction of her authority grants her power that is absolute and divine rather than provisional and subject to governance by other (male, clerical) authorities.

Furthermore, Martín counsels Isabel to have more fear of God than average citizens because she must fear God in order that her people fear her: "Si a Dios la reyna no teme, tan poco será temida por sus pueblos, antes ella temerá aellas" [If the queen does not fear God, she will be little feared by her people, and then she will fear them] (*Jardín*, 216).[49] Martín's formulation of ideal queenship is not, then, merely a matter of maternal care and intercession for one's people; it also entails inspiring fear in one's subjects. Indeed, even the passage in which Martín reassuringly and conventionally defines the role of queen as "madre" and "abogada" contains elements that suggest a stronger form of queenly power and a more menacing version of queenly identity. Martín does not stop with "abogada"; he continues by saying that the queen also should be an "escudo" for her people (*Jardín*, 199). He elaborates, "Lo tercero, la señora, es escudo, ca no sólo ha de ser piadosa como madre, ni como abogada cerca del rey, mas ha de ser paués & adaraga & escudo, defendiendo los menudos de las fuerças delos mayores" [Third, the lady is a shield; she must be not only merciful like a mother and an advocate with the king, but she must also be a shield, defending the weak from the force of those who are stronger] (*Jardín*, 202). Martín's assertion that a queen should defend the weak from the strong implies that she has the right to define these categories and so to decide who is deserving of her defense, an implication that further extends queenly agency. Additionally, although Martín does describe the queen's protective role with the feminine image of the Virgin's mantle, the choice of terminology drawn from the world of arms (*escudo, paués*, and *adaraga* all refer to types of shields), combined with his reference to the queen's personal defense of the weak from the strong, suggest a militaristic component to queenship.

An even more pointed insertion with great potential to legitimate Isabel's military endeavors in Granada appears right in the middle of the very conventional passage discussed above describing the need for queens to be devout and to undertake traditional spiritual practices. Just after saying that queens should be an example to all in their honor and service to God, and just before indicating the desirability of queens' hearing Mass daily, Martín writes that queens "deuen . . . defender la Yglesia & las personas della" [ought to . . . defend the Church and its people] (*Jardín*, 204). The idea that queenship involves defending not only one's subjects but also the Church resonates particularly well with the ways in which the war with Granada was framed. This military endeavor was promoted as a defensive campaign to protect the realm from incursions and to take back territory illicitly occupied, but it was simultaneously presented as a campaign to defend the Christian faith.[50]

As early as the spring of 1483, bulls of crusade were disseminated to encourage support for the campaign against Granada. Such bulls "deepened the public sense that this was a holy crusade against unbelievers— Turks and Moors—and waging war a religious duty."[51] A history of Isabel and Ferdinand's reign, written by Andreas Bernaldes in 1514, makes clear

the degree to which the Granada campaign was seen as a holy war undertaken in defense of the Christian faith. Chapter 102 describes "del Partido
del Alhambra e como sedio la ciudad de Granada" [the fall of the Alhambra
and how the city of Granada ceded].⁵² In the description of the surrender
of the city in to Isabel and Ferdinand in 1492, Bernaldes emphasizes the
role of "fe de Jesu Christo" [faith in Jesus Christ] in the Spanish monarchs'
victory. He also reports that the king, queen, prince, "e toda su hueste"
[and all his entourage] humbled themselves publicly before "la santa Cruz
que el Rey traia siempre en la Santa Conquista" [the holy cross that the
king always carried in the Holy Conquest] (BL MS Add. 28, 490 fol. 114v).

Bernaldes goes on to recount the triumphant celebrations in Granada,
in which "Arcobispos, ecleresia dixeron tedeum laudamus eluego mostra-
non los dedentro el pendon de santiago traia ensu hueste e junto conel
pendon Real del Rey Don Fernando" [Archbishops and clergy said, "Te
deum laudamus," and later exhibited to those within the banner of St.
James carried in his entourage and beside it the royal banner of King Fer-
dinand] To complete the scene, the crown shouted "a muy allas voses
Castilla Castilla" [very loudly, "Castile, Castile"] (BL MS Add. 28,490 fol.
114v). In spite of this seemingly complete Christian triumph, as the fifteenth century drew to a close Isabel and Ferdinand still had a great deal
of anxiety about the extent to which a strong Muslim presence survived in
Granada, always potentially threatening their Catholic monarchy. By mid-
November 1499, Archbishop Cisneros had arrived in the region, likely
summoned by Isabel and Ferdinand, to begin an all-out campaign of conversion, by violent means if necessary. His efforts led to armed resistance
from Muslims who had been assured under the *capitulaciones* that they
could keep their faith. Two years of fighting and bribed—or forced—conversions ensued; those who resisted becoming Christian were enslaved or
executed. By July 1501, a royal decree was promulgated forbidding Muslims to reside in the kingdom of Granada, and by February of the next
year the prohibition was extended to Castile. Indeed, Isabel's complete turn
away from even the limited tolerance of Islam set out in the post-conquest
agreements is clear when, in 1501, she writes that all Muslims "must either
convert or leave our kingdoms, for we cannot harbor infidels."⁵³

When the *Jardín* was first printed in 1500, Granada was at once a great
victory of recent memory and a ongoing source of trouble still occupying
the minds of the monarchs and their subjects. Martín's version of queenship would have thus been doubly useful. Not only does he legitimate
Isabel's role as a holy warrior on a mission from God, but his version of

queenship, with its emphasis on pity, compassion, and maternal intercession, would have been equally beneficial. The warm, ultra-feminine queenly
identity Martín constructs would have helped to counter any tarnish Isabel's
image might have collected through her involvement in the violent processes of the Inquisition, the expulsion of the Jews in 1492, and the harsh
treatment of conquered Muslims, supposedly protected by the *capitulaciones* signed following the fall of Granada in 1492. While brutal treatment
of their Islamic neighbors might not have necessarily disturbed Christian
inhabitants of Isabel's realm, a queen with blood on her hands—even non-
Christian blood—would not have been an especially acceptable prospect.
A letter Isabel wrote in defense of the Spanish Inquisition makes clear that
she did in fact need representational strategies to defend herself from those
who opposed her at-times-violent exercise of authority; furthermore, it also
reveals the extent to which her spirituality could serve just such a legitimating purpose. Isabel claimed, "'I have . . . caused great calamities, and
depopulated towns, lands, provinces, and kingdoms;'" however, as David
A. Boruchoff notes, "she protested that she had acted thus from love of
Christ and his Holy Mother."[54]

In closing this section on the *Jardín*, I turn to Martín's version of the
story of Judith and Holofernes, which provides in many respects a micro-
cosmic version of the representational strategies mobilized on Isabel's behalf by the text as a whole. Judith is, of course, one of the women whose
lives are frequently included in catalogues of famous women. As a savior
of her people, she is also an obviously attractive figure to connect with
Isabel. The context into which Martín inserts her story gives his account
of Judith special significance. He tells the story of Judith's victory over
Holofernes to illustrate his argument that women, though naturally weak
and fearful, can accomplish great things if they overcome their innate
timidity. Judith is not only a useful political model; she is also a useful
example of what women are capable of achieving.

However, as woman who bravely takes armed action against her people's enemy—a woman with blood on her hands—Judith might well also
be perceived as a threatening manifestation of female power, much as Joan
of Arc, Margaret of Anjou, and Margaret of York were in fifteenth- and
sixteenth-century England. As the *Jardín* as a whole does for Isabel, Martín's
account of Judith recasts the anxiety-producing figure of a politically active,
armed and assertive woman to make her seem less menacing. He emphasizes Judith's piety and her beauty, calling her "biuda & sancta & muy hermosa" [a widow, holy and very beautiful] (*Jardín*, 247). So, although

Judith is not a typical woman in her bravery and armed political action, she does fit into accepted, even idealized, categories of feminine virtue and conduct.

Martín also makes an important addition to the story of her visit to Holofernes's tent, adopting a modified version of the strategy embraced by English redactors of Christine de Pizan's works. Turning Judith into a devout holy women, Martín says that, before killing Holofernes, she "con su servienta en lugar apartado oraua toda la noche" [prayed all night with her maid in an isolated place] (*Jardín*, 248).[55] Martín further sanctifies Judith and her actions by directly invoking a medieval tradition of reading Judith as a type of the Virgin Mary (an association that, as we have seen, he also uses for Isabel). He writes of Judith, "por quanto figuró en muchas cosas la Virgen María que es archa de santas escrituras, ca ella conseruaua todas las palabras & las retenía en su coraçón" [in many respects she figures the Virgin Mary, who is the ark of the Holy Scriptures, because she kept all these words and held them in her heart] (*Jardín*, 247).[56]

Martín's account of Judith, like the *Jardín* as a whole, thus accomplishes several things at once, all of which help Isabel's representational efforts in some fashion. It introduces models of female virtue—Judith herself and the Virgin Mary—that have clear political value for Isabel's cause. It reinforces traditional understandings of feminine weakness and inferiority, but says that there can be exceptions to the rule; Isabel, like Judith, can overcome feminine frailty and save her people. It then reframes the exceptional woman, a potential source of anxiety (especially when such a woman takes up arms), in non-threatening terms, showing her practicing accepted and idealized forms of feminine conduct and associating her with long-standing models of piety and holiness. It therefore simultaneously makes a case for the divine legitimacy of potentially transgressive political action by a woman and makes that action appear to be part of an uncontroversial system of female virtue and devotion.

Isabel "la Católica" and "St. Joan"

That the image of Isabel as a holy queen continued to be reproduced even after her death attests to the success of the type of representational strategy present in the *Jardín*. In the early 1550s, Alonso de Santa Cruz describes Isabel with language that strikingly resembles the model of holy queenship that Martín de Córdoba sets out. Alonso writes:

Fue fiel amiga, sujeta y muy amada a su marido, favorecedora de las mujeres bien casadas y de lo contrario muy enemiga. Católica y cristianísima, fidelísima a Dios. Madre muy piadosa a sus vasallos. Heredada a contemplación. Ocupávase continuamente en los oficios divinos. Fue religiosa y devota, y tenía gran caridad con todas las religiones.[57]

[She was a faithful friend, submissive and very loving to her husband; she favored chaste women and was very hostile to unchaste ones. She was Catholic, Christian, extremely faithful to God. She was a merciful mother to her subjects. She was heiress to contemplation. She constantly occupied herself with divine service. She was religious and devout and had great love for all the religious orders.]

Successful though it was, the strategy of relying on a model of queenship so strongly connected to traditions of medieval female spirituality also had some fairly obvious drawbacks. One was that the representation of Isabel as a holy queen provided raw material for those who wished to limit her power in ways similar to those employed by Tudor Englishmen when they were confronted with Margaret of Anjou and Margaret of York. While during her lifetime, Isabel of Castile could not be contained any more easily than they could, the neutralizing strategy used by Christine de Pizan's English redactors and in modified form by Martín in his description of Judith was available to writers who reoriented Isabel's self-representations her after her death. Writers of "creative and didactic literature of the sixteenth and seventeenth centuries" took a leaf from English books, so to speak, in their efforts to transform Isabel into "an emblematic figure used to transmit moral and social . . . values."[58] In the *Instrucción*, written, as we have seen, for Isabel's daughter Katherine of Aragon to educate her daughter Mary, Juan Luis Vives "not surprisingly included Isabel among his exemplary women."[59] However, the nature of her exemplarity in Vives's eyes is striking. As if desiring, consciously or unconsciously, to shape a very different sort of queen than Isabel had been, Vives praises Isabel not for her political skill or for her part in the reconquest of Granada but rather for teaching her daughters spinning and needlework. As Elizabeth Howe points out, "Like latter-day Penelopes, Isabel and her daughters (all queens in their own right) exemplify faithful wives and mothers busy at their looms, rather than with their statecraft."[60]

Among the later texts effecting Isabel's transformation is one which resembles not only the English texts' transformation of Christine but also the post-World War II French pamphlet's "makeover" of St. Colette into an icon of traditional, domestic femininity discussed at the beginning of Chapter 1. A report by the royal archivist Santiago Riol submitted to the

crown in 1726 literally places Isabel inside the cloister walls. Riol "explains
the queen's success in reforming monastic institutions by declaring that
she would spend her afternoons spinning thread in the company of cloistered nuns."[61] An Isabel "la Católica" who spends her days spinning with
nuns presents a rather different mobilization of female holiness than the
ones she and her supporters advanced, and indeed, Boruchoff contrasts
the sixteenth- and seventeenth-century Isabel with the one found in "chronicles written during or shortly after her lifetime."[62]

Pro-Isabelline representational strategies did not, however, end with
the model of holy queenship constructed in the *Jardín* and so widely disseminated and reoriented after Isabel's death. Other strategies that drew
on religious material were readily at hand, as we have begun to see in our
examination of some of Martín's innovations in the *Jardín*. Indeed, in her
own will, a text which created a symbolic as well as a material legacy, Isabel
strikingly combines expressions of conventional feminine piety (including
bequests to enable poor women to enter religion) with suggestions of a
more overtly militaristic form of queenly power also grounded in spirituality. She begins with the traditional invocations of God and Father, God
the Son, and God the Holy Spirit, accompanied by expressions of devotion to the Virgin Mary, whose advocacy she craves. Isabel also invokes
the aid of the "Muy excelente Principe de la Iglesia e Caballeria Anxelical
Sr Miguel" [most excellent prince of the Church and of angelic chivalry
Lord Michael]—that is, the sword-bearing Archangel Michael.[63] She then
prays that at her judgment she will be supported by "el Apostal Santiago
. . . patron destos mis Reynos" [the apostle St. James . . . patron of my
realms].[64] St. James was known as "Matamoros," or the "Moor-slayer," and
was frequently upheld as a patron of the reconquest. Both of these peti-
tions are remarkably appropriate ones for a queen who "spent most of her
life at war."[65]

The anonymous text *La Poncella de Francia*, like Isabel's will, also
mixes expected models of female religiosity with symbolic support for
female military and political authority. Like the *Jardín*, *La Poncella* responds,
albeit in a different fashion, to objections both spiritual and practical concerning female rule and military participation. While the afterlife of Joan
of Arc was a factor in the textual "cloistering" of Christine de Pizan and
the vilification of Margaret of Anjou and Margaret of York in fifteenth-
and sixteenth-century England, in fifteenth-century Spain Isabel of Castile
was able to harness that afterlife to her own benefit through clever self-
representation as a carefully crafted "latter-day Joan."[66]

La Poncella de Francia has often been read as a romance in which Joan of Arc is depicted as a chivalric hero.[67] The text thus by extension presents Isabel as a chivalric hero, since Joan is explicitly held up as a model for Isabel. For instance, the Prologue speaks of "la Poncella de Francia, que de sus notables fechos mejor enxemple se puede dar a Vuestra Alteza que de ninguna de las otras señoras por grandes que ayan sido comparar" [the Maid of France, who by her notable deeds may give Your Highness a better example than any of the other ladies, no matter how great they may have been in comparison] (*Poncella* 90). As Cristina Guardiola observes, "Chivalry . . . serves as a framework from which to identify the queen and elaborate her propagandistic aspirations."[68] Through the conventions of the chivalric genre, the text addresses questions of women's mental and physical abilities to fight and rule.

I would like to consider, however, another tradition in which I believe *La Poncella* participates—that of medieval female hagiography. Joan is not only a chivalric model for Isabel but also a saintly one. The hagiographic elements in the text are by no means contrary to its chivalric ones; indeed, as Jocelyn Wogan-Browne has observed, saints' lives and chivalric romances can have much in common.[69] The editors of *La Poncella de Francia* argue against reading the text as hagiography, saying that the author "does not need to recount a work of hagiography, because Isabel is not presumed to be a saint."[70] Jules Quicherat similarly rejects the presence of hagiographical elements, saying that *La Poncella* presents Joan as a "fierce character, devoid of religious inspiration."[71] I contend, on the contrary, that the text manifests many qualities of medieval female saints' lives, and that the construction of Isabel as a saintly figure was quite important to her representational initiatives.[72]

By recasting Joan's history in not only a chivalric but also a hagiographic mode, *La Poncella* makes Joan into a valuable tool for Isabel's representational program. *La Poncella* engages in a Žižekian "rewriting of history," and its revised Joan retroactively receives new "symbolic weight" in fifteenth-century Castile, aiding efforts to counter objections about women's mental and physical capacities in the realms of war and politics.[73] Even more pointedly, the *Poncella*'s version of Joan helps Isabel to perform the vital task of addressing doubts about the *spiritual* dimensions of women's rule and military involvement. Through astute manipulations of hagiographic conventions, *La Poncella* not only emphasizes that women can be the equals of men, but it also counteracts objections like those raised in Vives's *Instrucción*. *La Poncella*'s Joan demonstrates that women can be chaste, virtuous, and devout while involved in traditionally masculine activities. Indeed, much as does Martín's treatment of Judith in the *Jardín*, *La Poncella* makes a case that the pursuit of arms and active political involvement are divinely sanctioned for Isabel. In short, *La Poncella* emphasizes that, for Isabel "la Católica," her interests in independent rule, military conquest, and empire-building are indeed, contrary to Vives's view, "muy católico" [truly Catholic].

Joan was not canonized until the twentieth century, but she was officially rehabilitated in 1456, a few years before the composition of *La Poncella*, which was written sometime between 1474 and 1492.[74] Although Joan's voices are de-emphasized in *La Poncella* and Joan avoids a martyr's death at the stake, the text exhibits several generic elements commonly found in medieval female hagiography, so in effect textually "canonizing" Joan. Indeed, in *La Poncella de Francia* Joan has many traditional saintly qualities: she is sent by God, she effects conversions, she speaks with unexpected eloquence, and she is a chaste virgin. Particularly striking are *La Poncella*'s intertextual echoes of the lives of St. Margaret and St. Katherine of Alexandria, saints who spoke to Joan in her voices and whose *vitae* have, in several later medieval versions, distinctly political dimensions.[75] Like these saints' *vitae*, *La Poncella* too is hagiography with markedly politicized valences.

Joan's saintly dimensions initially appear in the repeated descriptions of her as heaven-sent, as a miraculous divine emissary. The King of France, for example, views her "como a persona del cielo venida" [like a person come from heaven] when she arrives at his court (*Poncella*, 109). Later, we are told that he is "atónito" [astonished] to think of the accomplishments and the "esfuerço de esta donzella" [strength of this young woman] whom he does not see "como a muger humana" [as a human woman] but rather "como a cosa del cielo venida" [as something come from heaven] (*Poncella*, 165). Even her textual presence suggests that there is something divine about her. When Juan II receives her letter, "toda la corte miravan la firma de la Poncella y la mostrava el Maestre a los grandes d'este reino, como si aquella letra viniera del cielo" [all the court regarded the Maid's signature, and the Master showed it to the nobles of this realm, as if that letter had come from heaven] (*Poncella*, 171).

Joan is heaven-sent, however, not to save souls but to save a state. The conversions her miraculous deeds inspire are not those traditionally found in saints' lives where hoards of pagans are brought to Christianity by the spectacular ability of the female body to survive gruesome tortures.

Rather, they are political conversions bringing support to the King of France effected by Joan's female body's extraordinary feats of arms. These feats are accomplished, like virgin martyrs' endurance of torture, by the grace and will of God. Similarly, Joan's amazing deeds strike fear not into the hearts of pagan rulers but rather into the hearts of the analogously god-less Anglo-Burgundian leaders. For instance, at Poitiers a "fraile de obser-vancia" [Observant friar] who accompanies Joan because she is "cuidosa de su honra" [scrupulous concerning her honor] tells the "Almirante de Francia" [Admiral of France] of the "maravillas de la Poncella" [marvels of the Maid] (*Poncella*, 123–24).[76] The friar also stresses to the Admiral the divinely-sanctioned nature of Joan's mission. He declares his certainty that "la voluntad de Dios era por esta donzella remediar el reino" [God's will was for this young woman to reform the kingdom], and he indicates that he "tenía por fe que todos los de contraria opinión serían perdidos" [held it as an article of faith that those of the contrary opinion would be lost]. Upon hearing these things, the Admiral "de puro temor, vino a querer ver la Poncella y d'ella mesma tomar seguridad de su vida y palabra de las mer-cedes que el Rey por aquel servicio le prometiesse" [from pure fear, came to desire to see the Maid and receive from her herself assurance of his life and word of the king's mercy for that service he had promised]. Ultimately, he "prometió servir al Rey con todas sus gentes" [promised to serve the king with all his people]. After his "buelta" [turn] and Joan and the king's subsequent victory at Poitiers, "cresció mucho el partido del Rey, y cada día su favor y sus gentes crescían y el de los contrarios menguava" [the king's party increased greatly, and each day his favor and his people grew and that of the enemy diminished] (*Poncella*, 124). Similarly, in a description that echoes the accounts of conversions of thousands in virgin martyrs' lives, the author of *La Poncella* recounts that "con la fama de la Poncella infinitos se juntan en al partido del Rey" [through the Maid's renown, infinite numbers joined the king's party] (*Poncella*, 126).

An identity of heaven-sent political savior was one which, as many critics have observed, Isabel cultivated;[77] it shows up frequently in pro-Isabelline chronicles and other propagandist texts, where Isabel is often connected with the Virgin Mary not only as one who is pure, as in the *Jardín*, but also as one who brings redemption. For instance, Iñigo de Mendoza "began the dedication to his *Dechado del regimiento de príncipes* by comparing Isabel with the Virgin in her specific function of repairer and restorer, the latter of mankind, the former of the realm of Castile."[78] Diego de Valera specifically connects the Virgin Mary and Isabel as bringers of salvation in political terms, writing to Isabel that "just as our Lord wished that our glorious Lady might be born in this world because from her would proceed the Universal Redeemer of the human lineage, so he determined that you, My Lady, would be born to reform and restore these kingdoms and lead them out from the tyrannical government under which they have been for so long."[79]

Isabel's connection with Joan in *La Poncella* enhances her self-representation as a political savior in significant ways. Not only is Isabel, like the Virgin Mary, a conduit for redemption (a parallel important in its own right, especially after the birth of Isabel's first son Juan in 1478[80]), but Isabel, like Joan, is also capable of acting directly to bring about her people's salvation. *La Poncella* thus expands Isabel's redemptive labor beyond the traditional female redemptive work of maternity. Linkage with Joan helps Isabel positively highlight her efforts to save her people in proactive, traditionally masculine, ways—that is, through political action and military campaign.

The Joan of *La Poncella* also resembles medieval female saints in her striking rhetorical skill. Joan, like the "sharp-tongued, confident" heroines of hagiography, possesses, in addition to her ability to wage war successfully with weapons, the ability to wage war successfully with words.[81] In *La Poncella*, Joan, like St. Katherine of Alexandria, triumphs in debates with male authority figures. While St. Katherine engages pagan philosophers, in another politicized twist on a hagiographic trope Joan takes on the Duke of Savoy concerning definitions of nobility and the code of dueling (*Poncella*, 132–37); she also spars verbally with the Duke of Brittany concerning matters of political policy (*Poncella*, 181–87).[82]

Joan's eloquence, her political savvy, and her knowledge of wise policy all provide helpful parallels for Isabel, since these traits demonstrate the strength of feminine political abilities. Joan exhibits intellectual and rhetorical abilities that allow her to come out "on top" in her debates with male authority figures; even more significantly for Isabel's cause, Joan's victories are also clearly to the benefit of her country and people. *La Poncella* thus makes the point that a woman can indeed be equipped by God to wage war (with both weapons and words) successfully and to make political decisions effectively. At the same time, it strongly suggests that when a woman divinely endowed with such skills is allowed to undertake the deeds she has been commissioned by God to perform, the public, civic good is advanced.[83]

Foremost of all hagiographic conventions present in *La Poncella* is the text's emphasis on Joan's virginity and chastity, those essential female virtues that appear so prominently in the *Jardín* and that Vives says cannot coexist with even a woman's *thoughts* of arms. Virginity and chastity are also *the* defining characteristics of medieval female sanctity, being, as Wogan-Browne argues, basically coextensive in hagiography with Christian faith itself. She writes that the "boundaries of Christian polity are policed on the bodies of virgins: represented bodily integrity serves as an exclusionary definition of Christian community asserted against the 'pagan.'"[84] In the rewritten "happy ending" of *La Poncella*, Joan does not die at the stake but instead receives multiple offers of marriage, which she refuses. We are told, succinctly, that like St. Margaret, St. Katherine, and so many other virginal saints, "la Poncella jamas quiso casar" [the Maid never wished to marry] (*Poncella*, 203–4).[85] It is particularly significant that in the *Poncella*, Joan of Arc is never called Joan (*Juana*). Rather, we learn:

E no sabía que nombre poner a aquella pastora, y porque ella tan bien supo defender su virginidad llamóla la Poncella, que en francés dizen por virgen y aun se entiende donzella. Assi que fallado el nombre que mejor le convenía, de allí delante y para siempre su nombre más alto tenido fue llamarse Poncella de Francia. (*Poncella*, 117)

[And no one knew what name to call this shepherdess, and because she had known so well how to defend her virginity, she was called the Maid, which in French signifies virgin and also young woman. Thus this was pronounced the name that suited her best, and from thence and forever she was given the high name of the Maid of France.]

Her very name comes from her virginity and her unstinting defense thereof.[86]

Joan must indeed defend her virginity in *La Poncella*; as in many female saints' lives, a high-born suitor attempts to deflower the holy virgin. In a scene which recalls the prefect Olibrius's "wooing" of that other saintly shepherdess St. Margaret, the son of the Marshal of France "començo a reqüestarla de rústicos amores, según a labradoras semejantes tentar" [began to demand uncouth embraces of her, as is his habit to try with working-class girls]. Joan rejects his advances and "con muchas lágrimas y piadosas razones" [with many tears and pious reasons] pleads with him to desist in his campaign to take her virginity, which she significantly calls "mi tesoro" [my treasure]. Her pleas are in vain, and he continues his efforts to "corromper la limpieza de su castidad" [corrupt the purity of her chastity]. In fact, her tears and supplications merely increase his dishonest desire:

"E cuanto más ella llorando le suplicava tal fuerça no le fiziesse, tanto más en su desonesto desseo se encendía" [And however much she, crying, pleaded forcefully with him not to do it, just so much his dishonest desire was inflamed] (*Poncella*, 112–13). Like Judith, who goes to the tent of Holofernes (a story that, as we have seen, appears in the *Jardín*), Joan pretends to acquiesce to the young man's desires, but, when they are alone, she is able to fight off his advances. Indeed, in spite of her lesser physical strength, she manages not only to prevent his assault on her virginity but also to kill her attacker and cut off his finger "para señal de su vitoria." We subsequently learn that she wanted his head, but, unlike Judith with Holofernes, she could not manage the decapitation because her knife was too small (*Poncella*, 113).

The seemingly miraculous preservation of virginity, and the maiming and / or demise of the evil suitor who tries to violate it, are hallmarks of virgin martyrs' lives. A prime example appears in the life of St. Agnes, who is thrown into a brothel where a patron who looks at her with lascivious intent is struck blind, falling to the floor as though dead. Another occurs in the life of St. Christine. In an act that in some respects parallels Joan's symbolic castration of the Marshal's son, this virgin martyr puts out the pagan judge Julian's eye by biting off a piece of her tongue and spitting it at him. The blinding of Julian foregrounds the virgin martyr's extraordinary power to end the violating male gaze and to foil all attempts to corrupt her virginity.[87]

Association with Joan's passionately, even violently, defended virginity helps Isabel in the same ways that her association with the Virgin Mary does in contrasting her purity with the corruption of Enrique and Juana.[88] *La Poncella*'s stress on Joan's virginity is especially beneficial to Isabel, though, because of the ways in which this saintly virtue, like so many others, is politicized. Joan is quite concerned with protecting not only her own virginity but also the chastity of other women. When she initially appears before the king of France, she speaks of the evils plaguing the realm that she will help remedy, and in this speech a key issue is "la castidad de las duenas y donzellas forçada y corrompida" [the forcibly corrupted chastity of ladies and young women] (*Poncella*, 107). Joan's speech to the king makes clear that virginity and chastity are more than private, personal virtues that benefit the individual. They are also civic virtues that have value for the common good, and the corruption of them is symptomatic of the degradation of the ruler's authority.

Joan's concern with protecting other women's chastity, the corruption of which she sees as a pressing problem in the realm of France, resonates with Isabel's objections to the corruption of female chastity in Castile. Virginity and chastity were such important pillars in constructing the edifice of Isabel's authority that they were concomitantly perceived as critical political issues.[89] For Isabel, as for Joan in *La Poncella*, it behooved the state to preserve not only the personal purity of the leader but also female virginity and chastity more generally. Doing so was an important step in imposing order, consolidating royal authority, and representing the monarch as one who enacts the law and will of God.

In Isabel's view, the source of degradation of virginity and chastity in her realm was not rape, as in Joan's France, but rather moral decline, especially in female religious communities. The solution for Isabel therefore did not lie in leading a military campaign but rather in instigating a personally-directed campaign of monastic reform. The imposition of strict claustration for nuns was, not surprisingly, a chief element in her monastic reform program. She and Ferdinand appointed visitors and, in instructing their appointees, the monarchs "particularly insisted on the introduction of claustration."[90] Isabel's intense interest in claustration for women religious is abundantly evident in a letter she herself wrote to the nuns of Alguaire, saying, "No queriamos que se nos dijese mas . . . que monja alguna sale fuera del monasterio, ni habla con otras personas, porque desto se siguen muchos inconvenientes y mal ejemplo" [We did not want it said to us again . . . that any nun goes out of the monastery, nor speaks with other people, because many inconveniences, as well as a bad example, come from this].[91] In fact, according to Isabel, "en ésta [claustration] consiste el mayor bien de la reformación" [the greatest benefit of the reform consists of this (claustration)].[92] Claustration was the "mayor bien" of reform because it benefited the spiritual condition of the nuns (not to mention that of the people of the realm for whom the nuns were to serve as an example) and it enhanced the credibility of Isabel's representational program. Isabel found her own sort of symbolic value in "cloistering," yet again making something very traditional and potentially limiting work for her. In this case, her enforcement of enclosure for women religious enabled her to receive the benefits of cloistered status without experiencing its restrictions. Her insistence on claustration foregrounded her devotion to the highest standard of virtue and suggested that she too was on the same spiritual level as the most strictly enclosed, irreproachable holy women.[93]

Joan's virginity provided still more specialized benefits for Isabel, because Joan was a useful conduit for channeling the ideology of virginity to suggest the legitimacy of Isabel's "masculine" undertakings. The idea that virginity allows women to "shed their cultural gender and become more like men" is rooted in the writings of the early church fathers and survived into the later Middle Ages, even as it came to coexist with a "refeminized" discourse of virginity as marriage to Christ.[94] Virginity, the well-known argument goes, allows a woman to overcome innate feminine weakness in body, mind, and spirit, so making her more masculine. Such transformation is evident in the *Poncella* when Joan tells the king, for example, that, although she is "muger flaca" [weak woman] she has been able to "perder el natural temor de las mugeres" [lose a woman's natural fear] in order to accomplish her divinely-ordained mission (*Poncella*, 108). Joan's amazing abilities to transcend "natural" female limitations are similarly evident in the king of England's lament. In its expressions of disbelief about a virginal holy woman's power, his complaint echoes the one uttered by the likewise befuddled demon defeated by St. Margaret. Henry VI says:

E quien tan pacífico rey de Francia se vio, y por una muger de las salvajes montañas ser el muerto resuscitado y el bivo muerto; yo lo veo y no lo puedo creer. Y a gran passión lo siento que las flacas manos de una muger ganen contra mí tan crecidas vitorias. (*Poncella*, 189–90)

[And this was seen by the very placid king of France: the dead to be resuscitated and the living killed by a woman from the wild mountains; I see it and I cannot believe it. And I feel a great passion that the weak hands of a woman win such increasing victories against me.]

Speaking, one might say, more truly than he knows, the King continues, "Que cierto es que no una muger, mas Dios y sus maravillas me fazen la guerra" [It is certain that it is not a woman who makes war against me, but rather God and His marvels] (*Poncella*, 190). Joan is, of course, physically female; since she is a virgin, however, she also is not a "normal" woman. Instead, as the inspired and pure agent of God through whom He works, she is endowed with powers beyond the limited abilities typically ascribed to the female sex.

In *La Poncella*, virginity thus underwrites Joan's—and so Isabel's—participation in the masculine activities of politics and war. By identifying herself with Joan, Isabel took advantage of the constructions of the virile holy woman or virgin as *virago*, in spite of the inherently anti-feminist premises that underlie such constructions.[95] Isabel was thus able to embrace the positive "masculinity" of female saints to illustrate that her own political and military abilities were on par with those of men. Identification with the virginal Joan enhanced Isabel's credentials as a military leader and ruler, credentials "which . . . increase in a durable way the value of their bearer by increasing the extent and the intensity of the belief in their value."[96]

Virginity brings feminine "masculinity" into the realm of the possible; it also helps to make feminine "masculinity" culturally palatable. It is no accident that in the historical Joan's trial her accusers frequently called her virginity into question in their attempts to portray her adoption of male clothing and her military leadership as transgressive acts. *La Poncella*'s juxtaposition of Joan and Isabel as virile holy women demonstrates that Isabel's "masculine" activities were spiritually acceptable, even desirable, since the alignment of Joan and Isabel effected a sort of "sanctification by association" for Isabel. This process, like the ceremonies of investiture described by Bourdieu, "transform[ed] the representations" others had of Isabel and, concomitantly, transformed "the behaviour they adopt[ed]" towards her.[97]

The possibility of transferring desirable spiritual qualities from Joan to Isabel offered rather extensive opportunities to make that which would typically be out-of-bounds for women permissible for Isabel. As hagiography reveals, female saints can behave in ways forbidden to ordinary women.[98] Wogan-Browne notes, for instance, that virgin martyrs "rhetorically reappropriate their bodies as territory they own or rule,"[99] so exhibiting a kind of autonomy routinely denied to ordinary women. Similarly, "virgin heroines can both gaze and answer back,"[100] again demonstrating self-assertive behavior frowned upon for other women. In their saintly guises both Joan and Isabel enjoyed something like the "privileges of consecration," one of which consists, as Bourdieu notes, "in the fact that, by conferring an undeniable and indelible essence on the individuals consecrated, it [consecration] authorizes transgressions that would otherwise be forbidden."[101]

Joan's saint-like "permission to transgress" extends to a range of activities and qualities traditionally reserved for men, all of which *La Poncella* celebrates as parts of Joan's divine mission.[102] On one occasion, when the king of France is hesitant to engage the enemy in battle, Joan pleads with him to do so, saying that she "tenía tan gran esfuerço en Dios de los desbaratar y vencer" [had such great strength in God to thwart and vanquish them] (*Poncella*, 151). Her eagerness to fight, something that would otherwise be perceived as problematic in a woman, stems from her knowledge that God has given her great strength and skill; she also has divine assurance that she is authorized to use these abilities in God's service. She continues to attempt to persuade the king to enter the fray by expressing her confidence in God's endorsement of her military initiative, saying definitively that God, "que la avía sacado de las prisiones, le daría victoria en todo cuanto en aquella empresa començasse, como fasta allí avía fecho" [who had liberated her from prisons, would give her victory in everything when this venture would commence, as He had done before] (*Poncella*, 152).

By suggesting that Isabel, like Joan, enjoys God's permission—is even under His command—to do that which would ordinarily be forbidden, *La Poncella* helps to make creditable the necessity and validity of Isabel's own transgressive acts. The latitude afforded by this "sanctification" was particularly useful for addressing difficulties present at the very foundations of Isabel's authority. In addition to the dynastic complications surrounding her succession, Isabel's coronation raised questions of a different kind of legitimacy, the legitimacy of the way in which she symbolized her identity as monarch. As part of the festivities, Isabel rode in procession behind Gutierre de Cárdenas, who carried an unsheathed sword. In a controversy that foregrounds the vital importance of the symbolics of power, this phallic and militaristic representation of her regal authority caused, according to one chronicler, "murmuring at the insolence of a woman appropriating attributes rightfully belonging to a husband."[103] The "murmuring" illustrates that Isabel had to deal with the difficulties of being perceived as a usurper of masculine dominance as well as of the throne. Isabel's association with the saint-like Joan of *La Poncella*, sent by God to fight to restore the legitimate ruler, helpfully emphasized Isabel's own divine right to be queen as well as the divine sanction given to her adoption of masculine roles and identities in enacting her queenship.

The privileges accorded to Isabel through her "consecration by association" with Joan also validated other instances of Isabel's taking up the sword, so to speak, including her involvement in the campaigns to squelch rebellions of noblemen and, as we have seen, to retake Granada. Significantly, *La Poncella*, like the *Jardín*, approvingly alludes to Isabel's actions in Granada. The author says that "en vuestro famoso tiempo torne toda la ley una" (*Poncella*, 94–95), a phrase that refers to the creation of an entirely Christian realm purified of Islam and unified under Catholic monarchy. The Prologue to *La Poncella* portrays Isabel's reconquest of lost territory (and the most notorious of such losses was Granada) as a difficult yet sacred obligation resembling the necessary obedience of a professed religious to the three substantial vows. The author tells Isabel that "cobrar sus reinos ocupados" [to recover her occupied territories] is "muy más fuerte cosa" [a much more important thing] than "conquistar los ajenos" [to conquer other people's lands] because "la una guerra es de fuerça que se ha de hazer y la otra sin vergüença se puede retraer de la conquista" [the one war is so important that you must undertake it, and you may without shame withdraw from the other campaign]. He continues, "Porque fallan por más grave religioso guardar los tres votos que prometen, que acá en al mundo otro que muy más estrechos los guardasse, porque lo que es de fuerça se faze con trabajo y lo que se faze con voluntad no es pena" [Because it is held to be more important for a religious to keep the three vows he makes, than for another in the world to keep stricter ones, because that which one does compulsorily is accomplished with difficulty, and that which one does willingly is no trouble] (*Poncella*, 93). In a new twist on the trope of "cloistering," the author aligns Isabel's obligation to retake occupied territories to the obligation of a religious to keep the monastic vows. *La Poncella* thus frames behavior that might otherwise be construed as transgressive in a woman as holy obedience for Isabel, who like Joan is doing God's work.

Epilogue: "St. Isabel"

Isabel "la Católica," who found hagiography and models of female holiness so useful in advancing her political aims, became, like St. Colette of Corbie, herself a politicized exemplar of female sanctity in the twentieth century. In 1958, in Francisco Franco's Spain, José García Goldarez, bishop of Valladolid, set in motion an investigation to determine whether canonization proceedings should be begun for Isabel. After twelve years, the commission concluded that "a Canonical process for the canonization of Isabel the Catholic could be undertaken with a sense of security, since there was not found one single act, public or private, of Queen Isabel that was not inspired by Christian and evangelical criteria; moreover there was a 'reputation for sanctity' uninterrupted for five centuries and as the investigation was progressing, it was more accentuated."[104] The process of canonization was approved, and in March 1974, the year before Franco's death, the Sacred Congregation for the Cause of the Saints in the Vatican granted Isabel the title "Servant of God."

While the stated motivation for initiating the investigation was the growing popular acclaim for Isabel's sanctity, Franco's support for the process was no less political than Burgundian support for Colette's canonization had been. Indeed, advancement of the canonization process had distinct political benefits for Franco's political and propagandist agendas. In 1936, when Franco played a key role in leading the insurrection against the Republican government of Spain, a pastoral letter written by Enrique Plá y Deniel, bishop of Salamanca, represented Franco as a new Catholic crusader. As Paul Preston observes in his biography of Franco, in this letter "For the first time, the word 'crusade' was used to describe the Civil War."[105] By invoking the model of a crusade, "Franco could project himself not just as the defender of his Spain but also as the defender of the universal faith."[106] Franco would continue to cultivate a "carefully constructed self-image as the medieval warrior-crusader, defender of the faith and restorer of Spanish national greatness" throughout his career.[107]

Such a self-representation precisely resembles the one Isabel cultivated through her associations with female sanctity. It is not surprising, then, that Franco encouraged a connection of himself with Isabel, evidently aiming for the same sort of "sanctification by association" that Isabel sought through association with Joan of Arc. The linkage of Franco and Isabel is made quite explicit in his use of "images of the *Reconquista* of Spain from the Moors . . . to reinforce the notion that he was the heroic leader" called by God to undertake "a 'Crusade' to liberate Spain from the godless hordes of Moscow."[108] Franco compared himself to Isabel in a speech he made on May 29, 1942, at Medina del Campo during the inauguration of a training school for the *Sección Femenina* of the Falange.[109] Strikingly, the Falangist movement employed "a coat of arms in which the yoke (with the 'Y' of *Ysabel* and the 'F' of *Fernando*) are conjoined in a bond of shared imperial rule."[110] Just as Isabel found value in the creation of "St. Joan" to legitimate her authoritarian rule and religious reconquest, so Franco found it worthwhile to try to create "St. Isabel" to legitimate another authoritarian, militaristic regime.

5

The Mystic, the Monarch, and the Persistence of "the Medieval": Elizabeth Barton and Henry VIII

Medieval Female Spirituality and the English Reformation

Although Joan of Arc's legacy shaped perceptions of Margaret of Anjou's and Isabel of Castile's reigns in dramatically different ways, both queens' careers illustrate that gendered authority, religious authority, and political authority existed interwoven in an elaborate tapestry in which national and international affairs crossed as warp and woof. With the advent of the "Great Matter" of Henry VIII's proposed divorce from Katherine of Aragon, the interface of gender, religion, and temporal authority became even more complex, as did the relationships of national and international politics.[1] Scholars often draw the dividing line between the Middle Ages and the early modern era in this tumultuous period during the first half of the sixteenth century, typically placing it to correspond with the English break with the Roman Catholic Church, in the process reconfiguring the relationship of church and state. Such scholars as Christopher Haigh, Norman Jones, and Eamon Duffy have shown, however, that the transition from the Catholic to the Protestant religion was not an absolute one. After Henry VIII's break with Rome, he exhibited an "essential Catholicism," and many aspects of religious services did not change dramatically despite his denial of papal authority. [2]

The importance of Christine de Pizan's writings in the Henrician court, as well as the ongoing influence in Tudor chronicles, literature, and political culture of Joan of Arc and Margaret of Anjou, further suggest that perhaps the line separating "the medieval" and "the early modern" is not so easy to draw. Indeed, in the "Great Matter" on which this chapter focuses, the figure of that latter-day Joan, Henry VIII's first mother-in-law Isabel of Castile, loomed large as an example of the continuing political power inherent in manifestations of medieval female spirituality. In the liminal period spanning the reigns of Henry VIII and Elizabeth I, the persistence of medieval religion, and particularly of medieval female spirituality, took a central part in the "continuous 'play' of history, culture, and power" to which identity of persons and nations alike is always subject.[3] Through this continuous play, the constitutions of English identities both personal and corporate were informed by Catholic and Protestant cultural groups' competing, yet interconnected, visions of self and state; these visions were in turn dependent on distinctive, yet also mutually informing, understandings of past and present.

Elizabeth Barton, the "Holy Maid of Kent," is a "medieval" visionary at the advent of what is typically called the "early modern" age.[4] She is best known for inserting herself into the fraught political struggle to define English identity by proclaiming her revelations condemning Henry VIII's divorce. She declared that "God commanded her to say to the late cardinal and also to the said Archbishop of Canterbury that, if they married or furthered the King's Grace to be married to the Queen's Grace that now is [Anne Boleyn]—they both should be utterly destroyed."[5] Even more pointedly, she said "that if the King's Grace married the Queen's Grace that now is, he should not be king a month after."[6]

In turning her attention to such a matter, Elizabeth was following a very traditional pattern for medieval female visionaries. Elizabeth Barton's predecessors St. Birgitta of Sweden and St. Catherine of Siena both had politically oriented revelations and made controversial prophecies; as we have seen, we might also add St. Colette of Corbie to this list.[7] In fact, Diane Watt suggests that St. Birgitta and St. Catherine may have been "role models" for Barton, a possibility that also did not escape Barton's contemporaries.[8] In the sermon preached against her at St. Paul's on November 23, 1533, Dr. Capon, bishop-elect of Bangor, insisted that her spiritual father Bocking had "daily rehearsed matter enough unto her, out of St. Bridget's and St. Catherine of Senys revelations, to make up her fantasies and counterfeit visions."[9]

The beginnings of Elizabeth Barton's story also closely resemble those of Colette of Corbie, Joan of Arc, and many other medieval female mystics. Barton was a servant in the house of Thomas Cobb, a farmer of the archbishop of Canterbury, in Aldington, Kent. Her visionary career began during a serious illness that she suffered during the Easter season of 1525. Once her revelations became publicly known, Richard Masters, the rector of Aldington, brought the matter before William Warham, the archbishop of Canterbury. Slightly less than a year after her mystical experiences began, an archepiscopal commission was appointed, led by the Benedictine monk Edward Bocking.[10] Nothing unorthodox was found in her case, and her public healing from her illness by the Virgin Mary at Court-at-Street increased both the fame of the Holy Maid of Kent and that of the Marian shrine. In response to another revelation from the Virgin Mary, Elizabeth became a nun at the Benedictine house of St. Sepulchre near Canterbury, placing herself under Bocking's spiritual direction. In 1527, at roughly the same time that Henry VIII's struggle to obtain a divorce began, the London printer Robert Redman published the first account of her miracles, revelations, and prophecies, entitled *A marueilous woorke of late done at Court of Streete in Kent*.

Elizabeth Barton has been the focus of competing interpretations since her own lifetime. The attention paid her has typically concentrated on arguing either for her sanctity or for her unholy fraudulence.[11] The priests and friars who perished with her on the scaffold at Tyburn in 1534 clearly took the former position, as did later Catholic historians and devotionally oriented writers.[12] Thomas Cranmer, not surprisingly, held the latter opinion, saying that Elizabeth "passed all others in devilish devices" and that "she could, when she list, feign herself to be in a trance."[13] A similar attitude, and the corresponding vision of Elizabeth as an easily manipulated pawn in political plots organized by others, inform the writing of such later scholars as Leslie Stephen and Sidney Lee, as the entry for Elizabeth Barton in the *Dictionary of National Biography* demonstrates.[14]

My concern is not to resolve the still-disputed question of Elizabeth Barton's legitimacy as a holy woman and a visionary. Her political and cultural importance, and that of the divine knowledge to which she declared herself (and was declared by others) to be privy, do not depend on her "true" sanctity or the "truth" of her mystical experiences. Similarly, I do not simply want to argue that Elizabeth Barton's revelations were political in nature and problematic for Henry VIII; as the examples mentioned above demonstrate, one could hardly argue otherwise. Rather, I want to explore *how* and *why* her political revelations, like those of Joan of Arc, who also publicized divine displeasure with an English king, took on such great significance and were deemed worthy of intensive prosecutory efforts, while other expressions of dissent—even dissent similarly indicative of God's disapproval—were dealt with in far less elaborate fashion.

The case of William Peto, Minister of the English Province of the Observant Friars (an order which had, since its introduction in Edward

IV's reign, enjoyed special royal favor), provides an instructive comparison. On Easter Sunday, 1532, at a mass for the king and court at the chapel of Greenwich Palace, Peto preached a sermon on the topic of King Ahab, with pointed reference to Henry's relationship with Anne Boleyn. The sermon, not surprisingly, caused a scandal, and on the following Sunday, Hugh Curwen, one of the royal chaplains, was commissioned to preach a sermon denouncing Peto. During the course of this sermon, a shouting match broke out between Henry Elstow, Guardian of the Greenwich Observants, who supported Peto, and the Earl of Essex, who supported the king.[15] Peto, Elstow, and the whole order of the Observant Friars fell from royal grace in an instant and were irrevocably inscribed on the king's blacklist; Peto and Elstow were in due course imprisoned for a time. The Holy Roman Emperor Charles V's ambassador to England, Eustache Chapuys, reports on May 2, 1532, that "The Observant Fathers are still under arrest. They have been told that the king has sent to Rome for a commission to the provincial of the Broadsleeved Order . . . to try them" (L and P, vol. 5, no. 9).

Unlike Elizabeth Barton and her associates, Peto and Elstow did not end up facing an elaborate judicial procedure. Rather, they were set free and went to the Continent. That the government allowed them their liberty indicates the comparatively low priority their case received. Indeed, immediately after the fateful sermon, Henry was unconcerned enough with the danger Peto posed to permit him to go to Toulouse (L and P, vol. 5, no. 941). On the Continent, Peto and Elstow continued to work against the king; Peto, who eventually became a cardinal, is repeatedly mentioned in correspondence as an author of writings opposing the king's marriage to Anne Boleyn.[16]

With his influential position in the church and his ready access to publication opportunities, Peto would, on the face of things, seem to be a far more dangerous figure for Henry VIII than Elizabeth Barton. Although Peto was included in 1539 "in the sweeping bill of attainder passed against Cardinal Pole and others" (DNB, vol. 15, 975), he and his writings were actually the target of far fewer, and far less highly choreographed, official demonstrations of ire than were Elizabeth and her revelations. After Peto arrived on the Continent, Henry VIII's agents made efforts to obtain copies of his writings, and a few expressions of hatred toward Peto show up in letters from the king's supporters.[17] In general, however, the royal attitude concerning Peto seems to have been that having him out of sight, and so largely out of mind, was a sufficient containment strategy. The sheer number of official documents concerning Elizabeth Barton, the campaign undertaken to eradicate all written accounts of her revelations,[18] and the carefully crafted spectacle of her condemnation, confession of fraudulence, and execution all suggest, in contrast, her extraordinary power.

The King's Mass at Calais

Elizabeth Barton is, as I mentioned previously, well known for her opposition to the Act of Supremacy and the royal divorce, but her visions' disruptive political power did not end with the king's "Great Matter." Just as the controversy surrounding the divorce spilled over into, and indeed largely shaped, Henry VIII's foreign policy, so too, her revelations took on international importance as Henry endeavored to secure England's position in the European political sphere. To consider the how's and why's of Elizabeth Barton's political significance, I want to focus in some detail on a revelation from 1532, the same year as Peto's sermon, around which a constellation of key factors converge. The year 1532 was an important one for Henry VIII in his related efforts to divorce Katherine of Aragon, marry Anne Boleyn, and carve out a position of absolute authority for himself within the English church. By late in that year, he appeared to be making progress on all fronts. In January, 1532, Parliament had passed a bill halting the payment of papal annates to Rome, and Henry, having taken on the Convocation of the Clergy, at length had forced them to pass the Act for the Submission of the Clergy on May 15, 1532.

As Henry battled with the English clergy and the Pope, he also engaged in negotiations to solidify his position within Europe, particularly vis-à-vis the Holy Roman Emperor Charles V. The emperor was the pope's chief military supporter and, as Katherine's nephew, he played a central role in the efforts to prevent the divorce. The mainstay of Henry's foreign policy at this time was his plan to form an alliance with Francis I of France. The two monarchs had attempted to do so some years earlier in 1520, in the famous interlude of the Field of the Cloth of Gold, but the relationship had not prospered particularly well. A meeting between the English and French kings to hammer out a new alliance was accordingly scheduled to take place in October, 1532, at Boulogne-sur-Mer and Calais.[19]

From Henry's perspective, the meeting on the Continent was of the utmost importance. Chapuys writes, "The King seems never to have desired anything so much as this journey, for he does not care to talk of anything else" (L and P, vol. 5, no. 1292). As if the importance of securing an alliance with Francis I were not enough, the expedition to the Continent took on added significance because it was widely rumored that Henry VIII would marry Anne Boleyn while they were abroad. On September 1, 1532, prior to setting sail for France, Henry had created Anne "Marchioness of Pembroke in her own right and granted her lands to the value of a thousand pounds a year."[20] The ceremony in which Anne's title and lands were conferred was fairly splendid. It took place "at the castill of Wyndsor," where the king was "accompanied with the duke of Norffolk the duke of Suffolk with dyuers Erlis barons & oþer noble men as the Ambassador of fraunce & oþer of his councell." Anne was "convaid with diuers noble men afor hir ii and ii," accompanied by "the Lady Mary doughter to þe duke of Norffolk," the Countess of Rutland, the Countess of Sussex, and "diuers Ladies & gentilwomen." All were elaborately dressed in ermine-trimmed velvet, and they came before Henry "standing under the cloth of astate" for the exchange of letters patent and for the placement of "þe crownett on hir hed."[21] The ostentation and publicity of the ceremony surely provided support for the widely circulating rumors that Henry and Anne's marriage was imminent.

Henry's desire for the French alliance was, of course, largely driven by his desire to marry Anne. The extent to which the two undertakings were connected for Henry emerges not only in the French ambassador's presence at the aforementioned ceremony but also in one of Chapuys's letters to Charles V, dated September 5, 1532. He writes, "On Sunday, before mass, lady Anne was created marchioness of Pembroke, with an income of 4,000 ducats. After mass, which was performed by the bishop of Winchester, the King and the French ambassador drew near to the altar, and signed and swore to certain articles" (L and P, vol. 5, no. 1292).

It was not only important to Henry that his attempt to secure an alliance with Francis succeed, but it was also crucial that his skilful diplomatic efforts, and their ultimately successful outcome, be well known and well publicized. Strong outward representations of power and authority were vital for Henry, given the precariousness of his position both at home and within Europe. As the ceremony in which he created Anne marchioness of Pembroke begins to suggest, he realized that representation was all. Furthermore, he was well aware that his ability to achieve his political aims depended on the successful public promotion of his agenda. Accordingly, although not as elaborate in its pageantry as the meeting in 1520, the conference of 1532 was no quiet, private undertaking.[22]

To emphasize the representational importance of the occasion, Henry took an enormous contingent to the Continent with him; the party included "140 lords and knights arrayed in velvet, and a body of 600 horse."[23] Furthermore, Henry VIII did not hold back in displays of all-important "magnificence," which, as Roy C. Strong points out, had become a necessary "princely virtue."[24] In addition to electing key French nobles to the Order of the Garter in return for the induction of English dukes into the order of St. Michael, "the kynge of Englond had made a costly banqwete" during the course of the festivities (*Chronicle of Calais*, 43). The Privy Purse accounts also include several entries for payments for losses at dice and tennis in Calais, a reward to the French king's jester, as well as monies given to "the singers of the French King's Privy Chamber" and to "Parker, yeoman of the Robes, for doublets for the guard to wrestle in before the King and French king at Calais."[25] Sydney Anglo argues that the interview was "primarily a business meeting"; as the accounts reveal, however, there was no shortage of entertainments, with their concomitant opportunities for lavish self-representation and self-promotion, to accompany the business dealings. Indeed, in Henry VIII's case, it is not entirely possible to separate ceremony, entertainment, and "business." Ceremony and entertainment clearly *were* business for Henry; they attest to "the symbolic power of the whole political theatre which actualizes and officializes visions of the world and political divisions."[26]

Henry particularly needed to mobilize the symbolic power of political theater on the home front in 1532. Prior to the king's departure, the mission had been very unpopular. Chapuys reports that, despite Henry's enthusiasm for the venture, "No one else wishes it except the lady, and the people talk of it in a strange fashion. The Council, and especially the duke of Suffolk, have spoken so plainly that the King insulted him several times. The earl of Oxford . . . said a week ago to a friend that he feared this interview would be the cause of great evils to the kingdom" (*L and P*, vol. 5, no. 1292). Henry accordingly made sure that the details of his elaborate meeting with Francis and his friendly relationship with the French monarch were well known in England. Wynkyn de Worde printed under royal privilege an account emphasizing the richness and pageantry of the interview, significantly entitled "The maner of the *tryumphe* at Caleys and Bulleyn" (emphasis added), before Henry even made it back across the Channel.[27]

As it turned out, the interview was also a great success for Henry, at least in the short term. Perhaps Wynkyn de Worde's text had the desired

positive impact, because public opinion evidently altered somewhat in
Henry VIII's favor following the meeting in Calais (or at least Henry's
supporters were saying it had done so, perhaps hoping that reports of good
publicity would engender more good publicity). Sir Thomas Audeley,
keeper of the Privy Seal, reports to Cromwell on November 4, 1532, that
"the Commons are delighted at the amicable interview between the King
and the King of France, and Henry's personal trouble therein" (*L and P*,
vol. 5, no. 1518); similarly, Christopher Hales writes, also to Cromwell, "I
am glad to hear of the amicable entertainment between the King's highness and the French king" (*L and P*, vol. 5, no. 1527).

The meeting also had the effects Henry desired in the arena of foreign policy. The *Chronicle of Calais* reports that the kings "departed lyke
louynge bretherne in greate amytie" (43), and the newly solid relationship
between the English and French monarchs got the pope's attention, as
Henry had hoped it would. Although the pope did officially command
Henry, under pain of excommunication, to end his relationship with Anne
Boleyn and take Katherine back, he issued the orders "with extreme unwillingness, especially the last, which was dated 15th November 1532, just
after the interview between Henry and Francis I at Calais."[28] The pope
clearly feared that the alliance between Henry VIII and Francis I would be
strong enough to allow Henry to resist Charles V.[29]

Henry's triumphal diplomatic success on the Continent was, however,
somewhat tarnished, and the carefully orchestrated dissemination of the
news of the splendid meeting was somewhat disrupted, when one of Elizabeth Barton's revelations became publicly known:

> when the Kynges highnes was at Caleis in the entreview betwene hys Majestie and
> the Frenche Kyng and heryng masse in the Churche of our Lady at Caleis . . . God
> was so displeased with the Kynges Highnes that hys grace sawe not that tyme at
> the masse the blessed Sacrament in forme of breade, for it was takyn away from
> the Prest . . . by an angell, and mynystred to the seid Elizabeth then being there
> present and invysible, and sodenly conveyed and rapte thens ageyn by the power
> of God in to the seid Nonnerie where she is professed.[30]

God's displeasure, expressed in this fashion at Calais, where the marriage
of Henry VIII and Anne Boleyn was so widely believed to be impending,
would have been a welcome endorsement of Katherine's cause to those
who opposed the divorce. But, there was more at stake in this revelation
than an indication of divine condemnation of Henry VIII's intention to
marry Anne.[31] As did the divorce and marriage themselves, the revelation

had significant implications for Henry's broader foreign and domestic policy strategies.

Elizabeth Barton in her nunnery near Canterbury was likely well aware of the magnitude of the royal meeting, since the great entourage gathered there before departing for Calais. Her revelation, publicized in this politically important town, had the potential to circulate quickly among powerful English clerics and laymen whose support Henry needed. Furthermore, as Ethan H. Shagan has shown, Barton's location in Canterbury, "for centuries . . . England's most popular pilgrimage destination," likely helped to spread her fame among the general population. "The coincidence of Barton's location at one of England's most popular tourist-traps may have given her access to a national audience she could not otherwise have reached."[32]

Canterbury was also an important international space, through which far-reaching currents of power flowed. J. R. McKee calls attention to the significance of the town's location, noting that "it lay on the high-road between London and Dover, along which all the great functionaries of Church and State must pass on their way to and from the Continent."[33] A revelation concerning God's rejection of the English king that originated in Canterbury could, therefore, also rapidly have reached the ears of some of the most influential figures in European political circles—the very figures on whom Henry's success in obtaining the divorce and resisting the forces of Charles V depended.[34]

Indeed, Barton's troubling revelation about events at the royal conference did become widely known. It appears in the catalogue of her revelations recorded in a letter written to Cromwell by the examiner of the Observant Friar Hugh Rich, and it is mentioned by the Prior of Christ Church in his letter to Cromwell concerning Elizabeth. [35] Thomas More too reports knowing of the revelation. In a letter written to Cromwell to defend himself on the subject of his former relationship with Elizabeth Barton (whom he here denigrates as "that huswife"), More declares that he has heard "the tale of the hoste, with which . . . she saide she was houseled, at the Kingis Masse at Calice."[36]

Furthermore, other letters concerning Elizabeth demonstrate her perceived power to turn people against the king, suggesting that wide and rapid circulation of her vision would have been disquieting indeed. According to Cranmer, for instance, Archbishop Warham and Cardinal Wolsey supported the divorce until she persuaded them to change their minds. He writes, "She also had communication with my lord Cardinal and with

my lord of Canterbury, my predecessor in the matter; and [in] mine opinion . . . she stayed them, very much in the matter."[37]

As problematic as the factors of Elizabeth Barton's location and her
evident persuasive ability were, the most serious danger posed by the holy
woman and her revelations was not directly to Henry's foreign or domestic policy initiatives themselves; rather, it was to his *representations* of them,
and, even more importantly, of himself. The "political labour of representation," which "gives the objectivity of public discourse and exemplary
practice to a way of seeing or experiencing the social world" was, as we
have seen, of the utmost importance for Henry.[38] Through successful representation, he could shape experiences and perceptions. If his representations were successful, the state of political affairs as he represented them
would, in effect, *be* the state of political affairs. The most important struggle in which Elizabeth Barton was involved was thus not that concerning
the royal divorce. It was not even that among Henry VIII, Francis I, and
Charles V. Rather, it was the struggle waged by "different ideological groups
or fractions" to "command and deploy common and very potent symbols
and tropes."[39] Indeed, she was inescapably involved in such competition,
because medieval female spirituality was such a rich source of precisely these
symbols and tropes. The competition was particularly fierce, because what
was at stake were the very definition of English identity and the nature of
English royal authority.

Canterbury, as the seat of the most important English archbishop,
was a critical location for Henry's religious and political undertakings in
representational as well as practical terms.[40] That Elizabeth's damning report of the events at the mass issued from the seat of the English church
(the Supreme Headship of which Henry claimed as early as 1530), and that
she had been given the seal of approval by the archbishop himself, intensify the revelation's suggestion that the divinely endorsed stance for the
English church and the English people to take would be to oppose the
divorce and, concomitantly, to reject Henry as God had done. Thomas
Cranmer, appointed as archbishop in 1533, felt no small amount of chagrin
that this obstinate visionary uttered her inconvenient prophecies under
his very nose, and, furthermore, had received the official endorsement of
his predecessor, Warham. He writes, "This monster was convented both
before William Warham, archbishop of Canterbury, and Thomas Wolsey,
cardinal and archbishop of York: who, either because that generation of
the clergy hath alway defended idolatry and superstition, or because she

knew too much of their incontinency and other wickedness of living . . . they clearly discharged her without finding any fault in her at all."[41] Given the town's symbolic as well as practical importance, it is thus not surprising that Elizabeth Barton's public humiliation and the sermon preached against her at St. Paul's were repeated at Canterbury.

That Elizabeth's revelation of 1532 transpired at a mass also had serious consequences for Henry's representational project. God's expression of displeasure during the divine office undermined Henry's promotion of his alliance with Francis as a sacred one. The initial signing of an agreement between Henry and the French ambassador at the mass celebrated prior to Henry's departure illuminates the English king's aim to promote his union with Francis as one engineered by God and so in effect a *fait accompli* even before the interview transpired. On that occasion, Dr. Foxe praised "the alliance between England and France, of which God, not man, must have been the inventor," adding that it "was inviolable and eternal" (*L and P*, vol. 5, no. 1292).[42]

A description of the part of the royal interview that took place at Boulogne dramatically illustrates the ways in which the mass as a ceremony functioned to unify the kings and publicly to demonstrate the sacred quality of that union. The anonymous French writer says that the king of England, wearing clothes sent to him by the French king, attended a mass accompanied by "all his men between the ages of 30 and 60." At the service:

There were with him "le comte de Richemonte," and the dukes of Suffolk and Norfolk. Two oratories for the Kings were fitted up near the high altar of the church of Our Lady. The King of England went into that on the right, and heard a low mass, and then as he was waiting for the King another was begun. Francis came in at the beginning of the Gospel accompanied by princes, cardinals, and noblemen. The king of England came out of his oratory and embraced him, and then returned with the Cardinal of Lorraine to his oratory, to hear the end of the mass, and the French king went to his oratory to hear mass, while the singers sang "motez." (*L and P*, vol. 5, no. 1485)

Furthermore, descriptions suggest that the mass at Boulogne was an elaborate occasion, allowing once again for the display of royal "magnificence" as well as for public demonstrations of the monarchs' piety. Hamy reports that on Henry VIII's oratory "the canopy and the hangings" were "of curly-queued gold and silver cloth" while on Francis I's "the decoration was made of velvet, sprinkled with gold fleurs-de-lys." He confirms the splendor of the ceremony when he notes that the French king's account of expenses for the meeting "includes twenty-seven ells of black velvet, at a cost of 209 *l* 10 *s* to make four mantles for the singers."[43] Given each monarch's careful efforts never to let himself be outdone or overshadowed by the other, one expects that the mass in Calais was no less a glittering, elaborate affair where worldly aims of self-representation mixed with sacred observance.[44]

Henry endeavored to portray his alliance with Francis not only as being divinely engineered but also as having a holy purpose, a characterization countering the impious motives many saw it advancing. In these efforts too the mass did useful ceremonial work,[45] and as it had for Isabel of Castile, the rhetoric of holy war played a valuable political role. The official reason given for holding the meeting in 1532 was to plan for the defense of Christendom from the Turks. At the mass that Henry attended prior to departure for the Continent, Dr. Foxe called the alliance between Henry and Francis "the best means for resisting the Turks" (*L and P*, vol. 5, no. 1292).[46] Similarly, the treaty the two kings signed on October 28, 1532, at Calais begins by invoking "l'exaltation, augmentation, conservation et deffense de nostre saincte foy et religion chrestienne" [the exaltation, augmentation, conservation, and defense of our holy faith and Christian religion] with particular reference to putting an end to the "dampnées conspirations et machinations que le Turq, ancien ennemy de nostre saincte foy, a, puis peu de temps en ça, entrepriese sur ladicte chrestienté" [damned conspiracies and machinations that the Turk—ancient enemy of our holy faith—has, quite recently, undertaken against the said Christian faith].[47] In Elizabeth's revelation, on the contrary, Henry and Francis's alliance is far from being divinely blessed as a union of defenders of the faith. Rather, it appears to be under a serious cloud. Henry, from whom the host is taken, seems little better than the "infidels" he is meant to be fighting, in contrast to the saintly Elizabeth, who receives the host in his place.

Perhaps most distressing for Henry were the ways in which Elizabeth Barton's revelation concerning events at the mass struck at the very heart of his representation of the English monarchy. Henry's royal identity in 1532 was inseparable from his self-identification as Supreme Head of the English Church. He occupied this latter position by virtue of his self-proclaimed status as bearer of the sacred *imperium* transmitted from Constantine, who "had borne equal sway" over both the temporal and ecclesiastical spheres.[48] The famous preamble to the Act in Restraint of Appeals, passed by Parliament in 1533, sets out Henry VIII's sacred, imperial identity very clearly:

Where by divers sundry old authentic histories and chronicles it is manifestly declared and expressed that this realm of England is an empire, and so hath been accepted in the world, governed by one supreme head and king having the dignity and royal estate of the imperial crown of the same, unto whom a body politic, compact of all sorts and degrees of people divided in terms and by names of spirituality and temporality, be bounded and owe next to God a natural and humble obedience.[49]

Henry's self-transformation from the king of England to the English Emperor and Supreme Head of the English Church, his versions of self and state, depended for success on the process that Pierre Bourdieu terms "symbolic alchemy." Bourdieu writes, "Symbolic alchemy . . . produces, to the benefit of the one who accomplishes acts of euphemization, transfiguration, or imposition of form, a capital of recognition which permits him to exert symbolic effects."[50] Henry's efforts to perform symbolic alchemy and so consolidate the model of royal power set forth in the Act in Restraint of Appeals reached back some years prior to 1532. In 1530, Henry had demanded that the clergy "should acknowledge him 'the only Protector and Supreme Head of the Church and clergy of England,'" and he received such acknowledgement in 1531, with the qualifier, largely ignored by the king and his supporters, "as far as the laws of Christ allow."[51] Henry saw himself, and required others to see him, not simply as a divinely annointed and divinely approved monarch, but as "the ymage of God vpon earthe."[52]

Henry sought to enact in extraordinarily literal terms the sacerdotal kingship, the identity of priest-king, used to great propagandistic effect by his Lancastrian ancestor Henry V in his own project of legitimating his claim to the English throne.[53] Henry VIII's retention of the mass, more or less unchanged, after his break with Rome was likely connected not only to personal religious taste but also to a political desire to preserve a vital building block in the foundation of his sacral, sacerdotal royal identity.[54] Tellingly, as Strong observes, following the 1534 Act of Supremacy, "Henry . . . exercised in his own right the *potestas jurisdictionis* over the temporal affairs of the Church and also, at least in some degree, the *potestas ordinis*."[55] Strong further points out that, while Henry VIII "did not of course perform the duties of a priest," he did "by royal prerogative determine doctrine and ritual." In fact, by the end of his reign, "Henry had the right to make doctrinal decrees by letters patent."[56]

Henry VIII wrote himself into an apostolic lineage of holy kings fairly early in his reign, as we see in the pageant for the entry of Henry VIII and

Charles V into London on June 6, 1522. One of the tableaux, designed by William Lily, focused on Charlemagne. As John N. King observes, "By styling the founder of the Holy Roman Empire and his successors as ideal rulers deserving of a Christlike crown, Lily presents Charlemagne, and, by extension, Charles V and Henry VIII, as governors in an 'apostolic succession' from Christ."[57] Ultimately, though, Henry desired to *rewrite* apostolic succession, imposing a new form of sacerdotal kingship by presenting himself, rather than the pope, as the legitimate heir in the true line of succession from Christ.

Henry's transfigured version of the apostolic kingship embraced by earlier Lancastrian monarchs appears prominently in Hans Holbein's title page border in the 1535 Coverdale Bible. The border depicts the "descent" to Henry VIII of authority deriving "from the Old and New Testament models for sacred kingship."[58] On the right side, where images from the New Testament are portrayed, the text "Go youre vvaye in to all the vvorlde, & preach the Gospel" appears prominently. Accompanying the text is a picture of Christ surrounded by the apostles, all of whom hold keys.[59] As King points out, the use of the text from Mark 16:15 is "iconoclastic," since it represents an appropriation of a "text that the church of Rome had used as a precedent for the papal claim of apostolic succession from Christ."[60] Similarly, the "proliferation of keys . . . undermines the papal claim to primacy as the inheritor of the keys of St. Peter."[61] The expected "capital of recognition" accruing from these transformative efforts emerges in Miles Coverdale's preface to the 1535 Bible, in which he concisely lays out the power Henry VIII envisioned having. Coverdale says that the Bible "declareth most abountdauntly that the office, auctorite and power geven to God unto kynges, is in earth above all other powers: let them call themselves Popes, Cardynalles, or what so ever they will, the worde of god declareth them . . . to be obedient unto the temporall swerde."[62]

Imperial Identity and Elizabeth's Destruction

As the aforementioned examples indicate, Henry VIII took his "symbolic alchemy" quite seriously, and Elizabeth Barton's revelation of the host being denied to him at the mass at Calais threw a fairly serious spanner into the works of the transformations he was, in 1532, at the height of his efforts to realize. Central to Elizabeth's problematic force for Henry VIII and his supporters were her gender and her status as a professed nun. As I have argued, female spirituality and the revelations of holy women were valuable, and extremely malleable, sources of symbolic capital in the later medieval and early modern periods. Henry VIII recognized the symbolic potential inherent in Elizabeth Barton, and he evidently hoped to turn the impending disaster that she represented into success.

In fact, both Henry and Anne may well have been particularly anxious to gain a holy woman's support to counteract popular opposition to Anne that seemed to be especially strong among women. For instance, when Henry traveled north on a hunting trip in July, 1532, he abruptly turned back, and Chapuys reports, "some say the cause is that, in two or three places that he passed through, the people urged him to take back the queen, and the women insulted the Lady [Anne Boleyn]" (*L and P*, vol. 5, no. 1202). One also finds evidence of perhaps more serious female opposition to Henry's relationship with Anne in the grants listed for July 1532. Included there is a "Writ to Sir Thomas Audeley, keeper of the Great Seal, to direct a commission of Oyer and Terminer to Sir Rob. Norwich, chief justice of the King's Bench, Sir Ric. Lester, chief baron of the Exchequer, and to other persons named . . . for an inquiry to be held at Yarmouth, immediately after the assizes at Norwich, touching a great riot and unlawful assembly of women at that town, which it is thought could not have been held without the connivance of their husbands" (*L and P*, vol. 5, no. 1207/45).[63] Another sinister, although perhaps exaggerated, report of popular feminine opposition to Anne appears in "a 1532 report to the French ambassador in Venice that 'a mob of from seven to eight thousand women of London went out of the town to seize Boleyn's daughter, the sweetheart of the king of England, who was supping at a villa on a river, the king not being with her; and having received notice of this, she escaped by crossing the river in a boat. The women had intended to kill her; and amongst the mob were many men, disguised as women.'"[64]

Henry seemed hopeful that Elizabeth Barton might be for his cause something like what St. Colette had been for the Burgundians. Even after her initial meeting with the king, in which she told him of her divine knowledge of the risks he ran in losing God's favor—and his kingdom—if he pursued the divorce, Henry offered to make her an abbess. Anne Boleyn too recognized the benefits Elizabeth could provide; she "asked her to remain at the Royal Court in attendance upon her."[65] They attempted, in effect, to enact the same strategy practiced by the English writers who exploited Christine de Pizan's works for their ends while minimizing her troubling dimensions. The English king and queen hoped to make the most of the symbolic resources of Elizabeth Barton's spirituality while evading associated symbolic costs.

Watt observes, "Henry VIII's apparent acceptance of Barton, despite her troublesome revelations, may have reflected his continuing sympathies with the old order."[66] Henry certainly did have "continuing sympathies with the old order"; indeed, as we have seen, the old order provided much grist for his representational mill. Elizabeth Barton's revelations did, however, finally get too troublesome, and her own connections with the old order do much to elucidate why this was so. Her revelation of 1532 transformed a longstanding aspect of female Eucharistic piety into political polemic.[67] She mobilized religious tradition in a way that was quite detrimental for the king's attempts to cloak innovation in the guise of tradition and to portray a dramatic break with the past as a return to a correct, originary state of affairs.[68]

The revelation of 1532 suggested that Henry VIII was not merely unworthy to occupy a sacerdotal role as God's vicar and Christ's legitimate heir on earth to be obeyed, as Coverdale claims, by prelates and popes, but he was in fact not even worthy to receive the body of Christ produced by another priest. Rather than being God's image on earth, and the Head of the Church that is the body of Christ, Henry had been separated from that body altogether, and so was less than a lowly nun.[69] Far from being the divinely ordained recipient of sacred *imperium* and head of a holy English empire like the Holy Roman Empire ruled by his nemesis Charles V, he was not even a legitimate king of England, having been in effect excommunicated by the revelation (something that happened soon enough afterward by the pope's hand).[70]

The wording of the Treason Act of 1535, passed the year following Elizabeth Barton's execution, demonstrates just how highly Henry valued the place of the symbolic in politics, and it highlights just how seriously transgressive Elizabeth Barton's revelations were. The act declares it to be high treason, not surprisingly, to "wish, will, or desire by words or writing, or by any craft imagine, invent, practice, or attempt any bodily harm" to the person of the king, queen, and their heirs apparent. It also declares the crime of high treason to include any efforts "to deprive them of their dignity, title or name of their royal estates, or *slanderously and maliciously* publish and pronounce, by express writing or words, that the King our sovereign lord should be heretic, schismatic, tyrant, infidel or usurper of the crown."[71] Elizabeth Barton's revelation of 1532 did nearly all of these, depriving Henry of the dignity, title, and name to which he laid claim and portraying him as a heretic, schismatic, infidel, and illegitimate king. While William Peto might have suggested similar things in his sermon, the form (a divine revelation), the source (a professed nun renowned for sanctity), and the timing (at the moment of Henry VIII's publication of his important successes in France) all made Elizabeth Barton's declaration of God's disapproval far more symbolically damaging and so more politically detrimental. The fact that Elizabeth Barton's revelation of 1532 is recounted in great detail in the Act of Attainder, from which the description of it given above is taken, foregrounds the vision's symbolically destructive force.

The elaborate machinations undertaken to attaint and execute Elizabeth Barton reveal Henry's need to separate her from the traditions of medieval female sanctity which were clearly still a powerful force to be reckoned with and which ultimately proved so dangerous to his religiopolitical efforts. The cloister could not in the end provide Henry with even the partial, temporary solution that it had provided in the 1521 edition of the *City of Ladies*, because Elizabeth's connection to the cloister and all it represented was a fundamental aspect of the obstacles she offered to Henry's representational success. As we have seen, while Isabel of Castile embraced elements of medieval female spirituality to craft models of queenship that allowed her strong political agency, Juan Luis Vives still envisioned traditional female piety as a sort of antidote to the unnerving ramifications of that very queenship. Henry's position was more difficult than Vives's. Henry could not simply invoke tradition, because Elizabeth Barton had its valuable symbolic resources too firmly in her grasp. His strategy had to be, in effect, the opposite of Vives's; his attempt at retaining what was valuable in medieval female spirituality while minimizing what was damaging had failed, so rather than mobilizing female holiness, he had to destroy it. He could not afford to let Elizabeth Barton follow in the footsteps of Isabel of Castile as a successful exploiter of female spirituality in supporting the cause of Isabel's daughter Katherine of Aragon. Much as he had dissolved the monasteries, Henry VIII had to "dissolve" the threatening embodiment of female piety that was Elizabeth Barton.

The insistence in the official charges against Elizabeth Barton that her revelations were feigned, really originating with her spiritual advisors, underscores the ongoing symbolic value of female holiness, since Barton's opponents felt the need to try to remove it from the equation altogether. The official charges against Barton and Capon's sermon both place power back in the hands of men, so diminishing the potency of the threat by transforming the symbolically dangerous voice of a woman speaking God's words into the treasonous, but merely temporal—and therefore so much more easily counteracted—words of men. The charges begin, "Edward Bocking, D. D., frequently railed against the King's marriage before the 'false nun of St. Sepulchre's,' whose ghostly father he was. She, to please him, feigned to have a revelation from God" (*L and P*, vol. 7, no. 72). Capon preached that before Elizabeth "heard the said Dr. Bocking rail and jest like a frantic person against the King's Grace" she "all the time of her abode at Aldington . . . meddled not with the King's Grace's marriage, his reign, or his realm, neither with the acts of the King's Grace's parliament, neither yet she spake any word of maintenance of heresies within this realm."[72] Such erasure was necessary to enable Henry's symbolic alchemy to proceed unimpeded by a competing locus of divine authority and contrary visions of traditional religion and English kingship.

To the same end of destroying the foundations of Elizabeth Barton's holiness and transforming her into something more manageable, Capon used a technique reminiscent of that employed against Joan of Arc by her interrogators as well as by Henrician "reformers" in the visitations leading up to the Dissolution of the Monasteries: he repeatedly called Barton's chastity into question. He implied that she and Bocking engaged in an improper, apparently sexual, relationship, saying, "And she came with the said Bocking's servants to Canterbury in an evening; and Dr. Bocking brought her to the said Priory of St. Sepulchre's in the morning."[73] Capon also suggested that she engaged in other sexual misconduct when she violated the enclosure to which she was subject as a nun. He declared that she frightened her sisters by pretending to be "troubled and vexed with the devil" so that she "thereby might walk abroad in the night without controllment of any of them"; furthermore, "as her own maid hath confessed, she used twice or thrice a week to go out of her cell secretly, and to be absent for an hour and some times more, when she perceived her sisters in their deep sleep. And it is supposed that then she went not about the saying of her Pater Noster!"[74]

The methods chosen for Elizabeth Barton's humiliation and execution resonate with this deeply felt need to destroy her symbolically as well as bodily so that Henry's construction of himself as a divine English monarch and his realms as a holy English empire might avoid challenge. Just as Elizabeth Barton's revelations spread far and wide, so too her condemnation and the denial of her holiness had to be broadly disseminated. Elizabeth's public penance, along with the sermon preached against her, were, as I mentioned, enacted in both London and Canterbury. Initially, plans had been laid to perform this spectacle in every town in the realm.[75] Such an undertaking proved too overwhelming even for the powerful Henrician propaganda machine, so instead "it was decreed that a proclamation to the effect of the Act should be made throughout the realm."[76]

The way in which Elizabeth Barton was put to death represents a physical enactment of the verbal accusations of impurity present in Capon's sermon. As Watt points out, "Until the late seventeenth century, the appropriate form of execution in England for women found guilty of treason was burning at the stake . . . ; consequently, it is likely that Barton's death by public hanging was intended to be understood as a symbolic act, with her body shown to be vulnerable, broken, and therefore impure."[77] The female body, the intactness of which provided such a valuable symbolic resource in medieval female spirituality, was, in the method of Elizabeth Barton's execution, irrevocably violated to destroy that locus of value since Henry could not finally reframe it and turn it to his benefit.

Mary Tudor's "St. Elizabeth of Aldington"

For Henry VIII, constructing and then executing Elizabeth Barton as an embodiment of corrupt, Catholic femininity provided the necessary foil for the construction of masculine, Protestant, imperial identity. Her threats to his representational program were very like the ones that Joan of Arc had posed for his Lancastrian and earlier Tudor forebears, and Elizabeth met a correspondingly similar fate. The similarities in Joan's and Elizabeth's stories continue beyond their executions. Joan underwent a posthumous rehabilitation process every bit as implicated in secular politics as her condemnation had been. Elizabeth Barton too enjoyed a politically motivated transformation from harlot to holy woman after her death.

Although Henry VIII could not turn Elizabeth's brand of female spirituality to his benefit, his daughter Mary Tudor could. The Act of Attainder in which Elizabeth's revelation concerning the king's mass at Calais is recorded also reports another of God's revelations to Elizabeth. God told her that "the said Lady Catherine should prosper and do well, and that her issue, the Lady Mary, the King's daughter, should prosper and reign in the kingdom and have many friends to sustain and maintain her."[78] God also told Elizabeth that "no man should fear but she [Mary Tudor] should have succour and help enough, that no man should put her from her right that she was born into" (*L and P*, vol. 7, no. 72). When Mary Tudor came to the throne in 1554, her accession was "inextricably associated in men's minds" with these prophecies, which did much to support Mary's claims to return true rule along with the true Roman religion. [79]

Furthermore, Elizabeth Barton's form of medieval female spirituality harmonized well with Mary's self-representational strategies. Mary and her supporters adopted the iconography of the Virgin Mary "from the time she was a young princess."[80] The court poet Henry Parker called her "the secunde mary of this wo[r]lde," and John Proctor's 1549 attack on Protestants entitled *The Fal of the Late Arrian* "contains a woodcut of the Annunciation facing his address to the princess as the 'high resemblaunce and perfect imitation' of the Virgin Mary (A Iv-2v)."[81] This woodcut had originally appeared in the 1531 edition of John Lydgate's *Life of Our Lady*. That an image used to illustrate Lydgate's *Life of Our Lady*, that monumental tribute to characteristically medieval Marian devotion, was so readily transferred to Mary I highlights Mary's use of an explicitly medieval style of spirituality to proclaim her royal identity. A ballad from Mary's reign further emphasizes the importance of medieval religion, especially female sanctity, in her representational strategies. The ballad, entitled "An AVE MARIA in commendation of our most Vertuous Queene," begins: "Haile Quene of England, of most worthy fame / For vertue, for wisdome, for mercy & grace." The queen is also called "mirrour of mercifulnesse," and she is addressed as an intercessor for the love of whom "vnto this lande our Lorde . . . / Hath of his mercy most mercifull bene."[82]

Like Isabel of Castile, Mary was cast as a saintly queen. As we have seen, the textually "canonized" Joan of Arc of *La Poncella de Francia* added legitimacy to Isabel's political authority, suggesting by association Isabel's own holy status. Not surprisingly, Mary I and her supporters adopted the same strategy employed earlier by Charles the Bold and Margaret of York on Colette of Corbie's behalf and later by Franco on Isabel of Castile's behalf. Hoping to have a politically useful medieval holy woman officially given the title of saint, Mary and her advisors, including Cardinal Pole and Thomas Goldwell the younger, "considered petitioning the Pope" for Elizabeth Barton's canonization. As Neame observes, "Had the Queen's reign lasted, England might have gained a Saint Elizabeth of Aldington."[83]

6

Dissolution, Diaspora, and Defining Englishness: Syon in Exile and Elizabethan Politics

Exile and English Identity

Elizabeth Barton spoke in support of an oppositional vision of divinely ordained political authority in England. She thus participated in the sort of intellectual exile that Edward Said attributes to the "nay-sayers," to those "individuals at odds with their society."[1] Although her prophecies were undercut by her (likely forced) recantation and her voice silenced in her execution, the exilic voice of opposition itself lived on, embodied in, among others, the members of the Brigittine community of Syon, a house with which Elizabeth Barton had important connections.[2] In the periods after the instatement of the Oath of Supremacy and the dissolution of the monasteries under Henry VIII and the reinstatement and redissolution under Elizabeth I, intellectual exile became, for many English Catholics, physical exile.[3] A significant group of this English Catholic diaspora consisted of members of the Brigittine community of Syon.[4] This flight to the Continent solidified Syon's commitment to an oppositional vision of English religion and English identity grounded in medieval traditions.

Syon's experience of exile emphasizes that to some extent under Henry VIII, and to even greater extent under Elizabeth I, medieval religion became the displaced native Other of the official, "colonizing" Protestant religio-political system as religious and secular power become more closely joined—at least in official terms—than perhaps ever before. The relationship of Catholicism and Protestantism is more complicated than a simple binary pair, however. After the rather stringent policies of the reign of the Protestant Edward VI, many of the Catholic religious practices that had been made official once again under Mary I continued generally to be allowed to exist through the first dozen years or so of Elizabeth I's reign.[5]

Peter Lake and Michael Questier suggest that even in the 1580s and 1590s, "Catholics went about their business" with "relative impunity" as a result of the "uneven administration of the recusancy statutes, and indeed the ideological and political disagreements and incoherences which lay behind both the drafting and the enforcing of those laws."[6] To make matters of religion and identity even more complex, post-Reformation English Catholicism was strongly connected to pre-Reformation religion. Christopher Haigh claims persuasively that "the deepest foundations of post-Reformation Catholicism were medieval, in both its piety and its structure."[7] Furthermore, Alexandra Walsham has found a great deal of common ground, unexpected though its existence might be, between early modern Protestants and their Catholic predecessors.[8]

The history of the relationships between English Catholics and Protestants demonstrates that what each group claimed as "English" identity was characterized by the sort of ambivalent "interdependence and . . . mutual construction of . . . subjectivities" typical of colonizer / colonized relationships.[9] Catholicism in the early modern period was not simply "the great unifying Other for the English state and nation."[10] The Elizabethan regime both defined itself against Catholicism and incorporated elements of medieval religion into its representational schemes, competing with English Catholics to "own" traditions and to mobilize them in polemically useful ways. Medieval female spirituality continued to play vital roles in the political processes by which models of authority and national identity were put into action on a contemporary European stage. As the story of Syon in the sixteenth and seventeenth century illustrates, these processes included campaigns both textual and military as well as battles to "own" history.

Syon Nuns, Textual Battles, and Catholic Plots

After Henry VIII dissolved their foundation, nuns from Syon carefully preserved their distinctively English community first in Antwerp, where they found refuge with the Canonesses of St. Augustine.[11] Then, when additional nuns who had been living in an unofficial community in England with Agnes Jordan joined them on the Continent following Jordan's death, they all moved to the Brigittine house of Maria Troon in Termonde, Flanders. In both Antwerp and Termonde, the Syon nuns lived separately and held services separately from their hosts. A contemporary account of their stay in Termonde indicates that the English Brigittines "remained . . . in a distinct quarter of the monastery, making as it were two monasteries, one of the Flemish, the other of English nuns, each with their own different Abbess."[12] When Mary I came to the throne in 1553, they were granted a charter of restoration and returned home to England.[13]

The fulfillment of the exile's dream of homecoming, and the return to what the religious of Syon saw as an authentically English religio-political system, were, however, quite short lived. Upon Elizabeth's accession, the Brigittines entered a much more extended period of exile on the Continent, and during this second exile, Syon's political involvement became far more direct, and even more dangerous, than it had been during the Henrician era. As the stories of Elizabeth Sanders and Marie Champney reveal, Syon's "women of God" became "women of arms," returning illegally to England to work for the Catholic cause, allying themselves with Spain and the Catholic League, and quite possibly even engaging in plots against the queen. The cases of Elizabeth Sanders and Marie Champney emblematize the ways in which Syon involved itself in the conflict concerning "the legitimacy of the Elizabethan state . . . and . . . the whole structure of the English monarchy as the English reformation had recreated it."[14]

Elizabeth, a nun of Syon, was the sister of Dr. Nicholas Sanders.[15] Nicholas Sanders served as one of Philip II of Spain's almoners to the English Catholic community in exile in Louvain. He was also one of the leading Catholic intellectuals of his day, writing such treatises as *The Rise and Growth of the Anglican Schism* and *De visibili monarchia ecclesiae*, a defense of the bull of 1570 excommunicating Elizabeth. His voice was a strong one in the conflict over the ownership of history. As Sandra Johnson has observed, "The first three books Sanders published were part of a specific debate over who controlled tradition."[16] His opposition to Protestant rule went beyond rhetoric, though. He supported the Northern Rising of 1569, and after the 1570 papal bull "Sanders was the only exile to write political tracts urging rebellion. Sanders' support for military activity was immediate and public."[17] By the early 1570s, he was embracing the cause of Mary Stuart.[18] In doing so, he was "among the first to say that the only hope for English Catholicism was a foreign invasion."[19] He proposed that Mary Stuart and Archduke Ferdinand of Austria should marry, and that Philip II should engage in military efforts to put Ferdinand on the English throne.[20] Again, his interest in overthrowing Elizabeth went beyond the realm of words; in 1579 he took part in the failed papal military expedition in Ireland to "incite the chiefs to rise under the papal banner against the English government." He died for this cause in Ireland in 1581.[21]

Nicholas Sanders' sister Elizabeth was sent covertly from Malines to England in 1578, along with several other Syon nuns. The purpose of their voyage was reportedly to escape Protestant hostility in the Low Countries and to raise alms for the community abroad. While the nuns were successful in obtaining alms, there is, I would argue, a certain irony in claiming to seek safety from Protestant hostility by returning to England where the penal laws were in effect. Thus, it seems to me worth considering that motives beyond that of self preservation may have prompted Syon to send these nuns—especially Elizabeth Sanders—back to England at this particular juncture.[22]

Elizabeth sailed from Gravelines to Billingsgate, London, and entered England safely; Marie Champney and Anne Stapleton likewise managed undetected entries.[23] Once in England, Elizabeth went to Fulham, probably to the house of Thomas and Magdalen Heath, where she was supposed to meet with the rest of the nuns, but they had not arrived. Anne Stapleton did finally make it to Fulham, but she was seriously ill and died there in December, 1578. In order to avoid capture in the post-mortem inquest, Elizabeth went to her sister's house in Abingdon, and then on to Francis Yates's house at Lyford, where she remained until the middle of 1580. When this situation became unsafe, Elizabeth Sanders again took refuge with her family, going to the house of one of her sisters (also called Elizabeth), who was married to Henry Pitts. It is through her association with Elizabeth Pitts and her son William that Elizabeth Sanders became involved in dangerous, and extremely subversive, political activity—the distribution of Edmund Campion's "Challenge."

Elizabeth's possession and distribution of this notorious text link her to a chain of well-known members of the recusant community. The copies of the "Challenge" that came into the hands of Elizabeth Sanders and William Pitts originated with Thomas Pounde, at whose urging Edmund Campion wrote the text in the first place.[24] While in Marshalsea Prison, Pounde wrote letters to Bishop Aylmer and Privy Council member Sir Christopher Hatton, letters that "convinced the Council that a conspiracy was under way."[25] Pounde was subsequently transported to solitary confinement at the castle of Bishop Stortford, but before the transfer he managed to pass on a copy of Campion's text that made its way to Benjamin Tichborne; Tichborne then gave copies to William Horde, who sent copies to several people, including Pitts and Elizabeth Sanders.[26] William Pitts passed along a copy of the "Challenge" to "one Lichepoole,"[27] who was caught with it, and, upon apprehension, confessed where he had gotten it, leading authorities to the Pitts's house. William Pitts eluded capture, but the authorities found "there a syster of Doctour Saunderes, who is a professed nunne, and diverse unlawfull bookes."[28] Elizabeth Sanders was promptly taken into custody and imprisoned at Winchester.[29]

Upon capture, Elizabeth's response to the magistrates' questioning was "that she was a woman and a nun, that the first reason was proof enough that she would not disturb the kingdom and the second to let them know that she was a Catholic."[30] When Elizabeth invoked her female sex and her status as a professed nun to suggest her harmlessness, she played upon received, idealized versions of both womanhood and religious life. Her self-defensive, gendered claims of non-threatening piety resemble the creation of an identity of devout, politically disengaged queenship for Isabel of Castile in the *Jardín des nobles donzellas*, as discussed in chapter four. As was the case for Isabel, though, Elizabeth's declared identity was something of a smokescreen. Isabel was certainly quite involved in hands-on, politico-military activity, and Elizabeth Sanders was not as far outside this sphere of action as she would have liked her captors to believe.[31]

Elizabeth Sanders's rather disingenuous protestation that her sex would prevent her, Catholic though she was, from disturbing the kingdom resembles Campion's protest in the "Challenge" that he had no political mission, only a religious one. He declares, "I never had mind, and am strictly forbidden by our Father that sent me, to deal in any respect with matters of State or Policy of this realm, as things which appertain not to my vocation, and from which I do gladly restrain and sequester my thoughts."[32] However much Campion, Sanders, and other Catholics might have wanted to separate matters of Church and State, in England in the 1570s and 1580s it was entirely impossible to do so. James Holleran observes that even though the missionaries "were ordered neither to involve themselves in political matters nor to speak against the queen," all the "elaborate instructions and detailed advice" that they were given "could not alter the fact that Pope Pius V had excommunicated Elizabeth and all who obeyed her laws. The missionaries themselves knew well that this was the petard on which they would be hoisted."[33] Furthermore, the very claim that Church and State were separate spheres, upon which Campion's argument for his political disengagement rests, was a deeply political one to make. Lake and Questier point out, "A good deal of the struggle between the Elizabethan regime and its Romish subjects and opponents centered on rival constructions of those different domains and powers and the lines of demarcation that should stand between them."[34] Much as the timing of Anne d'Orléans's "mission" to Edward IV suggests that she had political as well as spiritual aims, so too the Jesuits' timing in launching their mission to England strongly implies a political agenda. In 1580, the turmoil occasioned by the Anjou Match was at its height, and many Catholics believed the time was ripe to try to better their position in England.[35]

Campion was, then, deeply engaged in political activities, and his "Challenge" is without doubt a political document, whether or not he acknowledged these facts or indeed was even consciously aware of them.[36] To distribute this text was thus also to participate in a serious type of political "disturbance," in spite of Elizabeth Sanders's protestations; indeed, doing so went a long way towards making this women of God into a woman of arms. To Protestant officials such action would have closely resembled the military efforts in which Nicholas Sanders was involved at the very time his sister was captured and interrogated in prison. Such Protestant attitudes to a certain extent stemmed from polemical efforts to stir up anti-Catholic feeling by allying religious dissent with threats of treason, invasion, and deposition.[37] There seems to have been at least some germ of truth behind Protestant anxieties, however, since Catholic writers also repeatedly likened their textual campaigns to military ones, suggesting an awareness, at least on some level, that their undertakings were not purely spiritual. Sir Francis Englefield, who was closely involved with the Syon community in exile, wrote in 1586, "In stede therfore of the sword, which we cannot obtayne, we must fight with paper and pennes, which can not be taken from us."[38] Similarly, a ballad published with a Catholic account of Edmund Campion's martyrdom speaks of fighting "with word & not with sword."[39]

An examination of the text of Campion's "Challenge" alongside the Protestant response to it provides insights into the overlap of textual assaults and politico-military action, illuminating the ways in which Elizabeth Sanders's activities were politically disruptive. Campion's "Challenge" is fundamentally an invitation to Protestants to debate and a declaration of the inevitable triumph of the truth of the Catholic faith ("Challenge," 180). It also proclaims Campion's fervent belief that, if only the Queen would listen to his arguments, she would change her mind on matters of religion ("Challenge," 181). Such assertions alone were surely enough to rouse the ire of government authorities. On more than one occasion, though, the "Challenge" resorts to militaristic language resembling that of

Englefield and the anonymous ballad. For instance, in proposing a debate with Protestant doctors and masters, Campion describes the debate as battle, saying, "I am to sue most humbly and instantly for the combat with all and every of them" ("Challenge," 180). In the first of the nine articles, Campion also declares that he has been "vowed now these viii years into the Religion of the Societe of Jhesus." He continues, "Hereby I have taken upon me a special kind of warfare under the banner of obedience" ("Challenge," 179).

Metaphorical descriptions of the religious life in terms of battle have a long tradition; the prologue to the Rule of St. Benedict proclaims, "This message of mine is for you, then, if you are ready to give up your own will, once and for all, and armed with the strong and noble weapons of obedience to do battle for the true King, Christ the Lord."[40] However, such a description of monastic life cannot escape an accretion of meanings beyond the metaphorical in a sixteenth-century English context. In his account of Syon's history, discussed in more detail below, Parsons describes Syon's monastic life of prayer and contemplation in military terms that directly suggest links among metaphorical battle, "fighting with words," and armed endeavors. He writes of Syon and Sheen:

So that these two monasteries of religious persons giving themselves to prayer and contemplation, are Moses, Aaron, and Hur, lifting up their hands to God for redress of their country, and for victory over the enemies of the Church of God. And in like manner the five seminaries perform the office of Joshua and the other valiant captains of the People of God against the Amalakites, that is, against the heretics. God in His infinite Mercy give them all both Religious and Seminaries, their desired victories.[41]

For the Jesuits, praying, writing and distributing texts, and participating in armed combat were perceived as analogous activities undertaken in service of a common goal.

Meredith Hanmer's response to the "Challenge," printed in 1581, reveals the depth of Protestant concerns that verbal assaults might become armed attacks, correspondingly illustrating the Protestants' own politicized textual maneuvering to manage the threats. One of Hanmer's strategies to rebut Campion's claims is to denigrate the Jesuit order as one only recently established. He calls it "a fond order, neuer heard of, the space of fifteene hundred and odde yeares after Christ," and he casts aspersions on its founder, "a certain Souldier by name Ignatius Layole."[42] In one passage, Hanmer condemns the superstitious and false practices of all religious

orders, but adds, "You for nouelties sake haue found out a newe rule, and
ye lousiest order of all. They had some colour, either they fathered their
inuention vppon the virgine Mary, or upon some sainct. You addict your
selfe to a maymed souldier, and brynge forth vnto us an haulting religion"
(*Great Bragge*, 5b). Hanmer's repeated references to Ignatius Loyola as a
soldier, and an unsuccessful one at that, support his case that the Jesuit
order, with its new, base, and secular origins, is rotten at its very roots.
They also suggest that the order is in some respect military in nature and
so inflame suspicions that the Jesuits were engaged in a politico-military
mission against England. Hanmer comfortingly asserts, however, that this
mission is certain to mirror its founder's military failures.

Perceptions that Catholic textual battle and actual fighting are intimately related, and are both doomed to failure, emerge strongly in
Hamer's frequent connections of Campion's "enterprise" with the papal
military expedition in Ireland defeated shortly before his text's publication.
In responding to Campion's claim to have nothing to do with matters of
state or policy, Hanmer declares that, since Campion is "a Romanist, a
fauorer of ye Pope," he is necessarily involved in papal efforts to stir up
"mortall warres," to depose kings, and to take territory unlawfully; "the
late enterprise in Ireland is a witnes of part thereof," he claims (*Great
Bragge*, 7b). Similarly, in espousing the futility and falsity of Campion's
claims, Hanmer says, "Beholde the fall of your Mates in Ireland and such
as the Pope had blessed in a bad howre and directed thither to his great
shame and their biter destruction" (*Great Bragge*, 25b-26a).

As Hanmer's response to the "Challenge" demonstrates, Protestants
clearly suspected that verbal "fighting" and spiritual "battles" were not the
only sorts they might have to face, and they suspected that those who
authored or distributed such texts as the "Challenge" could equally be involved with plans for military action. Such concerns did have some basis
in fact, as Nicholas Sanders' involvement in both the authorship of "seditious texts" and the failed papal endeavors in Ireland demonstrate. They
may equally have some justification in relation to Elizabeth Sanders and
the Syon nuns who returned with her to England, since, in spite of her
claims that she was a nondisruptive nun, Elizabeth Sanders was at the very
least participating as a footsoldier in a textual campaign by disseminating
one of that campaign's key weapons.

Like Elizabeth Barton before her, Elizabeth Sanders attracted a fair
amount of official attention. Part of this anxious response was tied to her
kinship with Nicholas Sanders, who was such a thorn in the side of the

Protestants, but records suggest that Elizabeth was judged to be an independent political threat as well. [43] In prison she was examined by such notable figures as Sir Henry Radcliff, Sir William Kingsmill, Sir Richard Norton, and the bishop of Winchester. In the report of the examination to the Privy Council, they tell of her possession of "certain lewd and forbydden bookes" as well as of "the copye of a supplication, protestation, or challendge." They go on to say, "we finde . . . grete dissimulation and varietie in her, and also grete obstinancie in her perseverance of her profession."[44] She "was closely questioned about priests, about the support Syon received from England, why she had come to this country, etc.,"[45] and the Privy Council's report on her questioning indicates that "the said Elizabeth remaineth obstinate in refusing to confesse where she was harbored since she came into England, and where she had that seditious challenge about her."[46]

Events that occurred after the Abbess of Syon ordered the sisters in England to return to the Continent show, furthermore, that Elizabeth Sander was both capable of shrewd, independent political action and able to turn expectations of female religious identity to her benefit, as she attempted to do upon her original capture. She managed multiple escapes from prison, and, on one of these occasions, she was told by three priests "that she must return to the prison 'and ther abyde tyll God should delyver her by some better meane.'"[47] She did return, but her honesty in doing so, and her subsequent model conduct, so impressed her jailers that eventually "the Governor's wife told her that she might leave when she liked, the Governor apparently giving a tacit consent."[48] So, she departed once again, benefiting from the perceived qualities of the Syon nuns in England praised by A. Dolm, in a letter written to Douai in 1578: "passinge great constancy in theyre fayth, singular modesty in ther behaviour and wise and discrete answers."[49] Elizabeth Sanders, disguised as a servant, at last managed to leave England, and, after a nine year absence, she rejoined the Syon community in May, 1587, in Rouen, where they had moved while she was in England.

While there is no definite evidence to indicate that Elizabeth Sanders was actually engaged in helping to plan military action, given her connection to Nicholas Sanders and the fact that she and her sisters were sent to England in 1578, just in advance of the papal military expedition to Ireland in 1579, it remains a tantalizing possibility. There is, however, evidence in the *Life of Sister Marie Champney* (London, British Library MS Add. 18,650) to hint that the nuns may have been involved in plotting to depose Queen

Elizabeth by force. Marie was one of the nuns sent to England with Elizabeth Sanders, and her entry into religion, episodes from her life with the
community, and (in extensive hagiographic detail) her "good death" were
recorded by an anonymous author.[50] At one point, before the author tells
of the nuns' voyage to England and their tribulations there, he or she
recounts a conversation between Marie and an unnamed male speaker. In
a formulation that heightens the significance of Parsons's description of
Syon's prayers as a sort of "military action," this speaker says, "But nowe
good virgin . . . thou must praye for the speedie conversion of Englande
by name, . . . and by name also for gods cheife prisoner (you knowe what
good Ladye I meane) that shee may be fullye delivered out of miscreantes
handes, to be an instrument for it, as to many mens hope and expectacion
it seemeth likelye."[51] Marie responds to the male speaker's command, "O
sweete Ladye . . . to remember her by name likewise that I will. . . . it is
for such a Susanna, by whome (for her heavie crosse [)] in deede we maie
hope for some grete worke of god, to all our comfortes, when we ar at the
lowest" (*Life*, fol. 8r).

   Given that the date of this conversation had to be after 1569 when
Marie was professed, and before 1578 when she was sent to England, the
good lady who is "God's chief prisoner" and the hope of many for the conversion of England must be Mary Stuart, who had been taken into English
custody in 1568. Additionally, the allusive as well as elusive narrative elements of the speaker's command to pray by name for one explicitly not
named are characteristic of language produced by and about Mary Stuart.[52]
Jayne Lewis has observed that "Mary menaced so many of her contemporaries because together her blood and faith did indeed seem to put her
everywhere, or at least at the intersection of several places which included
England, Scotland, France and, more remotely, the Catholic powers of
Spain and Italy."[53] The Syon nuns too inhabited precisely such intersections. Many of the Syon nuns in exile on the Continent had connections
to prominent Catholic families in England, and the community had close
ties to the Spanish court; they were therefore advantageously situated to
support those who opposed Elizabeth I in the name of Mary Stuart.

   The suggestions of involvement with Marian plots inherent in the conversation between Marie Champney and the male speaker intensify when
the author inserts a personal remembrance. The author interjects that
Marie's remarks "made me to thinke of certayne wordes, which I hearde
her speake, how she had hearde by some secret hope of such a thinge a
longe tyme spoken of in their house, since their firste suppression: that

their order shoulde be erected againe in the northe partes of Englande who-
soever shoulde liue to see it" (*Life*, fol. 7v-8r). The idea that Syon, whose
foundation had been on the banks of the Thames, should be re-established
in the north of England links the community with the persistent Catholic
opposition to Protestant rule in the North. That Marie reportedly says such
a possibility had been discussed since the order's first suppression under
Henry VIII recalls both the Pilgrimage of Grace during his reign and the
more recent Northern Rising of 1569, which Nicholas Sanders supported.

The connections between Mary Stuart and the Brigittines evident in
the *Life of Marie Champney* are suggestive in other ways as well. The nuns
of Syon were not only well placed to help Mary's cause, but they also
embodied a gendered and religious threat quite similar to that posed by
Mary. The similarity of the situations of Mary Stuart and the Syon nuns
clarifies the symbolic as well as practical problems that Elizabeth Sanders
and her fellow nuns caused. Lewis's observation that "Mary stood for an
England ominously other than the one Elizabeth mirrored back to it, its
borders dangerously open rather than tidily closed, its texture of religious
faith oppressively Catholic instead of autonomously Protestant"[54] might
equally be applied to the religious of Syon. Once the nuns entered England
as Mary did, they too "became paranoia's catalyst" and "ignited fears" that
England "might be engulfed by . . . Catholic interests . . . from within."[55]
Just as Elizabeth Barton did in the reign of Henry VIII, these nuns suggested an alternative version of English identity, one that, in Elizabethan
England, was relentlessly subjected to efforts to make it "Other." Elizabeth
Barton and Marie Champney demonstrate, though, that this "Other" was
always uncomfortably close to home, especially for a queen who had herself coopted medieval history and medieval female spirituality in her representational efforts.

Owning the Middle Ages

The case of the nuns sent to England was not the only instance in which
Syon was suspected of participating in attempts to overthrow England's
Protestant government. In 1594, following the submission of Rouen to
the newly Catholic Henry IV, the Syon community, which was closely
allied with the Catholic League and so not prepared to accept Henry IV
as king, found themselves in a dangerous situation. The community was
no longer welcome in Rouen, where they had spent several years after their

flight from the Low Countries. While deciding upon their course of action, the Confessor General Seth Foster received "a report that the English Ambassador was coming to Rouen, with what object . . . [he] could not discover." Foster knew "Queen Elizabeth's anger against her Catholic subjects abroad," and he was aware of "the intimate relations which now existed between the English and French Governments." The confessor general accordingly "feared that the visit boded no good to Syon."[56]

Foster had good reason to fear the queen's anger and to suspect that the ambassador's impending visit likely promised trouble for Syon. In addition to sharing in the general hostility toward English Catholics abroad, Syon was suspected of particularly nefarious treachery. A rumor was circulating (possibly started by the English ambassador) "that the Bridgettines had in their possession £10,000, the blood money promised by the King of Spain to Rodrigo Lopez for the removal of Queen Elizabeth by poison."[57] Lopez, the queen's physician, had confessed on the rack to "having entertained a suggestion to poison the Queen for the sum of 50,000 ducats but only with the design of cheating the King of Spain."[58] While the Syon community was in the process of fleeing from Rouen, he was in prison awaiting execution.

Elizabeth Sanders did participate in textual assaults on Protestant government in England and was connected—at least through her brother if not by other means—with military action undertaken against Elizabeth; furthermore, the *Life of Sister Marie Champney* hints at Syon's involvement with plots to depose Elizabeth in favor of Mary Stuart. In this case, however, there is nothing whatsoever to suggest Syon's involvement with the Lopez plot. Indeed, Fletcher points out, "neither at the trial nor in any records of the time were the Bridgettines mentioned as having any connection with Lopez. On the contrary the blood money was said to be in the hands of certain conspirators at Brussels."[59] Why, then, was Syon singled out for such a damning accusation?

Part of the reason may lie in Syon's close ties to the Spanish, so hated in England in the years after 1588. When they were forced to leave England under Elizabeth I, Syon began a long period of intimate association with the rulers of Spain. This relationship began when Jane Dormer, the English wife of the Duke of Feria, the Spanish ambassador to England, interceded with Elizabeth to persuade her to allow her husband to take the newly dispossessed religious with him as he retired from his ambassadorship. Some accounts say that "Elizabeth gave a grudging consent" out of a desire to keep good relations with Spain.[60] However, others say that the "request was officially denied."[61] In any case, the religious did reach the Continent, and Philip II of Spain did become one of their most important supporters, granting a yearly pension of 1,200 florins for the community, thanks to the Duchess of Feria's request.[62] Although it went unpaid at times, the Spanish pension was a major source of income for Syon throughout the years of exile on the Continent. Upon leaving Rouen in 1594, the religious of Syon made their way to Lisbon, which was at that time under the control of the King of Spain; the community remained in that city until it returned to England in the nineteenth century.

Guilt by close association with the Spanish crown was only part of what led to official Elizabethan hostility toward Syon. While the religious of Syon were *suspected* of abetting Spanish Catholic plots to remove Elizabeth from the throne, they indisputably *were* engaged in rewriting history in ways that conflicted with accepted Tudor Protestant versions. Elizabeth's Protestant and Syon's Catholic accounts of the past reveal the fraught "process of appropriation and reappropriation, of interpretation and reinterpretation, whereby . . . 'the traditional' . . . [was] taken over by a variety of ideological factions and fractions,"[63] the same process we find at work in the conflict between Henry VIII and Elizabeth Barton. Syon's histories also share something else with Elizabeth Barton's revelation of 1532. Her revelation profoundly called into question Henry VIII's strategies for self-representation, his "symbolic alchemy." Such symbolic processes were, if anything, even more important to Elizabeth I, and Syon's histories, like the earlier revelation, complicate and undermine official representational projects. Syon's alternative vision of the medieval past both reframed the nature of the relationship between England and Spain and called into question some of the most fundamental elements of Elizabethan triumphal narratives.

The competing interpretations of the past disseminated by Syon and Elizabeth's supporters are part of the "struggle for the control of some of the central ideological, rhetorical, and material weapons" used to forge English identity.[64] The rhetorical strategies used in claiming and defining England's medieval heritage evident in the writings of Syon and Elizabeth's supporters are rooted in the larger competition between Catholics and Protestants to appropriate ecclesiastical history. Norman Jones writes of the Catholic / Protestant conflict to "own" the past and its traditions, "It is hardly surprising that history became the common battleground where men of the Reformation met in violent intellectual warfare. . . . [H]istorical argument was the only weapon of reason that could dent the bastions of faith.["]65 And, as we have seen in the case of Hanmer and Campion, prevailing in textual battles was every bit as crucial as winning in armed combat.

One key skirmish in the battle for ownership of the medieval past was that for the right to claim the Lancastrian inheritance. An important element of Elizabeth's representational program was her identification with the Lancastrian line. She repeatedly pressed what John N. King calls the "incessant Tudor claim to Lancastrian descent" in order to emphasize the Tudor monarchs' legitimate inheritance of the English throne by blood.[66] Because the legitimacy of Elizabeth's own birth, and so her legitimacy to rule, were frequently challenged, the claim to Lancastrian heritage was particularly useful in her reign. One way in which Elizabethan representational efforts flaunted her Lancastrian ancestry was through the image of the Tudor rose tree, which invoked the iconography of the Tree of Jesse. In a woodcut border in John Stow's *Annales of England* (1600), the genealogy of the house of Tudor is depicted "as a rose tree rising from its stock, the sleeping figure of Edward III, to Queen Elizabeth."[67] As King notes, this image is "a redefinition of the Tudor rose tree from the title page of Edward Hall's *Union . . . of Lancaster and York* (1550; 2nd ed.); that plant grows upward from the recumbent figure of John of Gaunt to Henry VIII."[68]

A particularly interesting example of Elizabethan Lancastrianism appears in Richard Grafton's interpretations of the pageant series produced for Elizabeth's entry into London preceding her coronation. In his *Abridgement of the Chronicles of England*, Grafton reports that the "firste Pageant was the mariage of king henry the vii with Elizabeth the daughter of king Edward the iiii. Whereby the ii houses of Lancaster and yorke were united together."[69] Grafton then glosses the marriage of Henry VII and Elizabeth of York that effected this union as symbolizing "the coniunction and coupling together of our soveraigne Lady with the Gospell and veritie of Goddes holy woord, for the peaceable gouvernement of all her good subiectes."[70] This description firmly connects Queen Elizabeth to the Lancastrian line; it also suggests, through a sort of typological reading, that Elizabeth's Protestantism is prefigured not just by her father Henry VIII, with whom she took such pains to link herself,[71] but by her firmly Catholic grandfather Henry VII, founder of the Tudor dynasty. This quintessentially Lancastrian move of dramatically recasting the past (witness, for instance, Henry V's erasure of the deposition of Richard II by adopting him as a revered ancestor and father figure[72]) is especially significant. Earlier, one of Henry VII's strategies to solidify his claim to the throne "involved a formal effort to claim legitimacy and authority on the basis of his fealty to the pope in Rome."[73]

In the sixteenth and early seventeenth centuries, Syon produced several accounts of its history telling of its foundation and life in exile. These texts craft versions of the past and set up understandings of English identity that serve the cause of those opposed to Elizabeth's Protestant government, a stance particularly evident in their framing of Lancastrian history. One of these accounts is by Robert Parsons. Shortly after Syon arrived in Lisbon, the Confessor General Seth Foster sent information about the community and its travels to Parsons, who compiled a brief account of the community's foundation and wanderings.[74] Since the source for this account was information provided by a member of the community, and since the author was one so committed to the cause of restoring English Catholicism, it provides a valuable source for examining the ways in which the past could be strategically shaped to shake up the Tudor historical narratives that underwrote Protestant rule.

Parsons begins, naturally enough, with Syon's foundation by Henry V, immediately establishing the house's Lancastrian pedigree: "This monastery in England . . . was founded and very richly endowed by King Henry the Fifth, who was the second king of the House of Lancaster, and one of the most famous princes that ever was in England."[75] He goes on to emphasize that Henry V is famed not only for military skill and success but also "particularly for matters of religion and piety."[76] Parsons's narrative thus insists on the Lancastrian line's Catholic orthodoxy. Then, in a move that in some ways resembles Grafton's reading of the marriage of Henry VII and Elizabeth of York as a prefiguring of Elizabethan Protestant rule, Parsons turns the tables on Elizabethan imperialism by manipulating the past. He attaches the very sort of imperial language, so important to both Henry VIII and Elizabeth I in justifying their status of head of the English church, to Henry V, whose orthodox piety he has just extolled and who was, as Dale Hoak observes, the first to adopt the imperial crown.[77] Parsons ends his account of Syon's foundation by observing that Henry V "was so renowned that the historians of England call him the Alexander the Great of that isle."[78] In Parsons' account, Henry's example shows that true imperial greatness lies in embracing and defending, rather than denying, papal authority.

Indeed, for Parsons, Henry V's piety and power are enough to redeem, at least in a partial way, Henry VIII, who, in this as in all accounts Syon gives of its history, is depicted as the evil architect of their destruction. Parsons provides a rather curiously revised account of the dissolution in which he says that Syon's "great esteem and reputation," combined with "a certain reverence and respect which this king [Henry VIII] had to the great King Henry V," led Henry VIII to restrain himself from "casting down to the earth" Syon and Sheen as he did "all the other monasteries of England." Parsons continues, "although at length he did not spare them, yet they were the last against whom he executed his fury and madness; and even at their dissolution commanded that these two should not be pulled down but remain for the habitation of secular gentlemen.[79]

After outlining the course of Syon's peregrinations through the Low Countries and France, Parsons turns to their arrival in Lisbon. It is here that the subversive aspects of his interpretation of the Lancastrian heritage become most visible. He writes:

And now, considering the circumstances of these Religious, it certainly seems not to be without a mystery that by the particular Providence of God they have been brought through so many travels and banishment to the kingdom of Portugal, there to repose themselves securely within the protection of the descendants of the House of Lancaster and the blood royal of their founder King Henry the Fifth: for the kings of Portugal descend in a right line from the royal house of Lancaster.[80]

The logic of this passage strongly suggests that the true, legitimate heir of the house of Lancaster—and, by implication, the rightful occupant of the throne of England—was not the Protestant Tudor ruler who currently sat upon that throne but the Catholic monarch of Spain and Portugal.

The political implications of the emphasis on the Lancastrian line's continuance in Spain become even clearer in a document the community of Syon prepared during the reign of James I to present to the Infanta Maria, daughter of Philip III of Spain, when it was thought that she would marry Charles, Prince of Wales. Although this text was obviously written after Elizabeth's reign had ended, it recounts much the same story as Parsons's account does, revealing political stances and desires embraced by the community in the Tudor period. It also provides a glimpse into the nuns' own perspective on their history and their community's identity. The abbess and sisters, addressing the Infanta Maria, praise Mary I, daughter of Katherine of Aragon and wife of Philip II of Spain, as a blessed benefactor who "reduzio este convento de su destierro en Flandes"[81] ["resettled this convent following its exile in Flanders" (24)]. They go on to express their hope that the Infanta Maria, their expected savior, "lo redusiera esta

segunda vez de los Reynos estraños para adonde [e]stava otra vez dester-
rado" ["should resettle it a second time from the foreign kingdoms to
which it had again been exiled"] ("Petition," 12, 24). They stress that Syon's
"former home" ("su antiga Syon") was founded "por los Reales predeçessores destas dos serenissimas Marias" ["by the Royal predecessors of the
two Most Serene Marys"] ("Petition," 12, 24), again emphasizing the Lancastrian line's devolution onto Catholic, Spanish royalty. They subsequently
indicate their view that the Catholic, Spanish monarchs are the true Lancastrian heirs and, concomitantly, the right rulers of England. Thanking the
Spanish kings for their financial support, they write:

porque fultando la su dicha Real fundaçion *hecha y dotada por los Reys de Inglatierra
predeçeres de V. Magd.* como consta por los Anales del dicho Reyno todauia Nue-
stro Sñor no falto a estas sus sieruas de inspirar y tocar El Real pecho de V. Magd.
y de su Zelossissimo padre El Rey Phelippe segundo *como verdaderos descendientes
de los dichos Reys jnglezes sus fundadores dellas* Tomarlas a su quenta y sustentallas.

["driven out from their royal foundation, *founded and endowed by Your Majesty's
predecessors, the Kings of England,* as the Annals of that kingdom relate, these servants of Our Lord did not lack protection, for he touched and inspired the royal
hearts of Your Majesty and of Your Most Zealous father, King Philip II, *true descendants of their founders, the English Kings,* to take them to your charge and sustain
them. . . ."] ("Petition," 22, 33; emphasis added)

Although written before the marriage between the Infanta and Prince of
Wales took place—a marriage that, in fact, never did occur—the abbess
and sisters address the Infanta Maria as the Princess of Wales, heightening
the suggestion that the Spanish rulers are the right rulers of England by
textually turning a Spanish princess into an English one.

Pierre Bourdieu has astutely observed, "In politics, 'to say is to do,'
that is, it is to get people to believe . . . the *slogans*, which produce their
own verification by producing . . . a social order."[82] Syon's version of history was problematic because it had the potential to erode belief in the
"slogans" or representations of the "Tudor myth" and so erode the political structure and social order supported by this symbolic scaffolding.
Syon's challenge to Elizabeth's self-representation went beyond reframing
Lancastrian history to strike at some of the most potent symbolic weapons in Elizabeth's arsenal. One of Elizabeth's best-known and most discussed symbolizations of her monarchy is her self-representation as the
Virgin Queen.[83] In this guise, she famously adapted imagery from the cult
of the Virgin Mary. She capitalized on the Virgin Mary's popularity in

England, so highlighting once again the symbolic value of medieval female sanctity, which was so great that it was worth translating into a Protestant context even though it contradicted fundamental Protestant religious principles.[84]

Much of the evidence for the "cult" of Elizabeth as the Virgin Queen comes from late in her reign or even after her death. However, an unofficial cult associating Elizabeth with the Virgin Mary began to emerge by the late 1560s, albeit "without the approval of the goddess herself."[85] In 1569, John Day published a collection of prayers attributed to his son Richard Day called *Christian Prayers and Meditations* (also known as *Queen Elizabeth's Prayerbook*). This collection contains a "frontispiece of 'Elizabeth Regina' kneeling devoutly in prayer."[86] King points out:

> Nearly a decade later, the Days transferred the title page, frontispiece, and wood-cut borders to *A Booke of Christian Prayers* (1578). Elizabethan heraldic devices figure prominently in both of these collections. Richard and John Day collaborated in the production of what are, in effect, protestant books of hours that pay tribute throughout to Elizabeth as a Reformation queen. In an outstanding example of literary "iconoclasm," Elizabeth receives the place of honour in collections of prayers comparable to the *Horae* in which the Blessed Virgin Mary once reigned supreme as Mother of God and Queen of Heaven.[87]

Elizabeth's birthday, September 7, was the eve of the feast of the Nativity of the Virgin Mary, and, as Carole Levin observes, "Many of her loyal subjects regarded the fact that Elizabeth should share the nativity of the Virgin Mary as more than simply coincidence; they considered it a divine omen. It proved to them that Elizabeth and the Anglican Church were sustained and sanctified by divine providence."[88] The extent to which Elizabeth was identified with the Virgin Mary appears in an anonymous Latin elegy written soon after Elizabeth's death, which, coincidentally, occurred on March 24, the eve of the Annunciation of the Virgin Mary. The poet writes, "Mary was a Virgin, she, Elizabeth, was also; Mary was blessed; Beta was blessed among the race of women. . . . Mary bore God in her womb, but Elizabeth bore God in her heart. Although in all other respects they are like twins, it is in this latter respect alone that they are not of equal rank."[89] Similarly, a caption on a memorial engraving reads, "She was, she is (What can there more be said?) In earth the first, in heaven the second Maid."[90]

Devotion to the Virgin Queen spread far beyond poetry and the visual arts. The "cult" of the Virgin Queen took on actual cultic aspects when her

Accession Day of November 17 began to be celebrated as an official church holiday in 1576, "with a specific service and liturgy." From 1576 onward, November 17 had "'the forme of a Holy Day,' as Thomas Holland said in a sermon in 1599."[91] A marginal note in Maurice Kyffin's *The Blessednes of Brytaine*, published to celebrate Accession Day in 1587, indicates that "this day was 'more fit to be solemnized than many other days noted in the Calendar.'"[92] In some places, her birthday was similarly marked with prayers, bell-ringing, and sermons.[93] There were also occasionally sports and other celebrations held on November 19 "to celebrate St. Elizabeth's day, the queen's namesake."[94] As Louis A. Montrose indicates, the "cult of Elizabeth" was "a core component of Elizabethan statecraft, one within which elements of devotion and diversion were inextricably mixed."[95]

Extremely suggestive in the way that it highlights the political importance of medieval female spirituality for Elizabeth is her engagement with the cult of the Virgin Mary long before she became queen. At age eleven, she translated Marguerite de Navarre's *Le Miroir de l'âme pécheresse* and presented the text to her stepmother Catherine Parr. As Marc Shell observes, "the most profound themes in the 'Glass' involve the reworking and expansion in nationalist and secular terms of such medieval theological notions concerning kingship as universal siblinghood . . . and dormition, wherein the Virgin Mary plays at once the role of mother and daughter as well as wife."[96] In Marguerite's text, Elizabeth finds the raw materials that "allow for the transformation of the Catholic *sponsa Christi* . . . into such a Virgin Queen as Princess Elizabeth seems already in her eleventh year to comprehend."[97]

In Elizabeth's source and in the life of Marguerite, its author, one glimpses again the complex multivalence of medieval female spirituality as a reservoir of symbolic value. In the *Miroir* and in Marguerite's religious career one also finds fraught, even contradictory, dynamics among the imperatives to preserve, transform, and transcend tradition quite characteristic of Elizabeth's engagement with medieval religion—especially with the cult of the Virgin Mary. Marguerite, rather like Elizabeth herself, experienced opposition from both Catholics and Protestants. Marguerite was censured by Catholics for being too Protestant, for breaking with orthodoxy, since the *Miroir* does not mention "male or female saints, merits, or any purgatory other than the blood of Jesus."[98] However, John Calvin denounced Marguerite's spiritual libertinism, which aligned her too closely with what he saw as some of the worst aspects of Catholic tradition; as Shell notes, "many libertines . . . laid out in almost anthropological terms how both a spiritual libertine and a traditional nun, in imitating the Virgin Mary, ought to make God a father, husband, brother, and son."[99] Within Marguerite's libertinism, there is an affinity with conservatism, while conservatives find in her text alarmingly reformist aspects. One sees much the same contradictory reaction among Elizabeth's Catholic and Protestant subjects in regard to the queen's attitudes to the "old religion" and to Marian devotion.

Catholics, not surprisingly, were deeply offended by Elizabethan co-option of devotion to the Virgin Mary. In his continuation of Nicholas Sanders's *Rise and Growth*, Edward Rishton writes that the Protestants, "to show the greater contempt for our Blessed Lady . . . keep the birthday of queen Elizabeth in the most solemn way on the 7th day of September, which is the eve of the feast of the Mother of God, whose nativity they mark in their calendar in small and black letters, while that of Elizabeth is marked in letters both large and red."[100] In what Montrose calls a "spectacular instance of iconoclasm" the Irish rebel Sir Brian-na-Murtha O'Rourke reportedly took an image of a woman that had been previously removed from a church (presumably an image of the Virgin Mary), inscribed "Queen Elizabeth" on its chest, and dragged it through the muck tied to his horse's tail.[101] The official articles of O'Rourke's indictment for high treason charge that he did this "in despighte and contempt of her Majesty, tearmynge her highnes the mother and nurse of all herisies and heretiques."[102] As Montrose points out, the indictment's repetition of O'Rourke's calling Elizabeth the mother and nurse of heresies and heretics "ventriloquized a mocking Catholic perspective upon the Elizabethan regime's attempt to appropriate the maternal Marian cult for the benefit of the Protestant Virgin Queen."[103]

The nuns of Syon offered their own critical response to Elizabeth's takeover of devotion to the Virgin Mary, although they did not state it as directly as Rishton or enact it as dramatically as O'Rourke. Much as they textually reinterpreted Lancastrian history to a Catholic advantage, so too they textually—and quite polemically—invoked an alternative model of royal embodiment of Marian identity. Syon had an especially strong association with the Virgin Mary. In the Brigittine Order, the Virgin Mary is central to their distinctive form of monastic identity; according to the Brigittine Rule, the abbess holds the place of the Virgin Mary in the community, and Marian devotion shapes the Brigittine divine service. The abbess and nuns of Syon call attention to their Marian identification in their petition to the Spanish Infanta. They emphasize that the order "fue comensada y dedicada al honor de nuestra Señora Maria Madre de Dios, y Reyna de los cielos" ["was commended and dedicated to the honour of Our Lady, Mary Mother of God and Queen of Heaven"] ("Petition," 12, 24). They go on to say that divine providence has ordained that the Order "sea favoreçada y conservada por estas otras Reynas Marias muy devotas a la dicha divinissima Maria, y Reina de los Angeles" ["might later be favoured and protected by these other Queen Marys(themselves most devoted to the Most Divine Mary, Queen of the Angels"] ("Petition," 12, 24). The emphasis on the Virgin Mary as a queen, coupled with the mentions of Mary Tudor and the Infanta Maria as queens, imply that these Catholic monarchs, not Elizabeth, are the Virgin Mary's true earthly incarnation. The nuns' own close connection to the Virgin Mary gives special authority to their pronouncement. This reinterpretation of who the true "Virgin Queen" really is becomes even clearer when, simultaneously reinforcing their alternative view of Lancastrian succession, they write that Syon was "fundada por los Reales predeçessores destas dos serenissimas Marias las quales nuestra señora divinamente (como pareçe) escogio, y substituyo para suplir su proprio lugar, y veçes en la tierra" ["founded by the Royal predecessors of the two Most Serene Marys whom Our Lady divinely (it seems) chose and delegated to take her own role and place on earth"] ("Petition," 12, 24).

It might seem a rather small matter to recall medieval Marian devotion and so to suggest obliquely that Elizabeth was not in fact the legitimate Protestant replacement for the Virgin Mary. However, Elizabeth on occasion demonstrated marked hostility to surviving practices of Marian devotion, hostility perhaps indicative of an unconscious desire to remove any competing sacred virgins from the scene. For instance, during one of her royal progresses in 1578, Elizabeth stayed at Edward Rookwood's home. A piece of her plate reportedly went missing, so her officials searched the property. An eyewitness reports that in the investigations "suche an immaydge of *our* Lady was ther fownd, as for greatnes, for gayness, and woorkemanshipp, I did never see a matche." In a move that simultaneously served her representational agenda and helped mollify the Protestant iconoclasts who constantly pushed her fully to purify English religion from "popish" images, the queen "commanded it to the fyer, w*hi*ch in her sight by the contrie folks was quickly done, to her content."[104]

Brigittine assertions that Mary I and the Spanish Infanta were the true incarnations of the Virgin Mary, as well as the implied true heirs to the English throne, would furthermore have resonated with fears that the

English monarch would be deposed in favor of a foreign, Catholic replacement. Fears of a Catholic takeover of the English monarchy, so characteristic of much of Elizabeth's reign, were once again current in the early
seventeenth century, when the nuns' text was written, as I shall discuss
below. That Mary I had in fact made both the Virgin Mary and her Lancastrian lineage important building blocks of her own symbolic projects
would only have intensified the troubling force of Syon's assertions.[105]

Elizabeth's complex self-representational strategies were by no means
confined to fostering the "cult" of the Virgin Queen. An important strategy
for Henry VIII, as we have seen, was to connect himself with Constantine
as Emperor and restorer of ecclesiastical purity. Elizabeth too associated
herself with Constantine. Perhaps the most famous instance of this identification appears in the historiated initial "C" that graces the dedication
of the first edition of John Foxe's *Actes and Monuments*.[106] In the guise of
Constantine, Elizabeth was seen to usher in a new religious golden age,
bringing "peace and concord" represented in the Foxe woodcut "by the
fruitful yield of a cornucopia which forms the upper part of the initial capital 'C' (for 'Constantine')."[107] Elizabeth's frequent representations as Astraea,
the "just virgin of the golden age,"[108] capitalize on her gender and virginity to enhance further her identification as one who engineers a return to
a golden age. In addition, such representations suggest that her reign is
one of harmony and tranquility following a time of strife.[109]

Turning once again to texts originating with or associated with Syon,
we find a competing narrative of the "golden age" as a parallel to competing monastic accounts of the Lancastrian past and of the inheritance of
Marian identity. A petition from members of the community and other
English Catholics in exile in Rouen advances a vision of a medieval golden
age that is quite different from Elizabeth's portrayals of past and present.
This petition was circulated in England between 1587 and 1594 and was
ultimately confiscated by the English authorities. It requests aid for the
house on the grounds that Syon is under threat of being "utterly dissolvyd
and dispersed."[110] This eventuality is, the authors claim, to be avoided at
all costs because Syon "is ye onely religiouse couent remaynynge of our
country."[111] The petition presents Syon as the sole survivor of an English
past of holy Catholic community and true religion. The letter of the nuns
to the Spanish Infanta similarly remarks, "y no solamente començado con
los primeros desterrados por nuestra sancta fee catolica sino Tambien
estando nostras solas de todas las ordenes y monasterios de Religiosas yngle-
zas que continuaron, y perseveraron en esta dicho durissimo destierro"

["not only were we the first exiles for our Holy Catholic Faith, but also the only ones of all the orders and convents of English nuns, who have continued and persevered in this very hard exile"] ("Petition," 13, 25).

Intensifying the suggestion that Syon preserves the only remnant of England's sacred past are the frequent descriptions of the community as a relic. This choice of terminology portrays this remnant of medieval monasticism as a holy fragment of a society that has suffered martyrdom. The abbess and nuns call themselves "Unica y sola Reliquia de todas las Religiosas de Inglatierra" ["unique and only relic of all the houses of religious Sisters of England"] ("Petition," 21, 33), while Parsons calls Syon and Sheen "the only relics of all the Orders and Religious which in Catholick times were in England, which, as all know, were very many."[112] Indeed, Parsons even attributes to the community something like the power of a saint's relic to work miracles. When the community was residing in Malines, the town was sacked by William of Orange, whose troops included some English forces. Parsons reports that the nuns were "in extream danger . . . to lose their lives and honours." However, they were "miraculously delivered" when "the hearts of some English captains belonging to the Prince of Orange" were moved; these soldiers, "though hereticks, having respect to their honour and the reputation of their country, defended their poor countrywomen." One of these soldiers was even mystically inspired on several occasions to interrupt games of cards and dice to go help the nuns when they were in danger.[113]

In contrast to the Protestant England that Queen Elizabeth constructs as a peaceful, prosperous paradise, Elizabethan England appears in quite a different guise in *The Life of Sister Marie Champney*. The Syon nun Marie declares that England, unlike real "christian comonwealthes," is sunk in "this ranke tyme of synne & ryott, and comon decaye of christian charytye" (*Life*, fol. 7v). In recounting Marie's spiritual and temporal journeys to her profession, the author describes the greatest temptation that she had to overcome as her "marveilous longinge desire to returne againe into England" (*Life*, fol. 2v). Similarly, the author says that, after being educated by nuns in Antwerp, Marie did not "fully offe[r] her selfe to become a nunne" until she distanced herself "from her olde longinge homewarde into Egipte againe" (*Life*, fol. 3r). Protestant England represents sin, bondage, and heathen, paradoxically "foreign" customs for Syon, which often explicitly compared itself to the exiled Israelites.[114]

In the *Life of Marie Champney*, Marie's evocation of a past Catholic golden age to which a return is expected has markedly subversive aspects.[115]

She declares that "love of vertue and virginitye shall florishe & renewe
againe in gods little flocke like an eagle new mewed with golden eyes, and
that not leste in Englande for all this, where Syon yet I hope shalbe builded
vp againe most bewtifully, accordinge to father renolds hope and prayer."
Marie also praises "Gregorius 13^{tius}" and his "workes of mercye . . . to the
Germanes & to our nation moste afflicted with heresie" which "sownde
thoroughe all the Christian worlde for patrons to be followed, as they
before had a blessed patron of pius quintius to behold" (*Life*, fol. 8r).

Marie's assertion concerning the renewal of love for virtue and virginity among "gods little flocke" reads like another reappropriation of
Elizabeth's representational raw material of virginity and religious purity.
The fact that Marie mentions Pope Gregory XIII and Pope Pius V as the
ideal patterns for Christians to follow, and the fact that she invokes the
name of Richard Reynolds in predicting Syon's restoration, indicate that
the "golden age" she has in mind will not simply entail a return to a
Catholic past but rather a complete eradication of the Protestant present.
Each of these figures is known for vociferous opposition to, and in some
cases direct action against, English Protestant monarchs. Richard Reynolds
was the Syon brother executed by Henry VIII because he "maintained that
the Pope was the true Head of the Universal Church."[116] Since Reynolds
was executed before Syon was dissolved, there is an element of historical
revision in attributing to him the hope and prayer of Syon's restoration.
This revision highlights the close connection between his "intellectual"
exile and the community's later physical exile. It also draws parallels between the community's suffering and his martyrdom as well as between
his blessedness and their own. Pope Pius V is a particularly loaded figure
to hold up as a "blessed patron," since he was the pope who issued the
bull excommunicating Elizabeth in 1570. He also strongly supported Mary
Stuart, with whom Syon seems to have had some ties. The praise of Pope
Gregory XIII is the clearest indicator of the militant nature of the replacement Marie has in mind for the "false" golden age of Elizabeth. What
Marie calls his "workes of mercye . . . to our nation moste afflicted with
heresie" included founding the English Colleges at Rome and Douai, which
sent so many Jesuits—including Campion—to England as well as sponsor-
ing the military expedition in which Nicholas Sanders took part in Ireland
in 1579–1581. In the *Life of Sister Marie Champney*, it becomes abundantly
clear that the past, projected into the future, can have serious political
implications in the present.

An Epilogue to Syon's Elizabethan Exile

The medieval past continued to have political implications for the present well into the seventeenth century, and medieval female spirituality remained a powerful, ambivalent political force, serving as means both to lay claim to and to undermine political authority. The debate concerning the so-called "Spanish Marriage" between Charles, Prince of Wales, and the Infanta Maria of Spain is a case in point, and one in which Syon again figures prominently. The account of Syon's history addressed by the abbess and nuns to the Infanta Maria provides more than a record of the community's exile and its oppositional vision of Tudor history. It also represents Syon's continuing interventions in English political life.

As we have seen, Syon's address to the Infanta portrays the Catholic Marys (the past queen Mary I, wife of Philip II of Spain, and the current Spanish Infanta) as the recipients and transmitters of the true Lancastrian inheritance; correspondingly, they are positioned as the vehicles for the salvation of the community, and, more broadly, of England. The royal women's purity and holiness, their likeness to the Virgin Mary, underwrite the legitimacy of this version of succession and provide a stark contrast to the "false Virgin Mary" of Elizabeth, so frequently vilified by Catholic opponents (as well as by some Protestants opposed to female rule) as a wanton and a whore.[117] The holiness of the nuns of Syon, who themselves are closely connected to the Virgin Mary and who highlight their special resemblance to St. Birgitta (like the community, she spent a significant part of her life as a wandering pilgrim[118]), provides a further reserve of legitimating symbolic capital for the Catholic cause.

In England, however, the Protestant view of the Spanish Infanta was quite different, and there was great concern about the impact she would have as queen on English Protestant identity. As Cristina Malcolmson has shown, an association exists in the literature of the period "of women with Spanish infiltration," an association that "articulates a powerful fear about . . . the Spanish princess, who as queen would be mother to the future English king. . . . Like Queen Mary, the Spanish Infanta was seen as the avenue through which the Catholic Church and the Spanish empire would enter the English state and rob it of its national strength."[119] In the public debate regarding the Spanish Marriage, the flip side of Catholic representations of Elizabeth's unchastity—that is, the Protestant representation of the Catholic Church as the "whore of Babylon" or the "whore of Rome"—

often came into play.[120] Such equations were useful for elaborating the threat Protestants felt the Spanish marriage posed. William Prynne, for instance, writes that the Spanish sought to accomplish the downfall of the English through the "project of marrying us to the whore of Rome by matching the heire of the crowne of England to a *Romanist*."[121]

Furthermore, as was the case during the Lancastrian and early Tudor periods, when politically active French women prompted fears of English emasculation and political decline, there was a similar fear "of the emasculation of the English nation" through a Spanish, Catholic queen while the Spanish Marriage seemed a likely possibility.[122] These renewed, gendered political anxieties had deep roots in the long Elizabethan era which had witnessed much wrestling to maintain masculine authority under female rule. Exacerbating the situation were widespread feelings, much like those expressed earlier in William Worcester's *Boke of Noblesse*, that the English aristocracy "had become effeminate" through a long period of peace and prosperity.[123]

One consequent strategy to combat these fears was to urge "a more aggressive exercise and enforcement of male patriarchal authority" by waging war on Spain.[124] Interestingly, another strategy was also at work in dealing with anxieties about the Spanish, Catholic, feminine threat to Protestant, English, national identity. This strategy involved the English nuns of Syon who, from their home in Lisbon, supported the Spanish Marriage that was so unpopular in England. Earlier responses to the threat of foreign female power involved placing the offending women back into properly feminine roles outside the spheres of military and political action. The "cloistering" of Christine de Pizan is an ideal case in point, as we have seen in the discussions of English treatments of her work in chapter 3. Another kind of "cloistering" emerges in the Spanish Marriage debate. In this case, the cloister no longer represents a safe place to which politically inconvenient women can relegated; rather, it represents a means by which the unworthiness and corruption of politically inconvenient women can emphasized.

In 1622, Thomas Robinson published what he styled as an exposé of the dissolute life of the nuns of Syon in Lisbon. Robinson claimed to know from the perspective of an insider what really happened behind the convent walls. He says that "father Seth, alias Ioseph Foster . . . the sole Confessor of a Couent of English Nunnes . . . by his subtill and wily fetches inticed me to abide with him in the house."[125] Robinson then says he was put to work as a copiest and "depriued . . . of meanes to depart"

(*Anatomie*, 1); subsequently, he lived as a lay brother in the community for several years. This text appeared at a time when the Spanish Marriage seemed a virtual certainty, and it is also exactly contemporaneous with the document addressed by the abbess and nuns to the Infanta, which can "be dated with confidence to the early 1620s, probably to the year 1623."[126] If it is true, as Robinson claims, that he worked as a copiest for the Syon community, it seems quite likely he may even have seen some version of the nuns' text as it was prepared. Given these coincidences of time and place, it is difficult not to read the *Anatomie* as both a participant in the loud Protestant tirade against the Spanish Marriage and a targeted response to Syon's framing of its own identity and that of the English nation.

By far the most potent, and most frequently used, weapon in Robinson's arsenal is the charge of sexual corruption, the very sort of charge leveled at nunneries by Henrician "reformers" before the Dissolution as well as at Elizabeth Barton by her accusers. As in these two earlier cases, once again such charges are highly politicized. Robinson clearly aims to deny any sort of symbolic value to the Spanish Catholics who supported Syon and whose cause might benefit from association with Syon's holiness. He reports that he found the bones of nuns' illegitimate children in the walls (*Anatomie*, 12), and he discourses at length on the reign of sexual terror by which Seth Foster abused and oppressed the nuns (*Anatomie*, 14, 16, 19). He is moved to call for action, saying, "for such as haue either Daughters or Kinswomen in that house, in whose behalfe I am bound to intreat their friends to enter into a further search of their miserable estate and condition; and (hauing found my wordes true) to vse meanes, if it be possible, to free them from such horrible and sacrilegious rapine and spoile" (*Anatomie*, 30). This statement sounds rather like an encouragement to invade Lisbon to save English women, echoing contemporary calls for James I to go to war with Spain and so save the feminized English state threatened by Catholic violation.[127]

The way in which Robinson begins his account of the corruption in the nunnery has perhaps the greatest contemporary political significance in the Spanish Marriage debate. He claims that Syon's new postulants from England come largely from women who have fallen prey to the sexual advances of Jesuits and seminary priests hiding in their houses: "by such meanes hauing gotten a clap, diuers of them become Nunnes" (*Anatomie*, 7). A marginal gloss on this passage drives home the point, saying, "It is no great miracle for a whore to become a Nunne; nor for a Nunne to become a whore" (*Anatomie*, 7 note b). This characterization of English

Catholic women living in Spanish territory resonates with the characterization of the Catholic church as the whore of Babylon or Rome and with
the conflation of the Spanish Infanta, to whom the nunnery is so closely
linked, with the whore of Rome.

Robinson's *Anatomie* not only engages with contemporary political
issues but also with the political significance of representing the past. He
strongly refutes Syon's characterization of itself as a remnant of a holy
English past. He declares that "the successors of these banished runnagates" (that is, the successors of the religious who left England following the Henrician dissolution) are not a sacred relic but rather "now the
oneley stumpe which remaineth of that huge tree, that whilome ouerspred
and shaddowed our whole country" (*Anatomie*, 4). As Hanmer does with
Ignatius Loyola in his response to Campion's "Challenge," Robinson further discredits the community's claim to a sacred past by denigrating the
order's founder and origins. Robinson admits that "This Saint *Bridget* was
. . . a woman (questionlesse) of good vnderstanding and singular memory," but she was, much as Elizabeth Barton was said to have been, "miserably seduced and led away by the subtill allurements of her ghostly father"
whose "perswasions and counsell" led her to go to Rome. There "she pretended to have diuers reuelations from God" before the Pope. Among
these feigned revelations was "one . . . for the founding of this Order of
Nunnes." He goes on to deride the idea that Syon is imbued with mystical
or miraculous qualities, saying mockingly that "the Papists . . . do hold as
miraculous" Syon's continuing survival (*Anatomie*, 6, emphasis in original).

Even more strikingly, Robinson counters the idea that Syon will engineer a return to the "real" golden age of traditional religion. He writes,
"Some of the holiest of our vnholy Sisters, have not doubted (I thinke in
imitation of the old *Sybils*) to prophesie of another golden age, when they
shall againe be installed in *Syon*: but *Admiranda canunt, sed non credenda
sorores*. I know my Sisters at *Lisbon* for false prophets in more things then
one" (*Anatomie*, 4, emphasis in original). Finally, Robinson engages in
some historical rewriting of his own, blackening Syon's past by turning
the unsubstantiated rumor of their involvement with the Lopez plot into
documented historical truth about which the community apparently has
no compunction. He writes that while Syon was in France, "they had the
custodie of no small summe of money, which was sent to them to keepe
for Doctor *Lopez* the Portugese, as his reward for poysoning our late
Queene *Elizabeth* of famous memorie, which after that Traitor . . . was
executed, was remitted vnto them as an almes, as the Register-booke of

their house, (from whence I had it) shameth not to make mention" (*Anatomie*, 9–10, emphasis in original).

The *Anatomie* provides clear evidence that, as it did through the Henrician, Elizabethan, and Stuart eras, the medieval past persisted in animating the present into the seventeenth century. It demonstrates that manifestations of medieval female spirituality continued to shape contemporary political relations and to provide a battleground upon which conflicts to define identities were fought. In these regards, Robinson's text strikingly highlights the truth inherent in William Faulkner's memorable remark on the past: "The past is never dead. It's not even past."[128]

Conclusion: The Power of the Past

L. O. Aranye Fradenburg and Carla Freccero have argued, "we must see that positing the power of the past to disrupt and remake the present is not necessarily to adopt a naive continuism."[1] In this study, we have seen the multiple, complex ways in which manifestations of medieval female spirituality disrupted and remade cultural meaning both in its own present and in the early modern period for which the Middle Ages generally stands as "the past." We have also seen, however, the ways in which the Middle Ages were not simply "the past" for the early modern era, since medieval female spirituality lived on in the practices of such women as Elizabeth Barton, Elizabeth Sanders, and Marie Champney as well as in the representational strategies of Isabel of Castile and Elizabeth I. Furthermore, the battles to own and control the legacy of medieval religion were hard fought with high stakes, helping to shape European politics well into the seventeenth century. I want to close with a brief, and somewhat deliberately provocative, exploration of medieval female spirituality and political conflict in a time and place to which the adjective "medieval" by convention does not (but, I would argue, should) apply—the "Age of Discovery" and the New World.[2]

The New World and the Old Religion

For Isabel of Castile, 1492 was an extremely important year. It not only saw the long-desired reconquest of Granada, but also Columbus's first voyage to what would come to be known as the New World. Indeed, since at least part of the impetus for the reconquest of Granada and Columbus's New World enterprises was shared, resting in Isabel's desire to advance the Christian faith and correspondingly to expand her and Ferdinand's Catholic monarchy, it is thus entirely fitting that both events should have transpired in the same year.[3] Just as Isabel had a greater interest in, and a greater personal involvement with, the reconquest than did Ferdinand, so too she was more concerned with Columbus's voyages than he was. Emphasizing her independence in making Columbus's endeavor possible, José Luis Abellán observes that Isabel "lent extraordinary support to Columbus." He continues, "Although the *Capitulations of Santa Fe* of April 17, 1492, were signed by both monarchs, it is well known that the one who carried the preceding discussions was always Isabel, and it would be the kingdom of Castile that took the lead role in the enterprise of discovery. The new domains would thus fall to Castile alone."[4]

As we have seen, an important aspect of Isabel's self-representation was to portray herself as a latter-day Joan of Arc on a divinely inspired, divinely endorsed mission. Columbus's own version of the "Letter to the Sovereigns of 4 March 1493 Announcing the Discovery" makes clear the degree to which Isabel's royal identity as a Joan-like crusader was tied up with his framing of, and her involvement in, the expedition.[5] Peggy Liss observes that his "apocalyptic rhetoric," which was "culled from approved medieval and biblical sources . . . surely owes much to the language and imagery in which Isabel clothed her reign and its politics."[6] We see the influence of such language and imagery when, clearly hoping to gain continued sponsorship, Columbus appealed to Isabel's self-fashioning as a holy warrior:

I conclude here: that through the divine grace of Him who is the origin of good and virtuous things, who favors and gives victory to all those who walk in His path, in seven years from today I will be able to pay Your Highnesses for five thousand cavalry and fifty thousand foot soldiers for the war and conquest in Jerusalem, for which purpose this enterprise was undertaken. And in another five years another five thousand foot soldiers, which will total ten thousand cavalry and one hundred thousand foot soldiers; and all of this with very little investment now on Your Highness's part in the beginning of the taking of the Indies and all that they contain.[7]

Columbus planned for the wealth of the Indies to finance a crusade to retake Jerusalem, but the letter points the way to seeing the conquest of the Indies itself *as* crusade, *as* "holy war" undertaken under Isabel's banner.[8] One might go so far as to say that Isabel's engagement with medieval female spirituality is one of the points of origin for the so-called "Age of Discovery." Isabel's visions of self and state, shaped by medieval female spirituality, both helped to foster and to legitimate New World enterprises motivated (at least purportedly) by religious aims.[9] Indeed, the New World as Europeans would come to "discover" it, understand it, and transform it for the native populations owes much of its existence to the ongoing political clout of medieval religion.[10]

The conflict between the old Catholic religion and the new Protestant one was perhaps the most important force shaping England's involvement in the New World. Richard Hakluyt, a major promoter of English colonization efforts in the Elizabethan period, "was driven by a fear that if Protestant England did not establish an empire in the Americas, then Catholic Spain would dominate the known world for the foreseeable future."[11] As Andrew Hadfield observes, Hakluyt's "goal was to continue the sectarian conflict with Europe in the Americas."[12] A similar desire emerges in the letter patent of March 25, 1584, granting Walter Raleigh "free liberty and license . . . to discover search fynde out and view" territories in the New World. It specifies that his object should be "such remote heathen and barbarous landes Contries and territories not actually possessed of any Christian Prynce and inhabited by Christian people."[13] This passage suggests not only that lands possessed by "heathen" native peoples, but also those possessed by the Catholic—and so not really Christian—Spanish monarch were fair game.[14]

In English New World enterprises, as in the Spanish ones to which the English contrasted their own, we find manifestations of medieval female spirituality at work. Much as Isabel of Castile's creation of a version of queenship rooted in medieval female spirituality provided impetus and justification for Spain's New World expeditions, Elizabeth I's regal identity as the Virgin Queen, a self-representation crafted, as we have seen, in part of material drawn from medieval religion, provided the English name for their first-claimed piece of the New World—Virginia. In Arthur Barlowe's July 1584 report to Walter Raleigh, Barlowe describes the English arrival in America: "after thankes given to God for our safe arrivall thither, we manned our boates, and went to viewe the land . . . and to take possession of the same, in the right of the Queenes most excellent Majestie, as rightfull Queene, and Princesse of the same."[15] He goes on to say that the territory, called "Wingandacoa" by the natives has been renamed Virginia "by her Majestie."[16] As Louis Montrose observes, "Having authorized her subjects' acts of discovery and symbolic possession, the English monarch assumes the privilege of naming the land anew, and naming it for herself and for the gender-specific virtue she has so long and so successfully employed as a means of self-empowerment."[17] Montrose calls Barlowe's report a textualization of the "'inaugural scene' of Elizabethan New World colonialism."[18] I would also argue that the report draws our attention to the fact that, for England, as for Spain, "inaugural scenes" of New World colonialism have their own inauguration in the Middle Ages, and specifically in medieval female spirituality.

Women of Arms and Men of God

Both Isabel of Castile and Elizabeth I of England found valuable resources for self-empowerment as "women of arms" and self-representation as "women of God" in medieval female spirituality, although they deployed such resources in different ways.[19] That many Spanish and English New World ventures took place under such powerful female monarchs could not help but color the experiences and perceptions of the European men who engaged in them. In light of the inescapable presence of these powerful queens in enterprises of New World exploration and conquest, it is highly significant that one of the "native" populations that Europeans claimed, hoped, or perhaps feared, to encounter was that tribe of "women of arms" *par excellence*—the Amazons or Amazon-like women. Significantly, Isabel and Elizabeth both associated themselves, or were associated by their supporters, with Amazons. For instance, the pro-Isabelline writer Baltasar Gracián in *El Criticón* "calls Isabel 'that Catholic Amazon,'"[20] and in his report of Elizabeth I's famous Tilbury speech delivered to her troops in 1588, Thomas Heywood says that Elizabeth was "habited like an *Amazonian* Queene, Buskind and plumed, having a golden Truncheon, Gantlet, and Gorget, Arms sufficient to expresse her high and magnanimous spirit."[21]

Many scholars have read Raleigh's descriptions of the Amazons, and indeed of the land of Guiana itself in *The Discoverie of the large, rich and beautifull Empire of Guiana*, as bearing witness to his anxious view of female authority and his fraught efforts to fashion an identity under it.[22] Raleigh writes of his desire to "understand the truth of those warlike women," and continues:

they which are not far from Guiana doe accompany with men but once in a yere, and for the time of one moneth, which I gather by their relation to be in April: and at that time all kings of the borders assemble, and queenes of the Amazones. . . . If they conceive, and be delivered of a sonne, they returne him to the father; if of a daughter they nourish it and reteine it. . . . [T]hat they cut off the right dug of the brest, I doe not finde to be true. It was farther tolde me, that if in these warres they tooke any prisoners that they used to accompany with those also at what time soever, but in the end for certeine they put them to death: for they are sayd to be very cruell and bloodthirsty, especially to such as offer to invade their territories.[23]

Although Raleigh never actually found the Amazons, the parallels between these armed women and Raleigh's armed queen are easy enough to find. As Montrose observes, "Gender and rule, sex and power: these are the concerns that preoccupy Ralegh . . .; we might expect such concerns to be of more than incidental interest to a gentleman who is subject to a woman monarch."[24] Raleigh, like John Talbot, Stephen Scrope, and William Worcester before him, seems to fear that if women bear arms or hold political authority, he—and other English men—may share the fate of William Goddard's "maiden-chaunged Mick."[25] Ian Moulton observes that Goddard's Mick has been feminized by neglecting the manly practice of war to resort to women; Mick "is a man not because he has a prick, but because he knows how to use a pike."[26] In this case, when women use pikes, or other weapons, men seem in danger of losing rather than using their pricks—or, more accurately, losing the symbolic phallus (represented by the phallic pike or sword) that guarantees their masculine identity and its corresponding social privileges.

Columbus seems to have experienced similar anxieties about his identity and authority under a powerful ruling queen. As we have seen, Columbus says he will conclude his letter to Isabel and Ferdinand with his plan to finance the conquest of Jerusalem with the wealth of the Indies. This passage is not, however, the actual conclusion to the letter. The real conclusion is an account of the populations he had encountered on his voyage. It begins:

> Wherefore Your Highness should know that the first Island of the Indies, closest to Spain, is populated entirely by women, without a single man, and their comportment is not feminine, but rather they use weapons and other masculine practices. They carry bows and arrows and take their adornments from the copper mines, which metal they have in very large quantity. They call this island Matenino.[27]

He goes on to discuss Amazonian child-rearing practices and pairs the description of these armed women with one of feminized cannibals, who "are the ones who have intercourse with the women of Matenino." These men "eat human flesh" and "go about naked like the others, except they wear their hair very full, like women";[28] they are, in effect, "maiden-chaunged." This passage reenacts the very fears about maintaining masculinity (indeed, about maintaining civilization itself) in the face of the armed, powerful women that we saw in English treatments of Joan of Arc, Margaret of Anjou, Margaret of York, and Christine de Pizan. These women in no way occupy "another place" from which they confirm martial masculinity.

Rather, they occupy a place all too much the same. Indeed, that Columbus stresses these Amazon-like women live on the island "closest to Spain" precisely suggests that he feels the threat to be one very close to home, in every sense of the phrase.[29] Rather than being what the warrior is not, the women of Matenino are what the warrior is; as a consequence, masculinity is unmade and warriors become what the Amazon-like natives should be—women.

The English redactors of Christine de Pizan's work managed the threat she posed by transforming her into a pious patron and nun; her "cloistering" stood in for the more difficult work of containing Joan of Arc, Margaret of Anjou, and Margaret of York. Even though Columbus could not himself manage the anxieties prompted by female political and military might by cloistering either Isabel or the women of Matenino, an official chronicler of his voyages, the cleric Peter Martyr d'Anghiera, found a way to turn the strategy to his advantage. In his *De Orbe Novo Decades*, first published in 1516, Peter Martyr too describes "islands . . . inhabited only by women, who have no relations with men."[30] Rather than the fierce, Amazon-like women Columbus claimed to have encountered, or the bloodthirsty Amazons described by Raleigh, these women turn out to be something else altogether. Dismissing the existence of tribes of bow-wielding, one-breasted women as "a fable," he writes:

Some people think they live as did the Amazons, but others who have studied the question more closely believe they are virgins dedicated to God who take pleasure in solitude, just as those amongst us. . . . At certain epochs of the year, men cross to the islands, not to have intercourse with these religious women, but out of the spirit of piety to cultivate their fields and gardens, and thus assure their means of existence.[31]

For this man of God, women of arms turn out to be simply and comprehensibly women of God after all—safely "cloistered" in their "other place" of island solitude and virtuously chaste to boot.[32]

Interestingly, Peter Martyr's *De Orbe Novo Decades* was quickly translated into English by Richard Eden. Andrew Hadfield has argued that Eden's version demonstrates his support for Mary I and her husband Philip of Spain.[33] Claire Jowitt, however, sees Eden's "emphasis on monsters and strange births in the preface" as a factor that "complicates this apparently laudatory text."[34] She situates Eden's text in relation to John Knox's *First Blast of the Trumpet against the Monstrous Regiment of Women* and Anthony Gilby's *Admonition to England and Scotland to call them to Repentance*,[35]

suggesting that Eden under Mary I—like Columbus under Isabel and
Raleigh under Elizabeth I—found female rule troubling, perhaps even
monstrous, although he, like they, in many respects sympathized with his
monarch's policies.

Given the audience to whom Walter Raleigh addressed himself in the
Discoverie, "cloistering" was not the readily available containment strategy
it was for Peter Martyr. In dealing with Elizabeth and his Amazons, he
faced a more difficult task, one which he solved with some difficulty. His
strategy in the *Discoverie* is first to acknowledge Elizabeth's likeness to the
Amazons and then to turn to her self-representation as the Virgin Queen
to praise her as something better. He describes Elizabeth to the Natives as
"the great Casique of the north, and a virgine" (*Discoverie*, 353). Later, in
his attempt to convince Elizabeth to conquer Guiana, he writes, "And
where the South border of Guiana reacheth to the Dominion and Empire
of the Amazones, those women shall hereby heare the name of a virgin,
which is not onely able to defend her owne territories and her neighbours,
but also to invade and conquer so great Empires and so far removed"
(*Discoverie*, 431). As Schwarz observes of this passage, "In conquering
Guiana, Elizabeth will prove something to Amazons, opposing virginity
to whatever it is that Amazons do."[36]

Raleigh does not only suggest the virginal Elizabeth's similarity, and
ultimate superiority, to the Amazons, but he also aligns her with the virginal
land of Guiana itself, which he famously describes as "a country that hath *yet*
her maydenhead" (*Discoverie*, 428, emphasis added). Elizabeth named Virginia
after her virginity in an act that at once made visible her authority and
its symbolic underpinnings. Raleigh's description of Guiana, with its crucial
"yet," gives his flattery of the Virgin Queen an aggressive edge. It suggests
that virginity's value (the wealth of the land, the symbolic capital stemming
from physical intactness that guarantees female authority) is contingent. It
is something that can, perhaps even should, be seized by men, with force if
necessary. The description of Guiana raises the specter of rape, which, as
Montrose notes, is both an act of rage and an act that "must be contextual-
ized within a larger system of gender politics."[37] "Taking" virginity—either
through the sort of sexual violation the Marshal's son tries to perpetuate on
Joan in *La Poncella* or through the sort of sexual smear campaign employed
by Henry VIII's visitation officials, by Joan of Arc's and Elizabeth Barton's
accusers, and by Thomas Robinson in his account of the Syon nuns in
Lisbon—is the inverse of self-defensive "cloistering" and another sort of
containment strategy for female power with a very long history.

Nuns and Natives

One of the most important texts produced in the course of Elizabethan colonial enterprises is Thomas Hariot's *A briefe and true report of the new found
land of Virginia*. This account of Grenville's voyage of 1585 was reprinted
in 1590, accompanied by woodcut versions of John White's watercolors,
by Theodor de Bry as the first volume of his multi-year, multi-volume
America (published between 1590 and 1634). De Bry's version includes as
a sort of "afterword" a series of engravings of figures that were, as the title
page introducing the section states, "found . . . in an oold English chronicle."[38] De Bry's edition of Hariot's text bears witness to the complex relationships between the old and new religions, as well as between the Old
and New Worlds, that structured English identity in what was an unusually difficult period of English history.

As we have seen, in the 1580s the Elizabethan regime was dealing with
interrelated threats from Catholic recusants at home and English Catholics
abroad; furthermore, the Catholic monarchs of France and Spain were a
constant menace. Both Thomas Hariot and Theodor de Bry had personal
stakes in the English Protestant cause. De Bry was a Protestant who had
fled the Low Countries for England to escape Spanish Catholic rule.[39] As
Mary Campbell points out, "Thomas Hariot was a clergyman as well as a
scientist," and his voyage to Virginia, as well as his account of his mission
in the *Briefe and true report*, were shaped by both economic and religious
aims.[40] Hariot is straightforwardly partisan in his pro-colonization sentiments. He claims that he seeks to correct "diuers and variable reportes with
some slaunderous and shamefull speeches" that "haue not donne a litle
wrong to many that otherwise would haue also fauoured & aduentured in
the action, to the honour and benefite of our nation" (*Briefe and true report*,
5). To this end, the *Briefe and true report* consists of three sections, the first
of which outlines Virginia's marketable commodities, the second of which
describes the "victualls" to be found there, and the third of which describes
other commodities, plants, and "the nature and maners of the people of
the country" (*Briefe and true report*, 6). While in Virginia, Hariot not only
took notes on the natives, but he also "did some proselytizing," and, to further advance his pro-colonization agenda, he tends to describe the Algonquians "in terms of their potential for transformation into Christians."[41]

In light of Hariot's desire to present colonization as a good business
prospect and the natives as good prospects for conversion, he typically
portrays them as "civilized, reasonable people" who pose little threat to

Europeans;[42] they are, as he says, "not to be feared" (*Briefe and true report*, 24). When they do pose a threat, it is, he suggests, easily dealt with by Europeans' "superior" technical and intellectual resources. Hariot writes, "In respect of vs they are a people poore, and for want of skill and iudgement in the knowledge and vse of our things, doe esteeme our trifles before thinges of greater value." He also notes that in case of any war between the Algonquians and the English, the English will prevail, "hauing advantages against them so many maner of waies, as by our discipline, our strange weapons and deuises els; especialy by ordinance great and small" (*Briefe and true report*, 25).[43]

As other scholars have noted, there is an inevitable instability in Hariot's approach to the Indians—they are the same but different, they are inferior yet potentially equal before God, they exist in the present but represent his civilization's past.[44] The tensions inherent in the treatment of the Algonquians in De Bry's edition of Hariot's *Briefe and true report* coalesce in a rather surprising detail in the caption to the engraving entitled "Theirdanses vvich they vseatt their highe feastes." The caption states:

At a certayne tyme of the yere they make a great, and solemne feaste whereunto their neighbours of the townes adioninge repayre from all parts, every man attyred in the most strange fashion they can deuise. . . . The place where they meet is a broade playne, abowt the which are planted in the grownde *certayne posts carved with heads like to the faces of Nonnes couered with theyr vayles.* . . . Three of the fayrest Virgins, of the companie are in the mydds, which imbrassinge one another doe as yt wear turne abowt in their dancinge. (*Briefe and true report*, engraving XVIII, emphasis added)

If the aim of the Protestant Hariot and De Bry is to depict the Indians as a non-threatening people who, though godless are ready to "imitate us" and be "easelye . . . brougt to the knowledge of the gospel," this description of one of their religious ceremonies is jarring at best (*Briefe and true report*, engraving XXI entitled "Their Idol Kivvasa").

This description, with its unexpected reference to a form of female spirituality that would have been for Hariot and De Bry's Protestant target audiences distinctively Catholic and distinctively associated with the medieval past functions on multiple levels. Perhaps the simplest explanation for the reference to nuns is that it participates in the negative strand of "cloistering" seen in Robinson's *Anatomy* discussed in chapter 6. It emphasizes the inferiority of the natives by aligning their celebration involving carved posts with the idolatrous practices of Catholics, an equally godless people.

The juxtaposition of the carved posts said to resemble veiled nuns with the image of the nearly naked, definitely unveiled dancing, embracing young women adds ballast by calling to mind stereotypes of lasciviousness and sexual excess in nunneries, a stereotype which, as we have seen, Robinson mobilizes to great effect in his *Anatomy*. Medieval female spirituality remains a source of symbolic capital with as much value as it held for the dukes and duchesses of Burgundy and Isabel of Castile, although its value has been radically transformed.

That the text implies a negative association between Native American and Catholic religious practices is reinforced by the caption accompanying the engraving (number XXII) titled "The Tombe of their Werovvans." This caption states, "By the dead bodies they sett their Idol Kiwasa . . . : For they are persuaded that the same doth kepe the dead bodyes of their chieefe lords that nothinge may hurt them. Moreover vnder the foresaid scaffolde some on of their preists hath his lodginge, which Mumbleth his prayers nighte and day." This description echoes Protestant denigrations of Catholic veneration of saints' relics (which were, after all, for Protestants merely dead bodies with no supernatural powers whatsoever) and Catholic prayers for the dead, both frequently held up as contemptible hallmarks of corrupt papistry. Assigning the title of "preists" to the natives responsible for tending the "Idol Kiwasa" and the bodies of the dead chiefs draws a further parallel between this foreign, barbarous, and clearly "other" form of religious devotion and "superstitious," "idolatrous" Catholic practices.[45]

The captions that suggest parallels between native practices and Catholic devotion do not simply represent English efforts to make the natives "other." They also betray various kinds of anxieties. On the one hand, they resonate with a fear that this native population might *become* Catholic through Spanish influence, as so many others had done or were believed to have done. As William S. Maltby points out, Francis Drake's chaplain "claimed that 'the poisonous infection of Popery' is introduced wherever the Spaniards go, and there is therefore no city, village, or house in the Indies, 'wherein (amongst the other like Spanish virtues) not only whoredom, but the filthiness of Sodom . . . is not common without reproof.'"[46] If the Algonquians of Virginia already had a proclivity for Catholic-like practices, they might be all the more ready to fall under Spanish control. If the seeds of Catholicism were to sprout under Spanish cultivation, the Algonquians would be unlikely to fulfill the role that Hariot envisions for them: not that of a cloistered bride of Christ but that of a submissive, Christian spouse who will "honour, obey, feare and loue" a Protestant patriarch (*Briefe and true report*, 29).[47] On the contrary, Catholicized natives might behave more like the barbarous Spanish of the Black Legend, or worse yet like the women of Matenino or Raleigh's Amazons.

On the other hand, the anxieties that trouble Hariot's description of native religious practices go beyond fears about what the natives might become; they equally concern what the *English* might become. If the English feared the Catholicization of New World peoples through Spanish dominance, they feared even more the same fate for themselves. As Hadfield notes, "[T]he fear was that Europe could become like the New World if Spain were not stopped."[48] More fundamentally still, one discerns in the *Briefe and true report* anxieties about what the English were and what their past meant for their present. Greenblatt argues that Hariot sees the Algonquians as a representation of the English past, an understanding virtually inescapable when one considers the engravings of the Picts and their unnamed "neighbors" appended "to showe how that the Inhabitants of the great Bretanne haue bin in times past as sauuage as those of Uirginia." It is worth remembering in considering the representations of this "savage" past that it was, by and large, a Catholic past.

As we have seen, fears that this past would "rise again" were current in Elizabeth's day—especially in the 1580s—and well into the seventeenth century. For both Protestant Elizabethans and those opposed to the Spanish Marriage the embodiment of the threat posed by the Catholic past was a foreign, Catholic woman—Mary I; Mary, Queen of Scots; the Infanta Maria. It is thus important to examine the women who represent the past in De Bry's edition of the *Briefe and true report*. Hadfield sees a two-fold strategy at work in the collection of engravings appended to the account of Virginia and its natives. First, he draws attention to "the emphasis . . . placed on the Picts."[49] Indeed, from the title page introducing this section of the edition, one gets no inkling that the pictures are not all of Picts, since it proclaims what follows are "SOM PICTVRE, OF THE PICTES WHICH IN THE OLDE type dyd habite one part of the great Bretanne." The Picts, Hadfield says, are portrayed as being considerably more savage than their unnamed neighbors, who are "obviously the Britons."[50] He argues that the reader is meant to see the contrast between the savage Picts and the gentle Algonquians; the relationship of continuity is between the Britons and the Native Americans. Second, one is to make a connection between the Picts, who "were associated solely with Scotland" and the threat posed by the Scottish claim to the English throne.[51] He argues, "In this context it cannot be an entirely innocent detail that two of the three

Picts are female. Both women are recognizable as Amazons or warrior women"; these women evoke, and demonize, the recently executed Mary, Queen of Scots and Arabella Stuart.[52] The Pictish "Amazons" are, for Hariot, in a sense both Joan of Arc's ancestors and stand-ins for recent incarnations (Mary Stuart et al) of the same threats she as a Catholic, foreign woman posed to the English throne. It seems more than coincidental that Shakespeare created a Joan of Arc who embodies menacing, armed, Catholic, foreign femininity and who is described as "an Amazon" in a play first produced at almost exactly the same time as De Bry's edition of the *True Report* appeared.[53]

Matters are complicated, though, in the final section of De Bry's edition by the "trvve picture of a vvomen nighbor to the Pictes." This figure, who lacks the exotic tattoos of the Pictish women and who sports somewhat more clothing, is still recognizably Amazonian. She bears, significantly enough, a pike and large sword. In Elizabeth's England, as Kathryn Schwarz has argued, Amazons are not simply exotic others who dwell elsewhere; they cannot simply represent a foreign threat or a curiosity relegated to the past, to the New World, or even to the cloister. Troubling though the thought might have been to her Protestant soul, Elizabeth I could in many respects have been seen, like Isabel of Castile, as a new incarnation of Joan of Arc. Indeed, as Raleigh's writings reveal, the anxieties about female authority that emerge even in flattery addressed to her suggest that for some of her male subjects, the parallels were all too close for comfort. Just as women of God do not always readily fulfill the functions desired by men of arms, so too women of arms cannot help but trouble men of God like Hariot and De Bry, even when they are meant to function positively.

But for Elizabeth, too, the parallels between herself, the Briton woman, and the Pictish women (as well as those more recent women with whom the Pictish women are associated) would have perhaps suggested some uncomfortable truths too close to home. Although for Elizabeth I England's medieval, Catholic past was a foil for her construction of a Protestant golden age, it also provided fodder for her representational schemes. The medieval past was not really past, as much as Elizabeth, or anyone else, might have wanted it to be; furthermore, the elements of that past which she so carefully shaped to her self-representational ends always had a life of their own. The images of Picts and Britons are at once the same and different just as the English and the Native Americans, Catholics and Protestants, the Middle Ages and the early modern era are at once the same and different. De Bry's edition of Hariot's *Briefe and true report* finally teaches us that sameness and difference collapse into each other, as do past and present. As a result, the question of whether women had a Renaissance may not be a terribly urgent one to answer, or even quite the right question to ask.[54] Exploring the ongoing significance of medieval female spirituality as an arena for political action reveals that so much that was so culturally potent never "died," and hence never needed to be "reborn."

Notes

Introduction

1. Manuscript description from British Library online catalogue (http://www. molcat.bl.uk; accessed October 28, 2003).

2. London British Library MS Add. 25,351, fol. 16v; here, as elsewhere, italics in quotations from manuscripts indicate expansions of abbreviations. Henceforth I cite this manuscript parenthetically by folio. Unless otherwise noted, all translations throughout are my own.

3. The phrase comes from Clifford Geertz, "Centers, Kings, and Charisma: Reflections on the Symbolics of Power," in *Culture and Its Creators: Essays in Honour of Edward Shils*, ed. Joseph Ben-David and Terry Nichols Clark (Chicago: University of Chicago Press, 1977), 152.

4. On this sort of liminality, see Homi K. Bhabha, *The Location of Culture* (London: Routledge, 1994), 4.

5. Peter Lake with Michael Questier, *The Antichrist's Lewd Hat: Protestants, Papists, and Players in Post-Reformation England* (New Haven, Conn.: Yale University Press, 2002), 230.

6. Edward Said, "Intellectual Exile: Expatriates and Marginals," in *Representations of the Intellectual*, 1993 Reith Lectures (New York: Pantheon, 1994), 52.

Chapter 1. Monastic Politics: St. Colette of Corbie, Franciscan Reform, and the House of Burgundy

1. Pierre Damien, *Sainte Colette de Corbie et l'action catholique féminine française* (Paris: Libraire Saint-François d'Assise, 1946), 23.

2. Alphonse Germain, *Sainte Colette de Corbie (1381–1447)* (Paris: Poussilegue, 1903), 100.

3. Ibid., 100–101.

4. Poligny, Monastère de Sainte-Claire, A8. The documents in the archive of the Colettine nunnery at Poligny consist of original medieval manuscripts; copies (both hand copies and photocopies) of medieval documents, for which the original is often lost; and documents from the eighteenth, nineteenth, and early twentieth centuries concerning the history of the house and the order. The archives of the Colettine house at Amiens were deposited at Poligny when the former house was closed; when I quote from these manuscripts, I identify them both by their original and present locations. When a manuscript I have used is a copy, I indicate this fact in the relevant note. In many documents in this archive, pages are not

numbered; when this is the case, I also provide indication in a note. In all cases, I reproduce spelling, capitalization, punctuation, and diacritics as they appear; expansions of abbreviations in medieval manuscripts are indicated by italics. I have not, however, expanded abbreviations in hand copies of medieval manuscripts, since it is not always clear whether the abbreviations were made by the copiest or are present in the original. I am grateful to the abbess and sisters of the monastery for making their archive available to me during August 2000. The painting discussed above is reproduced in André Ravier, *Sainte Colette de Corbie* (Poligny: Monastère de Sainte-Claire, 1976), 29.

5. Elisabeth Lopez, *Petite vie de Sainte Colette* (Paris: Desclée, 1998), 58.

6. J-Th. Bizouard, *Histoire de Sainte Colette et des Clarisses en Bourgogne* (Paris: Haton, 1881), 108.

7. Poligny, Monastère de Sainte-Claire, B4.

8. Jules Corblet, *Hagiographie du diocèse d'Amiens*, vol. 1 (Paris: Dumoulin; Amiens: Prevost-Allo, 1868), 369 n.2, hereafter cited parenthetically as *Hagiographie*. Corblet's chosen text for his account of St. Colette's life is the French *Vie de Sainte Colette* of Pierre de Vaux, and it is this version of Colette's *vita*, written before the Latin version used in her canonization, to which I refer in this essay. Corblet declares, "We have undertaken to publish an unedited work from 1448, the *Vie de Ste Colette*, redacted by her last confessor, Pierre de Vaux, a reformed Franciscan friar" (361). Concerning his choice of manuscript, he says, "We have a choice between two manuscripts: one, which belonged to the Claresses of Amiens, is an authentic copy, made in 1491 by John Brondin; the other, later by at least a century, comes from the monastery in Ghent." Corblet further indicates that he decided to use the latter manuscript, not only because its "slightly modernized style" makes it easier for a general readership to comprehend, but also "because it contains fairly numerous additions borrowed from the accounts of Sister Perrine; the original for these accounts is now lost" (362).

9. Ravier, *Sainte Colette*, 9.

10. Fredric Jameson, *The Political Unconscious: Narrative as a Socially Symbolic Act* (Ithaca, N.Y.: Cornell University Press, 1981), 20.

11. Elisabeth Lopez, *Culture et sainteté: Colette de Corbie (1381–1447)* (Saint-Etienne: Publications de l'Université de Saint-Etienne, 1994), 152–53.

12. Colette's letter is quoted, in modernized French, in Lopez, *Culture*, 159.

13. Poligny, Monastère de Sainte-Claire, A14. This manuscript is a hand copy of the original letter; the pages of the copy are not numbered.

14. Ibid.

15. Poligny, Monastère de Sainte-Claire, A21. This manuscript is a hand copy of the original, which is housed in the Colettine monastery in Ghent; the pages of the copy are not numbered.

16. Colette's letter to Charles VII is quoted, in modernized French, in E. Sainte-Marie Perrin, *La belle vie de Sainte Colette de Corbie (1381–1447)* (Paris: Plon, 1921), 249, hereafter cited parenthetically as *Belle vie*.

17. Pierre Bourdieu, *Outline of a Theory of Practice*, trans. Richard Nice (Cambridge: Cambridge University Press, 1977), 178.

18. Ibid., 178, emphasis in original.

19. Ibid., 181, emphasis in original.

20. Ibid., 179, emphasis in original.

21. Lopez, *Culture*, 158.

22. These symbolic diminutions could also, of course, therefore exacerbate the very financial consequences that the monks initially feared. Benefactors were drawn to the perceived advantages of reformed communities, which had the added attraction of requiring comparatively little material outlay while providing for patrons valuable spiritual benefits and enhancing donors' own symbolic capital.

23. Germain, *Sainte Colette de Corbie*, 58 n. 1.

24. For instance, Philippe de Forceville reports that Joan was in Moulins in 1429 "to prepare for the siege of la Charité." Simultaneously, Colette "was in Moulins in 1429" and she would have thus had "a chance at least to *see*, and perhaps to embrace, the miraculous Maid." *Sainte Colette de Corbie et son alliance avec Yolande d'Anjou, reine des Quatre Royaumes* (Paris: Picard, 1958), 38–39, emphasis in original. The connection of Colette with Jerome of Prague in particular resonates with the close connection, in English eyes, between Joan of Arc and the Lollards, a connection highlighted by the contemporaneous, thematically convergent trials of Joan in Rouen and Lollards in Norwich. For a discussion of the connections between Joan of Arc and the Lollards, see chapter 7 of Nancy Bradley Warren, *Spiritual Economies: Female Monasticism in Later Medieval England* (Philadelphia: University of Pennsylvania Press, 2001).

25. On the accusations made against Joan of Arc, see W. P. Barrett, *The Trial of Jeanne d'Arc Translated into English from the Original Latin and French Documents* (London: Gotham House, 1932), 83, 91, 216–17.

26. R. I. Moore, *The Formation of a Persecuting Society: Power and Deviance in Western Europe 950–1250* (Oxford: Blackwell, 1987), 112.

27. Lopez, *Culture*, 63–65. Colette did not have "juridical power granted by the Sovereign Pontiff" to reform the First Order Franciscans, but she did have "a moral authority based on her intelligence, virtue, and know-how"; as Ubald d'Alençon observes, "The title of reformer of the First and Second Orders may be granted to St. Colette of Corbie without difficulty. She is entitled to it." Ubald d'Alençon, *Lettres inédites de Guillaume de Casal à Ste Colette et notes pour la biographie de cette sainte* (Paris: Picard, 1908), 14–15.

28. L'Abbé Douillet, *Sainte Colette, sa vie, son culte, son influence* (Paris: Bray, 1869), 122.

29. Germain, *Sainte Colette de Corbie*, 87 n.2.

30. Douillet, *Sainte Colette, sa vie*, 129.

31. Colette "certainly laid claim to the Observant movement, but not to the form of Observance created by the Council of Constance in 1415 and definitively constituted by the bull of Pope Eugene IV." Ubald d'Alençon, "Le Livre des Annales du Pauvre Monastère des Clarisses d'Amiens," 37; photocopy of handwritten document sent by author to Claresses at Amiens; Archives d'Amiens, carton 19; now in archives of Monastère de Sainte-Claire, Poligny.

32. Lopez, *Culture*, 270.

33. Letter 56 from the "dossier Casal," uncatalogued manuscripts in the Bibliothèque municipale de Besançon, printed in Alençon, *Lettres inédites*, 7; on this letter, see also Lopez, *Culture*, 271.

34. Poligny, Monastère de Sainte-Claire, A21.

35. Ibid.

36. Casal's letter to St. Colette, written from Toulouse in 1439, quoted in French translation of the Latin original in Lopez, *Culture*, 269.

37. Lopez, *Culture*, 168.

38. Photocopy of the original manuscript letter, carton 19, Archives d'Amiens now in Monastère de Sainte-Claire, Poligny; brackets indicate supplied letter missing in the photocopy and possibly on the manuscript as well.

39. Poligny, Monastère de Sainte-Claire, A18.

40. Lopez, *Culture*, 168.

41. Ibid., 177.

42. Ibid., 293.

43. Ernst A. Kock, *Three Middle-English Versions of the Rule of St. Benet and Two Contemporary Rituals for the Ordination of Nuns*, Early English Text Society o.s. 120 (1902; reprint, Millwood, N.Y.: Kraus, 1987), "Northern Verse Version," l. 2268. Kock edits this translation of the Benedictine Rule from London, British Library, MS Cotton Vespasian A. 25. For a more detailed discussion of construction of authority in Middle English translations of monastic rules, see chapter 2 of Warren, *Spiritual Economies*. In the negotiations of power that structure visitation procedures, one sees a similar difference between the conceptions of female authority in Colette's *Constitutions* and John's *Declaratio*. While John insists on the "full powers . . . granted to visitors" and on the submission of the abbess and nuns to the minister performing the visitation, Colette, who managed to obtain the right for her communities to be visited by Colettine friars, constructs "a relationship of superior to superior" between the visitor and the abbess (Lopez, *Culture* 288).

44. Bizouard, *Histoire de Sainte Colette*, 41.

45. Furthermore, it is likely due to Blanche's connections at the papal court in Avignon through her relative Clement VII that Colette managed to get a papal audience.

46. Roger Chartier, *On the Edge of the Cliff: History, Language, and Practices*, trans. Lydia G. Cochrane (Baltimore: Johns Hopkins University Press, 1997), 23.

47. André Vauchez, *The Laity in the Middle Ages: Religious Beliefs and Devotional Practices*, trans. Margery J. Schneider (Notre Dame, Ind.: University of Notre Dame Press, 1993), 225.

48. In light of the Yorkist connection with the Brigittine Order, and in relation to Margaret of York, duchess of Burgundy's, frequent participation in the efforts to secure Anglo-Burgundian alliances, it is worth noting that Margaret was a patroness not only of Colettine but also of Brigittine houses. For instance, she was named a trustee of the Brigittine house of Gouda, and her death appears in the necrology of the Brigittine house at Termonde; see F. R. Johnston, "The English Cult of St. Bridget of Sweden," *Analecta Bollandiana* 103 (1985): 87. On the political implications of Margaret of York's support of reformed monastic orders, see chapter 2 below.

49. Paris, Bibliothèque nationale, MS F. fr. 17909 fol. 151r. Expansions of abbreviations are indicated by italics.

50. Ibid.

51. The son, who owes his survival as well as his birth to Mary Magdalene, is responsible for the foundation of a Christian realm in France. "Le second Roy" [the second king] named "estienne," is, at Mary Magdalene's request, divinely resuscitated. During his fifty-two-year reign, he takes the "croix de mons*ieu*r St andrieu . . . pour son ensseigne" [cross of St. Andrew . . . for his sign], and he orders that this sign be born "*par* tous ceulx qui seroient xpiens en son roiaulme" [by all the Christians in the realm]. Subsequently, he required that "tous ceulx quy ne se baptiseroient" [those who were not baptised], presumably recognizable by the lack of the aforementioned sign, "*par*tissent hors de sondit roiaulme de bourgne" [depart from his said realm of Burgundy].

52. Paris, Bibliothèque Arsenal MS 3902 fol. 331r.

53. "It was a great festival day for the imperial city of Besançon when, on March 14, 1410, Colette, accompanied by Father Henri, the countess of Geneva, her niece Mahaut de Savoie, and her nuns, made her entry. An innumerable crowd thronged her route from the village of Beure, where the archbishop Thiebault de Rougement, along with his clerics, had gone to await her." M. le Chanoine de Vregille, *Sainte Colette vierge et réformatrice de l'Ordre de Sainte Claire* (Besançon: Monastère de Sainte-Claire de Besançon, 1907), 10–11.

54. On the costs of the foundation see Ravier, *Sainte Colette*, 22–23.

55. Letter in Archives de Dijon, printed in Bizouard, *Histoire de Sainte Colette*, 42–43.

56. Ravier, *Sainte Colette*, 23.

57. Germain, *Sainte Colette de Corbie*, 84.

58. Ibid., 84 n. 2.

59. Georges Chastellain, *Oeuvres*, ed. Kervyn de Lettenhove, 2 vols (Brussels: Heussner, 1864), 1: 188.

60. Jesse D. Hurlbut, "The City Renewed: Decorations for the 'Joyeuses Entrées' of Philip the Good and Charles the Bold," *Fifteenth Century Studies* 19 (1992): 79.

61. Joseph Calmette, *The Golden Age of Burgundy: The Magnificent Dukes and Their Court*, trans. Doreen Weightman (New York: Norton, 1962), 152.

62. The bourgeois of Ghent became impatient; Colette wrote in 1438 or 1439, clearly in response to a letter she had received, reassuring her benefactors that she would send nuns to inhabit the convent as soon as the roads were safe for travel. The letter, preserved in the monastery of Claresses in Ghent as a relic, is reprinted in Lopez, *Petite vie*, 89–92.

63. Since the nuns sent to begin new Colettine foundations tended to be "toutes formées en Bourgogne" [entirely educated in Burgundy] and "pour la plupart bourguignonnes" [for the most part Burgundian] (*Petite vie*, 57), the establishment of an important house of a "[c]ongrégation à dominante bourguignonne" [predominantly Burgundian congregation] in Ghent was clearly a strong step in the ducal efforts to create in the region "une Eglise à caractère national, dont les plus hauts responsables ne soient pas français ou allemands" [a church of a nationalist

character, in which those in the highest positions of responsibility were neither French nor German] (*Petite vie*, 73).

64. On the cult of St. Anne, see Kathleen Ashley and Pamela Sheingorn, eds., *Interpreting Cultural Symbols: Saint Anne in Late Medieval Society* (Athens: University of Georgia Press, 1990).

65. Chastellain, *Oeuvres*, 5: 119.

66. Ghent, Monastery of Bethlehem, MS 8 fol. 163r; quoted in Auspicius van Corstanje et al, *Vita Sanctae Coletae* (Tielt: Lannoo; Leiden: Brill, 1982), 149.

Chapter 2. Strategic Saints and Diplomatic Devotion: Margaret of York, Anne d'Orléans, and Female Political Action

1. Paris, Bibliothèque Arsenal MS 3602 fol. 325r. Here, as elsewhere in this chapter, when I quote from a manuscript I have indicated expansions of abbreviations with italics; for the expansions, I follow the spellings used elsewhere in the manuscripts. I am grateful to the British Academy for a Neil Ker Memorial Grant that supported my research on British manuscripts associated with Margaret of York.

2. In its version of Burgundian history, the Arsenal chronicle also gives a spiritual twist to a representational tactic frequently employed by "provincial historians of the late fifteenth and early sixteenth centuries" who "attempted to subvert the prestige of the French national chronicles by demonstrating an origin for their own lands and princely houses even more ancient than that of the French." Robert B. Rigoulot, "Imaginary History and Burgundian State-Building: The Translation of the Annals of Hainault," in *Essays in Medieval Studies: Proceedings of the Illinois Medieval Association* 9 (1992): 36.

3. Quoted in Richard Vaughan, *Charles the Bold: The Last Valois Duke of Burgundy* (New York: Barnes and Noble, 1973), 51. Walter Prevenier and Wim Blockmans observe that the commission of "tapestries depicting the coronation of Clovis . . . for the wedding of Charles the Bold and Margaret of York" was "proof of the heights to which the dynasty aspired." *The Burgundian Netherlands, 1380–1530* (Cambridge: Cambridge University Press, 1986), 318.

4. Wim Blockmans, "The Devotion of a Lonely Duchess," *Margaret of York, Simon Marmion, and* The Visions of Tondal: *Papers Delivered at a Symposium Organized by the Department of Manuscripts of the J. Paul Getty Museum in Collaboration with the Huntington Library and Art Collections, June 21–24, 1990*, ed. Thomas Kren (Malibu, Calif.: J. Paul Getty Museum, 1992), 29. As Kathryn Hall points out, "Edward IV of England viewed in his sister's marriage a means of securing protection for the continued exportation of English wool, while Charles the Bold, as head of the duchy that controlled the Netherlands, sought to restore the wool trade previously ruptured by a perceived inequity in silver and gold exchange." Kathryn Hall, "'Ne trespassez la regle de la religion de lobedience des souuerains': Margaret of York and the Douce 365 *L'Abbaye du saint esprit*," unpublished paper, 2; my thanks to Professor Hall for providing me with a copy of her essay.

5. Jeffrey Chipps Smith links Margaret's manuscript commissions with her political role (a role which he sees a mostly that of providing an example of piety)

and argues that after Charles's death, Margaret's role at court, and with it her patronage, declined in importance ("Margaret of York and the Burgundian Portrait Tradition," *Margaret of York, Simon Marmion*, 54). In the catalog for an exhibition of manuscripts associated with Margaret of York, E. Sabbe, in contrast, says that Margaret "seems, at least in the political domain, scarcely to have played a role in her husband's court" but acknowledges that she did take an active part in Burgundian affairs after Charles's death. In Banque de Bruxelles, *Marguerite d'York et son temps: Exposition organisée par la Banque de Bruxelles* (Bruxelles: Banque de Bruxelles, 1967), 16. Luc Hommel astutely points out that Margaret "definitely played an important political role. If this role does not always clearly appear in the documents of the era, it is because with the title of dowager duchess Margaret did not possess any political power and did not *officially* intervene in acts of the state. Nonetheless, she made her mark in political affairs in the last quarter of the fifteenth century." *Marguerite d'York ou la duchesse Junon* (Paris: Hachette, 1959), 313, emphasis in original.

6. Blockmans, "Devotion," 32.

7. Hommel indicates, "The restoration of her brother Edward, and the part she played in it, without a doubt enhanced the duchess's authority in the eyes of her Burgundian subjects" (*Marguerite d'York*, 75).

8. Christine Weightman, *Margaret of York, Duchess of Burgundy* (New York: St. Martin's, 1989), 188. Weightman adds that Margaret "was entirely independent in the administration and management of her dower lands, and she appointed her own officials" (Ibid., 189).

9. For example, a "cloister near Binche twice received 22 lb. par. 'en consideration et regart a la povrete d'icelle eglise et couvent et au grant nombre de personnes qui y sont a entretenir pour oeuvre de pitié et en aulmosne'[as an act of mercy and alms in consideration and regard of the poverty of that church and convent and of the large number of people that need to be maintained]" (Blockmans, "Devotion," 34). The account quoted by Blockmans appears in Brussels, Algemeen Rijksarchief, Rekenkamer no. 8839, fol. 39v. For information regarding Margaret's involvement with various monastic and ecclesiastical reform movements, as well as her numerous gifts to churches and religious foundations, see chapter 7 of Weightman, *Margaret of York*.

10. Weightman, *Margaret of York*, 205; on Margaret's library see Muriel J. Hughes, "Margaret of York, Duchess of Burgundy: Diplomat, Patroness, Bibliophile, and Benefactress," *Private Library* 3rd ser. 7, 1 (1984): 3–17, and Muriel J. Hughes, "The Library of Margaret of York, Duchess of Burgundy," *Private Library* 3rd ser. 7, 2 (1984): 53–78.

11. Thomas Kren, introduction, Kren, ed., *Margaret of York, Simon Marmion*, 16.

12. Smith, "Margaret of York and the Burgundian Portrait Tradition," 52. Smith does seem to see some potential for political significance in Margaret's spirituality, though. He goes on to say, "Just as Philip's portraits show him primarily as a patron of culture, and Charles is presented as an authoritative but conscientious ruler, Margaret's portraits seem to suggest a quasi-official spiritual role" (54). In a recent article on Margaret of York's pilgrimages, Harry Schnitker also considers the

importance of politics in influencing Margaret's choices of destination. He writes, "With Margaret, as with most of her contemporaries, pilgrimage worked on various levels. Her choice of pilgrimage destination was partly determined by family tradition, in Burgundy as well as in England. . . . Elements of politics—an ostentatious group of pilgrims can be quite an efficient way to show the colours—and questions of status also surface in the pilgrimages of high-ranking individuals like Margaret of York." "Margaret of York on Pilgrimage: The Exercise of Devotion and the Religious Traditions of the House of York," *Reputation and Representation in Fifteenth-Century Europe*, ed. Douglas L. Biggs, Sharon D. Michalove, and A. Compton Reeves (Leiden: E.J. Brill, 2004), 82.

13. Prevenier and Blockmans, *The Burgundian Netherlands*, 244.

14. Ibid., 246, 248.

15. Kren, introduction, *Margaret of York, Simon Marmion*, 16.

16. Weightman, *Margaret of York*, 23.

17. In his discussion of Margaret's pilgrimages, Schnitker notes that "the question arises as to whether contemporaries differentiated between religious and worldly impulses for their devotional practices and whether this matters. Perhaps not" ("Margaret of York on Pilgrimage," 100). Again, I would go one step further to say that Margaret and her contemporaries at times purposefully conflated "religious and worldly impulses," and at other times productively exploited already blurred boundaries between the two.

18. Smith, "Margaret of York and the Burgundian Portrait Tradition," 49; on this miniature, see also Weightman, *Margaret of York*, 203–4.

19. Smith, "Margaret of York and the Burgundian Portrait Tradition," 49.

20. For instance, a miniature of Charles in a military *Ordinance* depicts an image of the crucified Christ at the top with Charles on the bottom. "Dressed half in armor as a knight and half in the ermine robe of a prince, Charles holds the sword of justice and a Bible, on which is inscribed Christ's monogram and the text 'Nihil sine me.' That is, Charles is nothing without Christ since it is from the Lord that his power and authority as vicar stem" (Smith, "Margaret of York and the Burgundian Portrait Tradition," 49–50).

21. On the importance of this gift for Burgundian political undertakings in Ghent, see chapter 1.

22. Blockmans, "Devotion," 42. This crown has typically been understood to be the one Margaret wore at her marriage to Charles the Bold. Alasdair MacDonald has persuasively suggested to me in private communication, though, that based on his interpretation of the crown's inscription, he believes it may be a votive crown crafted specially to donate to the statue of the Virgin. Others have suggested that the small size of the crown is a result of its having been made for the then-young Margaret for her brother Edward IV's coronation in 1461. On the debate about the origins of the crown, see Schnitker, "Margaret of York on Pilgrimage," 108.

23. Jean Squilbeck, in Banque de Bruxelles, *Marguerite d'York et son temps*, 47. Charles's royal ambitions may be seen in his requiring his subject to address him as "most dread and sovereign lord" rather than simply as "most dread lord" (Steven

Gunn, "Henry VII and Charles the Bold: Brothers Under the Skin?" *History Today* 46, 4 (1996): 30. On Charles's desire for a kingdom, see Vaughan, *Charles the Bold*, chapters 3, 4.

24. Vaughan, *Charles the Bold*, 38.

25. Ibid.

26. Ibid.

27. Blockmans, "Devotion," 42.

28. Schnitker, "Margaret of York on Pilgrimage," 111. Furthermore, he says, "Perhaps Margaret, the princess of England and descendant of kings, spurred on her husband in his attempts to gain the royal title. The symbolic act of donating the crown of a ruler to the Queen of Heaven to underline the rightfulness of a quest for the royal title was one that occurred once more in a Yorkist context. In 1487 the crown used in the coronation of Lambert Simnel, the Yorkist pretender to the English crown, was donated to the statue of the Virgin in Dublin" (110).

29. Rigoulot, "Imaginary History," 37.

30. Blockmans sees in Margaret's devotional choices a reflection of her un-fulfilled desire for children, since the saints to which she paid particular attention have associations with conception, pregnancy, and childbirth. He writes, "The coherence in Margaret's devotion is striking. It almost always involves children, childbearing, and family" ("Devotion" 39). While Margaret's reproductive desires may certainly have influenced her spiritual life, I would argue that, for a duchess of Burgundy, such desires are themselves profoundly political.

31. Vaughan, *Charles the Bold*, 5.

32. Ibid., 7.

33. Ibid., 9.

34. Roger Chartier, *On the Edge of the Cliff: History, Language, and Practices*, trans. Lydia G. Cochrane (Baltimore: Johns Hopkins University Press, 1997), 23.

35. Rigoulot, "Imaginary History," 37.

36. Peter Arnade, *Realms of Ritual: Burgundian Ceremony and Civic Life in Late Medieval Ghent* (Ithaca, N.Y.: Cornell University Press, 1996), 156.

37. Blockmans, "Devotion," 39.

38. Ibid., 38.

39. Weightman, *Margaret of York*, 85.

40. On Richard II, Anne, and the city of London, as well as for a discussion of queenly intercession more broadly, see the chapter entitled "Queens as Inter-cessors," in Paul Strohm, *Hochon's Arrow: The Social Imagination of Fourteenth-Century Texts* (Princeton, N.J.: Princeton University Press, 1992).

41. Kathleen Ashley and Pamela Sheingorn, "Introduction," in *Interpreting Cultural Symbols: Saint Anne in Late Medieval Society* (Athens: University of Georgia Press, 1990), 50–51. Ashley and Sheingorn also note that St. Anne was "a popular patron" of "confraternities or brotherhoods which had devotional, social, and charitable functions as well as craft or civic affiliations . . . perhaps because her status as a bourgeois wife and mother rendered her a particularly appropriate role model for confraternity members who were also in the comfortable married pious middle class" (51).

42. Arnade, *Realms of Ritual*, 171. Interestingly, there was also a rhetoricians' confraternity of St. Barbara, although there is little surviving information concerning it (170).

43. Ibid., 160.

44. Ibid., 171.

45. Ibid.

46. Blockmans, "Devotion," 39.

47. Ibid., 39. Eric Inglis indicates that "Charles . . . adopted George as a personal patron; he is depicted in the saint's company in the prayerbook of Charles the Bold in Malibu (J. Paul Getty Museum, MS 37)." "Commentary," *The Hours of Mary of Burgundy Codex Vindobonensis 1857 Vienna, Österreiscische Nationalbibliothek* (London: Harvey Miller, 1995), 46. Charles also presented a gold reliquary depicting himself kneeling with St. George standing behind him to St. Lambert's cathedral in Liège (Prevenier and Blockmans, *Burgundian Netherlands*, 310; a full page color photograph of the reliquary appears on 311).

48. Arnade, *Realms of Ritual*, 83.

49. Ibid., 71.

50. Ibid., 77.

51. Inglis notes that Maximilian was "later in his life . . . even depicted in the guise of the saint" ("Commentary" 46).

52. For extensive discussion of Margaret's participation in the Perkin Warbeck affair, see Hommel, chapter 15, and Weightman, *Margaret of York*, chapter 6. In a letter Warbeck wrote to Isabel of Castile to try to secure her support, he invokes his connections with the duchess of Burgundy, calling her "Dominam Ducissam burgundie parentis mei sororem" and making reference to the aid she has given him (London, British Library MS Egerton 616, fol. 3r). The letter did not, however, convince Isabel to help him.

53. On Charles's membership in the Order of the Garter, see Vaughan, *Charles the Bold*, 60.

54. Urbain Plancher, *Histoire générale et particulière de Bourgogne avec les preuves justificatives* 4 vols. (Dijon: A. de Fray, 1739–1781), 4: preuves, cclxxxix. Charles also aligned himself with the (in this case Yorkist) English party and again invoked St. George for distinctly propagandist purposes during an especially difficult period of Franco-Burgundian relations. In May 1470, he wrote a letter to Louis XI's royal counselors at Rouen protesting Louis's purported involvement in "Warwick's piratical escapades" (Vaughan, *Charles the Bold*, 65). Charles blustered, "Archbishop, and you admiral, the ships which you say were sent by the king against the English have now attacked my subjects' ships on their return to my territories; but, by St. George, if anything can be done, with the help of God, I shall do it, without waiting for your leave, nor your explanations or judicial decision" (Plancher, 4: no 215, quoted in translation in Vaughan, *Charles the Bold*, 65). In response to his enemy Louis XI's association with the Earl of Warwick after the latter's switch from the party of Edward IV to the party of Henry VI, Charles also declared, according to Chastellain, "Entre nous Portugalois avons une coustume deuers nous, que quand ceulx que nous avouns tenu à nos amis se font amis à nos ennemis, nous le commandons à tous les cent mille diables d'enfer" [We Portuguese

have a custom that when those whom we have considered to be our friends make friends with our enemies, we command them to all the hundred thousand devils of hell]. Quoted in John Foster Kirk, *History of Charles the Bold, Duke of Burgundy*, 3 vols. (Philadelphia: Lippincott, 1898), 2: 39 n. 36. As Chastellain observes of this declaration, Charles's calling himself Portuguese is in effect a code for calling himself "Anglois" [English] (2: 39 n.6).

55. London, British Library, MS Stowe 668 fol. 36v.

56. Vaughan, *Charles the Bold*, 60.

57. Weightman, *Margaret of York*, 98.

58. Vaughan, *Charles the Bold*, 67; first ellipses mine, second in original.

59. Kirk, *History of Charles the Bold, Duke of Burgundy*, 2: 79. Vaughan observes that Charles's "attitude toward English affairs was conditioned less by sentiment, and more by his relations with the other north-west European maritime powers: France especially, but also the Hanse and Denmark. Thus, though he had married Margaret of York, Charles still maintained two notable Lancastrian exiles at his court . . . : Edmund Beaufort, earl and duke of Somerset, and Henry Holland, duke of Exeter" (*Charles the Bold*, 61).

60. Kirk, *History of Charles the Bold, Duke of Burgundy*, 2: 116 n. 41.

61. During his exile in 1471, Edward IV sought refuge in Bruges with Louis de Gruuthuse. There, "he had the occasion . . . to admire a superb library of manuscripts" (Hommel, *Marguerite d'York*, 329). Edward "was so impressed by the ritual and organization of the Burgundian court that shortly thereafter he commissioned the duke's master of ceremonies, Olivier de la Marche, to describe for him the workings of the Burgundian household" (Kren, introduction, *Margaret of York, Simon Marmion*, 17).

62. Sabbe, *Marguerite d'York et son temps*, 15.

63. Hommel, *Marguerite d'York*, 124–25.

64. For details concerning the diplomatic hurdles Margaret faced during her negotiations with Edward IV in London, see Hommel, *Marguerite d'York*, 124–31.

65. Interestingly, Margaret was accompanied to London by her head household official, "le chevalier d'honneur," who was "un noble savoyard, le sire de la Beaume" (Hommel, *Marguerite d'York*, 161–62). He was part of the same family that had done so much to foster the Burgundians' politically useful connections with St. Colette and her Franciscan reform movements, as discussed in the previous chapter. As will become clear, my reading of the Margaret's role in introducing the Observant Franciscans into England differs dramatically from Schnitker, who argues that "the introduction of the Observant Franciscans into England, was definitely a side aspect to the main reason for her presence, the attempt at creating an Anglo-Burgundian alliance" ("Margaret of York on Pilgrimage," 84 n. 13). On the contrary, I see Margaret's interest in creating a presence for the Observants in England as *part* of her attempt to create an Anglo-Burgundian alliance.

66. On Edward's reversal of Henry VI's charter, see George James Aungier, *The History and Antiquities of Syon Monastery, the Parish of Isleworth, and the Chapelry of Hounslow* (London: Nichols, 1840), 69. On Edward IV's support for Syon and the larger implications of his status as the house's "second founder," see chapter 5

of Nancy Bradley Warren, *Spiritual Economies: Female Monasticism in Later Medieval England* (Philadelphia: University of Pennsylvania Press, 2001).

67. A. G. Little, "The Introduction of the Observant Friars in England," *Proceedings of the British Academy* 10 (1921–1923): 458.

68. Hommel, *Marguerite d'York*, 124.

69. In addition to supporting Observant Friars in Malines, records show that Margaret visited a house of Observants near Brussels in 1473 (Weightman, *Margaret of York*, 237 n. 41).

70. Little, "The Introduction of the Observant Friars," 459–60. Greenwich was the only house of Observants in England until 1498, when "three conventual houses were transferred to the Observants, not by any spontaneous movement in the Order, but by 'the king's commandment'" (465). Henry VII was very interested in the Observants, and he showed special favor toward the Greenwich friars. Henry VII left the Observant Friars of Greenwich £200 "to inclose their garden and orchard with a brick-wall, and bequeathed £200 to the prior of the Charterhouse in trust for the use of the friars at Greenwich, as he 'knew they had been many times in peril of ruin for lack of food.'" William Page, ed., *The Victoria County History of the County of Kent*, 3 vols (1926; reprint London: Dawsons, 1974), 2: 195. Henry VII's attraction to this religious community may represent, ironically enough, an effort to take over the symbolic and spiritual benefits it had provided to the Yorkist dynasty, much as the Yorkists had earlier done with the Lancastrian-founded Brigittine house of Syon. Interestingly, Henry VIII also favored the Greenwich friars, giving them "frequent grants of money" until the "question of the nullity of the marriage of Henry VIII with Catherine brought the friars into direct conflict with the king" (195–96). On this conflict, and especially on the friar William Peto's controversial sermon condemning Henry VIII, see Chapter 5 below.

71. A folio from this gradual was bound as folio 9 with London, British Library MS Arundel 71; it is now bound separately under the designation Arundel 71 fol. 9. A note at the bottom of the folio reads "A Booke called a graile given vnto the graie observant friars of greenwich by Margaret duchesse of Bourgoine sister vnto k: Edward :4: the booke was made beyond the seas" (fol. 9r).

72. Little, "Introduction of the Observant Friars," 460.

73. The ordination lists are reproduced by Little as Appendix II of "The Introduction of the Observant Friars," 470–71.

74. The friars of Malines clearly fit the bill in this regard. Margaret had a long and very close relationship with the Observant Friars of Malines. She had initially persuaded the Beghards of that city to become Observant Friars (Weightman, *Margaret of York*, 201). As in many such cases, there was opposition among some members of the community to the reforms, and, according to Hommel, "the conflict endured a long time." Some citizens supported the religious who opposed reforms, but Margaret "took under her protection those among the religious who had agreed to reform themselves" (Hommel, *Marguerite d'York*, 321). Margaret also was involved in the appointment in 1480 of a new superior of the Franciscans in Malines, "a religious of great authority, Théodore de Munster" (321). She gave substantial funds to the community for its enlargement, and in 1497, after a fire destroyed the library, she paid for its reconstruction (322).

75. Prevenier and Blockmans, *The Burgundian Netherlands*, 246.

76. Prevenier and Blockmans point out that the dukes' and duchesses' concentration "on a few selected religious orders . . . was by no means coincidence; by directing their sympathies towards the orders that were fashionable at the time . . . [they] ensured their popularity" (248). They also note that support for the "strict Observants, who placed less emphasis upon material possessions" was "in keeping with the dukes' policy to restrict the possessions of the church" (249).

77. London, British Library MS Add. 7970 fol. 30r. Hereafter I cite this work parenthetically as *Dyalogue*.

78. The manuscript reads, "Leurs ofices te*n*dro*n*t et exerseront en gra*n*t soing et crainte de dieu sans orguel et vanite prudenteme*n*t et dilligamment et mapelleront et inuoqueront songneuseme*n*t pour estre adrechiez de mon saint esperit en tous leurs affayres et ne querront point leurs propres prouffis delices et honneurs mais tous iours le prouffit du bien conmun" [They hold and exercise their offices with great care and fear of God, without pride and vanity, prudently and diligently, and they scrupulously call on Me and invoke Me to be guided by My Holy Spirit in all their affairs and never seek their own profits, desires, and honors but rather always the advancement of the common good] (*Dyalogue*, fols. 30r–v).

79. Jesus says, "Et se tu me dis que tue es flaive de corps, et ia anchienne de tamps Tu as ton mary prince trespuissant" [And if you tell Me that you are too weak of body, and too old, you have your husband a powerful prince] (*Dyalogue*, 100r).

80. Quoted in Hommel, *Marguerite d'York*, 335.

81. Hommel, *Marguerite d'York*, 337.

82. Quoted in Hommel, *Marguerite d'York*, 337. A French translation of the Latin appears in ibid., n. 1.

83. Margaret's tomb, in the church of the Observant Franciscans of Malines, was destroyed by iconoclasts in the late sixteenth century. Shortly before its destruction, however, it was described by a visitor to the church between 1550 and 1560. This description survives in Paris, Bibliothèque Arsenal MS CFR 62541, fol. 146. The folio is reproduced in J. J. Tricot-Royer, "A la recherche de Marguerite d'York," in *Science, Medicine, and History: Essays on the Evolution of Scientific Thought and Medical Practice Written in Honour of Charles Singer*, ed. E. Ashworth Underwood, 2 vols. (London: Oxford University Press, 1953), 1: 220. Tricot-Royer also includes a transcription of the description of the tomb on 221. The translation comes from Weightman, *Margaret of York*, 215.

84. Paris, Bibliothèque Arsenal MS CFR 62,541, fol. 146; for facsimile see Tricot-Royer, 220: for a transcription see 221.

85. On Margaret's tomb, see also Weightman, *Margaret of York*, 215.

86. Anne's cousin and predecessor as abbess and reformer of Fontevraud was Marie de Bretagne, sister of Duke Francis II of Britanny.

87. B. Palustre, "L'Abbesse Anne d'Orléans et le réforme de Fontevrault," *Revue des questions historiques* 66 (1899): 211. The spelling "Fontevraud" is now generally preferred, and that is the spelling I adopt. However, when I quote sources, I retain "Fontevrault" where it appears.

88. Berenice M. Kerr, *Religious Life for Women, c. 1100–c. 1350: Fontevraud in England* (Oxford: Clarendon, 1999), 66.

89. Ibid., 67.

90. Marjorie Chibnall, "L'Ordre de Fontevraud en Angleterre au XII s.," *Cahiers de civilisation médiévale* 29, 1–2 (1986): 43.

91. Ibid.

92. Alfred Jubien, *L'Abbesse Marie de Bretagne et la réforme de l'ordre de Fontevrault* (Angers: Barassé; Paris: Didier, 1872), 29 n.1.

93. Letter quoted in Jubien, *L'Abbesse Marie de Bretagne*, 30, continuation of note 1 from page 29.

94. This fact has led some scholars to argue that English daughter houses of Fontevraud became entirely denizen, breaking ties with the foreign mother-house. However, as I discuss below, evidence points to ties persisting between the French abbey and the English priories well into the fifteenth, and possibly even into the sixteenth, century.

95. H. F. Chettle, "The English Houses of the Order of Fontevraud," *Downside Review* (January 1942): 43.

96. Jubien, *L'Abbesse Marie de Bretagne*, 28–31.

97. R. B. Pugh and Elizabeth Crittall, eds., *The Victoria History of the County of Wiltshire*, 2 vols. (London: Oxford University Press, 1953–1957), 2: 253.

98. Yvonne Parrey, "'Devoted disciples of Christ': Early Sixteenth-Century Religious Life in the Nunnery at Amesbury," *Bulletin of the Institute of Historical Research* 164 (1994): 244.

99. Pugh and Crittall, eds., *Victoria History of the County of Wiltshire*, 2: 253.

100. Ibid.

101. The Fontevrauldine Order, from its inception, subjected male members to the rule of an abbess. Not surprisingly, this led at times to a certain amount of masculine resistance, and in the years leading up to Marie's introduction of reforms, power was largely seized, "if not officially, at least in practice" by "male religious." Like St. Colette in her reforms of the Franciscan Order, Marie, and Anne after her, had to face not only opposition by those who "desired to live in freedom" but also by those who denied the authority of a female reformer (Jubien, *L'Abbesse Marie de Bretagne*, 111). By the time of Marie's death in 1477, the reforms had spread only to three houses. Anne, with strong support from ecclesiastical and secular authorities alike, was able to implement more widely reaching reforms. As Jubien observes, "the pope, the kings Louis XI and Charles VII facilitated the accomplishments and the efforts of the newly elected abbess with their bulls and gifts" (27). In October of 1479, Louis XI confirmed all the Order's privileges, and in that same year the pope made the reforms obligatory for the whole order (23–24). Charles VIII also facilitated the introduction of the reforms into "three priories: l'Encloître in Gironde—Foicy in Champagne—Variville in Beauvoisis"; furthermore, he helped Anne "secure recognition of her authority by further-flung monasteries" (28).

102. Chibnall, "L'Ordre de Fontevraud," 41.

103. Pugh and Crittall, eds., *Victoria History of the County of Wiltshire*, 2: 253.

Chapter 3. The Sword and the Cloister: Joan of Arc, Margaret of Anjou, and Christine de Pizan in England, 1445–1540

1. I discuss *La Poncella de Francia* and Joan's afterlife in Spain in Chapter 4.

2. Earl Jeffrey Richards, "French Cultural Nationalism and Christian Universalism in the Works of Christine de Pizan," in *Politics, Gender, and Genre: The Political Thought of Christine de Pizan*, ed. Margaret Brabant (Boulder, Colo.: Westview, 1992), 75.

3. Christine's status in England was further complicated by the fact that, although during part of her career she was closely tied with the English court, where her son was in residence, after Henry IV usurped the throne from Richard II, her formerly good relationship with the English monarchy soured.

4. The period of highest regard for and widest circulation of Christine de Pizan's texts in England ranges roughly from 1445, when a copy of the *Le Livre de faits d'armes et de chevalerie* was included in a manuscript given to Margaret of Anjou upon her marriage to Henry VI, through the first half of the sixteenth century. The year 1521 saw Henry Pepwell's publication of Brian Anslay's translation of *Le Livre de la cité des dames*, which was followed, c. 1540, by the printer Robert Wyer's translation of *L'Epistre d'Othea*. This nearly hundred-year period is a particularly turbulent one, corresponding with the Wars of the Roses, their factional entanglements on the Continent, and their aftermath in the Tudor era. It also witnessed crushing English losses in France and the subsequent renewals of the English claim to the French throne by Edward IV and the Tudor monarchs.

5. Ian Frederick Moulton, *Before Pornography: Erotic Writing in Early Modern England* (Oxford: Oxford University Press, 2000), 72. He is speaking of the late sixteenth and seventeenth centuries, but the conflations he observes were already emerging in the later Middle Ages. Indeed, these anxieties began to coalesce, as I shall discuss, fairly early in the Lancastrian era.

6. On the retroactive construction of meaning, see Slavoj Žižek, *The Sublime Object of Ideology* (London: Verso, 1989), 56.

7. On repetition and trauma, see Sigmund Freud, "Fixation to Traumas—The Unconscious," in *Introductory Lectures on Psycho-Analysis*, Standard Edition, ed. and trans. James Strachey (New York: Norton, 1933), 340.

8. L. O. Aranye Fradenburg, *Sacrifice Your Love: Psychoanalysis, Historicism, Chaucer*, Medieval Cultures 31 (Minneapolis: University of Minnesota Press, 2002), 44.

9. Jennifer Summit has made a somewhat parallel argument in her excellent book *Lost Property*, where she claims that the figure of and the texts of Christine de Pizan paradoxically enable English recastings of aristocratic masculinity and authorship in the literary sphere. Jennifer Summit, *Lost Property: The Woman Writer and English Literary History 1380–1589* (Chicago: University of Chicago Press, 2000), 61–107. As this chapter will make clear, my reading of English versions of Christine's texts, and my understanding of what constitutes English masculinity in the later medieval and early modern periods, differ in important respects from Summit's interpretations.

10. For instance, in the will Henry V made in 1415 before departing for France, he endowed thousands of Masses to honor the mysteries and joys of the Virgin Mary. He also expressed his wish that an altar honoring the Annunciation of the Virgin be constructed at his tomb. The specification of the type of Masses and the choice of an altar dedicated to the moment in which the divine Word becomes flesh in a female body reveal Henry's concern with, and desire to associate himself with, women's ability to transmit the divine into the human realm. This association is especially significant given its emphasis in the will made at the very moment Henry was pressing by military means his claim to the throne of France, a claim dependent on descent through the female line. For the terms of Henry's 1415 will, see J. A. Lauritis, R. A. Klinefelter, and V. F. Gallagher, Introduction, *A Critical Edition of John Lydgate's* Life of Our Lady, Duquesne Studies Philological Series 2 (Pittsburgh: Duquesne University Press, 1961), 7. For a detailed discussion Henry's will, as well as of Lancastrian and Yorkist strategies for representing their claims to the thrones of England and France more generally, see chapter 5 of Nancy Bradley Warren, *Spiritual Economies: Female Monasticism in Later Medieval England* (Philadelphia: University of Pennsylvania Press, 2001).

11. Christine de Pizan played an interesting role in the French project of crafting a model of succession that excludes women from opportunities to rule, a project prompted in part by English claims. Sarah Hanley points out that Christine's *City of Ladies* "circulated in political quarters" among "Queen Isabelle of Bavaria (regent intermittently for the ill Charles VI) and men and women of the high nobility; jurists, *parlementaires*, academics, and royal officials," spreading the "striking conclusion" that "women are capable of rule, have ruled, do rule, and in the future may rule in a *body politic* if called to the task" ("Mapping Rulership of the French Body Politic: Political Identity, Public Law and the King's One Body," *Historical Reflections / Reflexions Historiques* 23 (1997): 131, emphasis in original). Hanley notes that in response to the *City*, Jean de Montreuil, with whom Christine had been engaged in the debate about women and the *Romance of the Rose*, "wrote two works, *To All the Knighthood* (1409) and *Treatise Against the English* (1413), which refuted Pizan's political arguments . . . and pressed the case for the exclusion of women from rule in France. In those works he introduced, for the first time, textual renditions of a Salic Law. . . . In order to thwart Pizan's influential *City of Ladies*, refurbish his reputation tarnished by the earlier exchanges and defend his own political agenda, Montreuil fabricated a Salic Law" (131–32).

12. For instance, Lydgate's "Ballade to King Henry VI Upon His Coronation" describes the king as the "Royal braunche descendid from twoo lynes / Of Saynt Edward and of saynt Lowys." John Lydgate, "Ballade to King Henry VI Upon His Coronation," *The Minor Poems of John Lydgate*, part 2, ed. Henry Noble Mac-Cracken, Early English Text Society e.s. 107 (London: Oxford University Press, 1933), lines 9–10.

13. Steven Weiskopf, "Readers of the Lost Arc: Secrecy, Specularity, and Speculation in the Trial of Joan of Arc," in *Fresh Verdicts on Joan of Arc*, ed. Bonnie Wheeler and Charles T. Wood, New Middle Ages 3 (New York: Garland, 1996), 124. Furthermore, Susan Schibanoff astutely notes that in Joan's trial, "what was

'at stake' was not merely God, King, and Nation but the traditional constituent of all three, manhood." "True Lies: Transvestism and Idolatry in the Trial of Joan of Arc," *Fresh Verdicts on Joan of Arc*, 53.

14. For a discussion of the contents of this manuscript, see Michel-André Bossy, "Arms and the Bride: Christine de Pizan's Military Treatise as a Wedding Gift for Margaret of Anjou," *Christine de Pizan and the Categories of Difference*, ed. Marilynn Desmond, Medieval Cultures 14 (Minneapolis: University of Minnesota Press, 1998), 236–56.

15. Ruth Mazo Karras usefully discusses "the importance of the male line in the understanding of aristocratic manhood" in the chapter entitled "Mail Bonding: Knights, Ladies, and the Proof of Manhood" in her recent book *From Boys to Men: Formations of Masculinity in Late Medieval Europe* (Philadelphia: University of Pennsylvania Press, 2003), 20–66 (quote from page 35).

16. Bossy, "Arms and the Bride," 245.

17. Ibid.

18. London, British Library MS Royal 15 E VI fol. 2v, lines 5–8, quoted in Bossy, "Arms and the Bride," 240.

19. Bossy, "Arms and the Bride," 241.

20. Ibid., 251.

21. Ibid., 252–53.

22. Christine de Pizan, *The Book of Deeds of Arms and of Chivalry*, trans. Sumner Willard, ed. Charity Cannon Willard (University Park: Pennsylvania State University Press, 1999), 16.

23. See William Worcester, *The Boke of Noblesse Addressed to King Edward the Fourth on his Invasion of France in 1475, with an Introduction by John Gough Nichols* (1860; reprint, New York: Burt Franklin, 1972), 6–7. Hereafter I cite this work parenthetically as *Boke of Noblesse*.

24. See Frances Teague, "Christine de Pizan's *Book of War*," in *The Reception of Christine de Pizan from the Fifteenth Through the Nineteenth Centuries: Visitors to the City*, ed. Glenda K. McLeod, Medieval and Renaissance Series 9 (Lewiston, N.Y.: Edwin Mellen, 1991), 36–37, and the head note to "William Caxton, Translation of Christine de Pizan's *Book of Fayttes of Armes and of Chyvalrye*: Prologue," in *The Idea of the Vernacular: An Anthology of Middle English Literary Theory, 1280–1520*, ed. Jocelyn Wogan-Browne et al. (University Park: Pennsylvania State University Press, 1999), 169. The epilogue appears in A. T. P. Byles, ed., *The Book of the Fayttes of Armes and of Chyvalrye Translated and Printed by William Caxton from the French Original by Christine de Pisan*, Early English Text Society o.s. 189 (London: Oxford University Press, 1932).

25. Patricia-Ann Lee, "Reflections of Power: Margaret of Anjou and the Dark Side of Queenship," *Renaissance Quarterly* 39 (1986): 185.

26. Christine's prologue is printed from London, British Library MS Royal 19 B xviii in Byles, ed., *The Book of Fayttes of Armes and of Chyvalrye*, 5–8. For a modern English translation of this prologue, see Willard and Willard, trans., *The Book of Deeds of Arms*, 11–13.

27. Louise Olga Fradenburg, *City, Marriage, Tournament: Arts of Rule in Late Medieval Scotland* (Madison: University of Wisconsin Press, 1991), 212.

28. On this connection, see Ann W. Astell, *Political Allegory in Late Medieval England* (Ithaca, N.Y.: Cornell University Press, 1999), 139.

29. *The Commentaries of Pius II, Book IX*, trans. Florence Alden Gragg, with historical notes by Leona C. Gabel, Smith College Studies in History 25 (Northampton, Mass.: Department of History, Smith College, 1939–40), 580. On Margaret's self-identification with Joan, see also Astell, *Political Allegory*, 147, and Lee, "Reflections of Power," 198–99.

30. Christine de Pizan, *Ditié de Jehanne d'Arc*, Agnes J. Kennedy and Kenneth Varty, eds., *Medium Aevum Monographs* n. s. 9 (Oxford: Society for the Study of Mediaeval Languages and Literatures, 1977), lines 265–72. Henceforth I cite this text parenthetically by line number; the translations are from the one included in Kennedy and Varty's edition and are cited parenthetically by page number.

31. Deborah A. Fraioli, *Joan of Arc: The Early Debate* (Woodbridge: Boydell, 2000), 118.

32. Ibid., 103.

33. Ibid., 123–24.

34. On the many ironic elements of the manuscript's history, see Teague, "Christine de Pizan's *Book of War*," 25–41.

35. On the negative associations of Margaret and Joan, which appear fullfledged in, for instance, Shakespeare's *Henry VI* plays, and on their development in the later fifteenth and early sixteenth centuries, see Lee, "Reflections of Power," especially 190–91, 198–210, as well as Astell, *Political Allegory*, 146–51.

36. Dhira B. Mahoney, "Middle English Regenderings of Christine de Pizan," *The Medieval Opus: Imitation, Rewriting, and Transmission in the French Tradition*, ed. Douglas Kelly, Faux Titre: Études de la langue et littérature françaises 116 (Amsterdam: Rodopi, 1996), 407–8. Fastolf also served as John, duke of Bedford's master of the household, and Bedford too brought many manuscripts of Christine's texts (including the famous London, British Library MS Harley 4431 presented to Isabeau of Bavaria) back to England from France as spoils of victory.

37. On this "genealogy" of textual transmission, see Summit, *Lost Property*, 68–81.

38. K. B. McFarlane, "William Worcester: A Preliminary Survey," in *Studies Presented to Sir Hilary Jenkinson*, ed. J. Conway Davies (London: Oxford University Press, 1957), 200. Fastolf was, significantly, assisted in this case by none other than William Worcester, who had in turn his own disquieting experience with the French when he was captured at Dieppe and only managed to escape by bribing some French seamen (200 n.7).

39. On Edward IV and Joan of Arc, see Astell, *Political Allegory*, 153–57.

40. P. G. C. Campbell, "Christine de Pisan en Angleterre," *Revue de littérature comparée* 5 (1925): 669.

41. Margery Kempe, *The Book of Margery Kempe*, ed. Lynn Staley (Kalamazoo: Western Michigan University Press, 1996), 41.

42. Jennifer Summit similarly argues that Christine's "cloistering" denies her a role as an active participant in "the communities of men who are imagined to be the true creators of her books" (*Lost Property*, 81).

43. Curt F. Bühler points out that "Not many French contributions of so

early a date aroused sufficient interest to call forth three separate English translations within the space of a hundred years." *The Epistle of Othea Translated from the French Text of Christine de Pisan by Stephen Scrope*, ed. Curt F. Bühler, Early English Text Society o.s. 264 (London: Oxford University Press, 1970), xii–xiii, hereafter cited parenthetically as *Epistle*.

44. Another likely, and not mutually exclusive, possibility is that discussed by Summit, who notes the ways in which the *Othea*, like the *Faits d'armes*, "works to dislodge chivalry from its medieval associations with courtly love" and to demonstrate that "study and learning are . . . as strenuous and demanding as the arts of war." The text thus participates in the process of "redefining the knight as a figure of learning and prudence" (Summit, *Lost Property*, 67).

45. *Christine de Pizan's Letter of Othea to Hector*, trans. Jane Chance (Newburyport, Mass.: Focus, 1990), 35. Subsequent citations are to this edition (hereafter *Othea*) and are made parenthetically by page number.

46. Chance, Introduction, ibid., 26.

47. For a discussion of this Introduction, and possible identifications of the "hye princesse," see *Epistle,* ed. Bühler, xix–xxi as well as A. I. Doyle's Appendix B to this edition, 125–27.

48. Chance, introduction, *Christine de Pizan's Letter of Othea to Hector*, 8.

49. *Othea*, 120 n.1.

50. Chance, "Christine's Minerva, the Mother Valorized," *Christine de Pizan's Letter of Othea to Hector*, 133.

51. Helen Solterer, "Figures of Female Militancy in Medieval France," *Signs* 16 (1991): 549.

52. Marilynn Desmond and Pamela Sheingorn make a parallel argument about female desire in the *Othea*. They examine the illuminations in London, British Library MS Harley 4431, considering their relationships to the text. Focusing particularly on the cases of Andromeda, Pasiphaë, and Circe, they write, "In the visual dynamics of the *Othea*, the goddess Othea directs the implied male reader to look differently on these images of bestial desire and to see in their outlaw status an alternate economy of female desire, one that is not paradigmatically heterosexual but draws instead on female agency and authority. . . . In the received mythological versions of their stories, these three women dance dangerously into the border region where human and beast mate. The *Othea*, through its combination of text and image, re-visions female sexuality at the boundary of bestiality as a performance constitutive of the power of female desire." Marilynn Desmond and Pamela Sheingorn, "Queering Ovidian Myth: Bestiality and Desire in Christine de Pizan's *Epistre Othea*," *Queering the Middle Ages*, ed. Glenn Burger and Steven F. Kruger, Medieval Cultures 27 (Minneapolis: University of Minnesota Press, 2001), 6.

53. Chance, "Christine's Minerva, the Mother Valorized," *Christine de Pizan's Letter of Othea to Hector*, 125.

54. Lee, "Reflections of Power," 191, brackets and ellipses in original. As Lee indicates, such queenly machinations were regarded with extreme disfavor, and "one of the motives for establishing the regency was the desire to prevent her from gaining power" (ibid.). Although published too late in the process of my work on this project for me to make extensive use of it, Helen E. Maurer's excellent study

Margaret of Anjou: Queenship and Power in Late Medieval England (Woodbridge, Suffolk: Boydell, 2003) provides a valuable account of Margaret's power and opposition to it; see especially chapter 9, "Conditions and Means."

55. The Preface is printed from London, British Library MS Longleat 253.

56. Summit, *Lost Property*, 68.

57. I think it is quite possible that the valorization of women's transmissive function in lineages in the *Othea* may have also made this text particularly attractive to the Yorkist Edward IV, who had it copied, sometime after 1473, in London, British Library MS Royal E II. On this manuscript, see Campbell, "Christine de Pisan en Angleterre," 665. Another manuscript, London, British Library MS Royal 19 XIX, containing Christine de Pizan's work (in this case the *Cité des dames*), also bears evidence of Yorkist ownership in its first decorated border; "the white rose of York appears on the left, and the fetter lock on the right." Diane Bornstein, Introduction, *Distaves and Dames: Renaissance Treatises for and About Women* (Delmar, N.Y.: Scholars' Facsimiles and Reprints, 1978), xiv. Bornstein notes that, according to the British Library catalogue, "these symbols may show ownership of Richard, Duke of York, who may have acquired the manuscript while he was Commander of the English forces in France." Furthermore, this manuscript too may have been owned by Edward IV (ibid.).

58. This assertion mitigates somewhat against Summit's argument for the text's full-fledged redefinition of English aristocratic masculinity in learned and literary terms. She says, for instance, that in the *Boke of Noblesse* "'manliness' becomes coterminous with prudence and policy, rather than strength; it is a virtue that is taught and cultivated rather than deriving from an innate virility and display of physical force" (*Lost Property*, 74). Karras discusses this passage from the *Boke of Noblesse* in *From Boys to Men* as illustrative of ways in which the "knightly model of masculinity came into conflict with other roles and responsibilities of the late medieval aristocracy" (66).

59. Lines 11–12; quoted in Moulton, *Before Pornography*, 70. The discreet dash marking the omission is present in the original.

60. Moulton, *Before Pornography*, 71.

61. *Boke of Noblesse*, 54–55, n. b.

62. Žižek, *Sublime Object*, 56.

63. See Christine de Pizan, *The Book of the City of Ladies*, trans. Earl Jeffrey Richards (New York: Persea, 1982), 32–62.

64. On Carmentis and law see ibid., 71; for Minerva and armor, see 73–75.

65. Summit, *Lost Property*, 99. The *Cité* had, as Susan Groag Bell has argued, very different political significance to several early modern reigning queens and female regents who owned sets of tapestries based on the text. For these women, Christine's work did much to promote and justify female power. See Susan Groag Bell, "A New Approach to the Influence of Christine de Pizan: the Lost Tapestries of the 'City of Ladies,'" in *Sur le chemin de longue étude . . . : Actes du colloque d'Orléans juillet 1995*, ed. Bernard Ribémont (Paris: Champion, 1998), 7–12. Henry VIII was aware of these tapestries; as Bell notes, he was present in Tournai in 1513 at the occasion when the Regent Margaret of Austria received her set of tapestries. Also

present was Anne Boleyn, who was then one of Margaret of Austria's attendants and who would, of course, later become Henry VIII's second wife (ibid., 10).

66. Summit, *Lost Property*, 99–100.

67. "Brian Anslay, Translation of Christine de Pizan's *Book of the City of Ladies*: Chapter 1, with Dedicatory Verses by Henry Pepwell," in Wogan-Browne et al., *The Idea of the Vernacular*, 306, lines 11–14.

68. Hyrd died in 1528, so the translation must have been completed before that date. On the dedications, see Bornstein, Introduction, *Distaves and Dames*, xvii–xviii. Bornstein indicates that the *Catalogue* of the British Museum "dates the edition as 1540, whereas the Short Title Catalogue lists it as 1529"; however, since in the preface Hyrd "dedicates the book to Queen Catherine and speaks of her as living" and since she died in 1536, "the first edition was likely to have been printed before that date" (xix). For a discussion of Vives's *Instruccion* in the context of Isabel of Castile's reign, see Chapter 4 below.

69. John Rooks, "*The Boke of the Cyte of Ladyes* and Its Sixteenth-Century Readership," in *The Reception of Christine de Pizan from the Fifteenth Through the Nineteenth Centuries*, 85.

70. *Instruction of a Christian Woman*, facsimile printed in Bornstein, *Distaves and Dames*, h2v; on this passage, see also Rooks, "*The Boke of the Cyte of Ladyes* and Its Sixteenth-Century Readership," 85. Hereafter citations of *Instruction of a Christian Woman* are made parenthetically.

71. Moulton, *Before Pornography*, 78.

72. Polydore Vergil, *Three Books of Polydore Vergil's English History Comprising the Reigns of Henry VI, Edward IV, and Richard III*, ed. Henry Ellis, Camden Society Publications 29 (London: Nichols, 1844), 38–39, hereafter cited parenthetically as *English History*. On the translation, see the preface to this edition, xxxi–xxxii.

73. Moulton, *Before Pornography*, 79.

74. Edward Hall, *Hall's Chronicle*, ed. Henry Ellis (London, 1809), 157, hereafter cited parenthetically as *Hall's Chronicle*.

75. Lee, "Reflections of Power," 202. Lee observes that Fabyan's *New Chronicles* was the "'principal vehicle by which the historiographical tradition and factual content of the London chronicles was transmitted to Tudor England,' which is to say to Polydore Vergil, Stow and Hakluyt, Hall, Grafton, Holinshed, and of course Shakespeare" (201–2).

76. J. O. Haliwell-Phillips, ed., *Letters of the King of England*, vol. 1 (London, 1846), 172–73; quoted in Christine Weightman, *Margaret of York, Duchess of Burgundy 1446–1503* (New York: St. Martin's, 1989), 155.

77. Polydore Vergil, *The Anglica Historia*, ed. and trans. Denis Hay (London: Royal Historical Society, 1950), 17, hereafter cited parenthetically as *Anglica Historia*. The original Latin reads, "persequebatur Henricum Regem odio inexpiabili, iraque simul accensa non cessabat omnia tentare dolis, quibus hominem ut alterius factionis opprimet" (16). Simnel represented himself as Edward, son of the duke of Clarence. Vergil admits that Margaret knew him to be false, but that her hatred of Henry was such that she supported Simnel anyway (16–17).

78. Weightman, *Margaret of York*, 154.

79. On this passage, see also ibid., 153.

80. "Brian Anslay, Translation of Christine de Pizan's *Book of the City of Ladies*," 306, lines 9–10.

81. Headnote to "Brian Anslay, Translation of Christine de Pizan's *Book of the City of Ladies*," 305.

82. Summit, *Lost Property*, 101. Summit cites Martha Driver on this point; see Martha Driver, "Christine de Pisan and Robert Wyer: *The C Historyes of Troye* or *L'Epistre d'Othea* Englished," *Sonderdruk aus Gutenberg-Jahrbuch* (1997): 137.

83. Summit additionally observes that the woodcut removes Christine "from the scene of gentlemanly reading and textual exchange that Pepwell invokes in his prologue" (*Lost Property*, 101).

84. Žižek, *The Sublime Object of Ideology*, 61.

85. Ibid.

86. On Henry VIII and Elizabeth Barton, see Chapter 5 below; on Elizabeth I, medieval female spirituality, and the English Brigittines see Chapter 6.

Chapter 4. Religion and Female Rule: Isabel of Castile and the Construction of Queenship

1. Quoted from the 1539 edition of George Coel, fol. xr in M. C. Marín Pina, "La mujer y los libros caballerías: Notas para el estudio de la recepción del género caballeresco entre el público femenino," *Revista de Literatura Medieval* 3 (1991): 134. I am grateful to Bill Warren for help with translations in this chapter. My efforts benefited greatly from his linguistic expertise; any errors that remain are entirely my fault and largely due to my stubborn insistence on having my own way.

2. Vives wrote the text in Latin in 1523, dedicating it to Queen Katherine of England (Isabel's daughter) for use in instructing the Princess Mary. Vives traveled to England in 1523 to serve in Katherine's entourage and to tutor Mary. Diane Bornstein, Introduction, *Distaves and Dames: Renaissance Treatises for and About Women* (Delmar, N.Y.: Scholars' Facsimiles and Reprints, 1978), xvii. On Vives's career in England, see also Margaret L. King and Albert Rabil Jr.'s introduction to Juan Luis Vives, *The Education of a Christian Woman: A Sixteenth-Century Manual*, ed. and trans. Charles Fantazzi (Chicago: University of Chicago Press, 2000), especially 8–16. Vives's text "became the leading theoretical manual on women's education in the sixteenth century and was translated into Spanish, French, and English" (Bornstein, Introduction xviii). In spite of the fact that it was written after Isabel's death it is, as Bornstein observes, "very conservative"; it "strongly reflects medieval ideals and conventional practice" (xvii–xviii).

3. José de Sigüenza, *Historia de la Orden de San Jerónimo*, ed. Juan Catalina García, 2 vols., Nueva Biblioteca de Autores Españoles, vols. 8 and 12 (Madrid: Bailly-Baillière, 1907–1909), 2: 295. Barbara Weissberger pointedly observes that the meeting between Isabel and Talavera highlights "the threat that a female monarch posed to the divinely instituted condition of woman's subordination to man." "'Me atrevo a escribir así': Confessional Politics in the Letters of Isabel I and Hernando de Talavera," in *Women at Work in Spain from the Middle Ages to Early Modern*

Times, ed. Marilyn Stone and Carmen Benito-Vessels (New York: Peter Lang, 1998), 149. She further notes that in the exchange of letters between Talavera and Isabel, Talavera "drives home the point . . . that Isabel's humility is the proper response to her intellectual, moral, and spiritual inferiority to Talavera, the representative of the Church closest to her" (158). Although it appeared too late in my work on this project for me to make use of it in my research, Weissberger's book *Isabel Rules: Constructing Queenship, Wielding Power* (Minneapolis: University of Minnesota Press, 2004) engages some of the same questions of interest to me in this chapter. On Isabel and Talavera's relationship, see also Ronald E. Surtz, "Female Patronage of Vernacular Religious Works in Fifteenth-Century Castile: Aristocratic Women and Their Confessors," in *The Vernacular Spirit: Essays on Medieval Religious Literature*, ed. Renate Blumenfeld-Kosinski, Duncan Robertson, and Nancy Bradley Warren, New Middle Ages 21 (New York: Palgrave, 2002), 263–82.

4. On the symbolics of power and its relationship to the nature of power itself, see Clifford Geertz, "Centers, Kings, and Charisma: Reflections on the Symbolics of Power," in *Culture and Its Creators: Essays in Honour of Edward Shils*, ed. Joseph Ben-David and Terry Nichols Clark (Chicago: University of Chicago Press, 1977), 152.

5. Pierre Bourdieu, *Language and Symbolic Power*, ed. John B. Thompson, trans. Gino Raymond and Matthew Adamson (Cambridge, Mass.: Harvard University Press, 1991), 192.

6. Weissberger, "'Me atrevo a escribir así,'" 152.

7. Weissberger further argues that Isabel, while calling attention to her female inferiority and concomitantly subordinate position vis-à-vis Talavera, "manages . . . to appropriate some of those same strategies, using them to subtly resist the priest's control even as she appears to welcome it" (ibid., 158).

8. Peggy Liss, "Isabel, Myth and History," in *Isabel la Católica, Queen of Castile: Critical Essays*, ed. David A. Boruchoff (New York: Palgrave Macmillan, 2003), 60.

9. As Surtz notes, "Isabella the Catholic's royal propagandists did an effective job of creating the image of a humble, maternal, and pious queen who was also a model wife" ("Female Patronage," 264).

10. The edition to which I refer in this chapter is *Jardín de Nobles Donzellas, Fray Martín de Córdoba: A Critical Edition and Study*, ed. Harriet Goldberg (Chapel Hill: North Carolina Studies in the Romance Languages and Literatures, University of North Carolina Department of Romance Languages, 1974). Hereafter I will cite this text, subsequently called *Jardín*, parenthetically by page number; when I refer to Goldberg's critical essay rather than to the text of the *Jardín* itself, I will cite it as Goldberg, Critical Study, *Jardín*.

11. The edition which I cite is *La Poncella de Francia: La "historia" castellana de Juana de Arco*, ed. Victoria Campo and Victor Infantes (Vervuert: Iberoamericana, 1997). Hereafter I will cite this text, subsequently called *Poncella*, parenthetically by page number.

12. The prologue twice mentions the death of Isabel's brother Alfonso, once speaking of mourning for him as though the death were recent. Additionally, it refers to Isabel as princess rather than queen; on the bases of these passages, it can therefore be dated to the period between 1468, when Alfonso died, and 1474, when

Isabel became queen. The first reference to Alfonso's death occurs when Martín says, "Por lo qual avn que nos deuamos doler del yllustrísimo varón hermano vuestro, por quanto lo perdimos" [For we should mourn for your most illustrious brother to an extent equivalent to that which we lost] (*Jardín*, 136). The second is in the last sentence of the prologue, which reads, "Allegóse a esto la grand beniuolencia que oue a mi Señor de gloriosa memoria, el Rey Don Alfonso, vuestro hermano & la grand deuoción que él en mí tenía, por su dulce & real clemencia" [In this respect is approached the great benevolence that my lord of glorious memory, King Alfonso, your brother, had, and the great devotion he had for me, through his sweet and royal mercy] (141). Goldberg dates the text to 1468, seemingly on the basis of the reference to mourning for Alfonso; however, I am not convinced the text can be so precisely dated on the basis of this passage. Additionally, the text, as I shall argue, has political resonances with the years leading up to Isabel's accession, not just with 1468 alone.

13. Weissberger, "'Me atrevo a escribir así,'" 150.

14. Elizabeth A. Lehfeldt, "Ruling Sexuality: The Political Legitimacy of Isabel of Castile," *Renaissance Quarterly* 53 (2000): 36. Lehfeldt too remarks on the ways in which Martín de Córdoba invokes several "popular tropes of medieval misogyny" even as he argues against them elsewhere in the text (ibid.). These tropes include frequent references to women's loquaciousness, carnality, and their spiritual and intellectual inferiority to men. After outlining the three good conditions for women, for instance, Martín declares that women have three bad qualities as well as one indifferent one. The three negatives are that women "son intemperadas" [are intemperate], "son parleras & porfiosas" [are chatty and quarrelsome] and "son variables sin constancia" [are variable, without constancy]. He continues, "la indiferente es que todo lo hazen por extremo & por cabo & ésta conlas buenas es buena & conlas malas es mala" [the indifferent aspect is that they do everything to the extreme, and this is good for good ones and bad for bad ones] (*Jardín*, 209).

15. The same set of issues feature in the closing paragraph of the prologue, which juxtaposes the legitimacy of Isabel's succession and the fitness of her character for governing: "Enestas presentes razones & enlas que porné después, como en jardín de donzellas, mire vuestro vivo entendimiento & tome deleyte por que, pues que la sucessión natural vos da el regimiento que no fallezca por defecto de sabiduría moral; antes la vuestra aprouada sabiduría vos haga digna de regir, como vos haze digna la real & primogénita sangre" [In these present reasons, and in those I will set out later, look to your lively comprehension and take pleasure, as in a garden of young women, that since the natural succession gives you the governance that may not die for defect of moral wisdom, therefore your approved wisdom makes you worthy to rule, just as royal blood and primogeniture make you worthy] (*Jardín*, 140).

16. Goldberg, Critical Study, *Jardín*, 87.

17. Ibid.

18. Ibid., 51. Goldberg reinforces her stance that the text is politically insignificant, saying, "The conclusion is inescapable: the *Jardín* could not have had any measurable partisan political influence, nor was it running in any way counter to the views of the moment" (ibid., 88).

19. Surtz, "Female Patronage," 270.

20. Lehfeldt's reading is typical of modern critical assessments of the text. She writes, "While its fundamental message and intent is positive—a woman can be an effective political leader—the argument that moves towards this conclusion is more tentative. . . . A woman could rule, but only by acknowledging her short-comings and perhaps by having checks (like a husband) on her power" ("Ruling Sexuality," 36). My position differs somewhat; I see the text's "tentative" approach as a complement to, and indeed a vehicle for, the construction of a strong, politically engaged model of queenship.

21. On tactics, see Michel de Certeau, *The Practice of Everyday Life*, trans. Steven Rendall (Berkeley: University of California Press, 1984), xvii–xx.

22. Ibid., 19.

23. For instance, in discussing pity, Martín writes, "Agora, por quanto todo esto se ordena a dotrina & instrución dela princesa, quiero aplicar esto alas grandes señoras & prouar por razones que, avn que todas las mugeres sean natural miente piadosas, pero las grandes lo deuen ser más que todas" [Now, as much as all of this is ordained to the education and instruction of the princess, I wish to apply it to great ladies, and to prove through reasons that, even though all women are naturally pious, great ladies must however be more so than all others] (*Jardín* 199).

24. See the chapter entitled "Queens as Intercessors" in Paul Strohm, *Hochon's Arrow: The Social Imagination of Fourteenth-Century Texts* (Princeton, N.J.: Princeton University Press, 1992).

25. In setting up his account of the creation of women Martín speaks, for example, of the need to avoid language that might scandalize "vírgines & donzel-las" [virgins and young women]. Such care to avoid "las palabras de toda torpedad" [lewd speech] is particularly necessary since he is a "religioso profeso" [professed religious]. The importance of this reticence is heightened by the status of his addressee, Isabel, who is associated with these most desirable feminine qualities when Martín writes that she "deue ser resplandor de castidad & limpieza en todo este reyno" [ought to be the shining example of chastity and purity in the whole kingdom] (*Jardín*, 144). Not only does Martín begin by connecting chastity with Isabel, he also ends in a similar fashion. His final point in Part 3 is that chastity gives immortal fame to women above all other virtues (*Jardín*, 288).

26. Jerome writes, "It is the saying of a very learned man that chastity must be preserved at all costs and that when it is lost all virtue falls to the ground. This holds the primacy of all virtues in women" (*Against Jovinianus* 1: 49, *A Select Library of Nicene and Post-Nicene Fathers*, 2nd series, 14 vols. [New York: Christian Literature Company; Oxford: Parker, 1890–1900], 6: 386).

27. Even if the text were actually written in 1468, it was already clear at that point that Isabel's days as a virgin were limited. Negotiations for her marriage were well underway in 1468; the terms for Fernando and Isabel's union were finalized on January 7, 1469. Indeed, the *Jardín* looks ahead to Isabel's marriage at several points. For instance, Martín gives advice about wifely conduct and the proper ways to bring up children. See *Jardín*, 207, 268.

28. Sherry Ortner, "The Virgin and the State," *Feminist Studies* 4 (1978): 32.

29. On virginity as a spiritual disposition and on attitudes concerning virginity

in relation to marriage, see Jocelyn Wogan-Browne, "The Virgin's Tale," in *Feminist Readings in Middle English Literature*, ed. Ruth Evans and Lesley Johnson (London: Routledge, 1994), especially 166–67.

30. Peggy K. Liss, *Isabel the Queen: Life and Times* (New York: Oxford University Press, 1992), 78.

31. Ibid.

32. Quoted in Goldberg, Critical Study, *Jardín*, 112.

33. Liss, *Isabel the Queen*, 83.

34. Ibid., 83–84. Juana had gone on to marry Alfonso V, and so she had supporters both in Portugal and in Spain among those who wanted union with Portugal (Goldberg, Critical Study, *Jardín*, 112–13). Although Juana's claim to the throne was relatively weak, there was enough uncertainty about who should replace Enrique to make Isabel and her supporters anxious, since Enrique had died without either reiterating his selection of Isabel or his acknowledgement of Juana as his heir (113).

35. This charge against Enrique IV comes from Alfonso de Palencia; see Antonio Paz y Melia, *El cronista Alonso de Palencia* (Madrid: Hispanic Society of America, 1914), lxii. On Isabelline characterizations of Enrique IV, see Barbara Wiessberger, "'¡A tierra, puto!': Alfonso de Palencia's Discourse of Effeminacy," *Queer Iberia: Sexualities, Cultures, and Crossings from the Middle Ages to the Renaissance*, ed. Josiah Blackmore and Gregory S. Hutcheson (Durham, N.C.: Duke University Press, 1999), 291–323.

36. Paz y Melia, *El cronista Alonso de Palencia*, lxiv; quoted in Goldberg, Critical Study, *Jardín*, 39 n. 64.

37. Liss further observes that Isabel is characterized in propaganda by a virginal *limpieza* that obligates her "to cleanse her realm of the stain, the defilement, infection, and impurity associated not only with original sin, but in Castile during the recent past with heaven's displeasure" (*Isabel the Queen*, 158–59). Goldberg points out that Juana is not "called La Beltraneja in the chronicles until well into the reign of Ferdinand and Isabel" (Critical Study, *Jardín*, 42). Previously, Juana was typically called "hija de la reina"(the queen's daughter] in chronicles, a "designation . . . apparently pointed enough to question her paternity without naming her putative father" (Ibid.).

38. One finds a parallel to Isabel's paradoxical negotiations of queenly power in the career of Anne of Bohemia, queen of Richard II of England. She similarly managed to transform the roles of intercessor and advocate into vehicles for wielding real power. On Queen Anne's political power, see Paul Strohm, "Queens as Intercessors," and David Wallace, *Chaucerian Polity: Absolutist Lineages and Associational Forms in England and Italy* (Stanford, Calif.: Stanford University Press, 1997), especially 357–70.

39. Indeed, one chronicler wrote, "By the solicitude of this Queen was begun, and by her diligence was continued, the war against the Moors, until all the kingdom of Granada was won." This anonymous interpolation is included in Hernando del Pulgar's *Crónica de los Señores Reyes Católicos Don Fernando y Doña Isabel*, cap. 24; quoted in translation in Liss, *Isabel the Queen*, 194. On this passage, see also Liss, *Isabel the Queen*, 367 n. 1 for chapter 12.

40. As Liss observes, especially during the siege of Granada itself, "resurgent chivalry . . . inspired the knights" while "chivalric and religious attitudes overlapped, mutually reinforcing her [Isabel's] prestige" (ibid., 229).

41. Ibid., 197.

42. On June 28, 1482, Isabel actually went into labor at the council table during negotiations concerning the Granada campaign (ibid., 197).

43. Ibid., 202; see Pulgar, *Crónica*, cap. 158.

44. Liss, *Isabel the Queen*, 203.

45. Ibid., 217.

46. Lehfeldt, "Ruling Sexuality," 45.

47. Liss, *Isabel the Queen*, 200.

48. Goldberg, Critical Study, *Jardín*, 39.

49. Martín follows his assertion with the example of Adam, who lost the fear of God and, consequently, all the beasts lost their fear of Adam (*Jardín*, 216).

50. Liss discusses Isabel's use of the rhetoric of holy war, stating, "Isabel's wars were always holy wars, whether affirming her right to rule or confronting heretic or infidel" ("Isabel, Myth and History," 58). She continues, "As a queen, Isabel . . . repeatedly drew on the time-honored and widely familiar language of holy war for a bundle of purposes: to convey her political theology, to justify her reign, to define her political agenda, to bring about social cohesion, to enhance royal popularity and power, and to effect a state-building consensus" (61).

51. Liss, *Isabel the Queen*, 199. Interestingly, a letter congratulating Ferdinand on victories in the campaign for reconquest written in 1485 by Diego de Valera recalls the *Jardín*'s efforts to cast Isabel's military involvement in traditional terms, suggesting perhaps the threat her participation in such activities posed to Ferdinand's reputation and his own self-representational program. In this letter, Isabel's participation in the reconquest is framed as fighting with alms and prayers, a fitting complement to Ferdinand's "real" fighting: "La qual no menos pelea con sus muchas limosnas e devotas oraciones, e dando hórden a las cosas de la guerra, que vos, Señor, con la lança en la mano" [She no less fights with her great alms and devout prayers, and putting matters of war in order, than you do, Lord, with lance in hand] (Diego de Valera, "Epístola XXIV," in *Prositas castellanos del siglo XV*, I, ed. Mario Penna, Biblioteca de Autores Españoles, vol. 116 [Madrid: Atlas, 1959], 31). On this letter, see Surtz, "Female Patronage," 264, 275 n. 5.

52. London, British Library MS Add. 28,490, fol. 113v, hereafter cited parenthetically.

53. Isabel's letter quoted in translation in Liss, *Isabel the Queen*, 332.

54. David A. Boruchoff, "Introduction: Instructions for Sainthood and Other Feminine Wiles in the Historiography of Isabel I," *Isabel la Católica*, 4. Boruchoff quotes from an extract of the letter given by Gustave Adolph Bergenroth in the introduction to *Calendar of Letters, Dispatches, and State Papers, Relating to the Negotiations Between England and Spain*, vol. 1, *Henry VIII, 1485–1509* (London: Longman, 1862), xlv–xlvi.

55. Goldberg points out, "Neither Scripture nor D. Álvaro de Luna include the night long prayer vigil spent with her maid that Fray Martín describe as part of the story of Judith" (Critical Study, *Jardín*, 247 n.10); she does not, however,

comment on what the significance of this added detail might be. Martín's treatment of Judith contrasts with that of Talavera in the *Colación de cómo se deben renovar en las ánimas todos los fieles cristianos en el tiempo de adviento*. While Martín, like Talavera, refers to Judith's holy widowhood, Talavera pointedly "fails to mention her miraculous empowerment to perform the 'masculine' deed of killing Holofernes and chooses instead to present her as a model of chastity and maturity, who is notable only because she spent her widowhood enclosed in her dwelling" (Surtz, "Female Patronage," 268). For the passage of the *Colación* in question, see José Amador de los Rios, *Historia crítica de la literatura española*, 7 vols. (Madrid: J. Rodríguez, 1861–1865), 7: 557.

56. Martín adds that upon her victory over Holofernes "el pueblo cantó della:—*Benedicta filia tua domine, quia per te fructum vite communicauimus*. E este canto dezimos dela Virgen María" [the people sing of her: "*Benedicta filia tua domine, quia per te fructum vite communicauimus*." And we sing this song of the Virgin Mary] (*Jardín*, 249, emphasis in original). This text comes from the Gradual Mass for the Feast of the Immaculate Conception (*Jardín*, 249 n.14). Goldberg notes, "In medieval iconography Judith was identified as 'une préfigure de la Vierge' [a prefiguring of the Virgin]. She was associated with Jaël and Tomyris (in the *Speculum Humanae Salvationis*) 'plongeant dans une vase de sang la tête du roi Cyrus' [plunging Cyrus's head in a vessel of blood], and appears as the 'Vierge victorieuse du démon' [Virgin victorious over the demon]. In fact, St. Bonaventure compares the Virgin directly with Judith and Holofernes" (*Jardín*, 247 n. 10). Significantly for Isabel's representational program, especially her campaign to present herself as the opposite of the corrupt Enrique IV and Juana, Judith is also connected with the Virgin of the Visitation "the symbol of sanctimony, chastity and humility who triumphs over lust and pride which Holofernes symbolizes" (*Jardín*, 247 n. 10).

57. Alonso de Santa Cruz, *Crónica de los Reyes Católicos*, ed. Juan de Mata Carriazo, 2 vols. (Seville: Escuela de Estudios Hispano-Americanos de Sevilla, 1951), 1: 304–5. On this passage, and on the legacy of Isabel's representational strategies, see Surtz, "Female Patronage," 264, 276 n. 9.

58. Boruchoff, "Introduction: Instructions for Sainthood," 3.

59. Elizabeth Theresa Howe, "Zenobia or Penelope? Isabel la Católica as Literary Archetype," *Isabel la Católica*, 97.

60. Ibid.

61. Boruchoff, "Introduction: Instructions for Sainthood," 3.

62. Ibid.

63. London, British Library MS Add. 14,014, fol. 17r.

64. Ibid., fol. 17v.

65. Liss, "Isabel, Myth and History," 58.

66. Interestingly, the idea of a "Joan-like" Isabel has a legacy equally as long, and equally as open to reinterpretation, as that of Isabel "la Católica." Liss points out that the Isabel "best known" in America "is William H. Prescott's romantic yet heroic queen of Spain, the praying and fighting Isabella, wearing armor into battle like Joan of Arc" ("Isabel, Myth and History," 68–69).

67. For instance, Campo and Infantes situate *La Poncella* in the chivalric

tradition (introduction, *Poncella* 20), as does Christina Guardiola, who argues that Joan is associated with the hero who possesses "chivalric strength and wide discretion" and who goes to the king's court "Like the knight in search of adventure" ("Legitimizing the Queen: Isabel the Catholic and the *Poncella de Francia*," unpublished paper; my thanks to Professor Guardiola for providing me with a copy of the paper).

68. Guardiola, "Legitimizing the Queen," 14.

69. Wogan-Browne observes, for instance, that the "Katherine Group provides a narrative romance of the life of the virgin" ("The Virgin's Tale," 172).

70. Campo and Infantes, introduction, *Poncella*, 34.

71. Jules Quicherat, ed., *Procès de condamnation et de réhabilitation de Jeanne d'Arc, dite La Pucelle*, 5 vols. (Paris: Renouard, 1841–1849), 5: 374. Adeline Rucquoi also argues, "The Maid does not appear especially devout, and one may at the same time say that faith is singularly absent in her actions." "De Jeanne d'Arc à Isabelle la Catholique: L'image de la France en Castille au XVᵉ siècle," *Journal des savants* 1 (1990): 167.

72. Indeed, Campo and Infantes go on to admit, somewhat contradictorily, that Isabel had propaganda, "in many cases official, that seeks to sanctify her" (Introduction, *Poncella*, 35).

73. Slavoj Žižek, *The Sublime Object of Ideology* (London: Verso, 1989), 56.

74. Scholarly opinion on the exact date of the text varies. Rucquoi dates the text, on the basis of passages relating to retaking occupied territory, to 1474–1479, 1474 being the date of Isabel's accession to the throne and 1479 the date of peace with Portugal ("De Jeanne d'Arc à Isabelle la catholique," 164). Campo and Infantes, however, place the text somewhat later, dating it to the period between 1484 and 1492 on the basis of references at the end of the Prologue that evoke fairly pointedly the campaign to reconquer Muslim-held Granada (introduction, *Poncella* 94 n. 27).

75. Karen A. Winstead has written about the ways in which John Capgrave redefines traditional hagiography in social and political terms in his *Life of St. Katherine*; see "Piety, Politics, and Social Commitment in Capgrave's *Life of St. Katherine*," *Medievalia et Humanistica* n.s. 17 (1990): 59–80. For other politically influenced versions of female hagiography, see Osbern Bokenham's *Legendys of Hooly Wummen*, ed. Mary Serjeantson, Early English Text Society o.s. 206 (London: Oxford University Press, 1938), which includes lives of both St. Margaret and St. Katherine. For analysis of the political dimensions of the *Legendys*, see Sheila Delaney, *Impolitic Bodies: Poetry, Saints, and Society in Fifteenth-Century England* (New York: Oxford University Press, 1998), and chapter 6 of Nancy Bradley Warren, *Spiritual Economies: Female Monasticism in Later Medieval England* (Philadelphia: University of Pennsylvania Press, 2001).

76. The "Almirante de Francia" is, according to Campo and Infantes, Charles de Recourt, of the Burgundian faction (*Jardín*, 124 n. 178). That Joan is accompanied and supported by an Observant Friar suggests another parallel between her and Isabel, since Isabel, like Margaret of York, was deeply interested in and connected to reformed Franciscan communities.

77. Campo and Infantes note that *La Poncella* constructs both Joan and Isabel

as figures chosen by divine providence to save their people from comparable political situations (introduction, *Poncella*, 32–33).

78. Ian Michael, "'From Her Shall I Read the Perfect Ways of Honour': Isabel of Castile and Chivalric Romance," *The Age of the Catholic Monarchs, 1474–1516: Literary Studies in Memory of Keith Whinnom*, ed. Alan Deyermond and Ian Macpherson (Liverpool: Liverpool University Press, 1989), 104.

79. Diego de Valera is quoted in translation in Liss, *Isabel the Queen*, 157. On Valera, see also Lehfeldt, "Ruling Sexualities," 44.

80. Lehfeldt calls attention to the importance of the alignment of Isabel and the Virgin Mary on the occasion of Juan's birth. She says, "Mary had offered the world the ultimate redemption: the son of God. Isabel offered a similar redemption. She gave Castile an indisputable male heir who stood in a direct line to the throne" ("Ruling Sexualities," 50–51).

81. The description of female saints' verbal skills is from Winstead, "Piety, Politics, and Social Commitment" (162); Wogan-Browne also points to female saints' unwillingness to be silenced and their skills with words in "The Virgin's Tale," 181.

82. On these debates, and on the ways in which they connect Joan with the tradition of the *doncella sabia*, see Guardiola, "Legitimizing the Queen," 12–14.

83. In this regard, although it in some ways echoes the life of St. Katherine, the *Poncella* advances a far different argument than Capgrave's politicized fifteenth-century version of this saint's life, which, as Winstead observes, argues against female rule (although allowing room for oppositional interpretations) and demonstrates, with reference to Henry VI as well as to St. Katherine, "that saints are poor rulers." Karen Winstead, "Capgrave's St. Katherine and the Perils of Gyneocracy," *Viator* 25 (1994): 371.

84. Wogan-Browne, "The Virgin's Tale," 177.

85. Interestingly, in the trial of Joan of Arc, Joan's refusal to marry is presented as one of the signs of her transgressive rebellion against paternal and ecclesiastical authority.

86. There is direct contemporary political significance to this refusal to use Joan's name as well. As Guardiola points out, the correspondence of Isabel and Joan "avoids the issue of birthright and usurpation of the throne. As Joan (in Spanish, *Juana*) and Isabel become one and the same, *Juana* (Isabel's niece and goddaughter) is carefully and deliberately sidelined. That is to say, by equating *Juana* / Joan with Isabel, the potential legal problems of usurpation and tyrannical rule are no longer issues that need be addressed" ("Legitimizing the Queen," 5, emphasis in original).

87. For a fifteenth-century version of the life of St. Agnes, see Bokenham, *Legendys of Hooly Wummen*, 110–29. For a later-medieval account of the life of St. Christine, see Christine de Pizan, *The Book of the City of Ladies*, trans. Earl Jeffrey Richards (New York: Persea, 1982), 234–60.

88. Lehfeldt in "Ruling Sexualities" and Guardiola in "Legitimizing the Queen" both also argue for the political significance of Isabel's association with Joan's virginity as part of Isabel's efforts to represent her purity and concomitant legitimacy as queen.

89. Lehfeldt astutely observes that in fifteenth-century Castile "religious and

political legitimacy were never far removed from each other" ("Ruling Sexualities," 39).

90. José García-Oro, *Cisneros y la reforma del clero español en tiempo de los Reyes Católicos* (Madrid, 1971), 113.

91. Archivo de la Corona de Aragón, Reg. 3611, fol. 85v; quoted in García-Oro, *Cisneros*, 113.

92. Ibid.

93. Lehfeldt also remarks on the political importance of an implied association between Isabel and Castilian nuns. She observes, "Much as Isabel's female nature threatened the stability of the Spanish throne, so, too, the sexuality, even of women who had taken religious vows, threatened the integrity of Spanish Catholicism, and, by association, Isabel's redemptive mission" ("Ruling Sexualities," 45).

94. Wogan-Browne, "The Virgin's Tale," 166.

95. Weissberger argues that some historians deal with Isabel's "threatening authority by . . . underscoring her 'manliness' as a marker of her difference from and superiority to her sex, in effect making her an honorary man." She goes on to observe that such historians "manage" Isabel, by making her, like Theresa of Avila, a "virile woman" ("'Me atrevo a escribir así,'" 149–50). Weissberger's comparison of the treatments of Isabel and Theresa of Avila by historians is instructive, in that it highlights the long-standing tradition of constructing a holy woman as a *virago*. I believe, however, that the identification of Isabel as a "virile woman" is not merely a defensive technique employed by anti-feminists past and present who are troubled by her authority. Rather, it serves a beneficial purpose in Isabel's efforts to craft a creditable model of female monarchy. As I discuss in chapter 6 on women religious in the reign of Elizabeth I, the English queen made comparable use of the ideology of virginity through self-construction as a positive *virgo/virago*.

96. Bourdieu, *Language and Symbolic Power*, 119.

97. Ibid.

98. Guardiola observes in the same vein that the encounter between Joan and the Marshal's son not only emphasizes Joan's commitment to virginity but also demonstrates "a sly quality in our protagonist" that is something positive ("Legitimizing the Queen," 11); furthermore, the scene illustrates that Joan has "a purity of being that atones for the murder of the Marshall's son" (Ibid.).

99. Wogan-Browne, "The Virgin's Tale," 179.

100. Ibid., 118.

101. Bourdieu, *Language and Symbolic Power*, 125.

102. The issue of Joan's male attire does not receive an inordinate amount of attention in *La Poncella*. She is, though, at one point described as wearing clothing about which Campo and Infantes remark, "It is evident that the text wishes to represent the Maid outside of her feminine condition and to have her appear as a warrior" (*Poncella*, 161 n. 341).

103. Liss, *Isabel the Queen*, 97.

104. Findings quoted on a website promoting the canonization of Queen Isabel (http://www.queenisabel.com/isabelcanonization_bl.html; accessed October 24, 2003) supported by Miles Jesu (http://www.milesjesu.org; accessed October 24, 2003). Miles Jesu is a Catholic lay organization that works to promote the

ongoing attempt to canonize Isabel. The findings of the commission, and the involvement of Miles Jesu in the canonization efforts, both highlight the degree to
which medieval female sanctity is still highly politicized. The commission's statement that all of Isabel's acts are in perfect harmony with the criteria for sanctity
has caused no small degree of outrage from those who view her expulsion of the
Jews and Muslims from Spain as less than ideal Christian behavior. Furthermore,
while Miles Jesu claims on its website to be apolitical ("Miles Jesu is neither 'conservative' nor 'liberal.' We are simply Catholic" [http://www.milesjesu.org/general_
mj.html; accessed October 24, 2003]) many of its aims (for instance, the promotion of "Boys Towns" and "Girls Towns" as well as anti-abortion activities) are
profoundly political—as is the activity the website terms "promoting culture and
true history."

105. Paul Preston, *Franco* (New York: Basic Books, 1994), 185.

106. Ibid.

107. Ibid., 323.

108. Ibid., 289.

109. On this occasion he particularly praised her expulsion of the Jews, suggesting, as Preston observes, Franco's affinities with Hitler (ibid., 459).

110. José Luis Abellán, "Isabel and the Idea of America," *Isabel la Católica*,
79.

Chapter 5. The Mystic, the Monarch, and the Persistence of "the Medieval": Elizabeth Barton and Henry VIII

1. As Guy Bedouelle and Patrick Le Gal observe, the process leading up to
the divorce, the act itself, and its aftermath are "an episode in the history of ideas
. . . which led to consequences of the first importance beyond the religious drama
(important in itself) and the political dimension of the Affair, already so often
demonstrated." Guy Bedouelle and Patrick Le Gal, *Le "Divorce" du Roi Henry VIII:
Etudes et Documents* (Geneva: Travaux d'Humanisme et Renaissance, 1987), 440,
quoted in translation in Diarmid MacCulloch, *Thomas Cranmer: A Life* (New
Haven, Conn.: Yale University Press, 1996), 41.

2. Roseanne Desilets, "The Nuns of Tudor England: Feminine Responses
to the Dissolution of the Monasteries," Ph.D. dissertation, University of California,
Irvine, 1995, 481. Not only were the versions of Catholicism practiced in England
before and after Henry's separation from Rome quite similar, but Alexandra Walsham also suggests that connections exist between the faith professed by more
purely Protestant early modern sects and that of medieval Catholics, observing that
there were "many elements of late medieval piety which its successor almost invol-
untarily enlisted and developed." She argues, for instance, that "early modern Catholics and Protestants shared the same frame of reference: providential beliefs cut
across the invisible iron curtain which contemporary polemic erected between
Geneva and Rome." Alexandra Walsham, *Church Papists: Catholicism, Conformity,
and Confessional Polemic in Early Modern England* (Woodbridge: Boydell, 1993), 225.
A great deal has been written on the transition from Catholicism to Protestantism

from a variety of perspectives. Although far from an exhaustive list, see as representative of those who argue for the persistence of traditional religious beliefs and practices Eamon Duffy, *The Stripping of the Altars: Traditional Religion in England c. 1400–c.1580* (New Haven, Conn.: Yale University Press, 1992); Eamon Duffy, *The Voices of Morebath: Reformation and Rebellion in an English Village* (New Haven, Conn.: Yale University Press, 2001); Norman L. Jones, *The English Reformation: Religion and Cultural Adaptation* (Oxford: Blackwell, 2002); Christopher Haigh, *English Reformations: Religion, Politics, and Society Under the Tudors* (Oxford: Clarendon, 1993); Peter Lake, *Anglicans and Puritans? Presbyterianism and English Conformist Thought from Whitgift to Hooker* (London: Allen and Unwin, 1988); Peter Lake with Michael Questier, *The Antichrist's Lewd Hat: Protestants, Papists, and Players in Post-Reformation England* (New Haven, Conn.: Yale University Press, 2002), especially sections I and II. For an alternative view, see Patrick Collinson, *The Birthpangs of Protestant England: Religion and Cultural Change in the Sixteenth and Seventeenth Centuries* (New York: St. Martin's, 1988); Patrick Collinson, *Godly People: Essays on English Protestantism and Puritanism* (London: Hambledon, 1983). In general, as the arguments in this chapter and the next will make clear, I agree with scholars who argue that Catholic traditions persisted, more or less officially under Henry VIII, and later increasingly illicitly under Elizabeth I. As these chapters will also make clear, I believe that medieval religious practices not only endured through the Tudor period but also played extremely important cultural and political roles.

3. Stuart Hall, "Cultural Identity and Diaspora," *Contemporary Postcolonial Theory: A Reader*, ed. Padmini Mongia (London: Arnold, 1996), 112. I am using the concept of liminality here in Homi Bhaba's sense of the term in relation to spaces between historical periods and cultural groups. See Homi K. Bhabha, *The Location of Culture* (London: Routledge, 1994), 4. I am grateful to my former colleague at Utah State, Pallavi Rastogi, for many enlightening discussions of postcolonial theory as well as for many helpful references. My arguments in this chapter and the following one concerning early modern representational politics are indebted to the work of such groundbreaking scholars as Stephen Orgel, Roy C. Strong, and Stephen Greenblatt on theatrical expressions of power in the Renaissance. See Stephen Orgel, *The Illusion of Power* (Berkeley: University of California Press, 1975); Roy C. Strong, *Art and Power: Renaissance Festivals 1450–1650* (Woodbridge: Boydell, 1984); Stephen Greenblatt, "Invisible Bullets: Renaissance Authority and its Subversions, *Henry IV* and *Henry V*," *Political Shakespeare: New Essays in Cultural Materialism*, ed. Jonathan Dollimore and Alan Sinfield (Ithaca, N.Y.: Cornell University Press, 1985), 18–47. As my analysis will demonstrate, though, I also agree with David Scott Kastan's criticism of Greenblatt's paradigm of theatricality and power. Kastan says, "It is not that Greenblatt is wrong, only that his argument is unnecessarily totalized." He points out, "Representation is powerful and dangerous, and its subversions are not . . . as easily contained as the New Historicists would suggest." "Proud Majesty Made a Subject: Shakespeare and the Spectacle of Rule," *Shakespeare Quarterly* 37, 4 (1986): 472.

4. I want to take this opportunity to express my thanks to Nicholas Watson, whose comments on some of my earlier work first sparked my interest in Elizabeth Barton's connections with medieval female spirituality and monarchical

representation. I also wish to thank my former colleague at Utah State University, Norman Jones, for reading drafts of this chapter and the next as well as for his valuable insights into early modern religion. His learning on the subject far surpasses mine, and any errors that remain are entirely my own.

5. L. E. Whatmore, "The Sermon Against the Holy Maid of Kent and her Adherents, delivered at Paul's Cross, November the 23rd, 1533, and at Canterbury, December the 7th," *English Historical Review* 58 (1943): 467. One of the difficulties in analyzing Elizabeth Barton's revelations is that the only sources in which they are preserved are authored by those who sought to condemn her. There is enough uniformity in such texts to be able to determine to some extent the content of her revelations, but the sources are also always slanted toward discrediting that content. The account of her revelations that was published during her lifetime, *A marueilous woorke of late done at Court of Streete in Kent*, was so effectively censored by Henry VIII's government that no surviving copies have ever been located. On this act of censorship, see E. J. Devereux, "Elizabeth Barton and Tudor Censorship," *Bulletin of the John Rylands Library* 49 (1966): 91–106.

6. Whatmore, "Sermon," 467.

7. Diane Watt discusses the similarities between Elizabeth Barton and these later medieval saints in her essay "Reconstructing the Word: the Political Prophecies of Elizabeth Barton (1506–1534)," *Renaissance Quarterly* 50,1 (1997): 138. See also chapter 3 on Elizabeth Barton in her book *Secretaries of God: Women Prophets in Late Medieval and Early Modern England* (Cambridge: D.S. Brewer, 1997).

8. Watt, "Reconstructing the Word," 139.

9. Whatmore, "Sermon," 469

10. In addition to Bocking, the commission included William Hadleigh of Christ Church, Canterbury; Dom Barnes of the same community; two friars of the Observant Franciscans of Canterbury; Thomas Lawrence, an official of the Archbishop; and Richard Master.

11. A notable departure from this trend is Diane Watt's work on Elizabeth Baron in "Reconstructing the Word" and *Secretaries of God*. Watt argues that Barton stands "within established traditions of female and popular prophecy which . . . had their own partial autonomy" ("Reconstructing the Word," 138).

12. For the interpretation of a Catholic historian, see, for instance, Dom David Knowles, *The Religious Orders in* England, vol. 3 (Cambridge: Cambridge University Press, 1959), 182. Examples of historical, but more devotionally oriented, works include Dom Adam Hamilton, *The Angel of Syon* (Edinburgh: Sands, 1905); J. R. McKee, *Dame Elizabeth Barton, O.S.B.: The Holy Maid of Kent* (New York: Benziger, 1925); and John Rory Fletcher, *The Story of the English Bridgettines of Syon Abbey* (Devon: Syon Abbey, 1933). In spite of their often pious tone, and their clear partisanship in regards to Elizabeth's holiness, these works provide much valuable historical material, as does Alan Neame, *The Holy Maid of Kent: The Life of Elizabeth Barton, 1506–1534* (London: Hodder and Stoughton, 1971). In this work, Neame openly admits his desire to "rescue" Elizabeth from the charges made against her in the historical records, authored by her enemies, in which her revelations are preserved. Neame's interest in doing so is less obviously motivated by religious feeling than that of Hamilton, Fletcher, and McKee; rather, his motive

seems to be family pride, as he claims descent from Thomas Cobb in whose house Elizabeth lived as a servant before her profession as a nun.

13. Thomas Cranmer, *A Confutation of Vnwritten Verities, Miscellaneous Writings and Letters of Thomas Cranmer*, ed. John Edmund Cox (Cambridge: Cambridge University Press, 1846), 65.

14. Leslie Stephen and Sidney Lee, *Dictionary of National Biography*, vol. 1 (Oxford: Oxford University Press, 1921–1922), 1263–66; hereafter I will use the abbreviation *DNB* with relevant volume and page numbers to cite quotations from this work parenthetically.

15. See Eustache Chapuys's letter of April 16, 1532, for an account of the sermon, the king's angry reaction, and the aftermath. *Letters and Papers Foreign and Domestic of the Reign of Henry VIII*, arranged and catalogued James Gairdner (London: HMSO; reprint New York: Kraus, 1965), vol. 5, no. 591. Hereafter passages from this collection will be cited parenthetically using the abbreviation *L and P* followed by volume and entry numbers. On the sermon see also Neame, *Holy Maid of Kent*, 156–57.

16. See, for instance, *L and P*, vol. 6, nos. 726, 899, 902, 1370.

17. For example, see Stephen Vaughan's letter of October 21, 1533, to Cromwell, *L and P*, vol. 6, no. 1324. Vaughan harbored particular animosity toward Peto; according to Stephen and Lee, "Vaughan tried hard to get him entrapped and sent to England, but failed" (*DNB*, vol. 15, 975).

18. See Devereux, "Elizabeth Barton and Tudor Censorship."

19. For a detailed account of this meeting, complete with a wide variety of primary documents printed in appendices, see P. A. Hamy, *Entrevue de François Premier avec Henry VIII, à Boulogne-sur-Mer, en 1532* (Paris: Gougy, 1898).

20. Neame, *Holy Maid of Kent*, 172.

21. London, British Library MS Add. 6113, fol. 67r, renumbered 70r.

22. *The Chronicle of Calais in the Reigns of Henry VII and Henry VIII to the Year 1540*, ed. John Gough Nichols (London: Camden Society, 1846), 43, hereafter cited parenthetically. Sydney Anglo writes that the 1532 "interview was not a demonstration of wealth and artistic virtuosity" and calls the "entertainments . . . insignificant and inexpensive." *Spectacle, Pageantry, and Early Tudor Policy* (Oxford: Clarendon; New York: Oxford University Press, 1997), 245. This assessment, however, depends on just how one interprets what counts as an outlay of expense and a demonstration of wealth. J. J. Scarisbrick describes the 1532 meeting somewhat differently, saying, "The meeting had been dressed in all the panoply of buoyant monarchy: trumpets, cloth of gold, jousts and revels, twenty-four-course banquet and the rest. . . . It had also been outrageously expensive. Henry had spared nothing on food . . . or his wardrobe; he had thrown away money in gambling . . . ; he had showered horses, jewels and cash on the French so generously that, when it was Francis's turn to emulate his gallant friend, he had to borrow money." *Henry VIII* (Berkeley: University of California Press, 1968), 307. In comparison with the all-out extravaganza of the Field of the Cloth of Gold, the 1532 interview was, I would agree, more modest in scale; given its political importance, though, I would not go so far as to say that its elements of monarchical self-display, or the sums paid to achieve them, are insignificant.

23. *L and P*, vol. 5, introduction, xxvii; see also Wynkyn de Worde, *The maner of the tryumphe at Caleys and Bulleyn*, 1532, STC (2nd ed.) 4350.

24. Strong, *Art and Power*, 22.

25. Accounts for October 1532 printed in *L and P*, vol. 5, pp. 760–61.

26. Pierre Bourdieu, *Language and Symbolic Power*, ed. John B. Thompson, trans. Gino Richmond and Matthew Adamson (Cambridge, Mass.: Harvard University Press, 1991), 129.

27. The text ends by telling of the king's departure from Calais on October 29 and concludes, "And he purposeth god wyllynge to be at Caunterbury the viii daye of November and so home / whome god of his goodness euer preserue and sende good passage and safe agayne in to Englande. Amen. God save the Kynge" (de Worde, *The maner of the tryumphe*, A ivr).

28. *L and P*, vol. 6, Introduction, i–ii.

29. A letter written on November 10, 1532, by Dr. Ortiz to the Empress reveals the Pope's position. Ortiz says, "The Pope will have the brief [that is, the brief directing Henry VIII to give up Anne and take back Katherine] dated now, but he will not have it used till after he has seen the Emperor. He is hindered by this meeting between the Kings of England and France" (*L and P*, vol. 5, no. 1532).

30. Quoted from the Act of Attainder in Devereux, "Elizabeth Barton and Tudor Censorship," 101.

31. As Anglo notes, the royal interview "was, in reality . . . a statement by Henry VIII, through the medium of public spectacle, that as far as he was concerned Anne Boleyn was already his Queen" (*Spectacle*, 246). Interestingly, when the marriage did not in fact take place during the trip to France, "a rumor began to be circulated" shortly after the king's return "that he had intended marrying Anne Boleyn at the interview, but found it advisable to defer such a step to a more convenient opportunity" (*L and P*, vol. 5, Introduction, xxvii; see no. 1538 and no. 1642 for examples of the rumor); Elizabeth Barton reportedly took credit for having prevented the marriage with her prayers (*L and P*, vol. 6, no. 1468).

32. Ethan H. Shagan, "Print, Orality and Communications in the Maid of Kent Affair," *Journal of Ecclesiastical History* 52.1 (2001): 30.

33. McKee, *Dame Elizabeth Barton*, 10. Calais, too, was an important international space, housing a large English merchant community organized into the Staple and serving as "a major route for England into Europe" (MacCulloch, *Thomas Cranmer*, 110). On the international importance of Calais, see the chapter entitled "At Calais Gate," in David Wallace, *Premodern Places: Calais to Surinam, Chaucer to Aphra Behn* (Oxford: Blackwell, 2004), 22–90. Calais was, significantly, also to prove to be a hotbed of the same sort of resistance to Henry VIII's religious and political agenda as Elizabeth Barton practiced. In the same month in 1533 as Cranmer was consecrated Archbishop of Canterbury, a new King's Deputy was appointed in Calais—Arthur Plantagenet, Lord Lisle, an illegitimate son of Edward IV. He, and perhaps to an even greater extent, his wife Honor Grenville, "had no sympathy for religious change" (MacCulloch, *Thomas Cranmer*, 111); in 1534, they decided to bring to Calais to preach two Observant Friars. One of these preachers was Thomas Roche, who "had been on the edge of the Maid of Kent's coterie" (112).

34. Significantly, as McKee observes of Canterbury during Elizabeth Barton's mystical career, "Perhaps never more than at this particular period did so many ambassadors, envoys, diplomatists, and secret agents . . . pass through the little city" (*Dame Elizabeth Barton*, 10).

35. Thomas Wright, ed., *Three Chapters of Letters Relating to the Suppression of Monasteries* (London: Camden Society, 1843), 15, 20. Shagan comments on the extent of Barton's fame, arguing that word of her holiness and revelations spread through "The same mechanisms that had advertised medieval saints and their shrines, from written hagiography to pulpit announcement and popular rumors" ("Print, Orality, and Communication," 33).

36. Elizabeth Frances Rogers, ed., *The Correspondences of Sir Thomas More* (Princeton, N.J.: Princeton University Press, 1947), 481, 483. More explains that he did not hear Barton herself recount the experience at Calais; rather, he heard it either "of Riche or Resbye or of neither of them bothe" or possibly "of some other man sins s < he > was in holde" (ibid.). These possibilities suggest that her account of her mystical experience at the mass was fairly widely disseminated. Shagan point out that "An anonymous government memorandum, apparently a compendium of various depositions, includes a list of the people to whom the ringleaders [Edward Bocking, John Dering, Hugh Rich, Richard Risby, and Henry Gold] told Barton's most seditious revelations. The lists are staggering" ("Print, Orality, and Communication" 31; the memorandum, which Shagan quotes at length, is PRO, SP 1/80, fols. 126r-126v printed in *L and P*, vol. 6, no 1468 [1]). As Shagan observes, the lists are significant because "virtually all of the laypeople mentioned occupied the highest level of society" and because "the large number of priests on these lists suggests that the news traveled not only though ordinary word-of-mouth but through the pulpit as well" (ibid., 32).

37. Cranmer, *Confutation*, 273.

38. Bourdieu, *Language*, 130.

39. Lake and Questier, *Antichrist's*, 231.

40. That the nun from the outskirts of Canterbury had a revelation concerning a mass at Calais adds insult to injury, increasing the potential for embarrassment and symbolic damage to Henry VIII's position, since Canterbury and Calais have an important ecclesiastical connection. Calais was "an anomalous part of the diocese of Canterbury. . . . [A]rchbishops of Canterbury exercised powers in its twenty-five parishes by a commissary as in other peculiars" (MacCulloch, *Thomas Cranmer*, 110).

41. Cranmer, *Confutation*, 65.

42. On Dr. Foxe's speech, see Anglo, *Spectacle*, 244.

43. Hamy, *Entrevue*, 66–67.

44. Hamy points out, for example, "A Calais, comme à Boulogne, il se fit grande chère et les Anglais rivalisèrent avec leur maitre pour donner aux Français la plus somptueuse hospitalité" (ibid., 80).

45. Similarly, I think it is no coincidence that prior to his departure, Henry created Anne Marchioness of Pembroke just before a mass and signed articles with the French ambassador immediately after the service, as discussed above.

46. This justification for the meeting is not only found on the English side.

A letter, presumed to be by Langeais, to an unknown recipient, describes the preparations for the interview and says the cause of the meeting is "that the offer by these princes of succour for Christendom was rejected by the Emperor, either because he thinks himself strong enough, or because he wishes alone to have the honor of fighting the Turk; but they, considering that if the Emperor (which God forbid!) should have the worst of it, the damage would be common to all Christendom, have determined to consult together beforehand as to what they ought to do, and in order to devise some means, perhaps by way of a council, for the reunion of Christendom" (*L and P*, vol. 5, no. 1308). This purported agenda was widely recognized as a pretext, though. In September, 1532, Rodrigo Niño writes to Charles V, "the kings of England and France will hold an interview. The French say it is for the benefit of Christendom, but most persons think they will treat of the divorce and new marriage" (*L and P*, vol. 5, no. 1345).

47. Hamy, *Entrevue*, Appendix 65, cxciv–cxcv.

48. Roy C. Strong, *Tudor and Stuart Monarchy: Pageantry, Painting, and Iconography*, vol. 1 (Woodbridge: Boydell, 1995), 8–9. Indeed, Richard Koebner notes that Henry's claim of imperial status did not change his relationship to parliament or to foreign monarchs, and, he continues, "The innovation which really mattered was not the Imperial Crown, but the authority said to be annexed to that Crown—the king's claim to be Supreme Head of the English Church." "'The Imperial Crown of this Realm': Henry VIII, Constantine the Great, and Polydore Vergil," *Bulletin of the Institute of Historical Research* 26 (1953): 48. Although an official imperial identity was only created by statute in 1533, Henry's embracing of imperial identity reached back further, at least to some time in the 1520s, when he "redrafted the form" of the promises kings made in the coronation ceremony. His revised version included the "new phrase 'a crown or imperial jurisdiction.'" Dale Hoak, "The Iconography of the Crown Imperial," *Tudor Political Culture*, ed. Dale Hoak (Cambridge: Cambridge University Press, 1995), 55 n.3. Furthermore, as Hoak has illustrated, use of the closed imperial crown has a still more ancient history in England. He observes, "Henry VII was the true architect of the symbolism of Tudor 'imperial' kingship, and his commissions for artistic images of himself wearing an arched crown leave no doubt of his purpose: he would show his subjects that his imperial magnificence exceeded that of the Yorkists and that his arms could stand comparison with those of any European sovereign. Proof of his 'imperial' legitimacy he would trace back to two sources, to Henry V, the father of his 'holy' step-uncle and the first to wear the crown imperial, and to Constantine" (101).

49. G. R. Elton, *The Tudor Constitution* (Cambridge: Cambridge University Press, 1960), 344; quoted in Strong, *Tudor and Stuart*, 7.

50. Pierre Bourdieu, *Practical Reason: On the Theory of Action*, trans. Randal Johnson (Stanford, Calif.: Stanford University Press, 1998), 102.

51. Madeleine Hope Dodds and Ruth Dodds, *The Pilgrimage of Grace 1536–1537 and the Exeter Conspiracy 1538*, vol. 1 (Cambridge: Cambridge University Press, 1915), 6.

52. Stephen Gardiner, "The oration of true obedience," 97, in Pierre Janelle, *Obedience in Church and State: Three Political Tracts by Stephen Gardiner* (Cambridge: Cambridge University Press, 1930).

53. Carole Levin argues that Henry VIII represented a departure from medieval ideas of kingship, saying, "Medieval monarchs had not made the claims of being God's lieutenant that began to emerge under Henry VIII." *The Heart and Stomach of a King: Elizabeth I and the Politics of Sex and Power* (Philadelphia: University of Pennsylvania Press, 1996), 12. I would not go so far as to say medieval monarchs did not make such claims; Henry V, for instance, clearly did desire to construct such an identity. I would say that rather than constructing an entirely new version of kingship, Henry VIII extended a traditional one into new territory.

54. In this respect, the mass benefited the male Henry as it could not later benefit the female Elizabeth I; Queen Elizabeth's mobilizations of, and innovations to, medieval religious tradition are discussed in the following chapter. Henry also had other political motives for his religious conservatism. As Koebner points out, Henry's desire to have the headship "wedded to a proclamation of 'imperial' rights . . . was also meant to avert religious misgivings which Henry's revolutionary step might arouse in his catholic subjects." If Henry cut ties with Rome, he wanted to avoid "walking in the footsteps of the German and Scandanavian princes who had assumed authority in ecclesiastical matters when embracing Lutheran heresy. . . . His claim to Church government, if carried to its extremes, ought to be based on a title which none of these princes had to offer. He was certain that the Catholic Church had accepted the authority of the Christian emperors of ancient Rome to determine her internal matters. This authority had devolved on the kings of England" ("'The Imperial Crown of this Realm'" 42).

55. Strong, *Tudor and Stuart*, 8.

56. Ibid.

57. John N. King, *Tudor Royal Iconography: Literature and Art in an Age of Religious Crisis* (Princeton, N.J.: Princeton University Press, 1989), 8.

58. Ibid., 54.

59. For a detailed discussion of the title page border, see ibid., chapter 2; the title page is reproduced there as figure 7, and the detail of Christ and the apostles appears as figure 9. For more on the iconography of the woodcut, see Strong, *Tudor and Stuart*, 16–17.

60. King, *Tudor Royal Iconography*, 62.

61. Ibid., 63.

62. Coverdale's preface quoted in ibid., 59.

63. On this incident, and on the incident that interrupted Henry's hunting, see also *L and P*, vol. 5, Introduction, xxiv-xxv.

64. James Christopher Warner, *Henry VIII's Divorce: Literature and the Politics of the Printing Press* (Woodbridge: Boydell, 1998), 6.

65. Watt, "Reconstructing the Word," 150.

66. Ibid.

67. Mystical experiences in which the host is miraculously delivered to a female visionary are relatively common in the Middle Ages. For instance, the Flemish mystic Hadewijch tells of Christ coming to her from the altar in a mass "in the form and clothing of a man" and proceeding to "give himself to me in the shape of the sacrament, in its outward form." Quoted in Caroline Walker Bynum, *Fragmentation and Redemption: Essays on Gender and the Human Body in Medieval Religion*

(New York: Zone, 1992), 120. This sort of miracle is strongly associated with holy women; as Caroline Walker Bynum notes, "There are very few male examples of the various distribution miracles, whereby the eucharist is brought by doves or angels or soars by itself through the air" (*Fragmentation*, 123). Watt too points out that "miracles in which the Eucharist is brought to the recipient by divine means are not unusual, especially amongst women mystics and saints" (*Secretaries of God*, 69).

68. As Strong says of Henry VIII, "to those who believed and built up the royal myth he embodied a return of Church and State to the ancient purity of his great ancestor," that is, Constantine (*Tudor and Stuart*, 9).

69. Watt observes that "Elizabeth Barton's eucharistic vision . . . confirmed her prophecies against the king: for Henry VIII to be deprived of the host in this way was a sign that he was no longer a member of the community of the Church and may have been intended as a prediction of his excommunication" ("Reconstructing the Word," 152).

70. Such a sentiment is similarly expressed in Elizabeth's claim, when Henry did remain on the throne more than the predicted month following his marriage to Anne Boleyn, that he "should not be king one month, nay, one hour, *in the acceptation or reputation of God*" following his marriage (Whatmore, "Sermon," 468, emphasis added).

71. 27 Henry VIII, c. 13, quoted in Dodds and Dodds, *Pilgrimage of Grace*, 10–11, italics in original. Capon's sermon emphasizes the fundamental importance of Elizabeth's symbolic treason; it opens by declaring that she engaged in "conspiracy . . . to distain His Grace's renown and fame in time to come" (Whatmore, "Sermon," 466). Similarly, the Act of Attainder declares that she had spoken "termes and sentences of reproche and slaunder ageynst the Kynges Highnes and the Quene" (quoted in Devereux, "Elizabeth Barton and Tudor Censorship," 101).

72. Whatmore, "Sermon," 466–67.

73. Ibid., 466.

74. Ibid., 469–70.

75. Watt, "Reconstructing the Word," 158–59; Watt references *Calendar of State Papers*, Sp 4 (pt. 2):1154.

76. Ibid., 159; Watt references *Statutes of the Realm*, 3: 451.

77. Ibid.

78. Quoted in Neame, *Holy Maid of Kent*, 178.

79. Neame, *Holy Maid of Kent*, 351. Henry Parker celebrated Mary's accession as a restoration of "all the plentye that was in your wyse graund fathers daies king henry the seventh, and my godly maistres the lady Margaret your great grandame, and in your worthy fathers dayes king henry the eight" (London, British Library MS Add. 12060, fol. 9v–10r, quoted in King, *Tudor Royal Iconography*, 185).

80. King, *Tudor Royal Iconography*, 197.

81. Ibid. The quote from Henry Parker comes from his inscription in the presentation copy of his translation of Erasmus's *Laude or prayse to be saide unto the virgyn mary mother of chryste Jesu*.

82. Hyder Rollins, ed., *Old English Ballads, 1553–1620, Chiefly from Manuscripts* (Oxford: Clarendon, 1920), 13–18. On this ballad and on other imagery of

the Virgin Mary associated with Mary Tudor, see Helen Hackett, *Virgin Mother, Maiden Queen: Elizabeth I and the Cult of the Virgin Mary* (New York: St. Martin's, 1995), 34–37.

83. Neame, *Holy Maid of Kent*, 351.

Chapter 6. Dissolution, Diaspora, and Defining Englishness: Syon in Exile and Elizabethan Politics

1. Edward Said, "Intellectual Exile: Expatriates and Marginals," in *Representations of the Intellectual*, 1993 Reith Lectures (New York: Pantheon, 1994), 52.

2. Elizabeth Barton's revelations and prophecies are "said to have been told to John Fewterer, the confessor of Syon, Richard Reynolds, the scholar and future martyr, Abbess Agnes Jordan, and some of the women there, including the wife of the Lieutenant of the Tower, Lady Kingston" (Diane Watt, "Reconstructing the Word: The Political Prophecies of Elizabeth Barton (1506–1534)," *Renaissance Quarterly* 50, 1 (1997): 150. There are also indications of personal correspondence between Barton and Agnes Jordan; in a letter Henry Gold wrote to Barton in 1532, he mentions a petition that the abbess sent to her. Alan Neame, *The Holy Maid of Kent: The Life of Elizabeth Barton, 1506–1535* (London: Hodder and Stoughton, 1971), 170. Elizabeth Barton and the religious of Syon were also tied into the same network of the king's political opponents. Both Barton and Agnes Jordan had close relationships with Gertrude Courteney, wife of Henry Courteney, marquis of Exeter, the last Yorkist claimant to the throne and, as such, one of the heirs apparent. Sharon L. Jansen reports that Barton met with Gertrude Courteney, who "traveled from Kew to Canterbury, in disguise, to consult with Elizabeth. There she had dined privately with the nun and Bocking, but the subject of their conversation is unknown." *Dangerous Talk and Strange Behavior: Women and Popular Resistance to the Reforms of Henry VIII* (New York: St. Martin's, 1996), 50. On Barton's relationship with Gertrude Courtenay, see also Watt, "Reconstructing the Word," 155; on the connection between Agnes Jordan and Lady Exeter, see *Letters and Papers Foreign and Domestic of the Reign of Henry VIII*, arranged and catalogued James Gairdner (London: HMSO; reprint New York: Kraus, 1965), vol. 6, no. 1468 (hereafter passages from this collection will be cited using the abbreviation *L and P* followed by volume and entry numbers).

3. The reinstatement of the Oath of Supremacy under Elizabeth I had controversial implications for Catholics and Protestants alike. Concerns with having a woman as the head of the church were present among members of both faiths; on such opposition see Carole Levin, *The Heart and Stomach of a King: Elizabeth I and the Politics of Sex and Power* (Philadelphia: University of Pennsylvania Press, 1994), chapter 2, especially pp. 14–16, and Norman L. Jones, *Faith by Statute: Parliament and the Settlement of Religion, 1559* (London: Royal Historical Society, 1982), 131–32. As a compromise, Elizabeth took the title of Supreme Governor rather than Supreme Head. As Jones observes, however, although Elizabeth would not take the title of Supreme Head, "neither would she relinquish the power over the Church

that she believed was hers by right. In terms of her prerogative, the change from headship to governorship was meaningless" (Jones, *Faith*, 132).

4. The term "diaspora" is much used in postcolonial criticism, with varying understandings of what groups properly should be termed "diasporic." As I shall demonstrate in this section of this chapter, the Syon religions, and indeed the other English Catholics, who fled to the Continent fit very well with the definition of diaspora proposed by William Safran. He argues that the "concept of diaspora" should be applied "to expatriate minority communities whose members share several of the following characteristics: 1) they, or their ancestors, have been dispersed from a specific original 'center' to two or more 'peripheral,' or foreign, regions; 2) they retain a collective memory, vision, or myth about their original homeland—its physical location, history, and achievements; 3) they believe that they are not—and perhaps cannot be—fully accepted by their host society and therefore feel partly alienated and insulated from it; 4) they regard their ancestral homeland as their true, ideal, home and as the place to which they or their descendants would (or should) eventually return—when conditions are appropriate; 5) they believe that they should, collectively, be committed to the maintenance or restoration of their original homeland and to its safety and prosperity; and 6) they continue to relate, personally or vicariously, to that homeland in one way or another, and their ethnocommunal consciousness and solidarity are importantly defined by the existence of such a relationship." "Diasporas in Modern Societies: Myths of Homeland and Return," *Diaspora* 1, 1 (1991): 83–84.

5. Roseanne Desilets points out, "Until 1581, when recusancy was declared a treasonous offense," religions dissidents "as a general rule . . . were not persecuted except in periods of political crisis, such as during the Northern Rising of 1569 and after the Bull of excommunication was issued in 1570." "The Nuns of Tudor England: Feminine Responses to the Dissolution of the Monasteries," Ph.D. dissertation, University of California, Irvine, 1995, 507.

6. Peter Lake and Michael Questier, "Agency, Appropriation, and Rhetoric under the Gallows: Puritans, Romanists, and the State in Early Modern England," *Past and Present* 153 (1996): 66.

7. Christopher Haigh, "The Continuity of Catholicism and the English Reformation," *Past and Present* 93 (1981): 69.

8. Alexandra Walsham, *Church Papists: Catholicism, Conformity, and Confessional Polemic in Early Modern England* (Woodbridge: Boydell, 1993), 225.

9. Bill Ashcroft et al., *Key Concepts in Post-Colonial Studies* (London: Routledge, 1998); for the ways in which this dynamic of ambivalence functions in colonizer/colonized relations, see Homi Bhabha's essay "Of Mimicry and Men: The Ambivalence of Colonial Discourse," in his collection *The Location of Culture* (London: Routledge, 1995), 85–92.

10. Lake and Questier, "Agency, Appropriation, and Rhetoric," 66.

11. The general history of the Dissolution of the Monasteries is too well known to need elaboration in detail here; it has been much rehearsed from various pro-Catholic and pro-Protestant perspectives; for examples, see Eamon Duffy, *The Stripping of the Altars: Traditional Religion in England c. 1400–c.1580* (New Haven, Conn.: Yale University Press, 1992); G. W. O. Woodword, *The Dissolution of the*

Monasteries (New York: Walker, 1966); G. G. Coulter, *The Last Days of Medieval Monachism*, vol. 4 of *Five Centuries of Religion* (Cambridge: Cambridge University Press, 1950); Francis Aidan Gasquet, *English Monastic Life* (1904; reprint Port Washington, N.Y.: Kennikat, 1971), Philip Hughes, *The Reformation in England*, 5th ed. (New York: Macmillan, 1963). The dissolution of Syon was accomplished by taking out a writ of Praemunire against the Bishop of London, the Abbess, and the Confessor-General. The offense was attributing authority to the See of Rome and its present bishop in the professions of brothers of Syon in 1537 and 1538. See John Rory Fletcher, *The Story of the English Bridgettines of Syon Abbey* (Devon: Syon Abbey, 1933), 35–36. For information on the choices made by the Syon nuns following the Dissolution, both those who remained in England and those who went abroad, see Deborah A. Luke, "The Religious of Syon Abbey and the Dissolution of the English Monasteries," MA thesis, Utah State University, 1999, and Desilets, "Nuns of Tudor England." Ann Hutchison also discusses the dissolution of Syon and its immediate aftermath, with special attention to the activities of Abbess Catherine Palmer, in "Syon Abbey: Dissolution, No Decline," *Birgittiana* 2 (1996): 245–59.

    12. Dom Adam Hamilton, *Angel of Syon*, (Edinburgh: Sands, 1905), 104–5.

    13. On the travels of the Brigittines, see Fletcher, *Story of the English Bridgettines*, 38–41.

    14. Peter Lake with Michael Questier, *The Antichrist's Lewd Hat: Protestants, Papists, and Players in Post-reformation England* (New Haven, Conn.: Yale University Press, 2002), 261–62. For a description of the activities of Elizabeth Sanders and Marie Champney in England, see Ann Hutchison, "Beyond the Margin: The Recusant Brigittines," *Analecta Cartusiana* 35 part 2, 19 (1993): 267–84.

    15. I have chosen to use the spelling "Sanders" throughout unless I am quoting a text that uses a different spelling; the name appears variously in primary texts and historical studies as Sander, Sanders, Saunder, Saunders.

    16. Sandra K. Johnson, "The Formation of a Rebel: Nicholas Sanders, from Winchester to Ireland," M.A. thesis, Utah State University, 1997, 50.

    17. Ibid., 83.

    18. Ibid., 77.

    19. Desilets, "Nuns of Tudor England," 535.

    20. Ibid.

    21. Leslie Stephen and Sidney Lee, *Dictionary of National Biography* (Oxford: Oxford University Press, 1921–1927), 17: 749.

    22. On the success of the nuns of Syon in raising alms in England, see Hutchison, "Beyond the Margin," 275.

    23. Five other fellow nuns were not so fortunate; they were arrested immediately upon landing at Dover, while three more were caught and arrested at Colchester (Fletcher, *Story of the English Bridgettines* 56; see also Desilets, "Nuns of Tudor England," 538–39).

    24. When Campion and Robert Parsons (aka Robert Persons) departed from London to avoid capture, they encountered Thomas Pounde, who was on a temporary release from prison, in Hogsdon. Pounde "warned that if the two missionaries were captured the Council would surely attempt to discredit them publicly

by charging that they had come to England for political purposes. He advised, therefore, that both should write a brief declaration explaining their mission in England and leave a copy of it with a trusted friend who would make it public in the event of their capture." *A Jesuit Challenge: Edmund Campion's Debates at the Tower of London in 1581*, ed. James V. Holleran (New York: Fordham University Press, 1999), 25.

25. Desilets, "Nuns of Tudor England," 541–42.

26. Henry Foley, *Records of the English Province of the Society of Jesus*, vol. 3 (London: Burns and Oates, 1878), 645. On the distribution of Campion's "Challenge," see also Desilets, "Nuns of Tudor England," 541–43.

27. Dom. Eliz. vol. cxllvii, no. 74; printed in Foley, *Records*, 646.

28. PRO SP 147/127; quoted in Desilets, "Nuns of Tudor England," 542.

29. On Elizabeth Sanders's capture, see also the letter of John Watson, the bishop of Winchester, dated November 18, 1580, printed in Foley, *Records*, 646.

30. Fletcher, *Story of the English Bridgettines*, 63–64.

31. For instance, as Desilets observes, "Although clear identification is problematic, the evidence suggests that families of several former nuns—in particular, nuns of Sion—provided a support system which enabled Jesuits and missionary priests to re-invigorate English Catholicism" ("Nuns of Tudor England," 529).

32. Edmund Campion, "Challenge to the Right Honourable Lords of her Majestie's Privy Council," *Jesuit Challenge*, 180; hereafter I cite this text from Holleran's edition parenthetically as "Challenge."

33. Holleran, Introduction, *Jesuit Challenge*, 22.

34. Peter Lake and Michael Questier, "Puritans, Papists, and the 'Public Sphere' in Early Modern England: The Edmund Campion Affair in Context," *Journal of Modern History* 72 (2000): 588.

35. Ibid., 612.

36. Lake and Questier observe, "by the time of Campion's capture . . . the aims of their project had long ceased to resemble (if, indeed, they ever had resembled) the spiritual purposes that the traditional narratives of the episode have seen in the Jesuit general's instructions. . . . Instead their mission had become a public challenge to the authority, and even the legitimacy, of the regime" (ibid., 613).

37. Lake and Questier, *Antichrist's*, 261.

38. PRO SP 53/15/552; quoted in D. C. Peck, "Government Suppression of Elizabethan Catholic Books: The Case of *Burleigh's Commonwealth*," *Library Quarterly* 47, 2 (1977): 164.

39. Ballad printed in Hyder Rollins, ed., *Old English Ballads, 1553–1620, Chiefly from Manuscripts* (Oxford: Clarendon, 1920), 178. On this ballad, Englefield's letter mentioned above, and the Catholic "linguistic" assault on England, with particular attention to Campion's "Challenge," see Phebe Jensen, "Ballads and Brags: Free Speech and Recusant Culture in Elizabethan England," *Criticism* 40,3 (1998): 333–54. Protestant polemicists had their own twist on the idea of words as weapons. In Hans Sebold Beham's woodcut *The Fall of the Papacy* (c. 1525), for instance, the pope "is toppled by the divine word, which strikes as arrows of biblical text, targeting cardinals, bishops, and all the papal clergy." Margaret Aston, *The King's Bedpost: Reformation and Iconography in a Tudor Group Portrait*

(Cambridge: Cambridge University Press, 1993), 138; the woodcut is reproduced as figure 94, page 140.

40. Timothy Fry et al., eds., *RB 1980: The Rule of St. Benedict in Latin and English with Notes* (Collegeville, Minn.: Liturgical Press, 1981), 157.

41. Parsons's history of Syon as quoted in Hamilton, *Angel of Syon*, 113.

42. Merideth Hanmer, *The Great Bragge and Challenge of M. Champion, Com-[m]onlye called Edmunde Campion . . . Co[n]futed & aunswered by Meredith Hanmer*, 1581, *STC* 2nd ed., 12745, 3a-4a; hereafter I cite this text parenthetically as *Great Bragge*.

43. Mentions that Elizabeth is the sister of Dr. Sanders occur repeatedly in documents from her case. Indeed, as Desilets points out, the English government felt that all the Brigittines were potentially tainted by their relationship to Nicholas Sanders; she says, "Nicholas Sander's association with the nuns of Sion made them . . . suspect" (Desilets, "Nuns of Tudor England," 537). .

44. Printed in Foley, *Records*, 646.

45. Fletcher, *Story of the English Bridgettines*, 63.

46. *Acts of the Privy Council* XII, 270; quoted in Desilets, "Nuns of Tudor England," 543–44.

47. Fletcher, *Story of the English Bridgettines*, 65–66

48. Ibid., 66–67.

49. Quoted in Desilets, "Nuns of Tudor England," 539–40. Since one of the prisons from which she was escaping was that at Winchester, her escapes are not necessarily as surprising as they might other wise seem. According to Lake and Questier, "The most outrageous and funniest story of prison disorder concerned Winchester jail," where it "emerged that the prison was actually being run by leading Hampshire recusants. . . . From the early 1580s the prison had been stuffed with altars, vestments, candles, and liturgical and polemical books" (*Antichrist's*, 196).

50. Hutchison says of the text's authorship, "The account of Sister Mary's life seems to have been written by someone attending her during the period she was in (or near) London, from Shrovetide until her death on April 27, 1580" ("Beyond the Margin," 273).

51. London, British Library MS Add. 18,650, fol. 8r, hereafter cited parenthetically by folio as *Life*.

52. Mary Stuart's many correspondences in codes, some of which she devised herself, are well known, and Sir Thomas Randolph said of her speech that "sometimes I seem willing to take some of her words as answer, but I see them drawn back again from me as though they had not been spoken." Quoted in Jayne Elizabeth Lewis, *Mary, Queen of Scots: Romance and Nation* (London: Routledge, 1998), 26. I suspect that the male speaker in conversation with Marie Champney is probably either Nicholas Sanders himself or Sir Francis Englefield. Both of these men were on the Continent during the years between 1569 and 1578, both supported the cause of Mary, Queen of Scots, and both had ties to Syon—Sanders through his sister Elizabeth and Englefield through his kinship with the Yates family. Sir Francis Yates, who harbored some of the Syon nuns when they returned to England, married Catherine Fettiplace, who was kin to James Yates's wife Mary Fettiplace. As Deborah Luke observes, "Catherine's father, Sir Thomas Fettiplace (d. 1524),

called James his nephew, making Francis Englefield and James Yates cousins by marriage" ("The Religious of Syon Abbey," 83; see also Desilets, "Nuns of Tudor England," 444, 449–50). James Yates's daughter Elizabeth was a nun at Syon before the Henrician Dissolution, and two Fettiplace women, Eleanor and Ursula, appear in pension records for Syon following the Dissolution (see Luke, "The Religious of Syon Abbey," Appendix A 103–104). Sanders seems a particularly likely candidate, given his later construction of Mary Stuart as "a saintly martyr for her religion." Helen Hackett, *Virgin Mother, Maiden Queen: Elizabeth I and the Cult of the Virgin Mary* (New York: St. Martin's, 1995), 132. Hackett points out, "as early as 1572 he had included the sufferings of Mary in England in a Catholic martyrology" (ibid.).

53. Lewis, *Mary, Queen of Scots*, 4. Lewis also discusses the "push and pull" inherent in the name "Mary, Queen of Scots," a name that "suggests that to the extent that she is a queen—commanding subjection—Mary rules over no land (the modern touchstone of national identity), but rather over something at once more nebulous and heritable, . . . something which is internal and intangible rather than visible and readily demarcated. By consigning Mary Queen of Scots to nowhere, her popular name actually acknowledges her potential presence everywhere" (ibid.).

54. Ibid., 21.

55. Ibid., 4.

56. Fletcher, *Story of the English Bridgettines*, 97–98.

57. Ibid., 106–7.

58. Ibid., 107 n.1.

59. Ibid.

60. Ibid., 43.

61. Desilets, "Nuns of Tudor England," 531.

62. Fletcher, *Story of the English Bridgettines*, 44.

63. Lake and Questier, *Antichrist's*, 324.

64. Ibid., 230.

65. Norman L. Jones, "Matthew Parker, John Bale, and the Magdeburg Centuriators," *Sixteenth Century Journal* 12,3 (1981): 35. The tactics of both the religious of Syon and Elizabeth's supporters resemble those used by Nicholas Sanders in relation to the early Christian period. He laid claim to Antiquity for the Catholics, insisting that "Antiquite is ours altogether" (*Rocke of the Churche* fol. 16v; quoted in Johnson, "Nicholas Sanders" 52.) and that "the Protestants do not have any connection to the time of Christ" (Johnson, "Nicholas Sanders" 54). They also resemble, however, the tactics of the Protestant writers known as the Magdeburg Centuriators who "made it their business to collect and study the records of the medieval past in order to create a potent polemical tool" (Jones, "Matthew Parker" 35).

66. John N. King, *Tudor Royal Iconography: Literature and Art in an Age of Religious Crisis* (Princeton: Princeton University Press, 1989), 216.

67. Ibid., 200.

68. Ibid.

69. Richard Grafton, *Graftons Adbrigement of the Chronicles of Englande*, 1570, STC 2nd. ed. 12151, 178v.

70. Ibid.

71. For instance, in a 1566 speech to Parliament rebuking members for attempting to force her to settle the question of succession, Elizabeth said, "though I be a woman, yet I have as good a courage, answerable to my place, as ever my father had." John E. Neale, *Elizabeth I and Her Parliaments*, vol. 1 (London: Cape, 1953), 149. Hackett observes of this speech, "This rhetoric was not only a means of laying claim by inheritance to the masculine qualities considered necessary to a ruler, but also a way of refuting doubts cast on Elizabeth's legitimacy" (*Virgin Mother, Maiden Queen*, 58).

72. On this strategy of Henry V, see chapter 4 of Paul Strohm's *England's Empty Throne: Usurpation and the Language of Legitimation, 1399–1422* (New Haven, Conn.: Yale University Press, 1998).

73. King, *Tudor Royal Iconography*, 201.

74. On Foster's and Parsons's texts, see Hutchison, "Beyond the Margin," 269 n.5.

75. Parsons's history of Syon as quoted in Hamilton, *Angel of Syon*, 97–98.

76. Ibid.

77. Dale Hoak, "The Iconography of the Crown Imperial," *Tudor Political Culture*, ed. Dale Hoak (Cambridge: Cambridge University Press, 1995), 101.

78. Parsons's history of Syon as quoted in Hamilton, *Angel of Syon*, 97–98.

79. Ibid., 100–101.

80. Ibid., 111.

81. "Petition a La Altissima Señora Prinçesa de Walia," in Christopher de Hamel and John Martin Robinson, *Syon Abbey: The Library of the Bridgettine Nuns and Their Peregrinations After the Reformation* (London: Roxburge Club, 1991), 12. In quoting from the Spanish text in this volume, I have reproduced abbreviations as printed. The English translations I give for this text also come from this edition. Further citations are given parenthetically, with the page number for the Spanish text followed by the page number for the English text.

82. Pierre Bourdieu, *Language and Symbolic Power*, trans. Gino Raymond and Matthew Adamson (Cambridge, Mass.: Harvard University Press, 1991), 190.

83. On Elizabeth as the Virgin Queen, see King, *Tudor Royal Iconography*, especially chapter 4; Hackett, *Virgin Mother, Maiden Queen*; Levin, *Heart and Stomach*; Frances A. Yates, *Astraea: The Imperial Theme in the Sixteenth Century* (London: Routledge, 1975); Roy C. Strong, *Cult of Elizabeth: Elizabethan Portraiture and Pageantry* (Wallop, Hampshire: Thames and Hudson, 1977); Louis A. Montrose, "Idols of the Queen: Policy, Gender, and the Picturing of Elizabeth I," *Representations* 68 (1999): 108–61.

84. As King observes, "Although explicit references to the Blessed Virgin were effaced by Protestants hostile to the Mariological cult, Elizabeth I took over many of the Virgin's epithets as part of an effort to channel traditional devotional forms in support of her regime" (*Tudor Royal Iconography*, 203).

85. Wallace MacCaffrey, *Queen Elizabeth and the Making of Policy, 1572–1588* (Princeton, N.J.: Princeton University Press, 1981) 265–66.

86. John N. King, "The Royal Image, 1535–1603," in *Tudor Political Culture*, ed. Hoak, 128.

87. Ibid., 128–29.

88. Levin, *Heart and Stomach*, 30.

89. Quoted in ibid., 30.

90. Quoted in Yates, *Astraea*, 79; see also Levin, *Heart and Stomach*, 30.

91. Levin, *Heart and Stomach*, 29. On Accession Day celebrations, see also Hackett, *Virgin Mother, Maiden Queen*, 83–87, and David Cressy, *Bonfires and Bells: National Memory and the Protestant Calendar in Elizabethan and Stuart England* (Berkeley: University of California Press, 1989), especially chapter 4. As Cressy observes, November 17 "was marked by the ringing of church bells, the holding of special services, and by other manifestations of joy and respect. The occasion was went by many names, but, significantly, was often referred to as 'the queen's holy day'" (ibid., 50).

92. Strong, *Cult of Elizabeth*, 123.

93. Ibid., 125.

94. Levin, *Heart and Stomach*, 29.

95. Montrose, "Idols of the Queen," 133. I tend to agree with Montrose's view that the "cult" is not, as Yates and Strong suggest, simply "a collective substitute or compensation for the world of sacred rituals and images that the Elizabethans had lost by virtue of the Reformation and its attendant iconoclasm;" rather, there are also "Machiavellian calculations . . . at work" motivated "not only by devotion but also by self-interest" on the parts of the queen and her subjects (Ibid. 131).

96. Marc Shell, *Elizabeth's Glass* (Lincoln: University of Nebraska Press, 1993), 6–7.

97. Ibid., 15.

98. Ibid., 32.

99. Ibid.

100. Nicholas Sanders, *The Rise and Growth of the Anglican Schism Published A.D. 1585 with a Continuation of the History by the Rev. Edward Rishton*, trans. David Lewis (1877; reprint Rockford, Ill.: Tan, 1988), 284–85; see also Levin, *Heart and Stomach*, 30.

101. Montrose, "Idols of the Queen," 114–15.

102. Quoted in Montrose, "Idols of the Queen," 115.

103. Montrose, "Idols of the Queen," 115.

104. John Nichols, ed., *The Progresses and Public Processions of Queen Elizabeth*, vol. 2 (London: Nichols, 1823), 215–19. On this incident, see also Susan Brigden, *London in the Reformation* (Oxford: Oxford University Press, 1989), 318. As Hackett points out, in this incident "The Virgin Mary is set up against the Virgin Queen Elizabeth; the 'false' virgin is destroyed, thereby reinforcing the authority of the 'true' Virgin," the Protestant Elizabeth, Supreme Governor of the Church (*Virgin Mother, Maiden Queen*, 2–3). On Elizabeth and iconoclasm, see Aston, *The King's Bedpost*, especially 97–127.

105. As I discuss in the previous chapter, Mary I's court poet Henry Parker called her a "second Mary," and John Proctor also emphasized her spiritual resemblance to the Blessed Virgin. He says, " . . . in some mans head, wytte might well gather, and reason conclude not a misse one, and the same soule to be of bothe, the bodyes only chaunged accordyng to Pythagoras lawe" (*The Fal of the Late Arrian*, quoted in King, *Tudor Royal Iconography*, 198). On Queen Mary's use of

Marian imagery as well as Lancastrian associations, see King, *Tudor Royal Iconography*, especially chapter 4.

106. Here, Elizabeth is depicted as Constantine "[s]eated on her throne and carrying the sword of justice, as she surmounts the toppled pope who is entwined with demonic serpents beneath her feet" (King, *Tudor Royal Iconography*, 154–55; the initial is reproduced as plate 50). On this woodcut, see also Aston, *The King's Bedpost*, 148. As Hoak has demonstrated, the development of imperial identity was intimately connected to Tudor Lancastrianism, so for Elizabeth, as for Henry VIII, the two representational strategies reinforced each other. Hoak notes that the woodcut of Elizabeth as Constantine incorporates "three Tudor roses which have grown from the union of the two roses of Lancaster and York" ("Iconography of the Crown Imperial," in *Tudor Political Culture*, ed. Hoak, 94 in caption for plate 20).

107. Hoak, "Iconography of the Crown Imperial," in *Tudor Political Culture*, ed. Hoak, 94 in caption to plate 20. As Yates indicates, "the whole royal supremacy over both church and state—the key-stone of the whole Tudor position—owed its sanction to the tradition of sacred empire. Elizabethan Protestantism claims to have restored . . . pure imperial religion" (Yates, *Astraea*, 39).

108. Ibid., 31.

109. For a detailed description of Elizabeth's representations as Astraea, see Yates, "Queen Elizabeth I as Astraea," in *Astraea*, 29–87. Similarly, the painting of the *Allegory of the Tudor Protestant Succession* constructs an idealized Elizabethan age in contrast to the era of sufferings the English people had endured under the Catholic rule of Mary I and Philip II. Philip and Mary are depicted on the left side of the painting, accompanied by Mars, while the much larger figure of Elizabeth enters from the right, leading the figures of Peace, who tramples weapons, and Plenty, who carries a cornucopia (See King, *Tudor Royal Iconography*, 223–34 on this painting, which is reproduced as figure 72).

110. "A petition for aid from the religious of the Order of St. Bridget, formerly of Sion in England," in Thomas Francis Knox, *Records of the English Catholics Under the Penal Laws*, vol. 1 of *The First and Second Diaries of the English College, Douay, and an Appendix of Unpublished Documents* (London: David Nutt, 1878), no. 48 page 361; printed from PRO Dom. Eliz. vol. 146 n.114.

111. Ibid., 362.

112. Hamilton, *Angel of Syon*, 112.

113. Ibid., 109–10.

114. In the "Petition," for instance, the abbess and nuns address the Infanta: "clementissima prinçesa de oyrnos dezir (Como tambien el dicho pueblo de Israel pur el espacio de setenta años de su destierro, podia dexir) . . ." ["Most clement Princess, to hear us say (as also the people of Israel could say throughout the seventy years of their exile) . . ."] (12–13, 24–25). They also address her as "Nuestra Reyna Hester" ["our Queen Esther"] and compare themselves to Mordecai (ibid., 13, 25). Esther was, of course, also one of the Old Testament figures with whom Elizabeth I was frequently associated.

115. Parsons similarly views Syon as the hope for the future, envisioned as a return to an ideal past of Catholic rule and religion. He writes that Syon and Sheen "give great hope that our Lord in His good pleasure will bring them once

again home to their country, to be the seed and seminaries of many others, which shall serve Him in religious life" (Hamilton, *Angel of Syon* 112).

116. Ibid., 71.

117. Rishton, for instance, writes of Elizabeth's "pretense of a single life, which was the ruin of the state" (continuation of Sanders, *Rise and Growth*, 288).

118. The abbess and nuns begin their petition to the Infanta saying that they will tell of "la extraordinaria virtud, y dignidad de nuestra gloriosa madre sancta Brigida, y de sus devotissimas peregrinaçones, y destierros destas sus Religiosas hijas" ["the extraordinary virtue and dignity of our glorious mother, St. Bridget, and her most devout peregrinations, and the similar wanderings and exiles of her religious daughters"] ("Petition," 11, 23).

119. Cristina Malcolmson, "'As Tame as the Ladies': Politics and Gender in *The Changeling*," *English Literary Renaissance* 20,2 (1990): 333–34. My thanks to my former graduate student Stephanie Thompson Lundeen for bringing this article to my attention and for many stimulating discussions of early modern politics.

120. A prime example of such gendered Protestant characterization of Catholicism appears in the *Geneva Bible* of 1560, where Revelations 17:4 is rendered, "And the woman was araied in purple & skarlet, & guilded with golde, & precious stones, and pearles, and had a cup of golde in her hand, ful of abominations, and filthines of her fornication." The woman is glossed as "the Antichrist, that is, the Pope with ye whole bodie of his filthie creatures" (quoted in Montrose, "Idols of the Queen" 154 n.41). Similarly, William Whittingham's version of the *Geneva Bible* printed in London in 1582 glosses "skarlet" in this passage as "a red & purple garment: and surely it was not without cause that the Romish clergie were so much delighted with this colour" (*The Newe Testament of our Lord Iesus Christ*, 1582, STC 2nd ed. 2882, 398). An even more striking example of Catholic feminine corruption and Protestant feminine purity appears in a Protestant ballad written in response to the Northern Rebellion of 1569. The Protestant Church appears as Christ's chaste bride; the Catholic Church, in contrast, is described as follows: "The spouse of Christ that she is not / but Antichristes whoore" ("An Aunswere to the Proclamation of the Rebels in the North," W. C. Hazlitt, ed., *Fugitive Tracts, First Series, 1493–1600* [London: Chiswick, 1875], no. 22).

121. Quoted in Malcolmson, "'As Tame as the Ladies,'" 334, emphasis in original.

122. Ibid.

123. Ibid., 334–45.

124. Ibid., 334.

125. Thomas Robinson, *The Anatomie of the English nunnery at Lisbon in Portugall Dissected and laid open by one that was sometime a younger brother of the conuent*, 1622. STC, 2nd ed., 21123, 1, hereafter cited parenthetically as *Anatomie*.

126. Robinson, Introduction, *Syon Abbey*, 3.

127. Malcolmson describes such texts as Middleton's *A Game at Chesse* from the era of the Spanish Marriage in which "the vulnerable female body symbolizes the weakness of the body of the state, disturbingly open to the infiltration of foreign catholic powers who stand ready to enter England" ("'As Tame as the Ladies,'" 332).

128. William Faulkner, *Requiem for a Nun* (New York: Random House, 1951), Act I, Scene 3. My thanks to Howard Bahr for his kind advice about Faulkner.

Conclusion: The Power of the Past

1. Louise Fradenburg and Carla Freccero, Introduction, *Premodern Sexualities*, ed. Louise Fradenburg and Carla Freccero (New York: Routledge, 1996), xix.

2. Two important exceptions to the general view that "the medieval" does not apply to the New World are Claire Sponsler's exploration of the cultural work of medieval theater in the process of colonization, "Medieval America: Drama and Community in the English Colonies, 1580–1610," *Journal of Medieval and Early Modern Studies* 28, 2 (1998): 453–78 and David Wallace's ground-breaking book *Premodern Places: Calais to Surinam, Chaucer to Aphra Behn* (Oxford: Blackwell, 2004).

3. Peggy Liss points out, "In 1492, with Granada won, the enterprise proposed by Christopher Columbus fit with the commitment to imperial Christian expansion firmly associated with the reign"; see "Isabel, Myth and History," in *Isabel la Católica, Queen of Castile: Critical Essays*, ed. David A. Boruchoff (New York: Palgrave Macmillan, 2003), 66. As José Luis Abellán notes, the papal bulls issued by Alexander VI in 1493 to establish a line of demarcation dividing Spain's territories from Portugal's make clear that the pope viewed Isabel and Ferdinand as eminently suitable for the task of extending the Christian faith, and Isabel "fully assumed this papal intent as her own"("Isabel and the Idea of America," *Isabel la Católica*, 82–83).

4. Abellán, "Isabel and the Idea of America," 80.

5. Columbus's own version of this letter from his copybook (*Libro Copiador*) was first published by Antonio Rumeu de Armas in 1989; it differs substantially from the versions that circulated previously. For the textual history of the letter, see Margarita Zamora, "Christopher Columbus's 'Letter to the Sovereigns': Announcing the Discovery," in *New World Encounters*, ed. Stephen Greenblatt (Berkeley: University of California Press, 1993), 1–3. My quotations from the letter come from the translation she provides in this essay.

6. Liss, "Isabel, Myth and History," 66.

7. Zamora, "Christopher Columbus's 'Letter to the Sovereigns,'" 7.

8. It is worth remembering here that Joan of Arc too claimed her ultimate aim was the conquest of Jerusalem.

9. Liss argues that the study of "the history of European expansion to America" often manifests "an underappreciation of the interplay of religion and politics" ("Isabel, Myth and History," 68). This conclusion is one very small step to appreciate that interplay more fully.

10. I would emphasize here that I am not endorsing the view of Isabel as a "founding mother" of America or as an "American icon," views that are prominent still in the United States and in parts of Latin America. On these views, see Liss, "Isabel, Myth and History," 69 and Abellán, "Isabel and the Idea of America," 87.

11. Andrew Hadfield, "Bruited Abroad: John White and Thomas Hariot's Colonial Representations of Ancient Britain," in *British Identities and English Renaissance Literature*. ed. David J. Baker and Willy Maley (Cambridge: Cambridge University Press, 2002), 173.

12. Ibid.

13. Quoted in Louis Montrose, "The Work of Gender in the Discourse of Discovery," in *New World Encounters*, 183.

14. The letter's implied alignment of heathen natives' and godless Spanish Catholics' lands is borne out by England's (frequently unsuccessful) pirateering raids on Spanish ships and colonies. The binary pairing of the true Christian Protestant and the false Catholic follower of Antichrist is widespread in anti-Catholic and anti-Spanish propaganda during the Elizabethan period. See, for instance, a treatise by William Fulke which begins with the heading, "An Ansvver of a Trve Christian to a Covnterfait Catholike," *Tvvo treatises written against the papistes the one being an answere of the Christian Protestant to the proud challenge of a popish Catholicke: the other a confutation of the popish churches doctrine touching purgatory & prayers for the dead* (1577; STC 2nd ed. 11458), 2.

15. Arthur Barlowe, "The first voyage made to the coastes of America . . . ," in *The Roanoke Voyages, 1584–1590: Documents to Illustrate the English Voyages to North America under the Patent Granted to Walter Raleigh in 1584,* ed. David Beers Quinn, Hakluyt Society 2nd ser., nos. 104, 105 (London: Hakluyt Society, 1955), 94. On this passage, see also Montrose, "The Work of Gender," 183.

16. Barlowe, "First Voyage," 98–99.

17. Montrose, "The Work of Gender," 184.

18. Ibid., 183.

19. Interestingly, a letter from a colonial British American aligns the two queens as sponsors of New World enterprises. Written in 1650 to the wife of the governor of Virginia, the letter, which is a petition for her to "influence her husband to send an expedition to the East Indies," invokes the example of "'that Most renowned Lady Queene Isabella' who sent out Columbus" (quoted in Liss, "Isabel, Myth and History," 77 n.35). It continues, "Our most Famous Queen Elizabeth [was] willinge in a kind to be an Imitator of her heroyicke Spiritt" (ibid.).

20. Elizabeth Teresa Howe, "Zenobia or Penelope? Isabel la Católica as Literary Archetype," *Isabel la Católica,* 100 n. 18).

21. Thomas Heywood, *The exemplary lives and memorable acts of nine the most worthy women of the world* (London, 1640), 211; quoted in Montrose, "The Work of Gender," 203.

22. The foundational text is, of course, Stephen Greenblatt, *Sir Walter Ralegh: The Renaissance Man and His Roles* (New Haven, Conn.: Yale University Press, 1973). See also Kathryn Schwarz's recent work on Raleigh in chapter 1 of *Tough Love: Amazon Encounters in the English Renaissance* (Durham, N.C.: Duke University Press, 2000); Louis Montrose, "The Work of Gender," especially pages 190–210; Mary C. Fuller, "Ralegh's Fugitive Gold: Reference and Deferral in *The Discoverie of Guiana,*" in *New World Encounters,* 218–40.

23. Walter Raleigh, *The Discoverie of the large, rich and beautifull Empire of Guiana . . . ,* in Richard Hakluyt, *The Principall Voyages, Traffiques and Discoveries of the English Nation,* 12 vols. (Glasgow: James Maclehose and Sons, 1903–1905; reprint New York: A.M. Kelley, 1969), 10: 366–67, hereafter cited parenthetically as *Discoverie.*

24. Montrose, "The Work of Gender," 203.

25. William Goddard, Satire 62 in *A Mastiff Whelp*; quoted in Ian Frederick Moulton, *Before Pornography: Erotic Writing in Early Modern England* (Oxford: Oxford University Press, 2000), 70.

26. Moulton, *Before Pornography*, 71.

27. Zamora, "Christopher Columbus's 'Letter to the Sovereigns,'" 8.

28. Ibid.

29. On the need to place women in "another place" distinct from that of the male warrior, see Louise Olga Fradenburg, *City, Marriage, Tournament: Arts of Rule in Late Medieval Scotland* (Madison: University of Wisconsin Press, 1991), 212. Schwarz usefully examines the blurred boundaries between the domestic and the exotic, the *heimlich* and the *unheimlich*, in her discussions of Amazon encounters in *Tough Love*.

30. Peter Martyr d'Anghera, *De orbe novo: The Eight Decades of Peter Martyr d'Anghera*, trans. Francis Augustus MacNutt, 2 vols. (1912; reprint New York: Burt Franklin, 1970), 2: 218.

31. Ibid.

32. On this passage, see also Schwarz, *Tough Love*, 61–62.

33. Andrew Hadfield, "Peter Martyr, Richard Eden, and the New World: Reading, Experience and Translation," *Connotations* 5, 1 (1995/96): 1–22.

34. Claire Jowitt, "'Monsters and Straunge Births': The Politics of Richard Eden, a Response to Andrew Hadfield," *Connotations* 6, 1 (1996/97): 52.

35. Ibid., 55.

36. Schwarz, *Tough Love*, 77.

37. Montrose, "The Work of Gender," 208.

38. Thomas Hariot, *A briefe and true report of the new found land of Virginia* . . . (Frankfurt, 1590; *STC*, 2nd ed. 12786). Henceforth I cite this text parenthetically as *Briefe and true report*.

39. For an account of De Bry's career and the role his religion played in shaping it, see Hadfield, "Bruited Abroad," 174.

40. Mary B. Campbell, "The Illustrated Travel Book and the Birth of Ethnography: Part I of De Bry's *America*," in *The Work of Dissimilitude: Essays from the Sixth Citadel Conference on Medieval and Renaissance Literature*, ed. David G. Allen and Robert A. White (Newark: University of Delaware Press; London: Associated University Presses, 1992), 179,

41. Campbell, "The Illustrated Travel Book," 179–81.

42. Hadfield, "Bruited Abroad," 162–63.

43. On Hariot's belief in European superiority and his manipulations of what he saw as native credulity, see Stephen Greenblatt's seminal essay "Invisible Bullets: Renaissance Authority and its Subversions, *Henry IV* and *Henry V*," in *Political Shakespeare: New Essays in Cultural Materialism*, ed. Jonathan Dollimore and Alan Sinfield (Ithaca, N.Y.: Cornell University Press, 1985), 18–47. Hariot's characterization of the Native Americans as sometimes threatening yet ultimately ineffectual is very similar to contemporary Protestant characterizations of Catholics as menacing yet doomed to failure. Meredith Hanmer employs this approach in his response to Campion, as we saw in chapter 6. It is also evident in the address "To the Godly Reader" by William Fulke in *Tvvo Treatises Written Against the Papistes*. Fulke writes, "I confesse it kindled that final zeale of godlines that is in me, both to meinteine the common hope of Christians, against the insolent assaultes of so malicious and proud an adversary, and also to discover the infirmite

& feeblenesse of that fortress, vvich these vvilfully blinde Papistes do vaunt to be inunicible" (iib). This two-pronged strategy similarly resonates with some versions of the Black Legend in which the Spanish are portrayed as being at once barbarically cruel and cowardly. See William S. Maltby, *The Black Legend in England: The Development of Anti-Spanish Sentiment, 1558–1660* (Durham, N.C.: Duke University Press, 1974), and Andrew Hadfield, "Rethinking the Black Legend: Elizabethan Sixteenth-Century Identity and the Spanish Colonial Antichrist," *Reformation* 3 (1998): 303–22.

44. See, for instance, Greenblatt, "Invisible Bullets," and Campbell, "The Illustrated Travel Book."

45. See *The Injunctions of Elizabeth I* from 1559, which forbid extolling relics and images and which call for the removal of shrines. On the condemnation of Catholic prayers for the dead, see Fulke, *Tvvo treatises*. For an especially virulent attack on Catholicism as "damnable superstition" see Anthonie Marten's *An Exhortation to Stirre vp the mindes of all her Maiesties faithfull subiects, to defend their Countrey in this dangerous time, from the inuasion of Enemies* (1588; STC 2nd ed., 17489).

46. Maltby, *The Black Legend*, 31, ellipses added.

47. As Campbell observes, Hariot's explanation of his motives here echoes the Anglican marriage service ("The Illustrated Travel Book," 181); she further notes, "the colonial future is rehearsed in the words of the marriage vow" (189). William M. Hamlin makes a similar point, stating, "This echo of the Anglican bridal vow aptly sums up Hariot's vision of the English / Algonquian relation: an asymmetrical union based on notions of social subordination, technological disparity, and, paradoxically, ultimate equality in the potential for Christian salvation." "Imagined Apotheosis: Drake, Harriot, and Ralegh in the Americas," *Journal of the History of Ideas* 57, 3 (1996): 413.

48. Hadfield, "Rethinking the Black Legend," 310.

49. Hadfield, "Bruited Abroad," 171.

50. Ibid.

51. Ibid.

52. Ibid., 175–76.

53. William Shakespeare, *The First Part of King Henry VI*, I. 2. 104.

54. See Joan Kelly-Gadol, "Did Women Have a Renaissance," in *Becoming Visible: Women in European History*, ed. Renate Bridenthal and Claudia Koonz (Boston: Houghton Mifflin, 1977), 137–64.

Works Cited

MANUSCRIPT SOURCES

Brussels, Belgium

Algemeen Rijksarchief, Rokenkamer no. 8839

Ghent, Belgium

Monastery of Bethlehem MS 8

London, England

British Library MS Add. 6113
British Library MS Add. 7970
British Library MS Add. 14,014
British Library MS Add. 18,650
British Library MS Add. 25,351
British Library MS Add. 28,490
British Library MS Arundel 71
British Library MS Egerton 616
British Library MS Harley 4431
British Library MS Harley 4605
British Library Longleat 253
British Library MS Royal E II
British Library MS Royal 15 E VI
British Library MS Stowe 668

Oxford, England

Bodleian Library Add. A.42

Paris, France

Bibliothèque Arsenal MS 3602
Bibliothèque Arsenal MS 3902

Bibliothèque Arsenal MS CFR 62,541
Bibliothèque nationale MS F.fr.17,909

Poligny, France

Monastère de Sainte-Claire A8
Monastère de Sainte-Claire A14
Monastère de Sainte-Claire A18
Monastère de Sainte-Claire A21
Monastère de Sainte-Claire B4
Photocopy of manuscript letter from St. Colette of Corbie to Jehan Lanier; orig-
    inally in carton 19, Archives d'Amiens, now in Monastère de Sainte-Claire
Ubald d'Alençon, "Le Livre des Annales du Pauvre Monastère des Clarisses
    d'Amiens" (photocopy of handwritten document)

PRINTED PRIMARY SOURCES

Alençon, Ubald d'. *Lettres inédites de Guillaume de Casal à Ste Colette et notes pour
    la biographie de cette sainte*. Paris: Picard, 1908.
Alonso de Santa Cruz. *Crónica de los Reyes Católicos*. 2 vols. Edited by Juan de Mata
    Carriazo. Seville: Escuela de Estudios Hispano-Americanos de Sevilla, 1951.
Barrett, W. P. *The Trial of Jeanne d'Arc Translated into English from the Original
    Latin and French Documents*. London: Gotham House, 1932.
Bedouelle, Guy and Patrick Le Gal. *Le "Divorce" du Roi Henry VIII: Études et doc-
    uments*. Geneva: Travaux d'Humanisme et Renaissance, 1987.
Bizouard, J-Th. *Histoire de Sainte Colette et des Clarisses en Bourgogne*. Paris: Hatton,
    1881.
Bokenham, Osbern. *Legendys of Hooly Wummen*. Edited by Mary Serjeantson. Early
    English Text Society o.s. 206. London: Oxford University Press, 1938.
Campion, Edmund. *A Jesuit's Challenge: Edmund Campion's Debates at the Tower
    of London in 1581*. Edited by James V. Holleran. New York: Fordham Univer-
    sity Press, 1999.
Caxton, William, trans. *The Book of the Fayttes of Armes and of Chyvalrye Translated
    and Printed by William Caxton from the French Original by Christine de Pisan*.
    Edited by A. T. P. Byles. Early English Text Society o.s. 189. London: Oxford
    University Press, 1932.
Chastellain, Georges. *Oeuvres*. Vol. 1. Edited by Kervyn de Lettenhove. Brussels:
    Heussner, 1864.
Christine de Pizan. *The Book of the City of Ladies*. Translated by Earl Jeffrey Richards.
    New York: Persea, 1982.
——. *Christine de Pizan, The Book of Deeds of Arms and of Chivalry*. Translated by
    Sumner Willard, edited by Charity Cannon Willard. University Park: Penn-
    sylvania State University Press, 1999.
——. *Christine de Pizan's Letter of Othea to Hector*. Translated by Jane Chance.
    Newburyport, Mass.: Focus, 1990.

———. *Ditié de Jehanne d'Arc*. Edited by Agnus J. Kennedy and Kenneth Varty. Medium Aevum Monographs n.s. 9. Oxford: Society for the Study of Mediaeval Languages and Literatures, 1977.

The Chronicle of Calais in the Reigns of Henry VII and Henry VIII to the Year 1540. Ed. John Gough Nichols. London: Camden Society, 1846.

Columbus, Christopher. "Christopher Columbus's 'Letter to the Sovereigns': Announcing the Discovery." Translated by Margarita Zamora. In *New World Encounters*, edited by Stephen Greenblatt, 1–11. Berkeley: University of California Press, 1993.

The Commentaries of Pius II, Book IX. Translated by Florence Alden Gragg, with historical notes by Leona C. Gabel. Northampton, Mass.: Department of History, Smith College, 1939–1940.

Corblet, Jules. *Hagiographie du diocèse d'Amiens*. Vol. 1. Paris: Dumoulin; Amiens: Prevost-Allo, 1868.

Corstanje, Auspicius, Yves Cazaux, Johan Decavale, and Albert Derolez. *Vita sanctae Coletae*. Tielt: Lannoo; Leiden: E.J. Brill, 1982.

Cranmer, Thomas. *A Confutation of Vnwritten Verities, Miscellaneous Writings and Letters of Thomas Cranmer*. Edited by John Edmund Cox. Cambridge: Cambridge University Press, 1846.

Damien, Pierre. *Sainte Colette de Corbie et l'action catholique féminine française*. Paris: Libraire Saint-François d'Assisse, 1946.

Faulkner, William. *Requiem for a Nun*. New York: Random House, 1951.

Foley, Henry. *Records of the English Province of the Society of Jesus*. Vol. 3. London: Burns and Oates, 1878.

Fry, Timothy et al, eds. *RB 1980: The Rule of St. Benedict in Latin and English with Notes*. Collegeville, Minn.: Liturgical Press, 1981.

Fulke, William. *Two treatises written against the papistes the one being an answere of the Christian Protestant to the proud challenge of a popish Catholicke: the other a confutation of the popish churches doctrine touching purgatory & prayers for the dead*. London, 1577.

Gardiner, Stephen. *Obedience in Church and State: Three Political Tracts by Stephen Gardiner*. Edited by Pierre Janelle. Cambridge: Cambridge University Press, 1930.

Germain, Alphonse. *Sainte Colette de Corbie (1381–1447)*. Paris: Poussilegue, 1903.

Grafton, Richard. *Graftons Abridgement of the Chronicles of Englande*. London, 1570.

Haliwell-Phillips, J. O., ed. *Letters of the Kings of England*. Vol. 1. London, 1846.

Hall, Edward. *Hall's Chronicle*. Edited by Henry Ellis. London: J. Johnson, 1809.

Hanmer, Meredith. *The Great Bragge and Challenge of M. Champion, Com[m]onlye called Edmunde Campion . . . Co[n]futed & answered by Meredith Hanmer*. London, 1581.

Hariot, Thomas. *A briefe and true report of the new found land of Virginia. . . .* Frankfurt, 1590.

Hazlitt, William C., ed. *Fugitive tracts written in verse which illustrate the condition of religious and political feeling in England and the state of society there during two centuries*. First Series 1493–1600. London: Chiswick, 1875.

Heywood, Thomas. *The exemplary lives and memorable acts of nine the most worthy women of the world*. London, 1640.

Hyrd, Richard, trans. *Instruction of a Christian Woman*. Printed in facsimile in *Distaves and Dames: Renaissance Treatises for and About Women*. Delmar, N.Y.: Scholars' Facsimiles and Reprints, 1978.

Kempe, Margery. *The Book of Margery Kempe*. Edited by Lynn Staley. Kalamazoo: Western Michigan University Press, 1996.

Knox, Thomas Francis. *Records of the English Catholics Under the Penal Laws*. Vol. 1 of *The First and Second Diaries of the English College, Douay, and an Appendix of Unpublished Documents*. London: David Nutt, 1878.

Kock, Ernst A. *Three Middle-English Versions of the Rule of St. Benet and Two Contemporary Rituals for the Ordination of Nuns*. Early English Text Society o.s. 120. 1902. Reprint, Millwood, N.Y.: Kraus, 1987.

La Poncella de Francia: la "historia" castellana de Juana de Arco. Edited by Victoria Campo and Victor Infantes. Vervuert: Iberoamericana, 1997.

Letters and Papers Foreign and Domestic of the Reign of Henry VIII. Arranged and catalogued by James Gairdner. London: HMSO, 1862–1932. Reprint, New York: Kraus, 1965

Lydgate, John. "Ballade to King Henry VI Upon His Coronation." In *The Minor Poems of John Lydgate*. Part 2. Edited by Henry Noble MacCracken. Early English Text Society e.s. 107. London: Oxford University Press, 1933.

Marten, Anthony. *An Exhortation to Stirre vp the mindes of all her Maiesties faithfull subjects, to defend their Countrey in this dangerous time, from the inuasion of Enemies*. London, 1588.

Martín de Córdoba, *Jardín de Nobles Donzellas, Fray Martín de Córdoba: A Critical Edition and Study*. Edited by Harriet Goldberg. Chapel Hill: North Carolina Studies in the Romance Languages and Literatures, University of North Carolina Department of Romance Languages, 1974.

More, Thomas. *The Correspondences of Sir Thomas More*. Edited by Elizabeth Frances Rogers. Princeton, N.J.: Princeton University Press, 1947.

Nichols, John, ed. *The Progresses and Public Processions of Queen Elizabeth*. Vol. 2. London: Nichols, 1823.

Penna, Mario, ed. *Prositas castellanos del siglo XV*. Vol. 1. Biblioteca de Autores Españoles 116. Madrid: Atlas, 1959.

Peter Martyr d'Anghera. *De orbe novo: The Eight Decades of Peter Martyr D'Anghera*. Translated by Francis Augustus Macnutt. 2 vols. 1912. Reprint, New York: Burt Franklin, 1970.

"Petition a La Altissima Señora Prinçesa de Walia." In *Syon Abbey: The Library of the Bridgettine Nuns and Their Peregrinations After the Reformation*, by Christopher de Hamel and John Martin Robinson. London: Roxburghe Club, 1991.

Plancher, Urbain. *Histoire générale et particulière de Bourgogne avec les preuves justificatives*. 4 vols. Dijon: A. Fray, 1739–1781.

Quicherat, Jules, ed. *Procès de condamnation et réhabilitation de Jeanne d'Arc, dite la Pucelle*. 5 vols. Paris: Renouard, 1841–1849.

Quinn, David Beers, ed. *The Roanoke Voyages, 1584–1590: Documents to Illustrate the*

English Voyages to North American under the Patent Granted to Walter Raleigh in 1584. Hakluyt Society, 2nd ser. 104, 105. London: Hakluyt Society, 1955.

Raleigh, Walter. *The Discoverie of the large, rich and beautifull Empire of Guiana. . . .* In vol. 10 of Richard Hakluyt, *The Principal Voyages, Traffiques and Discoveries of the English Nation*. 12 vols. Glasgow: James Maclehose and Sons, 1903–1905. Reprint, New York, 1969.

Robinson, Thomas. *The Anatomie of the English nunnery at Lisbon in Portugall Dissected and laid open by one that was sometime a younger brother of the conuent*. London, 1622.

Rollins, Hyder, ed. *Old English Ballads, 1553–1620, Chiefly from Manuscripts*. Oxford: Clarendon, 1920.

Sanders, Nicholas. *The Rise and Growth of the Anglican Schism Published A.D. 1585 with a Continuation of the History by the Rev. Edward Rishton*. Translated by David Lewis. 1877. Reprint, Rochford, Ill.: Tan, 1988.

Sainte-Marie Perrin, Elisabeth Basin. *La belle vie de Sainte Colette de Corbie (1381–1447)*. Paris: Plon, 1921.

Scrope, Stephen, trans. *The Epistle of Othea Translated from the French Text of Christine de Pizan by Stephen Scrope*. Edited by Curt F. Bühler. Early English Text Society o.s. 264. London: Oxford University Press, 1970.

Jerome. *Against Jovinianus. A Select Library of Nicene and Post-Nicene Fathers*. 2nd ser. 14 vols. New York: Christian Literature Company; Oxford: Parker, 1890–1900. Vol. 6.

Sigüenza, José de. *Historia de la Orden de San Jerónimo*. 2 vols. Edited by Juan Catalina García. Nueva Biblioteca de Autores Españoles, vols. 8, 12. Madrid: Bailly-Ballière, 1907–1909.

Stephen, Leslie and Sidney Lee. *Dictionary of National Biography*. 63 vols. Oxford: Oxford University Press, 1921–1927.

Vergil, Polydore. *The Anglica Historia*. Edited and translated by Denis Hay. London: Royal Historical Society, 1950.

———. *Three Books of Polydore Vergil's English History Comprising the Reigns of Henry VI, Edward IV, and Richard III*. Edited by Henry Ellis. Camden Society Publications 29. London: Nichols, 1844.

Vives, Juan Luis. *The Education of a Christian Woman: A Sixteenth-Century Manual*. Edited and translated by Charles Fantazzi. Chicago: University of Chicago Press, 2000.

Whittingham, William. *The Nevv Testament of our Lord Iesus Christ. . . .* London, 1582.

Wogan-Browne, Jocelyn et al, eds. *The Idea of the Vernacular: An Anthology of Middle English Literary Theory, 1280–1520*. University Park: Pennsylvania State University Press, 1999.

Worcester, William. *The Boke of Noblesse Addressed to King Edward the Fourth on His Invasion of France in 1475, with an Introduction by John Gough Nichols*. 1860. Reprint, New York: Burt Franklin, 1972.

Worde, Wynkin de. *The maner of the tryumphe at Caleys and Bulleyn*. London, 1532.

Wright, Thomas, ed. *Three Chapters of Letters Relating to the Suppression of Monasteries*. London: Camden Society, 1843.

SECONDARY SOURCES

Abellán, José Luis. "Isabel and the Idea of America." In *Isabel la Católica, Queen of Castile: Critical Essays,* edited by David A. Boruchoff, 79–89. New York: Palgrave Macmillan, 2003.

Amador de los Rios, José. *Historia crítica de la literatura española.* 7 vols. Madrid, 1861–1865.

Anglo, Sydney. *Spectacle, Pageantry, and Early Tudor Policy.* Oxford: Clarendon; New York: Oxford University Press, 1997.

Arnade, Peter. *Realms of Ritual: Burgundian Ceremony and Civic Life in Late Medieval Ghent.* Ithaca, N.Y.: Cornell University Press, 1996.

Ashcroft, Bill, Gareth Griffits, and Helen Tiffin, eds. *Key Concepts in Post-Colonial Studies.* London: Routledge, 1998.

Ashley, Kathleen and Pamela Sheingorn, eds. *Interpreting Cultural Symbols: Saint Anne in Late Medieval Society.* Athens: University of Georgia Press, 1990.

Astell, Ann W. *Political Allegory in Late Medieval England.* Ithaca, N.Y.: Cornell University Press, 1999.

Aston, Margaret. *The King's Bedpost: Reformation and Iconography in a Tudor Group Portrait.* Cambridge: Cambridge University Press, 1993.

Aungier, George James. *The History and Antiquities of Syon Monastery, the Parish of Isleworth, and the Chapelry of Hounslow.* London: Nichols, 1840.

Banque de Bruxelles. *Marguerite d'York et son temps: exposition organisée par la Banque de Bruxelles.* Bruxelles: Banque de Bruxelles, 1967.

Bell, Susan Groag. "A New Approach to the Influence of Christine de Pizan: The Lost Tapestries of the 'City of Ladies.'" In *Sur le chemin de longue étude . . . : actes du colloque d'Orléans juillet 1995,* edited by Bernard Ribémont, 7–12. Paris: Editions Champion, 1998.

Berengroth, Gustave Adolph. Introduction to *Calendar of Letters, Dispatches, and State Papers, Relating to the Negotiations Between England and Spain, vol. 1, Henry VIII, 1485–1509.* London: Longman, 1862.

Bhabha, Homi K. *The Location of Culture.* London: Routledge, 1994.

Bizouard, J-Th. *Histoire de Sainte Colette et des Clarisses en Bourgogne.* Paris: Hatton, 1881.

Blockmans, Wim. "The Devotion of a Lonely Duchess." In *Margaret of York, Simon Marmion, and* The Visions of Tondal: *Papers Delivered at a Symposium Organized by the Department of Manuscripts of the J. Paul Getty Museum in Collaboration with the Huntington Library and Art Collections, June 21–24, 1990,* 29–46, edited by Thomas Kren. Malibu, Calif.: The J. Paul Getty Museum, 1992.

Bornstein, Diane. Introduction to *Distaves and Dames: Renaissance Treatises for and About Women.* Delmar, N.Y.: Scholars' Facsimiles and Reprints, 1978.

Boruchoff, David A. Introduction to *Isabel la Católica, Queen of Castile: Critical Essays,* edited by David A. Boruchoff. New York: Palgrave Macmillan, 2003.

Bossy, Michel-André. "Arms and the Bride: Christine de Pizan's Military Treatise as a Wedding Gift for Margaret of Anjou." In *Christine de Pizan and the Categories of Difference,* edited by Marilynn Desmond, 236–56. Minneapolis: University of Minnesota Press, 1998.

Bourdieu, Pierre. *Language and Symbolic Power*. Edited by John B. Thompson and translated by Gino Raymond and Matthew Adamson. Cambridge, Mass.: Harvard University Press, 1991.

———. *Outline of a Theory of Practice*. Translated by Richard Nice. Cambridge: Cambridge University Press, 1977.

———. *Practical Reason: On the Theory of Action*. Translated by Randal Johnson. Stanford, Calif.: Stanford University Press, 1998.

Brigden, Susan. *London in the Reformation*. Oxford: Oxford University Press, 1989.

Bynum, Caroline Walker. *Fragmentation and Redemption: Essays on Gender and the Human Body in Medieval Religion*. New York: Zone, 1992.

Calmette, Joseph. *The Golden Age of Burgundy: The Magnificent Dukes and Their Court*. Translated by Doreen Weightman. New York: Norton, 1962.

Campbell, Mary B. "The Illustrated Travel Book and the Birth of Ethnography: Part I of De Bry's *America*." In *The Work of Dissimilitude: Essays from the Sixth Citadel Conference on Medieval and Renaissance Literature*, edited by David G. Allen and Robert A. White, 177–95. Newark: University of Delaware Press; London: Associated University Presses, 1992.

Campbell, P. G. C. "Christine de Pisan en Angleterre." *Revue de littérature comparée* 5 (1925): 659–70.

Certeau, Michel de. *The Practice of Everyday Life*. Translated by Steven Rendall. Berkeley: University of California Press, 1984.

Chance, Jane. "Christine's Minerva, the Mother Valorized." In *Christine de Pizan's Letter of Othea to Hector*, 121–33. Newburyport, Mass..: Focus, 1990.

———. Introduction to *Christine de Pizan's Letter of Othea to Hector*. Newburyport, Mass.: Focus, 1990.

Chartier, Roger. *On the Edge of the Cliff: History, Language, and Practices*. Translated by Lydia G. Cochrane. Baltimore: Johns Hopkins University Press, 1997.

Chettle, H. F. "The English Houses of the Order of Fontevraud." *Downside Review* (January 1942): 33–55.

Chibnall, Marjorie. "L'Ordre de Fontevraud en Angleterre au XII s." *Cahiers de civilisation médiévale* 29,1–2 (1986): 41–47.

Collinson, Patrick. *The Birthpangs of Protestant England: Religion and Cultural Change in the Sixteenth and Seventeenth Centuries*. New York: St. Martin's, 1988.

———. *Godly People: Essays on English Protestantism and Puritanism*. London: Hambledon, 1983.

Coulter, G. G. *The Last Days of Medieval Monachism*. Vol. 4 of *Five Centuries of Religion*. Cambridge: Cambridge University Press, 1950.

Cressy, David. *Bonfires and Bells: National Memory and the Protestant Calendar in Elizabethan and Stuart England*. Berkeley: University of California Press, 1989.

Delany, Sheila. *Impolitic Bodies: Poetry, Saints and Society in Fifteenth-Century England*. New York: Oxford University Press, 1998.

Desilets, Roseanne. "The Nuns of Tudor England: Feminine Responses to the Dissolution of the Monasteries." Ph.D. dissertation, University of California, Irvine, 1995.

Desmond, Marilynn and Pamela Sheingorn. "Queering Ovidian Myth: Bestiality and Desire in Christine de Pizan's *Epistre Othea*." In *Queering the Middle Ages*, edited by Glenn Burger and Steven F. Kruger, 3–27. Minneapolis: University of Minnesota Press, 2001.

Devereux, E. J. "Elizabeth Barton and Tudor Censorship." *Bulletin of the John Rylands Library* 49 (1966): 91–106.

Dodds, Madeleine Hope and Ruth Dodds. *The Pilgrimage of Grace, 1536–1537 and the Exeter Conspiracy, 1538.* Vol. 1. Cambridge: Cambridge University Press, 1915.

Douillet, l'Abbé. *Sainte Colette, sa vie, son culte, son influence.* Paris: Bray, 1869.

Driver, Martha. "Christine de Pisan and Robert Wyer: *The C Historyes of Troye* or *L'Epistre d'Othea* Englished." *Sonderdruk aus Gutenberg-Jahrbuch* 72 (1997): 125–39.

Duffy, Eamon. *The Stripping of the Altars: Traditional Religion in England c.1400–c.1580.* New Haven, Conn.: Yale University Press, 1992.

———. *The Voices of Morebath: Reformation and Rebellion in an English Village.* New Haven, Conn.: Yale University Press, 2001.

Elton, G. R. *The Tudor Constitution.* Cambridge: Cambridge University Press, 1960.

Fletcher, John Rory. *The Story of the English Bridgettines of Syon Abbey.* Devon: Syon Abbey, 1933.

Forceville, Philippe de. *Sainte Colette de Corbie et son alliance avec Yolande d'Anjou, Reine des Quatres Royaumes.* Paris: Picard, 1958.

Fradenburg, Louise Olga Aranye. *City, Marriage, Tournament: Arts of Rule in Late Medieval Scotland.* Madison: University of Wisconsin Press, 1991.

———. *Sacrifice Your Love: Psychoanalysis, Historicism, Chaucer.* Minneapolis: University of Minnesota Press, 2002.

Fradenburg, Louise and Carla Freccero. Introduction to *Premodern Sexualities,* edited by Louise Fradenburg and Carla Freccero. New York: Routledge, 1996.

Fraioli, Deborah A. *Joan of Arc: The Early Debate.* Woodbridge: Boydell, 2000.

Freud, Sigmund. *Introductory Lectures on Psycho-Analysis.* Edited and translated by James Strachey. New York: Norton, 1933.

Fuller, Mary C. "Ralegh's Fugitive Gold: Reference and Deferral in *The Discoverie of Guiana.*" In *New World Encounters,* edited by Stephen Greenblatt, 218–40. Berkeley: University of California Press, 1993.

García-Oro, José. *Cisneros y la reforma del clero español en tiempo de los Reyes Católicos.* Madrid: Consejo Superior de Investigaciones Científicas Instituto Jerónimo Zurita, 1971.

Gasquet, Francis Aiden. *English Monastic Life.* 1904. Reprint, Port Washington, N.Y.: Kennikat, 1971.

Geertz, Clifford. "Centers, Kings, and Charisma: Reflections on the Symbolics of Power." In *Culture and Its Creators: Essays in Honour of Edward Shils,* edited by Joseph Ben-David and Terry Nichols Clark, 150–71. Chicago: University of Chicago Press, 1977.

Greenblatt, Stephen. "Invisible Bullets: Renaissance Authority and its Subversions, *Henry IV* and *Henry V.*" In *Political Shakespeare: New Essays in Cultural Materialism,* edited by Jonathan Dollimore and Alan Sinfield, 18–47. Ithaca, N.Y.: Cornell University Press, 1985.

———. *Sir Walter Ralegh: The Renaissance Man and His Roles.* New Haven, Conn.: Yale University Press, 1973.

Gunn, Steven. "Henry VII and Charles the Bold: Brothers Under the Skin?" *History Today* 46, 4 (1996): 26–33.

Hackett, Helen. *Virgin Mother, Maiden Queen: Elizabeth I and the Cult of the Virgin Mary.* New York: St. Martin's, 1995.

Hadfield, Andrew. "Bruited Abroad: John White and Thomas Hariot's Colonial Representations of Ancient Britain." In *British Identities and English Renaissance Literature*, edited by David J. Baker and Willy Maley, 159–77. Cambridge: Cambridge University Press, 2002.

———. "Peter Martyr, Richard Eden, and the New World: Reading, Experience, and Translation." *Connotations* 5, 1 (1995/1996): 1–22.

———. "Rethinking the Black Legend: Elizabethan Sixteenth-Century Identity and the Spanish Colonial Antichrist." *Reformation* 3 (1998): 303–22.

Haigh, Christopher. "The Continuity of Catholicism and the English Reformation." *Past and Present* 93 (1981): 37–69.

———. *English Reformations: Religion, Politics, and Society under the Tudors.* Oxford: Clarendon; New York: Oxford University Press, 1993.

Hall, Stuart. "Cultural Identity and Diaspora." In *Contemporary Postcolonial Theory: A Reader*, edited by Padmini Mongia, 110–21. London: Arnold, 1996.

Hamilton, Adam. *The Angel of Syon.* Edinburgh: Sands, 1905.

Hamlin, William M. "Imagined Apotheosis: Drake, Harriot, and Ralegh in the Americas." *Journal of the History of Ideas* 57,3 (1996): 405–28.

Hamy, P. A. *Entrevue de François Premier avec Henry VIII, à Boulogne-sur-Mer, en 1532.* Paris: Gougy, 1898.

Hanley, Sarah. "Mapping Rulership of the French Body Politic: Political Identity, Public Law, and the King's One Body." *Historical Reflections / Reflexions Historiques* 23 (1997): 129–49.

Hoak, Dale. "The Iconography of the Crown Imperial." In *Tudor Political Culture*, edited by Dale Hoak, 54–103. Cambridge: Cambridge University Press, 1995.

Hommel, Luc. *Marguerite d'York ou la duchesse Junon.* Paris: Hachette, 1959.

Howe, Elizabeth Theresa. "Zenobia or Penelope? Isabel la Católica as Literary Archetype. In *Isabel la Católica, Queen of Castile: Critical Essays*, edited by David A. Boruchoff, 91–102. New York: Palgrave Macmillan, 2003.

Hughes, Muriel J. "The Library of Margaret of York, Duchess of Burgundy." *Private Library* 3rd ser. 7, 2 (1984): 53–78.

———. "Margaret of York, Duchess of Burgundy: Diplomat, Patroness, Bibliophile, and Benefactress." *Private Library* 3rd ser. 7, 1 (1984): 3–17.

Hughes, Philip. *The Reformation in England.* 5th ed. New York: Macmillan, 1963.

Hurlbut, Jesse D. "The City Renewed: Decorations for the 'Joyeuses Entrées' of Philip the Good and Charles the Bold." *Fifteenth Century Studies* 19 (1992): 73–84.

Hutchison, Ann. "Beyond the Margin: The Recusant Brigittines." *Analecta Cartusiana*35, part 2, 19 (1993): 267–84.

———. "Syon Abbey: Dissolution, No Decline." *Birgittiana* 2 (1996): 245–59.

Inglis, Eric. Commentary on *The Hours of Mary of Burgundy Codex Vindobonensis 1857 Vienna, Österreicische Nationalbibliothek.* London: Harvey Miller, 1995.

Jameson, Frederic. *The Political Unconscious: Narrative as a Socially Symbolic Act.* Ithaca, N.Y.: Cornell University Press, 1981.

Jansen, Sharon L. *Dangerous Talk and Strange Behavior: Women and Popular Resistance to the Reforms of Henry VIII.* New York: St. Martin's, 1996.

Jensen, Phebe. "Ballads and Brags: Free Speech and Recusant Culture in Elizabethan England." *Criticism* 40, 3 (1998): 333–54.

Johnson, Sandra K. "The Formation of a Rebel: Nicholas Sanders, from Winchester to Ireland." M.A. thesis, Utah State University, 1997.

Johnston, F. R. "The English Cult of St. Bridget of Sweden." *Analecta Bollandiana* 103 (1985): 75–93.

Jones, Norman. *The English Reformation: Religion and Cultural Adaptation.* Oxford: Blackwell, 2002.

———. *Faith by Statute: Parliament and the Settlement of Religion, 1559.* London: Royal Historical Society, 1982.

———. "Matthew Parker, John Bale, and the Magdeburg Centuriators." *Sixteenth Century Journal* 12, 3 (1981): 35–49.

Jowitt, Claire. "'Monsters and Straunge Births': The Politics of Richard Eden, A Response to Andrew Hadfield." *Connotations* 6, 1 (1996/1997): 51–64.

Jubien, Alfred. *L'Abbesse Marie de Bretagne et la réforme de l'ordre de Fontevrault.* Angers: Barassé; Paris: Didier, 1872.

Karras, Ruth Mazo. *From Boys to Men: Formations of Masculinity in Late Medieval Europe.* Philadelphia: University of Pennsylvania Press, 2003.

Kastan, David Scott. "Proud Majesty Made a Subject: Shakespeare and the Spectacle of Rule." *Shakespeare Quarterly* 37, 4 (1986): 459–75.

Kelly-Gadol, Joan. "Did Women Have a Renaissance?" In *Becoming Visible: Women in European History,* edited by Renate Bridenthal and Claudia Koonz, 137–64. Boston: Houghton Mifflin, 1977.

Kerr, Berenice M. *Religious Life for Women, c.1100–c.1350: Fontevraud in England.* Oxford: Clarendon, 1999.

King, John N. *Tudor Royal Iconography: Literature and Art in an Age of Religious Crisis.* Princeton, N.J.: Princeton University Press, 1989.

King, Margaret L. and Albert Rabil Jr. Introduction to *The Education of a Christian Woman: A Sixteenth-Century Manual,* by Juan Luis Vives. Edited and translated by Charles Fantazzi. Chicago: University of Chicago Press, 2000.

Kirk, John Foster. *History of Charles the Bold, Duke of Burgundy.* 3 vols. Philadelphia: Lippincott, 1898.

Knowles, David. *The Religious Orders in England.* Vol. 3. Cambridge: Cambridge University Press, 1959.

Koebner, Richard. "'The Imperial Crown of this Realm': Henry VIII, Constantine the Great, and Polydore Vergil." *Bulletin of the Institute of Historical Research* 26 (1953): 29–52.

Kren, Thomas. Introduction to *Margaret of York, Simon Marmion, and* The Visions of Tondal*: Papers Delivered at a Symposium Organized by the Department of Manuscripts of the J. Paul Getty Museum in Collaboration with the Huntington Library and Art Collections, June 21–24, 1990,* edited by Thomas Kren. Malibu, Calif.: J. Paul Getty Museum, 1992.

Lake, Peter. *Anglicans and Puritans?: Presbyterianism and English Conformist Thought from Whitgift to Hooker*. London: Allen and Unwin, 1988.

Lake, Peter with Michael Questier. *The Antichrist's Lewd Hat: Protestants, Papists, and Players in Post-Reformation England*. New Haven, Conn.: Yale University Press, 2002.

———. "Agency, Appropriation, and Rhetoric Under the Gallows: Puritans, Romanists, and the State in Early Modern England." *Past and Present* 153 (1996): 64–107.

———. "Puritans, Papists, and the 'Public Sphere' in Early Modern England: The Edmund Campion Affair in Context." *Journal of Modern History* 72 (2000): 587–62.

Lauritis, J. A., R. A. Klinefelter, and V. F. Gallagher. Introduction to *A Critical Edition of John Lydgate's* Life of Our Lady. Pittsburgh: Duquesne University Press, 1961.

Lee, Patricia-Ann. "Reflections of Power: Margaret of Anjou and the Dark Side of Queenship." *Renaissance Quarterly* 39 (1986): 183–217.

Lehfeldt, Elizabeth A. "Ruling Sexuality: The Political Legitimacy of Isabel of Castile." *Renaissance Quarterly* 53 (2000): 31–56.

Levin, Carole. *The Heart and Stomach of a King: Elizabeth I and the Politics of Sex and Power*. Philadelphia: University of Pennsylvania Press, 1996.

Lewis, Jayne Elizabeth. *Mary, Queen of Scots: Romance and Nation*. London: Routledge, 1998.

Liss, Peggy. "Isabel, Myth and History." In *Isabel la Católica, Queen of Castile: Critical Essays*, edited by David A. Boruchoff, 57–78. New York: Palgrave Macmillan, 2003.

———. *Isabel the Queen: Life and Times*. New York: Oxford University Press, 1992.

Little, A. G. "The Introduction of the Observant Friars in England." *Proceedings of the British Academy* 10 (1921–1923): 455–71.

Lopez, Elisabeth. *Culture et sainteté: Colette de Corbie (1381–1447)*. Saint-Etienne: Publications de l'Université de Saint-Etienne, 1994.

———. *Histoire de Sainte Colette*. Paris: Desclée, 1998.

———. *Petite vie de Sainte Colette*. Paris: Desclée, 1998.

Luke, Deborah A. "The Religious of Syon Abbey and the Dissolution of the English Monasteries." MA thesis, Utah State University, 1999.

MacCaffrey, Wallace. *Queen Elizabeth and the Making of Policy, 1572–1588*. Princeton, N.J.: Princeton University Press, 1981.

MacCulloch, Diarmid. *Thomas Cranmer: A Life*. New Haven, Conn.: Yale University Press, 1996.

Mahoney, Dhira B. "Middle English Regenderings of Christine de Pizan." In *The Medieval "Opus": Imitation, Rewriting, and Transmission in the French Tradition*, edited by Douglas Kelly, 405–27. Faux Titre: Études de la langue et littérature françaises 116. Amsterdam: Rodopi, 1996.

Malcolmson, Cristina. "'As Tame as the Ladies': Politics and Gender in *The Changeling*." *English Literary Renaissance* 20, 2 (1990): 320–39.

Maltby, William S. *The Black Legend in England: The Development of Anti-Spanish Sentiment, 1558–1660*. Durham, N.C.: Duke University Press, 1974.

Maurer, Helen E. *Margaret of Anjou: Queenship and Power in Late Medieval Eng-land*. Woodbridge: Boydell, 2003.

McFarlane, K. B. "William Worcester: A Preliminary Survey." In *Studies Presented to Sir Hilary Jenkinson*, edited by J. Conway Davies, 196–221. London: Oxford University Press, 1957.

McKee, J. R. *Dame Elizabeth Barton, O.S.B.: The Holy Maid of Kent*. New York: Benziger, 1925.

Michael, Ian. "'From Her Shall I Read the Perfect Ways of Honour': Isabel of Castle and Chivalric Romance." In *The Age of the Catholic Monarchs, 1474–1516: Literary Studies in Memory of Keith Whinnom*, edited by Alan Deyermond and Ian Macpherson, 103–12. Liverpool: Liverpool University Press, 1989.

Montrose, Louis A. "Idols of the Queen: Policy, Gender, and the Picturing of Elizabeth I." *Representations* 68 (1999): 108–61.

———. "The Work of Gender in the Discourse of Discovery." In *New World Encoun-ters*, edited by Stephen Greenblatt, 177–217. Berkeley: University of Califor-nia Press, 1993.

Moore, R. I. *The Formation of a Persecuting Society: Power and Deviance in Western Europe 950–1250*. Oxford: Blackwell, 1987.

Moulton, Ian Frederick. *Before Pornography: Erotic Writing in Early Modern Eng-land*. Oxford: Oxford University Press, 2000.

Neale, John E. *Elizabeth I and Her Parliaments*. Vol. 1. London: Cape, 1953.

Neame, Alan. *The Holy Maid of Kent: The Life of Elizabeth Barton, 1506–1534*. Lon-don: Hodder and Stoughton, 1971.

Orgel, Stephen. *The Illusion of Power*. Berkeley: University of California Press, 1975.

Ortner, Sherry. "The Virgin and the State." *Feminist Studies* 4 (1978): 19–35.

Page, William, ed. *The Victoria County History of Kent*. Vol. 2. 1926. Reprint, Lon-don: Dawsons, 1974.

Palustre, B. "L'Abbesse Anne d'Orléans et le réforme de Fontevrault." *Revue des questions historiques* 66 (1989): 210–17.

Parrey, Yvonne. "'Devoted disciples of Christ': Early Sixteenth-Century Religious Life in the Nunnery at Amesbury." *Bulletin of the Institute of Historical Research* 164 (1994): 240–48.

Paz y Melia, Antonio. *El cronista Alonso de Palencia*. Madrid, 1914.

Peck, D. C. "Government Suppression of Elizabethan Catholic Books: The Case of Lancaster's Commonwealth." *Library Quarterly* 47, 2 (1977): 163–77.

Pina, M. C. Marín. "La mujer y los libros caballerías: Notas para el estudio de la recepción del género caballeresco entre el público femenino." *Revista de Lit-eratura Medieval* 3 (1991): 129–48.

Preston, Paul. *Franco*. New York: Basic Books, 1994.

Prevenier, Walter and Wim Blockmans, *The Burgundian Netherlands, 1380–1530*. Cam-bridge: Cambridge University Press, 1986.

Pugh, R. B. and Elizabeth Crittall, eds. *The Victoria History of the County of Wilt-shire*. 2 vols. London: Oxford University Press, 1953–1957.

Ravier, André. *Sainte Colette de Corbie*. Poligny: Monastère de Sainte-Claire, 1976.

Richards, Earl Jeffrey. "French Cultural Nationalism and Christian Universalism in the Works of Christine de Pizan." In *Politics, Gender, and Genre: The Political Thought of Christine de Pizan*, edited by Margaret Brabant, 75–94. Boulder, Colo.: Westview, 1992.

Rigoulot, Robert B. "Imaginary History and Burgundian State-Building: The Translation of the Annals of Hainault." In *Essays in Medieval Studies: Proceedings of the Illinois Medieval Association* 9 (1992): 33–40.

Rooks, John. "*The Boke of the Cyte of Ladyes* and its Sixteenth-Century Readership." In *The Reception of Christine de Pizan from the Fifteenth through the Nineteenth Centuries: Visitors to the City*, edited by Glenda K. McLeod, 83–100. Lewiston, N.Y.: Edwin Mellen, 1991.

Rucquoi, Adeline. "De Jeanne d'Arc à Isabelle la Catholique: L'Image de la France en Castille au Xve siècle." *Journal des savants* 1 (1990): 155–74.

Safran, William. "Diasporas in Modern Societies: Myths of Homeland and Return." *Diaspora* 1, 1 (1991): 83–100.

Said, Edward. "Intellectual Exile: Expatriates and Marginals." In *Representations of the Intellectual*. New York: Pantheon, 1994.

Scarisbrisk, J. J. *Henry VIII*. Berkeley: University of California Press, 1968.

Schibanoff, Susan. "True Lies: Transvestism and Idolatry in the Trial of Joan of Arc." In *Fresh Verdicts on Joan of Arc*, edited by Bonnie Wheeler and Charles T. Wood, 31–60. New York: Garland, 1996.

Schnitker, Harry. "Margaret of York on Pilgrimage: The Exercise of Devotion and the Religious Traditions of the House of York." In *Reputation and Representation in Fifteenth-Century Europe*, edited by Douglas L. Biggs, Sharon D. Michalove, and Albert Compton Reeves. Leiden: E.J. Brill, 2004.

Schwarz, Kathryn. *Tough Love: Amazon Encounters in the English Renaissance*. Durham, N.C.: Duke University Press, 2000.

Shagan, Ethan H. "Print, Orality, and Communications in the Maid of Kent Affair." *Journal of Ecclesiastical History* 52, 1 (2001): 21–33.

Shell, Marc. *Elizabeth's Glass*. Lincoln: University of Nebraska Press, 1993.

Smith, Jeffrey Chipps. "Margaret of York and the Burgundian Portrait Tradition." In *Margaret of York, Simon Marmion, and the Visions of Tondal: Papers Delivered at a Symposium Organized by the Department of Manuscripts of the J. Paul Getty Museum in Collaboration with the Huntington Library and Art Collections, June 21–24, 1990*, edited by Thomas Kren. Malibu, Calif.: J. Paul Getty Museum, 1992. 47–56.

Solterer, Helen. "Figures of Female Militancy in Medieval France." *Signs* 16, 3 (1991): 522–49.

Sponsler, Claire. "Medieval America: Drama and Community in the English Colonies, 1580–1610." *Journal of Medieval and Early Modern Studies* 28, 2 (1998): 453–78.

Strohm, Paul. *England's Empty Throne: Usurpation and the Language of Legitimation, 1399–1422*. New Haven, Conn.: Yale University Press, 1998.

———. *Hochon's Arrow: The Social Imagination of Fourteenth-Century Texts*. Princeton, N.J.: Princeton University Press, 1992.

Strong, Roy C. *Art and Power: Renaissance Festivals 1450–1650*. Woodbridge: Boydell, 1984.

——. *Cult of Elizabeth: Elizabethan Portraiture and Pageantry*. Wallop, Hampshire: Thames and Hudson, 1977.

——. *Tudor and Stuart Monarchy: Pageantry, Painting, and Iconography*. Vol 1. Woodbridge: Boydell, 1995.

Summit, Jennifer. *Lost Property: The Woman Writer and English Literary History, 1380–1589*. Chicago: University of Chicago Press, 2000.

Surtz, Ronald E. "Female Patronage of Vernacular Religious Works in Fifteenth-Century Castile: Aristocratic Women and Their Confessors." In *The Vernacular Spirit: Essays on Medieval Religious Literature*, edited by Renate Blumenfeld-Kosinski, Duncan Robertson, and Nancy Bradley Warren, 263–82. New York: Palgrave, 2002.

Teague, Frances. "Christine de Pizan's *Book of War*." In *The Reception of Christine de Pizan from the Fifteenth Through the Nineteenth Centuries: Visitors to the City*, edited by Glenda K. McLeod, 25–41. Lewiston, N.Y.: Edwin Mellen, 1991.

Tricot-Royer, J. J. "A la recherche de Marguerite d'York." In *Science, Medicine, and History: Essays on the Evolution of Scientific Thought and Medieval Practice Written in Honour of Charles Singer* vol.1, edited by E. Ashworth Underwood, 219–23. London: Oxford University Press, 1953.

Vauchez, André. *The Laity in the Middle Ages: Religious Beliefs and Devotional Practices*. Translated by Margery J. Schneider. Notre Dame, Ind.: University of Notre Dame Press, 1993.

Vaughan, Richard. *Charles the Bold: The Last Valois Duke of Burgundy*. New York: Barnes and Noble, 1973.

Vregille, M. le Chanoine de. *Sainte Colette vierge et réformatrice de l'Ordre de Sainte Claire*. Besançon: Monastère de Sainte-Claire de Besançon, 1907.

Wallace, David. *Chaucerian Polity: Absolutist Lineages and Associational Forms in England and Italy*. Stanford, Calif.: Stanford University Press, 1997.

——. *Premodern Places: Calais to Surinam, Chaucer to Aphra Behn*. Oxford: Blackwell, 2004.

Walsham, Alexandra. *Church Papists: Catholicism, Conformity, and Confessional Polemic in Early Modern England*. Woodbridge: Boydell, 1993.

Warner, James Christopher. *Henry VIII's Divorce: Literature and the Politics of the Printing Press*. Woodbridge: Boydell, 1998.

Warren, Nancy Bradley. *Spiritual Economies: Female Monasticism in Later Medieval England*. Philadelphia: University of Pennsylvania Press, 2001.

Watt, Diane. "Reconstructing the Word: the Political Prophecies of Elizabeth Barton." *Renaissance Quarterly* 50,1 (1997): 136–63.

——. *Secretaries of God: Women Prophets in Late Medieval England and Early Modern England*. Cambridge: D. S. Brewer, 1997.

Weightman, Christine. *Margaret of York, Duchess of Burgundy*. New York: St. Martin's, 1989.

Weiskopf, Steven. "Readers of the Lost Arc: Secrecy, Specularity, and Speculation in the Trial of Joan of Arc." In *Fresh Verdicts on Joan of Arc*, edited by Bonnie Wheeler and Charles T. Wood, 113–32. New York: Garland, 1996.

Weissberger, Barbara. "'¡A tierra puto!': Alfonso de Palencia's Discourse of Effeminacy." In *Queer Iberia: Sexualities, Cultures, and Crossings from the Middle Ages to the Renaissance*, edited by Josiah Blackmore and Gregory S. Hutcheson, 291–323. Durham, N.C.: Duke University Press, 1999.

———. *Isabel Rules: Constructing Queenship, Wielding Power*. Minneapolis: University of Minnesota Press, 2004.

———. "'Me atrevo a escribir así': Confessional Politics in the Letters of Isabel I and Hernando de Talavera." In *Women at Work in Spain from the Middle Ages to Early Modern Times*, edited by Marilyn Stone and Carmen Benito-Vessels, 147–73. New York: Peter Lang, 1998.

Whatmore, L. E. "The Sermon Against the Holy Maid of Kent and Her Adherents, delivered at Paul's Cross, November the 23rd, 1533, and at Canterbury, December the 7th." *Historical Review* 58 (1943): 463–75.

Winstead, Karen. "Capgrave's St. Katherine and the Perils of Gyneocracy." *Viator* 25 (1994): 361–76.

———. "Piety, Politics, and Social Commitment in Capgrave's *Life of St. Katherine*." *Medievalia et Humanistica* n.s. 17 (1990): 59–80.

Wogan-Browne, Jocelyn. "The Virgin's Tale." In *Feminist Readings in Middle English Literature*, edited by Ruth Evans and Lesley Johnson, 165–94. London: Routledge, 1994.

Woodward, G. W. O. *The Dissolution of the Monasteries*. New York: Walker, 1966.

Yates, Frances A. *Astraea: The Imperial Theme in the Sixteenth Century*. London: Routledge, 1975.

Žižek, Slavoj. *The Sublime Object of Ideology*. London: Verso, 1989.

Index

Saints are indexed under their given names (for instance, St. Colette of Corbie under "Colette") as are monarchs, dukes, and duchesses (Isabel of Castile under "Isabel," Charles the Bold under "Charles").

Chartier, Roger, 28, 41
Chastellain, George, 32, 34, 190 n. 54
Chibnall, Marjorie, 57
St. Christine, 112
Christine de Pizan, 4, 7, 8, 58–86, 88,
    92, 195 n. 3, 198 n. 36, 200 n. 57;
    and authorship, 64, 67, 72–77,
    82–86, 198 n. 42, 202 n. 83; *Ditié de
    Jehanne d'Arc*, 59, 66–68, 86; English
    redactors of, 59–60, 62–66, 69–78,
    82–86, 104, 105, 119, 133, 135, 172, 173,
    195 nn. 4, 9, 196 n. 11, 199 n. 43;
    L'Epistre d'Othea, 7, 59–60, 69–74,
    78, 195 n. 4, 199 nn. 43, 44, 52, 200
    n. 57; and female monasticism, 8,
    69, 73–77, 82–86, 106, 133, 135, 164,
    173, 198 n. 42; and Joan of Arc, 7,
    58–60, 66–69, 106; *Lamentacion sur
    les maux de la France*, 59; *Le Livre de
    faits d'armes et de chevalerie*, 7, 59–60,
    62–71, 74, 76–78, 85, 195 n. 4, 199 n.
    44; *Le Livre de la cité des dames*, 7,
    59–60, 77–78, 195 n. 4, 196 n. 11, 200
    nn. 57, 65; and Margaret of Anjou,
    58–60, 62–71. *See also* Anslay, Brian;
    Boke of Noblesse; *Othea*; Scrope,
    Stephen; Worcester, William
Cisneros, Francisco Jiménez, 102
St. Clare, 13, 16, 22
Clement VII, 184 n. 45
St. Clotilde, 36–38, 57
Clovis (king of France), 36–37, 57, 186
    n. 3
Cobb, Thomas, 120, 215 n. 12
St. Colette of Corbie, 2, 6–8, 11–35, 37,
    58, 77, 105, 117, 120, 182 n. 8, 183 n.
    24, 184 n. 45, 185 nn. 53, 62; and
    Benedictine monks of Corbie, 5,
    15–21, 27; and *Constitutions*, 22, 25,
    184 n. 43; and duchy of Burgundy,
    5–6, 12–17, 27–36, 39, 53, 58, 118, 133,
    138, 191 n. 65; "l'entention de Seur
    Colette," 17, 22, 26; and Franciscan
    friars of Dole, 5, 21, 24, 27; and
    Franciscan reform, 5, 13–15, 20–28,
    30, 33–34, 38, 50, 183 nn. 27, 31, 184

n. 43, 191 n. 65, 194 n. 101; and
    Joan of Arc, 19–20; and monastic
    foundation, 12–20, 27–33; and
    papacy, 13, 15–17, 20–22, 30, 32; and
    poverty, 16–20; *St. Colette de Corbie
    et l'action Catholique féminine
    française*, 11–12; *Vie de Sainte Colette*,
    25–26, 29, 34–35, 40, 49, 182 n. 8.
    See also Franciscan Order
Colettine nuns (reformed Claresses).
    See Franciscan Order
Columbus, Christopher, 168–70,
    172–74, 231 n. 3, 232 n. 19
confraternities, 43–45, 189 n. 41, 190
    n. 42
Congress of Auxerre, 30, 31
Constantine, 130, 160, 218 n. 48, 229
    n. 106
Conventual friars. *See* Franciscan
    Order
Corbie, 5, 13, 15–20, 21, 27
Corblet, Jules, 182 n. 8
Council of Basle, 16
Council of Constance, 19, 21–22, 24
Coverdale Bible, 132
Coverdale, Miles 132, 134
Cranmer, Thomas, 121, 127–29, 216
    n. 33
Cressy, David, 228 n. 91
Cromwell, Thomas, 126, 127
Chronicle of Calais, 126

Damien, Pierre, 11–14
Desilets, Roseanne, 222 n. 5, 224 n. 31,
    225 n. 43
Desmond, Marilynn, 100 n. 52
Dijon, 5, 12, 14, 29
*The Discoverie of the large, rich and
    beautifull Empire of Guiana* (Walter
    Raleigh), 171–72, 174
Ditié de Jehanne d'Arc (Christine de
    Pizan), 59, 66–68, 86
Dole, 5, 21, 24, 27
Dormer, Jane, 150–51
Douai, 147, 162
Drake, Francis, 177

Acknowledgments

The task of thanking those who helped bring a book into existence is perhaps the most pleasurable part of a process filled with enjoyment. My first thanks must go to my colleagues at the two universities where I wrote this book, Utah State University and Florida State University. I am fortunate enough to have had the experience of working in two institutions remarkably free from political conflict and filled with pleasant, astute interlocutors. I am deeply grateful to Utah State University for a New Faculty Research Grant that funded archival work for this project during the summer of 2000. A Neil Ker Memorial Grant from the British Academy enabled me to complete my archival research in 2003.

I am increasingly aware that writing, while seemingly one of the most solitary pursuits, is always, thankfully, conversational and collaborative. Wonderful groups of graduate students at Utah State and Florida State have accompanied me in the journey across the "great divide," and their enthusiasm and interest have made the trip all the more pleasant. I want to thank particularly my research assistant at FSU, David Swanson, for his hard work, good humor, and intelligence. I am delighted once again to thank my wonderful editor Jerry Singerman and the excellent staff at the University of Pennsylvania Press. Those friends who have answered my frequent questions and discussed with me chapter after chapter and draft after draft have my undying gratitude—David Aers, Tomeiko Ashford, Sarah Beckwith, Renate Blumenfeld-Kosinski, Theresa Coletti, Susan Dudash, Stephanie Thompson Lundeen, Miri Rubin, Lynn Staley, Lori Walters, Candace Ward, and so many others. Special thanks to Norm Jones, who sparked my interest in early modern religion and whose scholarship is both a valuable resource and an inspiration. Special thanks are due as well to Rita Copeland, Paul Strohm, and David Wallace for their extraordinarily insightful readings, for their faith in me and my work, and for their many and great kindnesses. I must end, conventional though it may be, by thanking those who have done the most to make this book possible—my families whose love sustains me. To my church families at St. John's Episcopal Church in Logan, Utah, and Old First Church in Tallahassee, Florida, thank you for allowing me to live among so many women and men of God. To my parents, thank you for always believing in me and for being, in so many things, my first and best teachers. To Bill, thank you for teaching me a new language, for living with me in true companionship, and, really, for everything! And to William Andrew, to whom this book is dedicated, thank you for giving me the purest joy I have ever known.

A version of Chapter 1 appeared previously as "Monastic Politics: St. Colette of Corbie, Franciscan Reform, and the House of Burgundy," *New Medieval Literatures* 5 (2002): 203–28, reprinted by permission of Oxford University Press. A version of Chapter 3 appeared as "French Women and English Men: Joan of Arc, Margaret of Anjou, and Christine de Pizan in England, 1445–1540," *Exemplaria* 16, 2 (2004): 405–36, reprinted by permission of Pegasus Press.